TABERNACLE OF MOSES

"Who serve unto the example and shadow of heavenly things, as Moses was admonished of God when he was about to make the tabernacle: for, See, saith he, that thou make all things according to the pattern shewed to thee in the mount."
Hebrews 8:5

Samuel Greene, *Ph.D.*

Glory Publishing, Inc.

Glory Publishing, Inc
GloryPublishingInc.com

About the Author:
www.nwmin.org

Printed in the United States of America
ISBN 978-1-937199-56-2

All Scriptures used in this book were taken from the King James Version.

TABERNACLE OF MOSES

Foreword

It is evident in our hearts when we read the Word of God found in Exodus 25:1-2, 8-9, *"Speak unto the children of Israel…and let them make me a sanctuary that I may dwell among them. According to all that I show thee, after the pattern of the tabernacle, and the pattern of all the furnishings thereof, even so shall ye make it"*, that a harvest of revelational truth awaits us as we *"…study to show ourselves approved"* (II Timothy 2:15) and *"…search the scriptures daily to see"* (Acts 17:11). Other translations of Exodus 25 read, *"For I want the people of Israel to make me a sacred temple"*, *"…I will make my habitation in their midst"*, *"…that I may shekinah…"*, and *"I will appear among you."*

One true Biblical principle is that *"It is the glory of God to conceal a thing: but the honour of kings is to search out a matter"* (Proverbs 25:2). God purposely hides deep precious truths for only those who will give themselves to finding them. *"Seek and ye shall find…"* (Matthew 7:7); *"I gave mine heart to know, and to search…"* (Ecclesiastes 7:25); Jesus said, *"search the scriptures…"* (John 5:39); David said, *"…the works of the Lord are great, sought out of all them that have pleasure therein"* (Psalms 111:2). We can and should know the deep mysteries of the Kingdom of God as Jesus told His disciples in Mark 4:11, *"Unto you it is given to know the mysteries of the Kingdom of God"*. Deuteronomy 29:29 tells us, *"The secret* (hidden realities) *things belong unto the Lord our God: but those things which are revealed belong unto us…"*

The truth is as we search, we find, and there is no greater reservoir of truth than the Tabernacle of Moses. Every object, mineral, number, color or measurement, literally all of the materials mentioned, speak of our Savior's great sacrifice as well as hidden realities of His person. They also speak of the way into the holiest, church ages, movements throughout church history, and personal and corporate truths. All of the most precious doctrines of the church are found herein. More than anything, however, Jesus is defined, described, demonstrated and revealed as the Saviour for all men. It shows His great personal sacrifices and the atonement for our whole man. It reveals to us our past, present, and future in God, which is your entire threefold salvation. I don't believe we can understand God's eternal purposes if we don't have a real and true understanding of the Tabernacle of Moses.

Just consider this with me. In the Tabernacle, we are actually given the revelation of how God came down to meet with, have mercy upon, and show us the way to where we can dwell with Him in fullness, *"And let them make me a sanctuary; that I may dwell among them"* (Exodus 25:8). Oh, how we long for this! *"For the Lord hath chosen Zion; He hath desired it for His habitation. This is my rest; here will I dwell…"* (Psalms 132:13-14). We are the temple of the living God (I Corinthians 6:19). So as we understand Moses' Tabernacle, we will understand our future and ourselves in His glorious kingdom, which is you and I becoming the habitation for the glory of God. This is our calling, *"That ye would walk worthy of God, who hath called you unto his kingdom and glory"* (I Thessalonians 2:12); *"…whereunto he called you… to the obtaining of the glory…"* (II Thessalonians 2:14); *"…who hath called us to glory"* (II Peter 1:3); *"But the God of all grace who hath called us unto his eternal glory by Christ Jesus…"* (I Peter 5:10). Well, it is ours to know, receive and ultimately live, so let's begin to study this wonderful "tent of meeting." For soon to come these Scriptures will become a reality in a people, *"For I, saith the Lord, will be unto her a wall of fire round about, and will be the glory in the midst of her"* (Zechariah 2:5); *"Behold the tabernacle of God is with men, and He will dwell with them, and they shall be His people and God himself shall be with them"* (Revelations 21:3). Unto that glorious end this manual has been prepared. To all of Jesus' true disciples everywhere, may the precious Holy Spirit enlighten our eyes to behold Him as we study (Ephesians 1:17-18). Breathe upon us Lord Jesus so that we can understand (Luke 24:45). Amen!

Jesus is Precious,

Samuel N. Greene, Ph. D.

TABERNACLE OF MOSES

Table Of Contents

Lesson 1

Introduction To "The Tabernacle"

I. Exodus 25:1-9 – Verse by verse overview:

*"1And the LORD spake unto Moses, saying, 2Speak unto the children of Israel, that they bring me an offering:
of every man that giveth it willingly with his heart ye shall take my offering. 3And this is the offering which ye
shall take of them; gold, and silver, and brass, 4And blue, and purple, and scarlet, and fine linen, and goats' hair,
5And rams' skins dyed red, and badgers' skins, and shittim wood, 6Oil for the light, spices for anointing oil, and for
sweet incense, 7Onyx stones, and stones to be set in the ephod, and in the breastplate. 8And let them make me a
sanctuary; that I may dwell among them. 9According to all that I shew thee, after the pattern of the tabernacle,
and the pattern of all the instruments thereof, even so shall ye make it."*

A. Verse 1 – God ordained this, not man; He is the one who spoke it.

B. Verse 2 – Speak to the children of Israel that they:

1. Bring me an offering
2. Every man is supposed to bring one
3. We are to give our offerings willingly
4. And give with our hearts

C. Verses 3-7

1. Things we should bring as an offering – All of these not only have a natural meaning as they were used to physically build the original tabernacle, but they also have tremendous spiritual significance; we will define their symbolic meaning later.

   a. Gold
   b. Silver
   c. Brass
   d. Blue
   e. Purple
   f. Scarlet
   g. Fine linen
   h. Goat's hair
   i. Ram's skin died red
   j. Badger's skin
   k. Shittim wood
   l. Oil for light
   m. Spices for anointing oil and sweet incense
   n. Onyx stone
   o. Stones to be set in ephod and breastplate

2. God wants a willing offering from every man:

The first step in God dwelling with us is revealed in the first seven verses. He requires a willing offering. We must pay a price to have His Presence. It is essential to understand this before even beginning this study. Are we willing to pay that price, to give that costly sacrifice? We cannot serve God and mammon. To have real fellowship with God we must be delivered from greed, the love of money, and the god of this world. Whether or not we will give of our material possessions always determines who is first in our lives. This is foundational.

D. Verse 8

1. *"Let"* – This means that doing this could be hindered. "Let" means somebody releases us to do it. Perhaps leadership might prevent us from building the true house of God. Somebody has to "let" us. Even if God ordained it, men could stop it. Moses didn't have to tell the people what God had said to him about and for them. Other places we see this:

a. Psalms 149:2-3, 5-6 – "[2]Let Israel rejoice in him that made him: let the children of Zion be joyful in their King. [3]Let them praise his name in the dance: let them sing praises unto him with the timbrel and harp...[5]Let the saints be joyful in glory: let them sing aloud upon their beds. [6]Let the high praises of God be in their mouth, and a twoedged sword in their hand;"
b. Psalms 68:1 – "*Let God arise, let his enemies be scattered: let them also that hate him flee before him.*"
c. Matthew 19:12 – "*For there are some eunuchs, which were so born from their mother's womb: and there are some eunuchs, which were made eunuchs of men: and there be eunuchs, which have made themselves eunuchs for the kingdom of heaven's sake. He that is able to receive it, let him receive it.*"
d. Luke 11:52 – "*Woe unto you, lawyers! for ye have taken away the key of knowledge: ye entered not in yourselves, and them that were entering in ye hindered.*"

2. "*Them*" – This means the people of God are supposed to do it. We are the "*them*." Just as these Israelites built Moses' Tabernacle, we are building the greatest house of God, the body of Christ. The Scriptures below show us that we are the house of God, God's building, God's temple, and the habitation of God.

a. I Corinthians 3:9, 16 – "[9]*For we are labourers together with God: ye are God's husbandry, ye are God's building...*[16]*Know ye not that ye are the temple of God, and that the Spirit of God dwelleth in you?*"
b. II Corinthians 6:16 – "*And what agreement hath the temple of God with idols? for ye are the temple of the living God; as God hath said, I will dwell in them, and walk in them; and I will be their God, and they shall be my people.*" – We are His temple, so essentially we must prepare ourselves in order for Him to have a dwelling place.
c. Ephesians 2:19-21 – "[19]*Now therefore ye are no more strangers and foreigners, but fellowcitizens with the saints, and of the household of God;* [20]*And are built upon the foundation of the apostles and prophets, Jesus Christ himself being the chief corner stone;* [21]*In whom all the building fitly framed together groweth unto an holy temple in the Lord:*"
d. Galatians 6:10 – "*As we have therefore opportunity, let us do good unto all men, especially unto them who are of the household of faith.*"
e. Luke 12:42 – "*And the Lord said, Who then is that faithful and wise steward, whom his lord shall make ruler over his household, to give them their portion of meat in due season?*"
f. I Peter 4:17 – "*For the time is come that judgment must begin at the house of God: and if it first begin at us, what shall the end be of them that obey not the gospel of God?*"
g. I Peter 2:5 – "*Ye also, as lively stones, are built up a spiritual house, an holy priesthood, to offer up spiritual sacrifices, acceptable to God by Jesus Christ.*"
h. Hebrews 10:21-22 – "*And having an high priest over the house of God; Let us draw near with a true heart in full assurance of faith, having our hearts sprinkled from an evil conscience, and our bodies washed with pure water.*"
i. Hebrews 3:6 – "*But Christ as a son over his own house; whose house are we, if we hold fast the confidence and the rejoicing of the hope firm unto the end.*"
j. I Timothy 3:15 – "*But if I tarry long, that thou mayest know how thou oughtest to behave thyself in the house of God, which is the church of the living God, the pillar and ground of the truth.*"
k. II Timothy 2:19-21 – "[19]*Nevertheless the foundation of God standeth sure, having this seal, The Lord knoweth them that are his. And, Let every one that nameth the name of Christ depart from iniquity.* [20]*But in a great house there are not only vessels of gold and of silver, but also of wood and of earth; and some to honour, and some to dishonour.* [21]*If a man therefore purge himself from these, he shall be a vessel unto honour, sanctified, and meet for the master's use, and prepared unto every good work.*"
l. Matthew 18:20 – "*For where two or three are gathered together in my name, there am I in the midst of them.*" – We are where He comes to dwell. When we gather together, He comes in the midst. We are the dwelling place He has longed for. The Old Testament Tabernacle

is a natural type of what God longs for in the spirit. We are the "living tabernacle" made up of living stones.

3. "*Make me*" – The word "make" speaks of a process. The word "*make*" in Hebrew means – to do or make, to create. We are to create, make, and be a dwelling place for the Lord. We are to build His house. We are to prepare a place, a habitation for Him. Where do we see this in Scripture?

   a. Exodus 15:2 – "*The LORD is my strength and song, and he is become my salvation: he is my God, and I will prepare him an habitation; my father's God, and I will exalt him.*"
   b. Ezra 1:2-7 – "*...3Who is there among you of all his people? his God be with him, and let him go up to Jerusalem, which is in Judah, and build the house of the LORD God of Israel, (he is the God,) which is in Jerusalem. 4And whosoever remaineth in any place where he sojourneth, let the men of his place help him with silver, and with gold, and with goods, and with beasts, beside the freewill offering for the house of God that is in Jerusalem. 5Then rose up the chief of the fathers of Judah and Benjamin, and the priests, and the Levites, with all them whose spirit God had raised, to go up to build the house of the LORD which is in Jerusalem. 6And all they that were about them strengthened their hands with vessels of silver, with gold, with goods, and with beasts, and with precious things, beside all that was willingly offered...*"
   c. I Kings 5:5 – "*And, behold, I purpose to build an house unto the name of the LORD my God, as the LORD spake unto David my father, saying, Thy son, whom I will set upon thy throne in thy room, he shall build an house unto my name.*"
   d. Zechariah 6:12-15 – "*12And speak unto him, saying, Thus speaketh the LORD of hosts, saying, Behold the man whose name is The BRANCH; and he shall grow up out of his place, and he shall build the temple of the LORD: 13Even he shall build the temple of the LORD; and he shall bear the glory, and shall sit and rule upon his throne; and he shall be a priest upon his throne: and the counsel of peace shall be between them both. 14And the crowns shall be to Helem, and to Tobijah, and to Jedaiah, and to Hen the son of Zephaniah, for a memorial in the temple of the LORD. 15And they that are far off shall come and build in the temple of the LORD, and ye shall know that the LORD of hosts hath sent me unto you. And this shall come to pass, if ye will diligently obey the voice of the LORD your God.*"
   e. Ezra 4:3-5 – "*3But Zerubbabel, and Jeshua, and the rest of the chief of the fathers of Israel, said unto them, Ye have nothing to do with us to build an house unto our God; but we ourselves together will build unto the LORD God of Israel, as king Cyrus the king of Persia hath commanded us. 4Then the people of the land weakened the hands of the people of Judah, and troubled them in building, 5And hired counsellers against them, to frustrate their purpose, all the days of Cyrus king of Persia, even until the reign of Darius king of Persia.*"
   f. Ezra 6:14-15 – "*And the elders of the Jews builded, and they prospered through the prophesying of Haggai the prophet and Zechariah the son of Iddo. And they builded, and finished it, according to the commandment of the God of Israel, and according to the commandment of Cyrus, and Darius, and Artaxerxes king of Persia. And this house was finished on the third day of the month Adar, which was in the sixth year of the reign of Darius the king.*"
   g. Ephesians 2:21-22 – "*In whom all the building fitly framed together groweth unto an holy temple in the Lord: In whom ye also are builded together for an habitation of God through the Spirit.*"
   h. Haggai – Chapter One
   i. I Chronicles 22:1-6 – "*1Then David said, This is the house of the LORD God, and this is the altar of the burnt offering for Israel. 2And David commanded to gather together the strangers that were in the land of Israel; and he set masons to hew wrought stones to build the house of God. 3And David prepared iron in abundance for the nails for the doors of the gates, and for the joinings; and brass in abundance without weight; 4Also cedar trees in abundance: for the Zidonians and they of Tyre brought much cedar wood to David. 5And David said, Solomon my son is young and tender, and the house that is to be builded for the LORD must be exceeding magnifical, of fame and of glory throughout all countries: I will therefore now make*

preparation for it. So David prepared abundantly before his death. [6]Then he called for Solomon his son, and charged him to build an house for the LORD God of Israel."

j. Luke 2:7 – "*And she brought forth her firstborn son, and wrapped him in swaddling clothes, and laid him in a manger; because there was no room for them in the inn.*" – Do we have room for Him?

4. "*A sanctuary*"

a. Hebrews 9:2 – "*For there was a tabernacle made; the first, wherein was the candlestick, and the table, and the shewbread; which is called the sanctuary.*" – The Greek word for sanctuary, "*hagion*", means "a sacred thing, holy place". Here, it refers to the holy place.

b. Hebrews 8:2 – "*A minister of the sanctuary, and of the true tabernacle, which the Lord pitched, and not man.*" – This refers to the true sanctuary in heaven, or as the deeper definition of the word in *Vines & Strong's* means – the immediate presence of God and His throne.

c. Sanctuary in Hebrew means – A consecrated thing, palace, an asylum. It comes from a root word that means "to pronounce clean". I believe the sanctuary is defined as the meeting place of God and men. It means the place that is holy or sanctified and it is where God dwells with His people. I believe this is the place of His presence. This could be compared to the Hebrew name "Bethel" which means "house of God."

1) Bethel – House of God (Genesis 28:12-19, Genesis 35:1-5, 9-15)

2) It is the place where God and man meet.

a) Mark 11:4 – "*And they went their way, and found the colt tied by the door without in a place where two ways met; and they loose him.*"

b) Genesis 32:1-2 – "*And Jacob went on his way, and the angels of God met him. And when Jacob saw them, he said, This is God's host: and he called the name of that place Mahanaim.*"

c) Matthew 18:20 – "*For where two or three are gathered together in my name, there am I in the midst of them.*"

d) John 15:4-10 – "*[4]Abide in me, and I in you. As the branch cannot bear fruit of itself, except it abide in the vine; no more can ye, except ye abide in me. [5]I am the vine, ye are the branches: He that abideth in me, and I in him, the same bringeth forth much fruit: for without me ye can do nothing. [6]If a man abide not in me, he is cast forth as a branch, and is withered; and men gather them, and cast them into the fire, and they are burned. [7]If ye abide in me, and my words abide in you, ye shall ask what ye will, and it shall be done unto you. [8]Herein is my Father glorified, that ye bear much fruit; so shall ye be my disciples. [9]As the Father hath loved me, so have I loved you: continue ye in my love. [10]If ye keep my commandments, ye shall abide in my love; even as I have kept my Father's commandments, and abide in his love.*"

5. "*...That I may dwell among them...*" – God has desired this from the beginning of time:

a. Genesis 3:8 – "*And they heard the voice of the LORD God walking in the garden in the cool of the day: and Adam and his wife hid themselves from the presence of the LORD God amongst the trees of the garden.*"

b. Psalms 132:13-14 – "*For the LORD hath chosen Zion; he hath desired it for his habitation. This is my rest for ever: here will I dwell; for I have desired it.*"

c. Revelation 21:3 – "*And I heard a great voice out of heaven saying, Behold, the tabernacle of God is with men, and he will dwell with them, and they shall be his people, and God himself shall be with them, and be their God.*"

d. Ephesians 3:17-21 – "[17]*That Christ may dwell in your hearts by faith; that ye, being rooted and grounded in love,* [18]*May be able to comprehend with all saints what is the breadth, and length, and depth, and height;* [19]*And to know the love of Christ, which passeth knowledge, that ye might be filled with all the fulness of God.* [20]*Now unto him that is able to do exceeding abundantly above all that we ask or think, according to the power that worketh in us,* [21]*Unto him be glory in the church by Christ Jesus throughout all ages, world without end. Amen.*"

e. How can we practically do this?

1) John 14:23 – "*Jesus answered and said unto him, If a man love me, he will keep my words: and my Father will love him, and we will come unto him, and make our abode with him.*" – Love and walk in His word
2) Psalms 22:3 – "*But thou art holy, O thou that inhabitest the praises of Israel.*" – Praise and worship

II. Other reasons why we should study "the Tabernacle":

A. Jesus is the most important revelation that should come out of the tabernacle. He is the antitype, the revelation, the fulfillment of every piece of furniture, every socket, tool, etc. Jesus fulfilled the symbolism of the tabernacle. Jesus is the person behind everything that is taught. (Hebrews 1:1-3 – "[1]*God, who at sundry times and in divers manners spake in time past unto the fathers by the prophets,* [2]*Hath in these last days spoken unto us by his Son, whom he hath appointed heir of all things, by whom also he made the worlds;* [3]*Who being the brightness of his glory, and the express image of his person, and upholding all things by the word of his power, when he had by himself purged our sins, sat down on the right hand of the Majesty on high;*")

1. Luke 24:27 – "*And beginning at Moses and all the prophets, he expounded unto them in all the scriptures the things concerning himself.*"
2. John 5:38-39 – "*And ye have not his word abiding in you: for whom he hath sent, him ye believe not. Search the scriptures; for in them ye think ye have eternal life: and they are they which testify of me.*"
3. Psalms 40:7 – "*Then said I, Lo, I come: <u>in the volume of the book</u> it is written of me,*" (Hebrews 10:7) – This Tabernacle is part of the volume of the book
4. John 1:14 – "*And the Word was made flesh, and dwelt among us, (and we beheld his glory, the glory as of the only begotten of the Father,) full of grace and truth.*" – He is the Word
5. Acts 26:22-23 – "*Having therefore obtained help of God, I continue unto this day, witnessing both to small and great, saying none other things than those which the prophets and Moses did say should come: That Christ should suffer, and that he should be the first that should rise from the dead, and should shew light unto the people, and to the Gentiles.*" – Ultimately it's not what we know, but **who** we know.
6. John 5:46-47 – "*For had ye believed Moses, ye would have believed me: for he wrote of me. But if ye believe not his writings, how shall ye believe my words?*" – Moses wrote of Jesus.
7. Galatians 3:21-24 – "[21]*Is the law then against the promises of God? God forbid: for if there had been a law given which could have given life, verily righteousness should have been by the law.* [22]*But the scripture hath concluded all under sin, that the promise by faith of Jesus Christ might be given to them that believe.* [23]*But before faith came, we were kept under the law, shut up unto the faith which should afterwards be revealed.* [24]*Wherefore the law was our schoolmaster to bring us unto Christ, that we might be justified by faith.*" – The Tabernacle, which was part of the law, was to bring us to Christ.

B. This Old Testament holds great truths within it that we can apply in our lives – The Old Testament is the New Testament concealed; the New Testament is the Old Testament revealed

1. Romans 15:4 – *"For whatsoever things were written aforetime were written for our learning, that we through patience and comfort of the scriptures might have hope."*
2. I Corinthians 10:6, 11 – *"[6]Now these things were our examples, to the intent we should not lust after evil things, as they also lusted...[11]Now all these things happened unto them for ensamples: and they are written for our admonition, upon whom the ends of the world are come."*
3. I Corinthians 15:45 – *"And so it is written, The first man Adam was made a living soul; the last Adam was made a quickening spirit."*
4. Hebrews 8:5 – *"Who serve unto the example and shadow of heavenly things, as Moses was admonished of God when he was about to make the tabernacle: for, See, saith he, that thou make all things according to the pattern shewed to thee in the mount."*
5. Romans 1:20 – *"For the invisible things of him from the creation of the world are clearly seen, being understood by the things that are made, even his eternal power and Godhead; so that they are without excuse:"*

C. Other several specific reasons:

1. We need to see the tabernacle as it is fulfilled in the life and ministry of Jesus.
2. We need to see how it speaks of the different dispensations of the church and church history.
3. We need to see how it speaks of the Church of Jesus Christ.
4. We need to see how the spiritual truth in the Tabernacle relates experientially in the life of every believer.
5. We need to see and remember that this earthly Tabernacle of Moses was simply a shadow or type of the true, heavenly sanctuary (Hebrews 9:21-24). Remember this principle: first the natural, then the spiritual (I Corinthians 15:46). As we see the natural, we discover the spiritual.
6. This earthly tabernacle with is the shadow of the real and gives us the steps whereby we can enter into His manifest glory in the Most Holy Place.
7. In studying the Tabernacle we see God's great <u>three-fold principle</u> as it relates to the Tabernacle

One	**Distinguished By Three**		
Tabernacle	Outer Court	Holy Place	Most Holy Place
Man	Spirit	Soul	Body
Salvation	Justification	Sanctification	Glorification
Baptisms	Blood	Holy Spirit	Water
God	Father	Son	Holy Spirit
Feasts of the Lord	Passover	Pentecost	Tabernacles
Worship	Thanksgiving	Praise	Worship
Heavens	First Heaven	Second Heaven	Third Heaven
Body of Christ	30-Fold	60-Fold	100-Fold
Faith	Measure of Faith	Fruit of Faith	Gift of Faith
Priestly Ministry	To the people	Before the Lord	To the Lord

I could go on and on, but for a complete listing of the threefold principle, in our book on the "Doctrine of Baptisms", it is fully and completely outlined.

D. Tabernacle – Type of local church (God's pattern for bringing forth a local church.)

1. Ark of Glory – Exodus 25:10-16

   a. Glory of God in the midst
   b. God's character

2. Mercy Seat – Exodus 25:17, 22 – *"[17]And thou shalt make a mercy seat of pure gold: two cubits and a half shall be the length thereof, and a cubit and a half the breadth thereof... [22]And there I will*

meet with thee, and I will commune with thee from above the mercy seat, from between the two cherubims which are upon the ark of the testimony, of all things which I will give thee in commandment unto the children of Israel."

a. No height or depth to mercy
b. Mercy must be a part of every local church
c. God meets here with his people

3. Cherubims of Gold – Exodus 25:18-21 – "[18]*And thou shalt make two cherubims of gold, of beaten work shalt thou make them, in the two ends of the mercy seat.* [19]*And make one cherub on the one end, and the other cherub on the other end: even of the mercy seat shall ye make the cherubims on the two ends thereof.* [20]*And the cherubims shall stretch forth their wings on high, covering the mercy seat with their wings, and their faces shall look one to another; toward the mercy seat shall the faces of the cherubims be.* [21]*And thou shalt put the mercy seat above upon the ark; and in the ark thou shalt put the testimony that I shall give thee."* – We must guard the glory and mercy.

4. Golden Altar of Incense – Exodus 30:1-10

   a. Worship (High level of worship)
   b. Intercession – Perpetual

5. Table of Shewbread – Exodus 25:23-30

   a. Bread of His Presence (the Living Word, anointed)
   b. Fellowship – Priests ate together
   c. 12 Loaves – Divine order

6. The Golden Candlestick – Exodus 25:31-40

   a. Gifts of the Spirit
   b. Fruits of the Spirit
   c. Divine light or vision

7. Brass Laver – Exodus 30:17-21

   a. Sanctification
   b. Baptisms
   c. Word and "expose" (mirrors)

8. Brass Altar – Exodus 27:1-8

   a. Judgment for sin
   b. Cross of Christ (Evangelism)

Lesson 2

According To The Pattern

We must first understand that our wonderful heavenly Father is a God of order. Everything He does has purpose and a reason. He is working all things together for good, for us, His people.

I. Everything In The Tabernacle Was Done According To The Heavenly Pattern

A. Exodus 25:9 – *"According to all that I shew thee, after the pattern of the tabernacle, and the pattern of all the instruments thereof, even so shall ye make it."*

1. Other translations:

a. *"...in exact agreement with all that I am about to show thee..."*
b. *"...The pattern of the habitation..."*
c. *"...this tabernacle's dwelling itself, must be of the pattern..."*
d. *"...and the pattern of all its vessels..."*
e. *"...and everything in it..."*
f. *"...and all its fittings..."*

2. Hebrews 8:5 – *"Who serve unto the example and shadow of heavenly things, as Moses was admonished of God when he was about to make the tabernacle: for, See, saith he, that thou make all things according to the pattern shewed to thee in the mount."* Other translations:

a. *"...For see: saith He – Thou shalt make all things..."*
b. *"...God said, see that you make everything..."*

Everything had a purpose not only naturally, but also symbolically, and spiritually. There is so much symbolism in this tabernacle. Every piece of furniture, every article, every color, every dimension, every cloth, utensil, etc., has a distinct and wonderful meaning. First it all will refer symbolically to our precious Saviour Jesus. Then it will speak to us both, individually and corporately as His church.

c. *"...according to the model which hath been pointed out to thee..."*
d. *"...like the design which you saw in the mountain..."*
e. *"...according to the example which was shewed thee..."*

3. Exodus 25:40 – *"And look that thou make them after their pattern, which was shewed thee in the mount."* – Other translations:

a. *"Note well, and follow the patterns for them..."*
b. *"...and beware that you make them from the design."*
c. *"...which thou wast called to behold in the mount..."*

4. Exodus 26:30 – *"And thou shalt rear up the tabernacle according to the fashion thereof which was shewed thee in the mount."* – Other translation, *"...after the standard shown you on the mountain."*
5. Exodus 27:8 – *"Hollow with boards shalt thou make it: as it was shewed thee in the mount, so shall they make it."* – Other translation, *"...on the pattern shown you on the mountain..."*

B. Our God always has a plan:

1. Ephesians 1:11 – *"In whom also we have obtained an inheritance, being predestinated according to the purpose of him who worketh all things after the counsel of his own will"*

2. Proverbs 8:10-16 – "[10]*Receive my instruction, and not silver; and knowledge rather than choice gold.* [11]*For wisdom is better than rubies; and all the things that may be desired are not to be compared to it.* [12]*I wisdom dwell with prudence, and find out knowledge of witty inventions.* [13]*The fear of the LORD is to hate evil: pride, and arrogancy, and the evil way, and the froward mouth, do I hate.* [14]*Counsel is mine, and sound wisdom: I am understanding; I have strength.* [15]*By me kings reign, and princes decree justice.* [16]*By me princes rule, and nobles, even all the judges of the earth.*"
3. Isaiah 46:10 – "*Declaring the end from the beginning, and from ancient times the things that are not yet done, saying, My counsel shall stand, and I will do all my pleasure:*"
4. Jeremiah 32:19 – "*Great in counsel, and mighty in work: for thine eyes are open upon all the ways of the sons of men: to give every one according to his ways, and according to the fruit of his doings*"

C. There is purpose behind all that He does:

1. Ephesians 1:9 – "*Having made known unto us the mystery of his will, according to his good pleasure which he hath purposed in himself:*"
2. Romans 8:28 – "*And we know that all things work together for good to them that love God, to them who are the called according to his purpose.*"
3. II Timothy 1:9 – "*Who hath saved us, and called us with an holy calling, not according to our works, but according to his own purpose and grace, which was given us in Christ Jesus before the world began*"
4. In the last two chapters of Exodus it is written seventeen times, "*...according as the Lord told Moses...*"

II. He Has Prepared For everything:

A. Acts 17:24-26 – "[24]*God that made the world and all things therein, seeing that he is Lord of heaven and earth, dwelleth not in temples made with hands;* [25]*Neither is worshipped with men's hands, as though he needed any thing, seeing he giveth to all life, and breath, and all things;* [26]*And hath made of one blood all nations of men for to dwell on all the face of the earth, and hath determined the times before appointed, and the bounds of their habitation;*" – He has appointed our times, and all that will happen to us according to our choices. He will shape and move heaven and earth to help us.

1. Hosea 6:3 – "*Then shall we know, if we follow on to know the LORD: his going forth is prepared as the morning; and he shall come unto us as the rain, as the latter and former rain unto the earth.*"
2. Psalms 74:16-17 – "[16]*The day is thine, the night also is thine: thou hast prepared the light and the sun.* [17]*Thou hast set all the borders of the earth: thou hast made summer and winter.*"
3. Psalms 103:19 – "*The LORD hath prepared his throne in the heavens; and his kingdom ruleth over all.*"
4. Jonah 1:17 – "*Now the LORD had prepared a great fish to swallow up Jonah...*" (Jonah 4:6-8) – Consider in these verses how the Lord was watching and preparing everything for Jonah.

B. Our time is in His hand:

1. Psalms 31:15 – "*My times are in thy hand: deliver me from the hand of mine enemies, and from them that persecute me.*"
2. Job 24:1 – "*Why, seeing times are not hidden from the Almighty, do they that know him not see his days?*"
3. Ecclesiastes 3:1, 11, 17 – "[1]*To every thing there is a season, and a time to every purpose under the heaven...*[11]*He hath made every thing beautiful in his time: also he hath set the world in their heart, so that no man can find out the work that God maketh from the beginning to the end...*[17]*I said in mine heart, God shall judge the righteous and the wicked: for there is a time there for every purpose and for every work.*"

4. Ecclesiastes 8:5-6 – "[5]*Whoso keepeth the commandment shall feel no evil thing: and a wise man's heart discerneth both time and judgment.* [6]*Because to every purpose there is time and judgment, therefore the misery of man is great upon him.*"

C. He is sovereign and knows all things:

1. Isaiah 45:21 – "*Tell ye, and bring them near; yea, let them take counsel together: who hath declared this from ancient time? who hath told it from that time? have not I the LORD? and there is no God else beside me; a just God and a Saviour; there is none beside me.*"
2. Isaiah 46:10-11 – "[10]*Declaring the end from the beginning, and from ancient times the things that are not yet done, saying, My counsel shall stand, and I will do all my pleasure:* [11]*Calling a ravenous bird from the east, the man that executeth my counsel from a far country: yea, I have spoken it, I will also bring it to pass; I have purposed it, I will also do it.*"
3. Jeremiah 29:11 – "*For I know the thoughts that I think toward you, saith the LORD, thoughts of peace, and not of evil, to give you an expected end.*"
4. Psalms 145:9 – "*The LORD is good to all: and his tender mercies are over all his works.*"

His mercy is over all His work. Though He knows everything and He has perfect knowledge of all, He allows us to make choices. He sets our pattern, our plan for life (the one He wants us to follow), and then waits and watches. He is always pointing us in the right direction. Some follow while others don't. One thing is for sure, "*Shall not the judge of the whole earth do right?*" (Genesis 18:25). The Tabernacle of Moses is a prime example of His plan, His will, and His preparation. It should forever teach us, "*His kingdom ruleth over all*" (Psalm 103:19).

Lesson 3

Jesus Symbolized In The Tabernacle

I. Everything In The Tabernacle Finds It's Fulfillment In Jesus

A. Scriptural foundation for this:

1. Luke 24:27 – *"And beginning at Moses and all the prophets, he expounded unto them in all the scriptures the things concerning himself."* – Other translations:

   a. *"Then going back to Moses and the whole line of prophets..."*
   b. *"...interpreted to them..."*
   c. *"...in every part of the Scriptures..."*
   d. *"...the passages that referred to himself..."*

2. Hebrews 10:7 – *"Then said I, Lo, I come (in the volume of the book it is written of me,) to do thy will, O God."* – Other translations:

   a. *"...the writing in the scroll of the Book tells about me..."*
   b. *"...in the heading of the scroll it is written concerning me..."*

3. Psalms 29:9 – *"The voice of the LORD maketh the hinds to calve, and discovereth the forests: and in his temple doth every one speak of his glory."* – Other translations:

   a. *"...surely through this His universal temple, everything speaks of His glory."*
   b. *"...meanwhile, in His sanctuary, there is no sound but tells of His glory."*
   c. *"...everything speaks of His glory."*

4. Revelation 1:8 – *"I am Alpha and Omega, the beginning and the ending, saith the Lord, which is, and which was, and which is to come, the Almighty."* – Other translation, *"...I am Alpha and Omega the beginning of all things and their end, says the Lord God."*

5. Hebrews 1:1-3 – *"[1]God, who at sundry times and in divers manners spake in time past unto the fathers by the prophets, [2]Hath in these last days spoken unto us by his Son, whom he hath appointed heir of all things, by whom also he made the worlds; [3]Who being the brightness of his glory, and the express image of his person, and upholding all things by the word of his power, when he had by himself purged our sins, sat down on the right hand of the Majesty on high"* – Other translations:

   a. *"...But in this final age, he has spoken to us..."*
   b. *"now at the end of this present age, given us the truth..."*
   c. *"...with a Son to speak for Him..."*

B. A listing of furniture, items, materials, etc. in the tabernacle and how it relates to Jesus:

1. Brass altar – He is our substitute, our justification, our lamb
2. Laver – He is our light, our sanctifier, cleanser
3. Candlestick – He is our light, our illuminator, our baptizer in the Holy Spirit
4. Table of Shewbread – He is the Word, he is the bread from heaven
5. Golden Altar – He is our intercessor; He has shown us the way of true worship in Spirit and in truth.
6. Ark – He is the manifest presence
7. Mercy seat – He is our propitiation
8. Table of Stone – He is our law giver

Jesus On The Cross

9. Golden pot of Manna – He is our food, He is the revealer of the hidden secrets of God
10. Aaron's Rod – He is the appointed one, our high priest, our Melchisedek
11. Glory Cloud – He is the express image of God, the revealer of the glory of God
12. The Cloud – He is our leader, our shepherd
13. The Veil – He has become our access to God
14. Door – He is our door, He said it himself; there is no other who can open the door for the sheep.
15. Curtains – He is our covering
16. Blue – He is the Lord from heaven
17. Gold – He is the divine nature
18. Silver – Jesus our wonderful redeemer
19. Brass – He is our Judge
20. Scarlet – He took our suffering and shed His blood
21. Purple – He is our royal King
22. Fine Linen – He is our righteousness; He also was sinless
23. Sacrificial Offering – He becomes our offering, the Lamb of God
24. Frankincense – He is our innocence, sinless and pure
25. Twelve Loaves – He is the living Word, and brings us order
26. Wood – It was His sinless humanity that saved us, His incorruptible humanity
27. Oil – He is our anointing; He gives us light
28. Utensils – Everything we need to minister is found in Him
29. Horns – He is our King, His kingdom ruleth over all
30. Crowns – He purchased for us the ability to win a crown, He is crowned King of Kings
31. Staves – He is our burden bearer, the Son of man; He is both divine and human
32. Incense – It is Him we worship, as He worshipped the Father, He taught us how to pray and worship
33. Foot at the laver – He helps us walk the walk of sanctification, He is our sanctification
34. Shaft and Branch – He is the righteous branch and connects us to His light
35. Priest – He is our high priest, our Melchisedek
36. Goat's hair – His atonement, our sin offering
37. Ram's Skin Dyed Red – He became our bloody sacrifice
38. Precious Stones – He has become for us all the glories and perfections of God to us
39. Gate – He is the way, truth and life; our Alpha, our beginning in God
40. Pillars – He is our foundation; our cornerstone
41. Silver Trumpets – He is the one who is heralding the news of our redemption
42. Cherubims – He is the guarder of God's glory, under His wings we have come to trust
43. Garments – He is our righteousness
44. Scapegoat – He died outside the camp
45. Badger Skins – Once again He is our substitution sacrifice; becoming all that was ugly in us to redeem us
46. Measurements – He is what we are to measure our lives to; He shows us the way to the stature and fullness of God
47. Willing Offerings – He willingly offered His life
48. Fifty Taches (Clasps) of Gold – he is our jubilee into the glory of God
49. Fifty Taches of Brass – He took us from judgment to jubilee
50. Boards and Bars –His incorruptible humanity overlaid with God's divine nature; this is what upholds our eternal salvation
51. Corners – Jesus is our precious cornerstone; He is the one that all others (builders) rejected, but He is become the head stone of the corner
52. Pins (nails) – He has fastened us to Himself; He will never leave us or forsake us; He holds us together with Him; He is nailing in to us His Word; Primarily that He took our judgment
53. Cords – He is the one who binds us together with Himself, the Holy Spirit and the Father
54. Spices – The fragrant graces and fruits of Jesus' Ministry
55. The Tabernacle Itself – Because of Jesus, God can now inhabit us.

II. The Centrality And All Importance Of The Lord Jesus Christ

A. I Peter 2:7 – "*Unto you therefore which believe* <u>*he is precious*</u>*: but unto them which be disobedient, the stone which the builders disallowed, the same is made the head of the corner,*" Other translations:

"*For those of you who trust, He is the dintinguished...*"
"*You believers therefore feel His value...*"
"*Now you believe, you hold him precious...*"
"*To you then who believe (who adhere to, trust in, and rely on Him) is he preciousness...*"

B. Jesus is the Pre-eminent One:

1. Colossians 1:15-19 – "[15]*Who is the image of the invisible God, the firstborn of every creature:* [16]*For by him were all things created, that are in heaven, and that are in earth, visible and invisible, whether they be thrones, or dominions, or principalities, or powers: all things were created by him, and for him:* [17]*And he is before all things, and by him all things consist.* [18]*And he is the head of the body, the church: who is the beginning, the firstborn from the dead; that in all things he might have the preeminence.* [19]*For it pleased the Father that in him should all fulness dwell;*"
2. Galatians 1:15-16 – "[15]*But when it pleased God, who separated me from my mother's womb, and called me by his grace,* [16]*To reveal his Son in me, that I might preach him among the heathen; immediately I conferred not with flesh and blood*"
3. Ephesians 4:13-15 – "[13]*Till we all come in the unity of the faith, and of the knowledge of the Son of God, unto a perfect man, unto the measure of the stature of the fulness of Christ:* [14]*That we henceforth be no more children, tossed to and fro, and carried about with every wind of doctrine, by the sleight of men, and cunning craftiness, whereby they lie in wait to deceive;* [15]*But speaking the truth in love, may grow up into him in all things, which is the head, even Christ:*"
4. Revelation 1:1 – "*The Revelation of Jesus Christ...*"
5. Colossians 2:10 – "*And ye are complete in him, which is the head of all principality and power:*"

Lesson 4

The Importance of the Name of Jesus

I. Jesus Is The Name Of The Godhead

A. Scriptural definition:

1. Zechariah 14:9 - "*And the Lord shall be king over all the earth: in that day shall there be one Lord, and his name one.*"
2. Colossians 1:19 - "*For it pleased the Father that in him should all fullness dwell;*"
3. Colossians 2:9 - "*For in him dwelleth all the fullness of the Godhead bodily.*"
4. Matthew 28:19 - "*Go ye therefore, and teach all nations, baptizing them in the name of the Father, and of the Son, and of the Holy Ghost:*"
5. Ephesians 1:20-21 - "[20]*Which he wrought in Christ, when he raised him from the dead, and set him at his own right hand in the heavenly places,* [21]*Far above all principality, and power, and might, and dominion, and every name that is named, not only in this world, but also in that which is to come.*"
6. John 8:58 - "*Jesus said unto them, Verily, verily, I say unto you, Before Abraham was, I am.*"
7. Matthew 1:21-23 – "[21]*And she shall bring forth a son, and thou shalt call his name JESUS: for he shall save his people from their sins.* [22]*Now all this was done, that it might be fulfilled which was spoken of the Lord by the prophet, saying,* [23]*Behold, a virgin shall be with child, and shall bring forth a son, and they shall call his name Emmanuel, which being interpreted is, God with us.*"
8. John 5:43 – "*I am come in my Father's name, and ye receive me not: if another shall come in his own name, him ye will receive.*"
9. John 10:25 – "*Jesus answered them, I told you, and ye believed not: the works that I do in my Father's name, they bear witness of me.*"
10. John 17:25-26 – "[25]*O righteous Father, the world hath not known thee: but I have known thee, and these have known that thou hast sent me.* [26]*And I have declared unto them thy name, and will declare it: that the love wherewith thou hast loved me may be in them, and I in them.*"

Jesus came in the name of name of the Father, Son, and Holy Spirit. God is not a name, but God has a name, and that name is the Lord Jesus Christ!

B. Jesus manifested the name of the Godhead:

1. John 17:6, 26 – "*I have manifested thy name unto the men which thou gavest me out of the world: thine they were, and thou gavest them me; and they have kept thy word...* [26]*And I have declared unto them thy name, and will declare it: that the love wherewith thou hast loved me may be in them, and I in them.*" – Jesus declared the name of the triune God and walked in His divine nature. He revealed God's character as He walked and ministered on the earth.

   a. John 14:7, 9 – "[7]*If ye had known me, ye should have known my Father also: and from henceforth ye know him, and have seen him...* [9]*Jesus saith unto him, Have I been so long time with you, and yet hast thou not known me, Philip? he that hath seen me hath seen the Father; and how sayest thou then, Shew us the Father?*"
   b. Colossians 1:15 – "*Who is the image of the invisible God, the firstborn of every creature.*"
   c. Colossians 2:9 – "*For in him dwelleth all the fulness of the Godhead bodily.*"

2. Hebrews 1:2-3 – "[2]*Hath in these last days spoken unto us by his Son, whom he hath appointed heir of all things, by whom also he made the worlds;* [3]*Who being the brightness of his glory, and the express image of his person, and upholding all things by the word of his power, when he had by himself purged our sins, sat down on the right hand of the Majesty on high.*" – Jesus is the brightness of His glory and the express image of His person.

a. Philippians 2:9-11 – "[9]*Wherefore God also hath highly exalted him, and given him a name which is above every name:* [10]*That at the name of Jesus every knee should bow, of things in heaven, and things in earth, and things under the earth;* [11]*And that every tongue should confess that Jesus Christ is Lord, to the glory of God the Father.*" – The Godhead has given us His name, and it is exalted above all, and that name is Jesus.
b. Colossians 3:17 – "*And whatsoever ye do in word or deed, do all in the name of the Lord Jesus, giving thanks to God and the Father by him.*"
c. Colossians 1:15-19 – "[15]*Who is the image of the invisible God, the firstborn of every creature:* [16]*For by him were all things created, that are in heaven, and that are in earth, visible and invisible, whether they be thrones, or dominions, or principalities, or powers: all things were created by him, and for him:* [17]*And he is before all things, and by him all things consist.* [18]*And he is the head of the body, the church: who is the beginning, the firstborn from the dead; that in all things he might have the preeminence.* [19]*For it pleased the Father that in him should all fulness dwell.*"
d. Ephesians 1:20-21 – "[20]*Which he wrought in Christ, when he raised him from the dead, and set him at his own right hand in the heavenly places,* [21]*Far above all principality, and power, and might, and dominion, and every name that is named, not only in this world, but also in that which is to come.*"
e. Psalms 22:22 – "*I will declare thy name unto my brethren: in the midst of the congregation will I praise thee.*"

II. The Power and Authority of the Name JESUS:

A. All the things scripturally associated with His name:

1. What we can do in His name and what His name does for us:

a. Psalms 20:1 – "*The LORD hear thee in the day of trouble; the name of the God of Jacob defend thee.*" – It defends us
b. Psalms 20:5 – "*We will rejoice in thy salvation, and in the name of our God we will set up our banners: the LORD fulfil all thy petitions.*" – Set up our banners
c. Psalms 44:5 – "*Through thee will we push down our enemies: through thy name will we tread them under that rise up against us.*" – Tread down our enemies

1) Psalms 118:11-12 – "[11]*They compassed me about; yea, they compassed me about: but in the name of the LORD I will destroy them.* [12]*They compassed me about like bees; they are quenched as the fire of thorns: for in the name of the LORD I will destroy them.*"

d. Romans 10:13 – "*For whosoever shall call upon the name of the Lord shall be saved.*" – Salvation in His name

1) Acts 10:43 – "*To him give all the prophets witness, that through his name whosoever believeth in him shall receive remission of sins.*"
2) Psalms 54:1 – "*...Save me, O God, by thy name, and judge me by thy strength.*"
3) Luke 1:31 – "*And, behold, thou shalt conceive in thy womb, and bring forth a son, and shalt call his name JESUS.*"
4) Joel 2:32 – "*And it shall come to pass, that whosoever shall call on the name of the LORD shall be delivered: for in mount Zion and in Jerusalem shall be deliverance, as the LORD hath said, and in the remnant whom the LORD shall call.*"
5) Acts 2:21 – "*And it shall come to pass, that whosoever shall call on the name of the Lord shall be saved.*"
6) I John 2:12 – "*I write unto you, little children, because your sins are forgiven you for his name's sake.*"

7) I Corinthians 6:11 – *"And such were some of you: but ye are washed, but ye are sanctified, but ye are justified in the name of the Lord Jesus, and by the Spirit of our God."*
8) Luke 24:47 – *"And that repentance and remission of sins should be preached in his name among all nations, beginning at Jerusalem."*

e. Psalms 91:14 – *"Because he hath set his love upon me, therefore will I deliver him: I will set him on high, because he hath known my name."* – We are set on high
f. Psalms 124:8 – *"Our help is in the name of the LORD, who made heaven and earth."* – Our help is in His name.
g. Proverbs 18:10 – *"The name of the LORD is a strong tower: the righteous runneth into it, and is safe."* – A strong tower from the enemy
h. John 17:12 – *"While I was with them in the world, I kept them in thy name: those that thou gavest me I have kept, and none of them is lost, but the son of perdition; that the scripture might be fulfilled."* – Kept by His name

i. Mark 16:17 – *"And these signs shall follow them that believe; In my name shall they cast out devils; they shall speak with new tongues."* – Cast out devils

1) Mark 9:38 – *"And John answered him, saying, Master, we saw one casting out devils in thy name, and he followeth not us: and we forbad him, because he followeth not us."*
2) Acts 16:18 – *"And this did she many days. But Paul, being grieved, turned and said to the spirit, I command thee in the name of Jesus Christ to come out of her. And he came out the same hour."*
3) Mark 16:17 – *"And these signs shall follow them that believe; In my name shall they cast out devils; they shall speak with new tongues."*

J. Mark 16:17 – *"And these signs shall follow them that believe; In my name shall they cast out devils; they shall speak with new tongues."* – Heal the sick in His name

1) James 5:14 – *"Is any sick among you? let him call for the elders of the church; and let them pray over him, anointing him with oil in the name of the Lord."*
2) Acts 4:30 – *"By stretching forth thine hand to heal; and that signs and wonders may be done by the name of thy holy child Jesus."*
3) Acts 3:6 – *"Then Peter said, Silver and gold have I none; but such as I have give I thee: In the name of Jesus Christ of Nazareth rise up and walk."*

k. Deuteronomy 18:18-22 – *"[18]I will raise them up a Prophet from among their brethren, like unto thee, and will put my words in his mouth; and he shall speak unto them all that I shall command him. [19]And it shall come to pass, that whosoever will not hearken unto my words which he shall speak in my name, I will require it of him. [20]But the prophet, which shall presume to speak a word in my name, which I have not commanded him to speak, or that shall speak in the name of other gods, even that prophet shall die. [21]And if thou say in thine heart, How shall we know the word which the LORD hath not spoken? [22]When a prophet speaketh in the name of the LORD, if the thing follow not, nor come to pass, that is the thing which the LORD hath not spoken, but the prophet hath spoken it presumptuously: thou shalt not be afraid of him."* – Prophesy in His name
l. Luke 10:17 – *"And the seventy returned again with joy, saying, Lord, even the devils are subject unto us through thy name."* – Devils are subject to us in his name
m. John 20:31 – *"But these are written, that ye might believe that Jesus is the Christ, the Son of God; and that believing ye might have life through his name."* – Life is in His name
n. Acts 4:30 – *"By stretching forth thine hand to heal; and that signs and wonders may be done by the name of thy holy child Jesus."* – Signs, wonders, miracles, done in His name

1) Mark 16:17 – *"And these signs shall follow them that believe; In my name shall they cast out devils; they shall speak with new tongues."*

o. Psalms 63:4 – *"Thus will I bless thee while I live: I will lift up my hands in thy name."* – Our ability to worship

p. Psalms 124:8 – "Our help is in the name of the LORD, who made heaven and earth." – Protection in His name

1) Psalms 91:10 – *"There shall no evil befall thee, neither shall any plague come nigh thy dwelling."*
2) Psalms 20:1 – *"The LORD hear thee in the day of trouble; the name of the God of Jacob defend thee."*
3) Psalms 89:36 – *"His seed shall endure forever, and his throne as the sun before me."*
4) Psalms 91:14 – *"Because he hath set his love upon me, therefore will I deliver him: I will set him on high, because he hath known my name."*

III. All The Other Aspects Of the Name

A. Awesome is the name of Jesus:

1. Philippians 2:9-10 – *"[9]Wherefore God also hath highly exalted him, and given him a name which is above every name: [10]That at the name of Jesus every knee should bow, of things in heaven, and things in earth, and things under the earth."*
2. Psalms 99:3 – *"Let them praise thy great and terrible name; for it is holy."*
3. Hebrews 1:4 – *"Being made so much better than the angels, as he hath by inheritance obtained a more excellent name than they."*
4. Malachi 1:11, 14 – *"[11]For from the rising of the sun even unto the going down of the same my name shall be great among the Gentiles; and in every place incense shall be offered unto my name, and a pure offering: for my name shall be great among the heathen, saith the LORD of hosts... [14]But cursed be the deceiver, which hath in his flock a male, and voweth, and sacrificeth unto the LORD a corrupt thing: for I am a great King, saith the LORD of hosts, and my name is dreadful among the heathen."*
5. Isaiah 42:8 – *"I am the LORD: that is my name: and my glory will I not give to another, neither my praise to graven images."*
6. Psalms 111:9 – *"He sent redemption unto his people: he hath commanded his covenant for ever: holy and reverend is his name."*
7. Acts 19:17 – *"And this was known to all the Jews and Greeks also dwelling at Ephesus; and fear fell on them all, and the name of the Lord Jesus was magnified."*
8. Ephesians 1:21 – *"Far above all principality, and power, and might, and dominion, and every name that is named, not only in this world, but also in that which is to come."*
9. Acts 4:12 – *"Neither is there salvation in any other: for there is none other name under heaven given among men, whereby we must be saved."*

B. His name can be trusted:

1. Psalms 33:21 – *"For our heart shall rejoice in him, because we have trusted in his holy name."*
2. Zephaniah 3:12
3. Matthew 12:21 – *"And in his name shall the Gentiles trust."*

C. His name is to be given glory:

1. Psalms 29:2 – *"Give unto the LORD the glory due unto his name; worship the LORD in the beauty of holiness."*

2. John 12:28 – *"Father, glorify thy name. Then came there a voice from heaven, saying, I have both glorified it, and will glorify it again."*
3. II Thessalonians 1:12

D. His name is to be praised:

1. Hebrews 13:15
2. Psalms 9:2
3. Psalms 18:49
4. Psalms 54:6
5. Psalms 61:8
6. Psalms 69:30
7. Psalms 66:2,4
8. Psalms 68:4
9. Psalms 74:21
10. Psalms 75:1
11. Psalms 89:16
12. Psalms 92:1
13. Psalms 96:2
14. Psalms 105:1, 3
15. Psalms 142:7
16. Psalms 149:3
17. Isaiah 12:4

E. His name is to be known

1. Psalms 9:10
2. Isaiah 52:6

F. His name is to be remembered

1. Psalms 20:7
2. Psalms 119:55
3. Malachi 3:16
4. Isaiah 26:8

G. His name is to be feared

1. Psalms 61:5
2. Psalms 86:11
3. Malachi 4:2
4. Revelation 11:18

H. His name is to be exalted

1. Psalms 34:3
2. Psalms 138:2
3. Isaiah 12:4

I. His name is to be loved

1. Psalms 69:36
2. Psalms 119:132

J. His name is excellent

1. Psalms 8:9
2. Psalms 148:13

K. His name is not to be polluted

1. Isaiah 48:11

2. Jeremiah 34:16
3. I Timothy 6:1
4. Ezekiel 20:39
5. Ezekiel 43:8
6. Leviticus 18:21
7. Ezekiel 36:21-23
8. Romans 2:24
9. James 2:7

L. His name will endure

1. Psalms 72:17
2. Psalms 135:13
3. Isaiah 63:16

M. His name not to be taken in vain, Exodus 20:7

N. His name is the highest

1. Ephesians 1:21
2. Ephesians 3:15
3. Deuteronomy 28:58
4. II Samuel 7:13, 23
5. I Chronicles 16:10, 29
6. I Chronicles 29:13

O. His name is to be delighted in

1. Psalms 5:11
2. Psalms 9:2
3. Psalms 34:3
4. Psalms 48:10
5. Psalms 66:2
6. Psalms 18:49

P. His name is holy

1. Isaiah 57:15
2. Matthew 6:9
3. Luke 1:49

Q. Religion hates His name

1. Acts 4:18
2. Acts 5:28, 40
3. Matthew 10:22
4. Matthew 24:9
5. Luke 21:12, 17
6. Acts 9:16
7. Acts 4:17
8. Acts 9:29
9. John 15:20-21

R. His name is to be seen

1. Micah 6:9

S. His name to be in the place of His choosing; in His city, upon His people

1. Exodus 20:24
2. I Kings 8:20, 29, 43
3. Deuteronomy 12:21
4. I Chronicles 13:6
5. II Samuel 6:2
6. I Kings 9:7
7. II Chronicles 7:20
8. II Chronicles 7:14
9. Jeremiah 7:12, 14

T. His name is blessed, Job 1:21

U. We are to gather in His name, Matthew 18:20

V. His name alone is worthy

1. Psalms 83:18
2. Psalms 113:2
3. Psalms 111:9

IV. What We Are To Do With His Name

A. Ask in His name

1. John 14:13-14
2. John 15:16
3. John 16:23-24

B. We are to have faith in His name

1. Acts 3:16
2. John 1:12
3. John 2:23
4. John 3:18
5. John 20:31
6. I John 3:23

C. His name is to be written in our minds

1. Revelation 14:1
2. Revelation 22:4
3. Revelation 3:12
4. II Thessalonians 1:12

D. We are to glorify His name in tribulation, Isaiah 24:15

E. Preach in His name

1. Acts 9:21
2. Acts 4:30

F. We must be willing to suffer and die for His name

1. Acts 9:16
2. Acts 21:13
3. Acts 5:41
4. I Peter 4:14
5. Matthew 19:29
6. Acts 5:40-41
7. Acts 15:26
8. Mark 3:13
9. Hebrews 13:13-15

G. We are to hold fast to His name

1. Revelation 2:13
2. Revelation 3:8

H. We are to walk in His name

1. Micah 4:5
2. Zechariah 10:12

I. We are to do things for His name's sake

1. I Samuel 12:22
2. Psalms 106:8
3. Revelation 2:3
4. III John 7
5. Mark 13:13
6. Acts 9:16
7. Isaiah 48:9

J. We are to make mention of His name – Isaiah 26:13

K. Everything we do we do in His name – Colossians 3:17

Lesson 5

The Encampment

The Tabernacle and its continual services, which lasted about 500 years, was and will always be a faithful and glorious teacher to Israel and presently to the church.

The Tabernacle, when set up in the wilderness, became the center of activity for all of Israel. It was also the meeting place between God and His people (Exodus 29:42-46). This would be the place where sin would be atoned for, God would be worshipped and His judgments appeased. This was also the place where God's glory would dwell. It was in this place that God would speak to Moses and to the priests. Throughout their journey, the Tabernacle was located at the center of the encampment.

I. Numbers 1:51-54 and Numbers 2

A. The Levites were separated - Numbers 1:47-51 - "[47]*But the Levites after the tribe of their fathers were not numbered among them.* [48]*For the LORD had spoken unto Moses, saying,* [49]*Only thou shalt not number the tribe of Levi, neither take the sum of them among the children of Israel:* [50]*But thou shalt appoint the Levites over the tabernacle of testimony, and over all the vessels thereof, and over all things that belong to it: they shall bear the tabernacle, and all the vessels thereof; and they shall minister unto it, and shall encamp round about the tabernacle.* [51]*And when the tabernacle setteth forward, the Levites shall take it down: and when the tabernacle is to be pitched, the Levites shall set it up: and the stranger that cometh nigh shall be put to death.*"

The Levites were not numbered. They were appointed to minister and take care of the tabernacle. They were to bear it, take it down, and set it up when it was moved. They were to encamp round about the tabernacle.

B. The rest of the tribes and where they were encamped - Every man knew his place; there was no confusion. This is obviously true of the church. God has an order for everything. There were four tribes chosen to lead the other eight tribes:

1. At the east side was Judah whose name means - praise; Judah was the head of the eastern tribes. Judah's standard was the lion. This speaks prophetically about the church; the worshippers and the overcomers will march forward toward the east. East in scripture always represents the coming of the Lord. Below are the tribes with Judah on the east side and their meaning in Hebrew:

   a. Zebulon - dwelling, habitation
   b. Issachar - He is hired, there is reward here

2. At the west side was Ephraim whose name means - two fold, increase, doubly fruitful. Its standard was an ox. West in the Scriptures speaks of going away from the Lord. Do you know the revelation here? God has placed a doubly fruitful tribe, one who is willing to work (ox) at being fruitful and one that will eventually bring increase. Below are the tribes with Ephraim:

   a. Manasseh - one who causes to forget, forgetfulness. Showing us our past will lead us to forget the Lord if not dealt with.
   b. Benjamin - son of the right hand, son of old age. This obviously is the best tribe to be in on the west side. These are symbolic of the overcomers, who will sit at Jesus' right hand (Psalms 45:9-11, 13-15, Matthew 20:20-23, Revelation 3:21). What better tribe would you want on the west side than Benjamin?

3. The south side (south in Scripture always represents prosperity and blessing) was led by Reuben whose name means - behold a son, or vision of a son. Reuben's standard was a man.

Though Reuben in his own life never made it, but failed miserably, still God had planned prophetically for him to prosper and become a full grown manifested son, who prospered and was blessed. Below are the tribes with Reuben

a. Simeon – hearkening, hearing with acceptance, hears and obeys. This speaks to us of when in prosperity and blessing we must continue to hear and obey the Lord.
b. Gad – good fortune, a troop, to cut through, and a seer. The south side obviously had the favor of the Lord and the ability to fight and overcome.

4. The north side was led by Dan. Dan's name means – judge, to rise, to execute judgment. We know that the north in Scripture always means judgment. Is it any wonder that Dan was to lead them? Dan's standard was an eagle. Eagles always represent overcoming. The judgments then of the overcomers mark this side. Other tribes with Dan:

a. Naphtali – A struggle, my wrestling, obtained by wrestling. As we are judged by the Holy Spirit, and wrestle with our own human natures, we overcome, line upon line, and we obtain His character. This is the struggle of sanctification (Romans 8:17-25, Romans 8:1, Galatians 4:22-31)
b. Asher – Happy, fortunate. This speaks to us of even in times of judgment we can continue to stay at peace. We can remain happy, knowing we are fortunate to be part of His people and His plans. As Paul said in Acts, "*I think* (Greek – command) *myself happy*" (Acts 26:2).

C. Placement for the tribe of Levi:

1. East – Numbers 3:38 – "*But those that encamp before the tabernacle toward the east, even before the tabernacle of the congregation eastward, shall be <u>Moses</u>, and <u>Aaron and his sons</u>, keeping the charge of the sanctuary for the charge of the children of Israel; and the stranger that cometh nigh shall be put to death.*"

a. Moses
b. Aaron and his sons

2. West – Numbers 3:23 – "*The <u>families of the Gershonites</u> shall pitch behind the tabernacle westward.*"

a. Gershon was the founder of the family of the Gershonites who were the oldest of Levi's sons
b. Gershon's name means – a stranger there, driven out, an outcast (Numbers 3:17)

3. South – Numbers 3:29 – "*The <u>families of the sons of Kohath</u> shall pitch on the side of the tabernacle southward.*"

a. Kohath – His name means, assembly, congregation; his name comes from a root that means to gather together.
b. He was the second son of Levi (Genesis 46:11). He founded the Kohathites.

4. North – Numbers 3:35 – "*And the chief of the house of the father of the <u>families of Merari</u> was Zuriel the son of Abihail: these shall pitch on the side of the tabernacle northward.*"

a. Merari – His name means, bitter, unhappy
b. He was the youngest son of Levi, and the founder of the Merarites (Numbers 26:57)

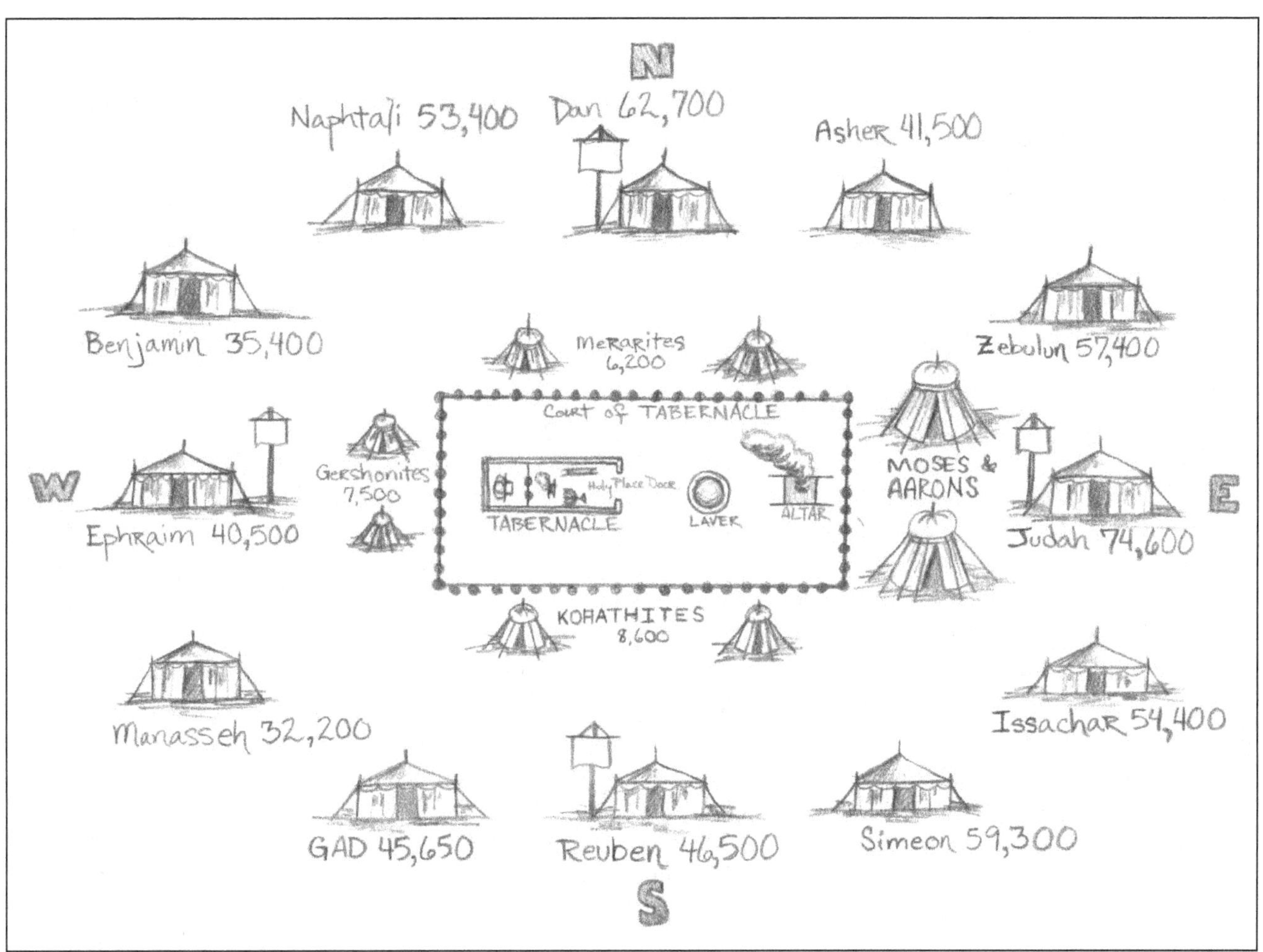

The Encampment

II. The Camp Was In The Shape of A Cross – Both the camp and furniture shaped in the form of a cross.

A. Revelation Israel's encampment around the tabernacle with the cross:

1. Israel's camp – compared with camp of the saints, Revelation 20:9 – *"And they went up on the breadth of the earth, and compassed the camp of the saints about, and the beloved city..."*

2. Israel armies of the Lord – compared with the church, His army:

a. Ephesians 6:10-18 – *"[10]Finally, my brethren, be strong in the Lord, and in the power of his might. [11]Put on the whole armour of God, that ye may be able to stand against the wiles of the devil..."*

b. II Timothy 2:3-4 – *"Thou therefore endure hardness, as a good soldier of Jesus Christ. No man that warreth entangleth himself with the affairs of this life; that he may please him who hath chosen him to be a soldier."*

c. II Corinthians 10:3-4 – *"For though we walk in the flesh, we do not war after the flesh: (For the weapons of our warfare are not carnal, but mighty through God to the pulling down of strong holds;)"*

3. Tabernacle in the midst of the camp – compared with Jesus is in the midst of His people, Matthew 18:20 – *"where two or three are gathered together in my name, there am I in the midst of them."*

4. Moses was their leader – Jesus is our captain:

   a. Hebrews 2:10 – *"For it became him, for whom are all things, and by whom are all things, in bringing many sons unto glory, to make the captain of their salvation perfect through sufferings."*
   b. Joshua 5:14 – *"And he said, Nay; but as captain of the host of the LORD am I now come. And Joshua fell on his face to the earth, and did worship, and said unto him, What saith my lord unto his servant?"*

B. The cross is the central theme throughout; it's symbolism in the Tabernacle is of great importance:

1. Galatians 6:14 – *"But God forbid that I should glory, save in the cross of our Lord Jesus Christ, by whom the world is crucified unto me, and I unto the world."*
2. I Corinthians 2:1-2 – *"And I, brethren, when I came to you, came not with excellency of speech or of wisdom, declaring unto you the testimony of God. For I determined not to know any thing among you, save Jesus Christ, and him crucified."*
3. Colossians 1:17-18 – *"And he is before all things, and by him all things consist. And he is the head of the body, the church: who is the beginning, the firstborn from the dead; that in all things he might have the preeminence."*
4. Ephesians 2:3-6 – *"[3]Among whom also we all had our conversation in times past in the lusts of our flesh, fulfilling the desires of the flesh and of the mind; and were by nature the children of wrath, even as others. [4]But God, who is rich in mercy, for his great love wherewith he loved us, [5]Even when we were dead in sins, hath quickened us together with Christ, (by grace ye are saved;) [6]And hath raised us up together, and made us sit together in heavenly places in Christ Jesus:"*
5. Philippians 2:5-10 – *"[5]Let this mind be in you, which was also in Christ Jesus: [6]Who, being in the form of God, thought it not robbery to be equal with God: [7]But made himself of no reputation, and took upon him the form of a servant, and was made in the likeness of men: [8]And being found in fashion as a man, he humbled himself, and became obedient unto death, even the death of the cross. [9]Wherefore God also hath highly exalted him, and given him a name which is above every name: [10]That at the name of Jesus every knee should bow, of things in heaven, and things in earth, and things under the earth;"*
6. Colossians 1:14-22 – *"[14]In whom we have redemption through his blood, even the forgiveness of sins: [15]Who is the image of the invisible God, the firstborn of every creature: [16]For by him were all things created, that are in heaven, and that are in earth, visible and invisible, whether they be thrones, or dominions, or principalities, or powers: all things were created by him, and for him: [17]And he is before all things, and by him all things consist. [18]And he is the head of the body, the church: who is the beginning, the firstborn from the dead; that in all things he might have the preeminence. [19]For it pleased the Father that in him should all fulness dwell; [20]And, having made peace through the blood of his cross, by him to reconcile all things unto himself; by him, I say, whether they be things in earth, or things in heaven. [21]And you, that were sometime alienated and enemies in your mind by wicked works, yet now hath he reconciled [22]In the body of his flesh through death, to present you holy and unblameable and unreproveable in his sight:"*
7. Colossians 2:13-14 – *"And you, being dead in your sins and the uncircumcision of your flesh, hath he quickened together with him, having forgiven you all trespasses; Blotting out the handwriting of ordinances that was against us, which was contrary to us, and took it out of the way, nailing it to his cross;"*
8. Hebrews 12:1-2 – *"Wherefore seeing we also are compassed about with so great a cloud of witnesses, let us lay aside every weight, and the sin which doth so easily beset us, and let us run with patience the race that is set before us, Looking unto Jesus the author and finisher of our faith; who for the joy that was set before him endured the cross, despising the shame, and is set down at the right hand of the throne of God."*
9. John 19:16-18 – *"[16]Then delivered he him therefore unto them to be crucified. And they took Jesus, and led him away. [17]And he bearing his cross went forth into a place called the place of a skull,*

which is called in the Hebrew Golgotha: [18]*Where they crucified him, and two other with him, on either side one, and Jesus in the midst."*

C. A picture of the symbolism and the revelation of the cross in the tabernacle:

1. The furniture placed in the form of a cross:

	The glory is our covering **Mercy Seat Ark** His head giving us the government of God. His Kingdom is ruled by mercy.	
Golden Candlestick His right hand to bless us with the Baptism of the Holy Ghost.	**Golden Altar** His heart of worship and intercession to the Father	**Table Of Shewbread** His left hand to minister His revealed Word to our hearts.
	Laver His knees bent in submission to the sanctification process **Brass Altar** His feet now stand over the judgments meant for us. He has conquered	

2. The camp and the placement of the tribes in the form of a cross:

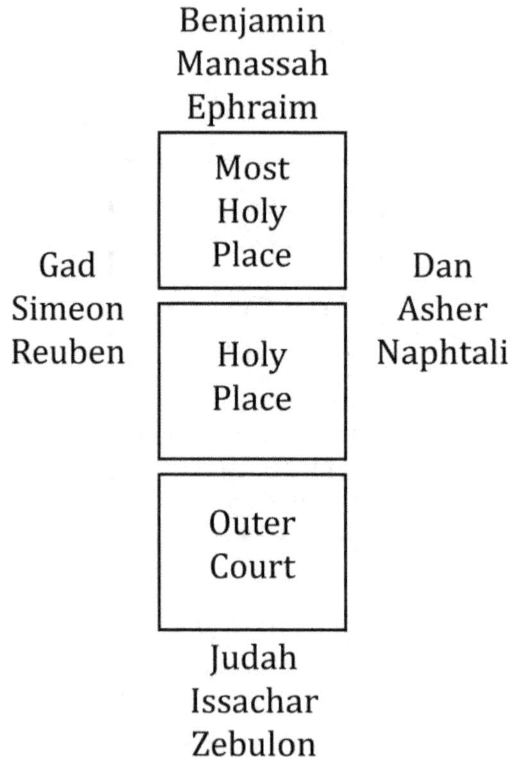

III. Other facts about the camp:

A. The camp was to be holy:

1. Hebrews 9:3, 8 – "[3]*And after the second veil, the tabernacle which is* <u>*called the Holiest of all*</u>*...*[8]*The Holy Ghost this signifying, that the way into the holiest of all was not yet made manifest, while as the first tabernacle was yet standing:*"
2. Psalms 93:5 – "*Thy testimonies are very sure: holiness becometh thine house, O LORD, for ever.*"

3. Not only was this true for our worship of our Holy God, but it was also practical for sanitary reasons.

   a. Dead to be buried outside of the camp – Leviticus 10:1-5
   b. Lepers lived outside the camp – Leviticus 13:38-46
   c. Unclean would defile the camp – Leviticus 15:1-33
   d. Dung was taken outside of the camp – Leviticus 9:11-12
   e. Those who cursed, taken outside of the camp – Leviticus 24:14
   f. Rebellious put outside of the camp – Numbers 12:1-15

B. Our lives are to be clean and holy (I Corinthians 3:17, Ephesians 2:21)

1. Clean

   a. II Corinthians 7:1 – "*Having therefore these promises, dearly beloved, let us cleanse ourselves from all filthiness of the flesh and spirit, perfecting holiness in the fear of God.*"
   b. Psalms 24:4 – "*He that hath clean hands, and a pure heart; who hath not lifted up his soul unto vanity, nor sworn deceitfully.*"

c. Psalms 51:10 – *"Create in me a clean heart, O God; and renew a right spirit within me."*
d. Isaiah 52:11 – *"Depart ye, depart ye, go ye out from thence, touch no unclean thing; go ye out of the midst of her; be ye clean, that bear the vessels of the LORD."*
e. Matthew 8:2-3 – *"[2]And, behold, there came a leper and worshipped him, saying, Lord, if thou wilt, thou canst make me clean. [3]And Jesus put forth his hand, and touched him, saying, I will; be thou clean. And immediately his leprosy was cleansed."*
f. Revelation 19:8, 14 – *"[8]And to her was granted that she should be arrayed in fine linen, clean and white: for the fine linen is the righteousness of saints…[14]And the armies which were in heaven followed him upon white horses, clothed in fine linen, white and clean."*
g. Psalms 119:9 – *"Wherewithal shall a young man cleanse his way? by taking heed thereto according to thy word."*
h. James 4:8 – *"Draw nigh to God, and he will draw nigh to you. Cleanse your hands, ye sinners; and purify your hearts, ye double minded."*
i. Ephesians 5:26 – *"That he might sanctify and cleanse it with the washing of water by the word,"*
j. John 15:3 – *"Now ye are clean through the word which I have spoken unto you."*

2. Holy

a. I Peter 1:15-16 – *"[15]But as he which hath called you is holy, so be ye holy in all manner of conversation; [16]Because it is written, Be ye holy; for I am holy."*
b. Hebrews 12:10 – *"For they verily for a few days chastened us after their own pleasure; but he for our profit, that we might be partakers of his holiness."*
c. Hebrews 12:14 – *"Follow peace with all men, and holiness, without which no man shall see the Lord:"*
d. I Thessalonians 3:13 – *"To the end he may stablish your hearts unblameable in holiness before God, even our Father, at the coming of our Lord Jesus Christ with all his saints."*
e. Romans 6:19-22 – *"[19]I speak after the manner of men because of the infirmity of your flesh: for as ye have yielded your members servants to uncleanness and to iniquity unto iniquity; even so now yield your members servants to righteousness unto holiness. [20]For when ye were the servants of sin, ye were free from righteousness. [21]What fruit had ye then in those things whereof ye are now ashamed? for the end of those things is death. [22]But now being made free from sin, and become servants to God, ye have your fruit unto holiness, and the end everlasting life."*
f. Ephesians 1:4 – *"According as he hath chosen us in him before the foundation of the world, that we should be holy and without blame before him in love:"*
g. II Timothy 1:9 – *"Who hath saved us, and called us with an holy calling, not according to our works, but according to his own purpose and grace, which was given us in Christ Jesus before the world began,"*
h. I Peter 2:9 – *"But ye are a chosen generation, a royal priesthood, an holy nation, a peculiar people; that ye should shew forth the praises of him who hath called you out of darkness into his marvellous light:"*

3. Just as the furniture made Israel clean, what all that those pieces represent make us clean.

IV. How The Camp Was Moved

A. Numbers 10:11-28:

"[11]And it came to pass on the twentieth day of the second month, in the second year, that the cloud was taken up from off the tabernacle of the testimony. [12]And the children of Israel took their journeys out of the wilderness of Sinai; and the cloud rested in the wilderness of Paran. [13]And they first took their journey according to the commandment of the LORD by the hand of Moses. [14]In the first place went the standard of the camp of the children of Judah according to their armies: and over his host was Nahshon the son of Amminadab. [15]And over

the host of the tribe of the children of Issachar was Nethaneel the son of Zuar. [16]And over the host of the tribe of the children of Zebulun was Eliab the son of Helon. [17]And the tabernacle was taken down; and the sons of Gershon and the sons of Merari set forward, bearing the tabernacle. [18]And the standard of the camp of Reuben set forward according to their armies: and over his host was Elizur the son of Shedeur. [19]And over the host of the tribe of the children of Simeon was Shelumiel the son of Zurishaddai. [20]And over the host of the tribe of the children of Gad was Eliasaph the son of Deuel. [21]And the Kohathites set forward, bearing the sanctuary: and the other did set up the tabernacle against they came. [22]And the standard of the camp of the children of Ephraim set forward according to their armies: and over his host was Elishama the son of Ammihud. [23]And over the host of the tribe of the children of Manasseh was Gamaliel the son of Pedahzur. [24]And over the host of the tribe of the children of Benjamin was Abidan the son of Gideoni. [25]And the standard of the camp of the children of Dan set forward, which was the rereward of all the camps throughout their hosts: and over his host was Ahiezer the son of Ammishaddai. [26]And over the host of the tribe of the children of Asher was Pagiel the son of Ocran. [27]And over the host of the tribe of the children of Naphtali was Ahira the son of Enan. [28]Thus were the journeyings of the children of Israel according to their armies, when they set forward."

1. First of all they went nowhere while the cloud of glory rested on the tabernacle. It was only when it lifted and moved that they moved and followed the cloud.
2. First place was Judah (Numbers 10:14); Judah again means "praise"; Their captain was Nashon. This name in Hebrews means – enchanting, ominous, and one that foretells. This speaks to us of the people who are true praisers always going out first. Worship defeats the enemy and keeps God very, very close. Also it tells us praisers have the ability to see in the spirit realm because of the illumination of the Holy Spirit.
3. Second place was Issachar (Numbers 10:15); His name means again in Hebrew – he is wages, reward there is here; Their captain was Nethaneel whose name means – God gave.
4. Third place was Zebulun (Numbers 10:16); His name means – wished for, habitation; Their captain was Eliab. Eliab's name in Hebrew means – my God is father.
5. Fourth place were the Gershonites (Numbers 10:17); His name means – a stranger, and driven out; The Merorites means bitterness or unhappy. These bore the burden of carrying the tabernacle. Spiritually this means it is very easy for those who bear the burden of ministry to have a tendency to become bitter and feel isolated (driven out). We who have this great and honorable calling must be very careful. They carried the curtains, coverings, and hangings (not the veil), boards, bars, pillars, pins, cards, and sockets.
6. Fifth place was Reuben (Numbers 10:18); His name again means – vision of a son; Their captain was Elizur whose name means – God the rock.
7. Sixth place was Simeon (Numbers 10:19); His name means in – hearkening, bearing with acceptance; Their captain was Shelumiel, which means in Hebrew – friend of God, God's peace, my reward.
8. Seventh place was Gad (Numbers 10:20); His name in Hebrew means – good fortune, to gather in troops; Their captain was Eliasaph, whose name means – who God added and God is gathered.
9. Eighth place were the Kohathites (Numbers 10:21); Their name means – assembly and comes from a root word that means – to gather together. These set forward bearing the sanctuary. They carried the ark, the table of shewbread, the brazen and golden altars, and the laver. It's interesting that the cloud of glory always goes out before His people, but yet the ark which is symbolic of His manifest presence is right in the midst of His people.
10. Ninth place was Ephraim (Numbers 10:22); Ephraim means again – two fold increase, doubly fruitful; Their captain was Elishama, whose name means God will hear, and God has heard.
11. Tenth place was Manasseh (Numbers 10:23); This name means – one who causes to forget, to forget and to be forgotten; Gamaliel was their captain whose name in Hebrew his name means – recompense of God, benefit of God, and God is the one who brings recompense.
12. Eleventh place was Benjamin (Numbers 10:24); His name means – son of the right hand; Their captain was Abidan whose name in Hebrew means – the father judges.
13. Twelfth place was Dan (Numbers 10:25); His name means – judge, he that judges, to rule, to execute judgment; Their captain was Ahiezer whose name in Hebrew means – brother of help,

to surround, gird and defend. This tribe brought up the rear along with Asher and Naphtali. They were last of all in battle array.

It is interesting to note that we begin with Judah (which means praise), in the middle are the Koathites (whose name means assembly; and they carried the ark, the manifest Presence of God), and finally at the end is Dan whose name means to rule, and to judge. Spiritually speaking this is where we are headed. By becoming worshippers and adoring His glory we will ultimately become like Him and will rule and reign with Him as full grown sons. We will be His overcomers. This obviously speaks of the manchild company.

a. Revelation 2:26-28 – "[26]*And he that overcometh, and keepeth my works unto the end, to him will I give power over the nations:* [27]*And he shall rule them with a rod of iron; as the vessels of a potter shall they be broken to shivers: even as I received of my Father.* [28]*And I will give him the morning star.*"
b. Revelation 12:5 – "*And she brought forth a man child, who was to rule all nations with a rod of iron: and her child was caught up unto God, and to his throne.*"

14. Thirteenth place (Numbers 10:26) was Asher; His name in Hebrew means – fortunate, fortress and happy; their captain was Pagiel, whose name in Hebrew means – prayer of God, answer from God, and God meets.
15. Fourteenth place (Numbers 10:27) was Naphtali; His name means – a struggle, my wrestlings, and obtained by wrestling; Their captain was Ahira, which means – brother of evil and it comes from a root that means – bad, noxious, to be evil. It's interesting to note that there is a struggle with evil, a wrestling with evil, all throughout our journey with the Lord. This should not come as a surprise. Jesus walked with Judas for three and one half years. Evil will always be present. It is there on purpose by God to challenge us, to trouble us, and ultimately to purify us. Never forget without our enemies we would never be overcomers.

a. Scriptural confirmation of this:

1) Hosea 2:15 – valley of trouble is our door of hope
2) Romans 5:3 – tribulation worketh
3) II Corinthians 4:17 – affliction works for us
4) I Peter 5:10 – suffering brings perfection and stability
5) Romans 7:15-25 – another law in my members, warring against the law of my mind
6) Psalm 110:2 – we need to rule in the midst of our enemies
7) Romans 12:19-21 – we overcome evil with good
8) John 16:33 – "*These things I have spoken unto you, that in me ye might have peace. In the world ye shall have tribulation: but be of good cheer; I have overcome the world.*"

This should not cause us to worry or fear. Our God is sovereign and "*...shall not the judge of the whole earth do right...*" (Genesis 18:25). Because Jesus overcame, so can we.

b. Never forget the promises to those who overcome:

1) I John 5:4-5 – Overcome the world
2) Revelation 2:7 – The tree of life
3) Revelation 2:11 – Not hurt of the second death
4) Revelation 2:17 – Hidden manna, a white stone, and a new name
5) Revelation 2:26 – Power over nations, ruling with a rod of iron, also the morning star
6) Revelation 3:5 – Clothed in white raiment, name confessed before the Father
7) Revelation 3:12 – Pillar in the temple, the privilege of staying in the presence of God, His new name written upon us
8) Revelation 3:21 – Sit with Him in His throne
9) Revelation 21:7 – Inherit all things

10) Revelation 12:11 – This is how we overcome: by the blood of the Lamb, word of our testimony, love not our lives unto death; below are other translations of this verse:

"*...Because of the blood, and because of the word...*"
"*...They defeated him by the blood of the Lamb and by the preaching of the Word...*"
"*Their victory was due to the blood of the Lamb, and to the message to which they bore testimony...*"
"*...Not by loving their own lives, they were willing to die...*"
"*...They did not hold their lives too dear to lay them down...*"
"*...They did not spare themselves, even unto death...*"
"*...They loved not their lies, even in the face of death...*"
"*...In their love of life they shrank not from death...*"

Lesson 6

Willing Offerings Build The Tabernacle

I. Exodus 25:2 – *"Speak unto the children of Israel that they bring me an offering; of every man that giveth it willingly with his heart, ye shall take my offering."*

A. This Scripture defined

1. *"They"* – God doesn't expect the world to provide for His house. He expects His people to prepare and give, then take those resources and do it.

a. Mark 6:34-44 – *"...Give ye them to eat..."*
b. Mark 8:1-9 – The disciples provided the initial food and then had to feed the people.
c. Acts 2:42-47 – All things common
d. I Corinthians 3:10-15 – *"[10]According to the grace of God which is given unto me, as a wise masterbuilder, I have laid the foundation, and another buildeth thereon. But let every man take heed how he buildeth thereupon. [11]For other foundation can no man lay than that is laid, which is Jesus Christ. [12]Now if any man build upon this foundation gold, silver, precious stones, wood, hay, stubble; [13]Every man's work shall be made manifest: for the day shall declare it, because it shall be revealed by fire; and the fire shall try every man's work of what sort it is. [14]If any man's work abide which he hath built thereupon, he shall receive a reward. [15]If any man's work shall be burned, he shall suffer loss: but he himself shall be saved; yet so as by fire."* – We need to take heed how and with what we build.

1) Gold, silver, precious stones are all of God:

a) Gold – God's divine character
b) Silver – God's redemption
c) Precious stones – all the characteristics of God's nature

2) Wood, hay and stubble speak of being man made:

a) Wood – Man's corrupt humanity won't stand the fire.
b) Hay – Consumes more rapidly; It is dried grass and flowers. It is only the traces of what was once something beautiful.
c) Stubble – Stubble is fit only to be burned. It has no fragrance and no beauty. Haggai 1:1-15

2. *"Bring Me"* - All of theirs as well as our offerings are never brought really to a man, but to God Himself. He says "bring me" when we give. It is to be to the Lord. We must never forget this. My responsibility stops once the offerings have been given. What others do with God's money (leaders, elders, etc.) is another story. They must answer to God for their stewardship over His offerings. Our responsibility is to give, and do it cheerfully.

a. II Corinthians 9:7 – *"Every man according as he purposeth in his heart, so let him give; not grudgingly, or of necessity: for God loveth a cheerful giver."*
b. II Corinthians 8:5 – *"And this they did, not as we hoped, but first gave their own selves to the Lord, and unto us by the will of God."*
c. Hebrews 13:15-16 – *"[15]By him therefore let us offer the sacrifice of praise to God continually, that is, the fruit of our lips giving thanks to his name. [16]But to do good and to communicate forget not: for with such sacrifices God is well pleased."*
d. III John 5-8 – *"[5]Beloved, thou doest faithfully whatsoever thou doest to the brethren, and to strangers; [6]Which have borne witness of thy charity before the church: whom if thou bring forward on their journey after a godly sort, thou shalt do well: [7]Because that for his name's*

sake they went forth, taking nothing of the Gentiles. [8]We therefore ought to receive such, that we might be fellowhelpers to the truth."

3. *"Every Man"*

   a. I Corinthians 16:2 – *"Upon the first day of the week let every one of you lay by him in store, as God hath prospered him, that there be no gatherings when I come."*
   b. II Corinthians 9:7 – *"Every man according as he purposeth in his heart, so let him give; not grudgingly, or of necessity: for God loveth a cheerful giver."*
   c. Exodus 35:20-29
   d. Proverbs 3:9 – *"Honour the LORD with thy substance, and with the firstfruits of all thine increase:"*
   e. Malachi 3:8-12 – *"[8]Will a man rob God? Yet ye have robbed me. But ye say, Wherein have we robbed thee? In tithes and offerings. [9]Ye are cursed with a curse: for ye have robbed me, even this whole nation. [10]Bring ye all the tithes into the storehouse, that there may be meat in mine house, and prove me now herewith, saith the LORD of hosts, if I will not open you the windows of heaven, and pour you out a blessing, that there shall not be room enough to receive it. [11]And I will rebuke the devourer for your sakes, and he shall not destroy the fruits of your ground; neither shall your vine cast her fruit before the time in the field, saith the LORD of hosts. [12]And all nations shall call you blessed: for ye shall be a delightsome land, saith the LORD of hosts."*
   f. Psalms 29:1-2 – *"[1]Give unto the LORD, O ye mighty, give unto the LORD glory and strength. [2]Give unto the LORD the glory due unto his name; worship the LORD in the beauty of holiness."*
   g. Psalms 96:7-9 – *"[7]Give unto the LORD, O ye kindreds of the people, give unto the LORD glory and strength. [8]Give unto the LORD the glory due unto his name: bring an offering, and come into his courts. [9]O worship the LORD in the beauty of holiness: fear before him, all the earth."*
   h. Ecclesiastes 11:1-7 – *"[1]Cast thy bread upon the waters: for thou shalt find it after many days. [2]Give a portion to seven, and also to eight; for thou knowest not what evil shall be upon the earth. [3]If the clouds be full of rain, they empty themselves upon the earth: and if the tree fall toward the south, or toward the north, in the place where the tree falleth, there it shall be. [4]He that observeth the wind shall not sow; and he that regardeth the clouds shall not reap. [5]As thou knowest not what is the way of the spirit, nor how the bones do grow in the womb of her that is with child: even so thou knowest not the works of God who maketh all. [6]In the morning sow thy seed, and in the evening withhold not thine hand: for thou knowest not whether shall prosper, either this or that, or whether they both shall be alike good. [7]Truly the light is sweet, and a pleasant thing it is for the eyes to behold the sun:"*
   i. II Corinthians 8:7 – *"Therefore, as ye abound in every thing, in faith, and utterance, and knowledge, and in all diligence, and in your love to us, see that ye abound in this grace also."*

   j. All of God's men and women who are in covenant with Him should and are required to honor Him with gifts. Giving is required in order to be a true disciple.

      1) Matthew 6:1-4 – *"[1]Take heed that ye do not your alms before men, to be seen of them: otherwise ye have no reward of your Father which is in heaven. [2]Therefore when thou doest thine alms, do not sound a trumpet before thee, as the hypocrites do in the synagogues and in the streets, that they may have glory of men. Verily I say unto you, They have their reward. [3]But when thou doest alms, let not thy left hand know what thy right hand doeth: [4]That thine alms may be in secret: and thy Father which seeth in secret himself shall reward thee openly."* – not if, but **when** you give
      2) Luke 21:1-4 – *"[1]And he looked up, and saw the rich men casting their gifts into the treasury. [2]And he saw also a certain poor widow casting in thither two mites. [3]And he said, Of a truth I say unto you, that this poor widow hath cast in more than they all: [4]For all these have of their abundance cast in unto the offerings of God: but she of her penury hath cast in all the living that she had."* – He was watching as people gave

k. Always remember, He is looking into our hearts as we give. It is not the amount that matters but the heart in giving.

   1) Matthew 10:8 – "*Heal the sick, cleanse the lepers, raise the dead, cast out devils: freely ye have received, freely give.*" – We are to freely give
   2) Luke 6:38 – "*Give, and it shall be given unto you; good measure, pressed down, and shaken together, and running over, shall men give into your bosom. For with the same measure that ye mete withal it shall be measured to you again.*" – We are told to give
   3) Deuteronomy 15:7-11

l. Our hands are to be always open to the poor and needy. We need always to be ready to bless and communicate; It is required in God's stewards (household managers) to be faithful in His giving.

   1) I Corinthians 4:1-2 – "[1]*Let a man so account of us, as of the ministers of Christ, and stewards of the mysteries of God.* [2]*Moreover it is required in stewards, that a man be found faithful.*"
   2) Matthew 5:42 – "*Give to him that asketh thee, and from him that would borrow of thee turn not thou away.*"
   3) Luke 6:30 – "*Give to every man that asketh of thee; and of him that taketh away thy goods ask them not again.*"

4. "*Willingly*"

   a. Psalms 110:3 – "*Thy people shall be willing in the day of thy power, in the beauties of holiness from the womb of the morning: thou hast the dew of thy youth.*" – In the day of His army, He will have a willing people
   b. I Chronicles 29:6-14, 17 – "[6]*Then the chief of the fathers and princes of the tribes of Israel, and the captains of thousands and of hundreds, with the rulers of the king's work, offered willingly,* [7]*And gave for the service of the house of God of gold five thousand talents and ten thousand drams, and of silver ten thousand talents, and of brass eighteen thousand talents, and one hundred thousand talents of iron.* [8]*And they with whom precious stones were found gave them to the treasure of the house of the LORD, by the hand of Jehiel the Gershonite.* [9]*Then the people rejoiced, for that they offered willingly, because with perfect heart they offered willingly to the LORD: and David the king also rejoiced with great joy.* [10]*Wherefore David blessed the LORD before all the congregation: and David said, Blessed be thou, LORD God of Israel our father, for ever and ever.* [11]*Thine, O LORD, is the greatness, and the power, and the glory, and the victory, and the majesty: for all that is in the heaven and in the earth is thine; thine is the kingdom, O LORD, and thou art exalted as head above all.* [12]*Both riches and honour come of thee, and thou reignest over all; and in thine hand is power and might; and in thine hand it is to make great, and to give strength unto all.* [13]*Now therefore, our God, we thank thee, and praise thy glorious name.* [14]*But who am I, and what is my people, that we should be able to offer so willingly after this sort? for all things come of thee, and of thine own have we given thee...*[17]*I know also, my God, that thou triest the heart, and hast pleasure in uprightness. As for me, in the uprightness of mine heart I have willingly offered all these things: and now have I seen with joy thy people, which are present here, to offer willingly unto thee.*"
   c. Ezra 1:5-6 – "[5]*Then rose up the chief of the fathers of Judah and Benjamin, and the priests, and the Levites, with all them whose spirit God had raised, to go up to build the house of the LORD which is in Jerusalem.* [6]*And all they that were about them strengthened their hands with vessels of silver, with gold, with goods, and with beasts, and with precious things, beside all that was willingly offered.*"

d. Ezra 7:13-16 – "*[13]I make a decree, that all they of the people of Israel, and of his priests and Levites, in my realm, which are minded of their own freewill to go up to Jerusalem, go with thee. [14]Forasmuch as thou art sent of the king, and of his seven counsellers, to inquire concerning Judah and Jerusalem, according to the law of thy God which is in thine hand; [15]And to carry the silver and gold, which the king and his counsellers have freely offered unto the God of Israel, whose habitation is in Jerusalem, [16]And all the silver and gold that thou canst find in all the province of Babylon, with the freewill offering of the people, and of the priests, offering willingly for the house of their God which is in Jerusalem.*"

e. Proverbs 31:13 – "*She seeketh wool, and flax, and worketh willingly with her hands.*"

f. II Corinthians 8:3 – "*[3]For to their power, I bear record, yea, and beyond their power they were willing of themselves... [11]Now therefore perform the doing of it; that as there was a readiness to will, so there may be a performance also out of that which ye have. [12]For if there be first a willing mind, it is accepted according to that a man hath, and not according to that he hath not.*"

g. I Timothy 6:18 – "*That they do good, that they be rich in good works, ready to distribute, willing to communicate.*"

h. Psalm 51:10-17

5. "*With His Heart*"

a. I Chronicles 29:9 – "*Then the people rejoiced, for that they offered willingly, because with perfect heart they offered willingly to the LORD: and David the king also rejoiced with great joy.*"

b. Luke 21:1-4 – "*[1]And he looked up, and saw the rich men casting their gifts into the treasury. [2]And he saw also a certain poor widow casting in thither two mites. [3]And he said, Of a truth I say unto you, that this poor widow hath cast in more than they all: [4]For all these have of their abundance cast in unto the offerings of God: but she of her penury hath cast in all the living that she had.*" He's watching with what attitude we give.

c. II Corinthians 9:7 – "*Every man according as he purposeth in his heart, so let him give; not grudgingly, or of necessity: for God loveth a cheerful giver.*"

d. Deuteronomy 15:7-10 – "*[7]If there be among you a poor man of one of thy brethren within any of thy gates in thy land which the LORD thy God giveth thee, thou shalt not harden thine heart, nor shut thine hand from thy poor brother: [8]But thou shalt open thine hand wide unto him, and shalt surely lend him sufficient for his need, in that which he wanteth. [9]Beware that there be not a thought in thy wicked heart, saying, The seventh year, the year of release, is at hand; and thine eye be evil against thy poor brother, and thou givest him nought; and he cry unto the LORD against thee, and it be sin unto thee. [10]Thou shalt surely give him, and thine heart shall not be grieved when thou givest unto him: because that for this thing the LORD thy God shall bless thee in all thy works, and in all that thou puttest thine hand unto.*"

e. Malachi 1:11 – "*For from the rising of the sun even unto the going down of the same my name shall be great among the Gentiles; and in every place incense shall be offered unto my name, and a pure offering: for my name shall be great among the heathen, saith the LORD of hosts.*"

f. Ultimately we are only giving back to Him what He has given to us:

1) I Chronicles 29:14-16 – "*[14]But who am I, and what is my people, that we should be able to offer so willingly after this sort? for all things come of thee, and of thine own have we given thee. [15]For we are strangers before thee, and sojourners, as were all our fathers: our days on the earth are as a shadow, and there is none abiding. [16]O LORD our God, all this store that we have prepared to build thee an house for thine holy name cometh of thine hand, and is all thine own.*"

2) Deuteronomy 8:17-18 – "*[17]And thou say in thine heart, My power and the might of mine hand hath gotten me this wealth. [18]But thou shalt remember the LORD thy God: for it is*

he that giveth thee power to get wealth, that he may establish his covenant which he sware unto thy fathers, as it is this day."

3) Psalm 50:7-15

6. *"My Offering"*

   a. Leviticus 27:30-34 – *"[30]And all the tithe of the land, whether of the seed of the land, or of the fruit of the tree, is the LORD's: it is holy unto the LORD..."*
   b. Nehemiah 10:35-39
   c. Malachi 3:10

II. The Principle Of Giving – As we saw in Exodus 25, without these offerings, God's house, both natural and spiritual, would never have been built.

A. There are two types of giving – disciplined/systematic (the tithe) and spontaneous (offerings); Proverbs 3:9 – *"Honour the LORD with thy substance, and with the firstfruits of all thine increase:"*

1. Systematic giving is tithing:

   a. The substance spoken of in Proverbs 3:9 is the tithe.

      1) Malachi 1:6-9
      2) Malachi 3:8-13
      3) Hebrews 7:2 – *"To whom also Abraham gave a tenth part of all; first being by interpretation King of righteousness, and after that also King of Salem, which is, King of peace."* (Genesis 14:26)

   b. Tithing Before The Law – Voluntary

      1) Genesis 14:18-20 – Abraham gave tithes
      2) Genesis 28:20-22 – Jacob promises the tithe

   c. Tithing under the Law of Moses was compulsory:

      1) Leviticus 27:30-32 – *"[30]And all the tithe of the land, whether of the seed of the land, or of the fruit of the tree, is the LORD's: it is holy unto the LORD. [31]And if a man will at all redeem ought of his tithes, he shall add thereto the fifth part thereof. [32]And concerning the tithe of the herd, or of the flock, even of whatsoever passeth under the rod, the tenth shall be holy unto the LORD."*
      2) Malachi 3:10
      3) Nehemiah 10:37-38

   d. Tithing under grace is done willingly

      1) Hebrews 7:1-17
      2) II Corinthians 8:5,11-12

Giving is a responsibility. God is a giver and we must be one too. Israel would take the best of their crop and give it to the Lord. We are called upon to do the same. The tithe belongs to God and obedience to the law of tithing brings blessing. We give ourselves to God first. Then He requires a tithe with which He promises to protect us from our adversary.

2. Spontaneous giving (offerings) – Offerings are special gifts we give to God, to our church, and to people under the spontaneous direction of the Holy Spirit. First fruits spoken of in Proverbs 3:9 are offerings. Offerings are our worship gifts to God.

   a. Luke 6:38
   b. Matthew 6:1-4

B. Some principles concerning giving

1. II Corinthians 8:5 – We give ourselves to the Lord first.
2. II Corinthians 9:7 – We give cheerfully (Greek – hilariously).
3. II Corinthians 8:3, 12 – We give willingly.
4. II Corinthians 8:2 (II Corinthians 8:9-13) – We are to give generously, liberally.
5. I Corinthians 16:1-2 – We are to give regularly, systematically (I Corinthians 9:7)
6. II Corinthians 9:12-13 – We are to give as a ministry to the Lord and His saints.
7. II Corinthians 9:11-12 – We are to give thankfully.
8. II Corinthians 8:24 – We are to give lovingly. Giving is a test of our love for Jesus. It is to be done with our heart and it really is a part of our worship and praise to the Lord.

C. God's promises are strongest to us concerning giving

1. His promises

   a. Proverbs 3:9-10 – "[9]*Honour the LORD with thy substance, and with the firstfruits of all thine increase:* [10]*So shall thy barns be filled with plenty, and thy presses shall burst out with new wine.*"
   b. Malachi 3:8-12 – "[8]*Will a man rob God? Yet ye have robbed me. But ye say, Wherein have we robbed thee? In tithes and offerings.* [9]*Ye are cursed with a curse: for ye have robbed me, even this whole nation.* [10]*Bring ye all the tithes into the storehouse, that there may be meat in mine house, and prove me now herewith, saith the LORD of hosts, if I will not open you the windows of heaven, and pour you out a blessing, that there shall not be room enough to receive it.* [11]*And I will rebuke the devourer for your sakes, and he shall not destroy the fruits of your ground; neither shall your vine cast her fruit before the time in the field, saith the LORD of hosts.* [12]*And all nations shall call you blessed: for ye shall be a delightsome land, saith the LORD of hosts.*"
   c. Ecclesiastes 11:1 – "*Cast thy bread upon the waters: for thou shalt find it after many days.*"
   d. Luke 6:38 – "*Give, and it shall be given unto you; good measure, pressed down, and shaken together, and running over, shall men give into your bosom. For with the same measure that ye mete withal it shall be measured to you again.*"

2. God simply wants us to be willing

   a. II Corinthians 8:11-14 – "[11]*Now therefore perform the doing of it; that as there was a readiness to will, so there may be a performance also out of that which ye have.* [12]*For if there be first a willing mind, it is accepted according to that a man hath, and not according to that he hath not.* [13]*For I mean not that other men be eased, and ye burdened:* [14]*But by an equality, that now at this time your abundance may be a supply for their want, that their abundance also may be a supply for your want: that there may be equality:*"
   b. II Corinthians 9:2 – "*For I know the forwardness of your mind, for which I boast of you to them of Macedonia, that Achaia was ready a year ago; and your zeal hath provoked very many.*"
   c. I Peter 5:2 – "*Feed the flock of God which is among you, taking the oversight thereof, not by constraint, but willingly; not for filthy lucre, but of a ready mind;*"
   d. Proverbs 31:13

e. Psalms 110:3

D. Common sense concerning giving

1. We are to give according to our ability
2. We give according to what we have. We are never to compare ourselves, or our giving with others. We are simply to do what we can with whatever we have.

    a. II Corinthians 8:12 – *"For if there be first a willing mind, it is accepted according to that a man hath, and not according to that he hath not."*
    b. II Corinthians 9:8 – *"And God is able to make all grace abound toward you; that ye, always having all sufficiency in all things, may abound to every good work:"*
    c. Deuteronomy 16:17 – *"Every man shall give as he is able, according to the blessing of the LORD thy God which he hath given thee."*
    d. Mark 14:8 – *"She hath done what she could: she is come aforehand to anoint my body to the burying."*
    e. Acts 11:29 – *"Then the disciples, every man according to his ability, determined to send relief unto the brethren which dwelt in Judaea:"*

Lesson 7

The Builders Of The Tabernacle

I. The Builders of the Tabernacle – Listed in Order

A. God Himself was the architect, Exodus 25:9 – "*According to all that I shew thee, after the pattern of the tabernacle, and the pattern of all the instruments thereof, even so shall ye make it.*" – It was God's idea and He gave all of the specific instructions for every aspect to the building of the Tabernacle. It was His idea, His diagram, His instructions, His particular choices of metals, colors, materials, numbers, arrangements, etc.

B. Moses

1. Exodus 25:1 – "*And the LORD spake unto Moses, saying,*"
2. Acts 7:44 – "*Our fathers had the tabernacle of witness in the wilderness, as he had appointed, speaking unto Moses, that he should make it according to the fashion that he had seen.*" – Over and over again, the Word declares God saying to Moses, "*...and thou shalt make...*" Moses was entrusted as the overseer of the building of the Tabernacle.

C. The children of Israel:

1. Exodus 25:8, 10 – "8*And let them make me a sanctuary; that I may dwell among them...*10*And they shall make an ark of shittim wood: two cubits and a half shall be the length thereof, and a cubit and a half the breadth thereof, and a cubit and a half the height thereof.*" – God required that every willing man of the children of Israel bring a willing offering from his heart. Out of these offerings were gold, silver, brass, linen, stones, skins, cloths, etc. It was out of these materials that the Tabernacle would be built.
2. Exodus 35:20-29 – "20*And all the congregation of the children of Israel departed from the presence of Moses.* 21*And they came, every one whose heart stirred him up, and every one whom his spirit made willing, and they brought the LORD's offering to the work of the tabernacle of the congregation, and for all his service, and for the holy garments.* 22*And they came, both men and women, as many as were willing hearted, and brought bracelets, and earrings, and rings, and tablets, all jewels of gold: and every man that offered offered an offering of gold unto the LORD.* 23*And every man, with whom was found blue, and purple, and scarlet, and fine linen, and goats' hair, and red skins of rams, and badgers' skins, brought them.* 24*Every one that did offer an offering of silver and brass brought the LORD's offering: and every man, with whom was found shittim wood for any work of the service, brought it.* 25*And all the women that were wise hearted did spin with their hands, and brought that which they had spun, both of blue, and of purple, and of scarlet, and of fine linen.* 26*And all the women whose heart stirred them up in wisdom spun goats' hair.* 27*And the rulers brought onyx stones, and stones to be set, for the ephod, and for the breastplate;* 28*And spice, and oil for the light, and for the anointing oil, and for the sweet incense.* 29*The children of Israel brought a willing offering unto the LORD, every man and woman, whose heart made them willing to bring for all manner of work, which the LORD had commanded to be made by the hand of Moses.*"
3. Exodus 36:3-8 – "3*And they received of Moses all the offering, which the children of Israel had brought for the work of the service of the sanctuary, to make it withal. And they brought yet unto him free offerings every morning.* 4*And all the wise men, that wrought all the work of the sanctuary, came every man from his work which they made;* 5*And they spake unto Moses, saying, The people bring much more than enough for the service of the work, which the LORD commanded to make.* 6*And Moses gave commandment, and they caused it to be proclaimed throughout the camp, saying, Let neither man nor woman make any more work for the offering of the sanctuary. So the people were restrained from bringing.* 7*For the stuff they had was sufficient for all the work to make it, and too much.* 8*And every wise hearted man among them that wrought the work of the*

tabernacle made ten curtains of fine twined linen, and blue, and purple, and scarlet: with cherubims of cunning work made he them."

D. The Egyptians – we must make mention of them here because it was with the spoils of Egypt that the people had something to willingly offer.

1. Exodus 12:35-36 – *"And the children of Israel did according to the word of Moses; and they borrowed of the Egyptians jewels of silver, and jewels of gold, and raiment: And the LORD gave the people favour in the sight of the Egyptians, so that they lent unto them such things as they required. And they spoiled the Egyptians."*
2. Exodus 3:21-22 – *"And I will give this people favour in the sight of the Egyptians: and it shall come to pass, that, when ye go, ye shall not go empty: But every woman shall borrow of her neighbour, and of her that sojourneth in her house, jewels of silver, and jewels of gold, and raiment: and ye shall put them upon your sons, and upon your daughters; and ye shall spoil the Egyptians."*
3. Exodus 11:1-3 – *"1And the LORD said unto Moses, Yet will I bring one plague more upon Pharaoh, and upon Egypt; afterwards he will let you go hence: when he shall let you go, he shall surely thrust you out hence altogether. 2Speak now in the ears of the people, and let every man borrow of his neighbour, and every woman of her neighbour, jewels of silver, and jewels of gold. 3And the LORD gave the people favour in the sight of the Egyptians. Moreover the man Moses was very great in the land of Egypt, in the sight of Pharaoh's servants, and in the sight of the people."*
4. Psalms 105:37-38 – *"He brought them forth also with silver and gold: and there was not one feeble person among their tribes. Egypt was glad when they departed: for the fear of them fell upon them."*

E. Bezaleel

Exodus 31:1-5 – *"1And the LORD spake unto Moses, saying, 2See, I have called by name Bezaleel the son of Uri, the son of Hur, of the tribe of Judah: 3And I have filled him with the spirit of God, in wisdom, and in understanding, and in knowledge, and in all manner of workmanship, 4To devise cunning works, to work in gold, and in silver, and in brass, 5And in cutting of stones, to set them, and in carving of timber, to work in all manner of workmanship."*

Exodus 35:30-35 – *"30And Moses said unto the children of Israel, See, the LORD hath called by name Bezaleel the son of Uri, the son of Hur, of the tribe of Judah; 31And he hath filled him with the spirit of God, in wisdom, in understanding, and in knowledge, and in all manner of workmanship; 32And to devise curious works, to work in gold, and in silver, and in brass, 33And in the cutting of stones, to set them, and in carving of wood, to make any manner of cunning work. 34And he hath put in his heart that he may teach, both he, and Aholiab, the son of Ahisamach, of the tribe of Dan. 35Them hath he filled with wisdom of heart, to work all manner of work, of the engraver, and of the cunning workman, and of the embroiderer, in blue, and in purple, in scarlet, and in fine linen, and of the weaver, even of them that do any work, and of those that devise cunning work."*

1. Bezaleel's name means in Hebrew – in the shadow of God, under God's shadow
2. His father Uri's name means in Hebrew – light of the Lord, enlightened, fiery burning
3. His grandfather Hur's name means in Hebrew – cavern, from a root meaning a hole, the idea of boring, a noble, splendor, white
4. Of the tribe of Judah; Judah means in Hebrew – praised, the Lord be praised, praise of the Lord

These definitions above reveal Bezaleel's heritage. He came from a tribe of praise (Judah), from a noble, clean line that was able to bore out a hole, a cavern. Judah was the first tribe. He came from an enlightened people who burned with God's fire, ending with himself one who lived under God's shadow. Bezaleel lived in the shadow of God. He was a worshipper and truly a man of the presence.

From the above two passages on Bezaleel, we see what God had done in him. He was filled with the Spirit of God, filled with wisdom, understanding, knowledge, and in all manner of workmanship, to devise cunning works, able to work in gold, silver, brass, and in cutting of stones and to set them, as well as skill in carving timber. God also called him by name. He was a teacher, his heart was stirred, and he had a willing heart. God knew his character and called him because of it.

5. This symbolizes to us the type of men or women who God will use to build His spiritual house. They will have these same qualities in them.

   a. They will have the same heritage as Him
   b. They will live under the shadow of the Almighty (Psalms 91:1 – *"He that dwelleth in the secret place of the most High shall abide under the shadow of the Almighty."*)
   c. Filled with the Holy Spirit
   d. Men of the Word which supplies them wisdom, knowledge, and understanding
   e. Creative, having the know how to build and shape God's people
   f. Able to work with gold (God's divine nature), silver (God's redemption), and brass (wise in judgment)
   g. They will have the ability to carve God's stones (His divine characteristics) in the people
   h. Knowing how to deal with man's flesh, the wisdom to know when to cut away at men's flesh without destroying the people
   i. A jack-of-all-trades, spiritually speaking
   j. One who God calls, not man and one whose character God knows
   k. Also a faithful, trustworthy persons
   l. Judah was the first tribe – the Alpha – He was able to start anything

F. Aholiab

Exodus 31:6 – *"And I, behold, I have given with him Aholiab, the son of Ahisamach, of the tribe of Dan: and in the hearts of all that are wise hearted I have put wisdom, that they may make all that I have commanded thee;"*

Exodus 35:34-35 – *"34And he hath put in his heart that he may teach, both he, and Aholiab, the son of Ahisamach, of the tribe of Dan. 35Them hath he filled with wisdom of heart, to work all manner of work, of the engraver, and of the cunning workman, and of the embroiderer, in blue, and in purple, in scarlet, and in fine linen, and of the weaver, even of them that do any work, and of those that devise cunning work."*

1. Hebrew definition of Aholiab – tabernacle of my father, tent of the father
2. His father Ahisamach's name means – brother of support, to sustain
3. Tribe of Dan – Dan means in Hebrew – judging, he that judges, to rule, to execute judgment, to contend
4. He was also a teacher, wise hearted, had the wisdom of God, filled with wisdom of heart
5. Dan was the last tribe

6. What these above Scriptures and definitions symbolize for the leaders who are to build the Tabernacle.

   a. One who knows the tent of their father's
   b. Comes from a heritage that will be a brother and a support to God's people
   c. One with authority (God given, not man given)
   d. One who has the ability to judge correctly
   e. A teacher of truths and one who is walking in or laboring to walk in them
   f. Has a wise heart – this speaks of one who will deal in wisdom and have a true heart while doing it

G. Cunning workmen of Israel – These are men who were skilled in every art. They were also men with wisdom and willingness of heart.

1. Exodus 36:1-3 – "[1]*Then wrought Bezaleel and Aholiab, and every wise hearted man, in whom the LORD put wisdom and understanding to know how to work all manner of work for the service of the sanctuary, according to all that the LORD had commanded.* [2]*And Moses called Bezaleel and Aholiab, and every wise hearted man, in whose heart the LORD had put wisdom, even every one whose heart stirred him up to come unto the work to do it:* [3]*And they received of Moses all the offering, which the children of Israel had brought for the work of the service of the sanctuary, to make it withal. And they brought yet unto him free offerings every morning.*"
2. Exodus 35:35 – "*Them hath he filled with wisdom of heart, to work all manner of work, of the engraver, and of the cunning workman, and of the embroiderer, in blue, and in purple, in scarlet, and in fine linen, and of the weaver, even of them that do any work, and of those that devise cunning work.*"

God is raising up leadership in the last days with different, distinct, and unique ministries. We need the help of the five-fold ministries to bring us to perfection. We need leaders with compassion, leaders who are wise, leaders who are willing and not hirelings, but true shepherds. These will be men and women who have a true heart. Obviously these will be leaders of meekness and humility like our Lord Jesus.

Lesson 8

The Entrances (Doors and Gates)

I. The Sanctuary Entrances

There were two entrances into the sanctuary itself – one to the Holy Place and one to the Most Holy Place. These will be covered in detail in later chapters. However, a searching of the Scriptures related to entrances, doors, gates, etc. would bring great light and understanding to the true Bible student

A. Comparison of the two sanctuary entrances:

HOLY PLACE	MOST HOLY PLACE
A Door	A Veil
Shut out people	Shut out priests
Priests could enter	Only the High Priest entered
5 pillars of gold (5 = grace)	4 pillars of gold (4 = new creation man)
5 sockets of brass (grace connected to judgment)	4 sockets of silver (creation connected to redemption)
Colors of blue, purple, scarlet, and fine linen (speaks to us of all things heavenly, royalty, suffering, and righteousness)	Colors of blue, purple, scarlet, and fine linen (speaks to us of all things heavenly, royalty, suffering, and righteousness)
No cherubims (the cherubim guard the glory – lesser dominion of His glory here)	Worked in cherubims (this room is full of God's glory – greater dimension of His glory here)
Crowns and fillets (the foundation is still being laid)	None mentioned (no need here, the foundation has already been laid)
Face east (looking for His coming)	Faced east (looking for His coming)

B. In looking at doors, windows, gates, etc, we are talking about an entranceway

An entrance does two things: it either lets you in to something or keeps you out of something. I think as we meditate on each gate, door, and window, curtain, veil, etc, perhaps we will find a deeper meaning in that passage. Below are Scriptures giving some thoughts on the principle of entering.

1. Deuteronomy 23:2 – *"A bastard shall not enter into the congregation of the LORD; even to his tenth generation shall he not enter into the congregation of the LORD."*
2. Psalms 100:4 – *"Enter into his gates with thanksgiving, and into his courts with praise: be thankful unto him, and bless his name."*
3. Matthew 7:13 – *"Enter ye in at the strait gate: for wide is the gate, and broad is the way, that leadeth to destruction, and many there be which go in thereat:"*
4. Acts 14:22 – *"Confirming the souls of the disciples, and exhorting them to continue in the faith, and that we must through much tribulation enter into the kingdom of God."*
5. Hebrews 3:18-19 – *"18And to whom sware he that they should not enter into his rest, but to them that believed not? 19So we see that they could not enter in because of unbelief."*
6. Hebrews 4:3 – *"For we which have believed do enter into rest, as he said, As I have sworn in my wrath, if they shall enter into my rest: although the works were finished from the foundation of the world."*
7. Hebrews 10:19 – *"Having therefore, brethren, boldness to enter into the holiest by the blood of Jesus,"*
8. Exodus 33:9 – *"And it came to pass, as Moses entered into the tabernacle, the cloudy pillar descended, and stood at the door of the tabernacle, and the LORD talked with Moses."*

In the following pages we will look exclusively into the Scriptures concerning what I call the "principle of the door." So as we continue to study lets remember what the Lord said to Ezekiel in Ezekiel 44:5, *"And the*

LORD said unto me, Son of man, mark well, and behold with thine eyes, and hear with thine ears all that I say unto thee concerning all the ordinances of the house of the LORD, and all the laws thereof; and mark well the entering in of the house, with every going forth of the sanctuary."

A door speaks of an entrance into something or being restrained from something. We will look at what the Scripture declare about the door or the doors of God, both in a natural sense and in a typical or spiritual way (i.e. in type or shadow). A good dictionary definition of the term door is "a usually swinging or sliding barrier by which an entry (as in a building) is closed or opened; a means of access or denied access".

We enter into something as we open. The The Scriptures speak of entering into something of God, such as spiritual truth or revelation as well as into things heavenly.. The Scriptures also speak of a door being a barrier preventing us from entering into some specific realm, position, or place of God.

The Word declares God Himself is a door and that He alone can open or shut doors. We must see this principle in a natural way as well as in a pictorial way, because sometimes a door is speaking of something other than itself and it represents a spiritual or typical truth about something God wants us to have. It is true that the Lord is the door, but also that there are particular doors of entryway we must go through. The onus then is on us to walk through or choose to enter in through the door.

The Scriptures also show us the horror of a shut door such as: Noah's ark, brideship, salvation, communion with God, all things heavenly, and so on. There is nothing more horrible then being shut out of something because you can't enter in through a doorway.

Let's take a look at some foundational information regarding doors and their meaning in Scripture. A door is the covering over an entrance into a tent, a house, or a public building. The doors of Bible times were made of a wide variety of materials that would include animal hides, wood, or metal. Many of these doors found in Scripture can only be understood by looking at them in the "symbolic" sense because it is obvious that they speak of something other than just the material that they consisted of. All one has to do is to look at the "Tabernacle of Moses" to know this. Every article, every piece of furniture and what they were made of (even down to the color, substance, height, depth, etc) all carries great spiritual truths that speak of something other than itself. This is also true in the other "houses of God" namely, the "Tabernacle of David" and the "Temple of Solomon" as well as the last day temple spoken of in the book of Ezekiel.

The word gate is almost the same as a door, meaning an entranceway or opening into something. So we will also look at this term "gate or gates" as it applies to God's door. In the Scriptures, it really appears to mean almost the same thing. A door or gate is a point of entry, especially when it comes to a house. The door frame was given special significance within the Law of Moses and the temple doorkeepers had special status. Remember we can see these terms both in natural and symbolic ways. Jesus spoke of Himself as the door which means to us symbolically that we now have a means of access to God the Father. The door symbolizes a gaining or a barring entry. It also speaks of entering into a new realm of revelation, opportunity, or access to something God wants us to have but have not entered into yet.

The term gate is also a point of entry into something, a walled city, or walled off area such as the temple of God. The gate also was a place where business was transacted, and where the elders would meet and dispense justice or punishment. It must also be seen to be used naturally and symbolically. It speaks of entry into life, death, or into a relationship with God. It also speaks of the entry to worship and to all things heavenly. We will look at all the gates and doors of significance in the Scripture and see what their true meaning is for us and for our lives.

I. Definitions of Important Words

A. Door, Doors

1. Hebrew words

a. *Pethach* – an opening, an entrance way, a gate; it comes from the root word, *pathach* that means – to open wide literally or figuratively, to loosen, begin, plough, carve.
b. *Deleth* – something swinging, the valve of a door; it comes from the root word, *dalah* that means – to dangle, to let down a bucket for water, to deliver.
c. *Mezuwzah* – a prominent doorpost

2. Greek word, *thura* – a portal or entrance, the opening or the closing literally or figuratively, a gate.

B. Gate, Gates

1. Hebrew word, *sha'ar* – an opening, a door; it comes from the root word, *sha'ar* – to split or eopen, to estimate, think.
2. Greek word, *pulon* – a gate way, a door way of a building or city, a portal; it comes from the root word *pule* which is also translated "gate" and it means – a gate, the leaf or wing of a folding entrance literally or figuratively.

II. The Principle Of The Door In Scripture – This is God's Door

A. Proverbs 8:34-35 – "[34]*Blessed is the man that heareth me, watching daily at my gates, waiting at the posts of my doors.* [35]*For whoso findeth me findeth life, and shall obtain favour of the LORD.*"

1. To those who hear the Lord, who watch daily at His gates and wait at the posts of His door, they will be blessed, find Him, find life, and shall obtain favour of the Lord!
2. Other translations: "*door-posts of my entrance*", "*waiting at my doorway*", "*waiting for me outside my home*", "*waits outside my doors*", "*waiting at my open doorway*", "*those who stay by my door every day*", "*watching at my doors day by day, keeping his place by the pillars of my house*"
3. This passage simply speaks of faithfulness in a disciple whose whole life is centered around the Lord Jesus and waiting upon Him.

4. This passage depicts those who are concerned about ministering to Him first and foremost, and not themselves being ministered unto. Below are other Scriptures where this attitude is seen in others:

a. I Samuel 2:18, 3:1 – "[18]*But Samuel ministered before the LORD, being a child, girded with a linen ephod...*[3:1]*And the child Samuel ministered unto the LORD before Eli. And the word of the LORD was precious in those days; there was no open vision.*"
b. Psalms 27:4 – "*One thing have I desired of the LORD, that will I seek after; that I may dwell in the house of the LORD all the days of my life, to behold the beauty of the LORD, and to inquire in his temple.*" – This was David's desire
c. Mark 3:13-15 – "[13]*And he goeth up into a mountain, and calleth unto him whom he would: and they came unto him.* [14]*And he ordained twelve, that they should be with him, and that he might send them forth to preach,* [15]*And to have power to heal sicknesses, and to cast out devils:*"
d. Luke 10:38-42 – "[38]*Now it came to pass, as they went, that he entered into a certain village: and a certain woman named Martha received him into her house.* [39]*And she had a sister called Mary, which also sat at Jesus' feet, and heard his word.* [40]*But Martha was cumbered about much serving, and came to him, and said, Lord, dost thou not care that my sister hath left me to serve alone? bid her therefore that she help me.* [41]*And Jesus answered and said unto her, Martha, Martha, thou art careful and troubled about many things:* [42]*But one thing is needful: and Mary hath chosen that good part, which shall not be taken away from her.*" The good part that Mary chose was sitting at the feet of Jesus and hearing His Word.

e. Psalms 123:1-2 – "[1]*Unto thee lift I up mine eyes, O thou that dwellest in the heavens.* [2]*Behold, as the eyes of servants look unto the hand of their masters, and as the eyes of a maiden unto the hand of her mistress; so our eyes wait upon the LORD our God, until that he have mercy upon us.*"

B. Exodus 21:2-6 – "[2]*If thou buy an Hebrew servant, six years he shall serve: and in the seventh he shall go out free for nothing.* [3]*If he came in by himself, he shall go out by himself: if he were married, then his wife shall go out with him.* [4]*If his master have given him a wife, and she have born him sons or daughters; the wife and her children shall be her master's, and he shall go out by himself.* [5]*And if the servant shall plainly say, I love my master, my wife, and my children; I will not go out free:* [6]*Then his master shall bring him unto the judges; he shall also bring him to the door, or unto the door post; and his master shall bore his ear through with an aul; and he shall serve him for ever.*"

1. We must look at this passage symbolically as a type of us being God's servant
2. God is giving instructions about Hebrew servants, how that after serving <u>six</u> years he is allowed his freedom in the <u>seventh</u>. Six is the number for man and the serpent (both created on the sixth day). It may seem to be a long time serving as a slave for six years. But this symbolizes that as we suffer through the dealings of God, to deliver us from our old Adamic nature, as well as being delivered from every aspect of Satan in our lives, we will enter into a place of rest (seventh year).
3. The question then, is what will we do upon obtain our freedom? Was it just all about us becoming free? Or will we understand that it was really all about being prepared to serve God continually and forever?
4. This particular servant shows us what God is really after. He is after a true son who chooses to stay as a servant even though he could be free.
5. In verse 5, He gives us the order of importance which should be in all of our lives: 1) "*I love my master...*" Jesus is first and foremost, 2) "*...my wife, and my children*" – then family
6. The servant makes an eternal commitment to belong to His master's servant forever.
7. Then the master brings him to "*the door*" and bores his ear with an aul – this speaks of the servants ability now to hear only what his master will speak.
8. He will now serve his master forever.

9. This principle seen in other Scriptures

   a. Matthew 11:29-30 – "[29]*Take my yoke upon you, and learn of me; for I am meek and lowly in heart: and ye shall find rest unto your souls.* [30]*For my yoke is easy, and my burden is light.*"
   b. John 13:13-17 – "[13]*Ye call me Master and Lord: and ye say well; for so I am.* [14]*If I then, your Lord and Master, have washed your feet; ye also ought to wash one another's feet.* [15]*For I have given you an example, that ye should do as I have done to you.* [16]*Verily, verily, I say unto you, The servant is not greater than his lord; neither he that is sent greater than he that sent him.* [17]*If ye know these things, happy are ye if ye do them.*"
   c. Matthew 10:24-25 – "[24]*The disciple is not above his master, nor the servant above his lord.* [25]*It is enough for the disciple that he be as his master, and the servant as his lord. If they have called the master of the house Beelzebub, how much more shall they call them of his household?*"
   d. Proverbs 29:21 – "*He that delicately bringeth up his servant from a child shall have him become his son at the length.*"
   e. II Kings 2:1-15 – Elisha receives double portion of his master's spirit (II Kings 3:11 – "*But Jehoshaphat said, Is there not here a prophet of the LORD, that we may inquire of the LORD by him? And one of the king of Israel's servants answered and said, Here is Elisha the son of Shaphat, which poured water on the hands of Elijah.*")
   f. II Chronicles 18:16 – "*Then he said, I did see all Israel scattered upon the mountains, as sheep that have no shepherd: and the LORD said, These have no master; let them return therefore*

every man to his house in peace." – This shows us the need for the master-servant relationship.

g. Proverbs 27:18 – *"Whoso keepeth the fig tree shall eat the fruit thereof: so he that waiteth on his master shall be honoured."*

h. Malachi 1:6 – *"A son honoureth his father, and a servant his master: if then I be a father, where is mine honour? and if I be a master, where is my fear? saith the LORD of hosts unto you, O priests, that despise my name. And ye say, Wherein have we despised thy name?"*

i. Matthew 23:8-12 – *"[8]But be not ye called Rabbi: for one is your Master, even Christ; and all ye are brethren. [9]And call no man your father upon the earth: for one is your Father, which is in heaven. [10]Neither be ye called masters: for one is your Master, even Christ. [11]But he that is greatest among you shall be your servant. [12]And whosoever shall exalt himself shall be abased; and he that shall humble himself shall be exalted."*

   1) Revelation 10:7-11 – *"...Give me the little book..."* – humility required to see your need for the revealed word of God in the last days

j. Luke 6:40 – *"The disciple is not above his master: but every one that is perfect shall be as his master."*

k. Romans 14:4 – *"Who art thou that judgest another man's servant? to his own master he standeth or falleth. Yea, he shall be holden up: for God is able to make him stand."*

l. Joshua 1:1-3, 7-10 – *"[1]Now after the death of Moses the servant of the LORD it came to pass, that the LORD spake unto Joshua the son of Nun, Moses' minister, saying, [2]Moses my servant is dead; now therefore arise, go over this Jordan, thou, and all this people, unto the land which I do give to them, even to the children of Israel. [3]Every place that the sole of your foot shall tread upon, that have I given unto you, as I said unto Moses...[7]Only be thou strong and very courageous, that thou mayest observe to do according to all the law, which Moses my servant commanded thee: turn not from it to the right hand or to the left, that thou mayest prosper whithersoever thou goest. [8]This book of the law shall not depart out of thy mouth; but thou shalt meditate therein day and night, that thou mayest observe to do according to all that is written therein: for then thou shalt make thy way prosperous, and then thou shalt have good success. [9]Have not I commanded thee? Be strong and of a good courage; be not afraid, neither be thou dismayed: for the LORD thy God is with thee whithersoever thou goest..."*

m. I Samuel 3:9 – *"...Speak, LORD; for thy servant heareth..."*

n. II Samuel 23:13-17 – David's mighty men heard Him sigh in his tent, then went and brought forth the water of the well of Bethlehem. They went in the jeopardy of their lives. David then poured the water on the ground which is a type of the last great move of God brought on my faithful servants.

o. Psalms 78:70-71 – *"[70]He chose David also his servant, and took him from the sheepfolds: [71]From following the ewes great with young he brought him to feed Jacob his people, and Israel his inheritance."* – David chosen to lead because he was a faithful shepherd.

p. Psalms 105:17-22 – *"[17]He sent a man before them, even Joseph, who was sold for a servant: [18]Whose feet they hurt with fetters: he was laid in iron: [19]Until the time that his word came: the word of the LORD tried him. [20]The king sent and loosed him; even the ruler of the people, and let him go free. [21]He made him lord of his house, and ruler of all his substance: [22]To bind his princes at his pleasure; and teach his senators wisdom."* – Joseph a servant made ruler over all of Egypt

q. Proverbs 14:35 – *"The king's favour is toward a wise servant: but his wrath is against him that causeth shame."*

r. Matthew 25:21-31 – *"[21]His lord said unto him, Well done, thou good and faithful servant: thou hast been faithful over a few things, I will make thee ruler over many things: enter thou into the joy of thy lord..."*

s. Luke 12:42-48 – *"[42]And the Lord said, Who then is that faithful and wise steward, whom his lord shall make ruler over his household, to give them their portion of meat in due season?*

[43]Blessed is that servant, whom his lord when he cometh shall find so doing. [44]Of a truth I say unto you, that he will make him ruler over all that he hath..."

t. Luke 16:10-13 – *"[10]He that is faithful in that which is least is faithful also in much: and he that is unjust in the least is unjust also in much. [11]If therefore ye have not been faithful in the unrighteous mammon, who will commit to your trust the true riches? [12]And if ye have not been faithful in that which is another man's, who shall give you that which is your own? [13]No servant can serve two masters: for either he will hate the one, and love the other; or else he will hold to the one, and despise the other. Ye cannot serve God and mammon."*

u. John 15:15-16 – *"[15]Henceforth I call you not servants; for the servant knoweth not what his lord doeth: but I have called you friends; for all things that I have heard of my Father I have made known unto you. [16]Ye have not chosen me, but I have chosen you, and ordained you, that ye should go and bring forth fruit, and that your fruit should remain: that whatsoever ye shall ask of the Father in my name, he may give it you."*

v. John 15:20 – *"Remember the word that I said unto you, The servant is not greater than his lord. If they have persecuted me, they will also persecute you; if they have kept my saying, they will keep yours also."*

w. I Corinthians 7:21-23 – *"[21]Art thou called being a servant? care not for it: but if thou mayest be made free, use it rather. [22]For he that is called in the Lord, being a servant, is the Lord's freeman: likewise also he that is called, being free, is Christ's servant. [23]Ye are bought with a price; be not ye the servants of men."*

x. I Corinthians 9:19 – *"For though I be free from all men, yet have I made myself servant unto all, that I might gain the more."*

y. Philippians 2:7 – *"But made himself of no reputation, and took upon him the form of a servant, and was made in the likeness of men:"*

z. II Timothy 2:24 – *"And the servant of the Lord must not strive; but be gentle unto all men, apt to teach, patient,"*

C. Genesis 28:10-19 – *"[10]And Jacob went out from Beer-sheba, and went toward Haran. [11]And he lighted upon a certain place, and tarried there all night, because the sun was set; and he took of the stones of that place, and put them for his pillows, and lay down in that place to sleep. [12]And he dreamed, and behold a ladder set up on the earth, and the top of it reached to heaven: and behold the angels of God ascending and descending on it. [13]And, behold, the LORD stood above it, and said, I am the LORD God of Abraham thy father, and the God of Isaac: the land whereon thou liest, to thee will I give it, and to thy seed; [14]And thy seed shall be as the dust of the earth, and thou shalt spread abroad to the west, and to the east, and to the north, and to the south: and in thee and in thy seed shall all the families of the earth be blessed. [15]And, behold, I am with thee, and will keep thee in all places whither thou goest, and will bring thee again into this land; for I will not leave thee, until I have done that which I have spoken to thee of. [16]And Jacob awaked out of his sleep, and he said, Surely the LORD is in this place; and I knew it not. [17]And he was afraid, and said, How dreadful is this place! this is none other but the house of God, and <u>this is the gate of heaven</u>. [18]And Jacob rose up early in the morning, and took the stone that he had put for his pillows, and set it up for a pillar, and poured oil upon the top of it. [19]And he called the name of that place Bethel: but the name of that city was called Luz at the first."*

1. This was Jacob's dream. It was a vision of a ladder set on earth, but reached to heaven.
2. This is a real place, though spiritual.
3. He called it "*the gate of heaven*" in verse 17.

4. This gives us insight into the spiritual realm and our ascent to the gate of heaven

   a. Song of Solomon 2:14 – *"O my dove, that art in the clefts of the rock, <u>in the secret places of the stairs</u>, let me see thy countenance, let me hear thy voice; for sweet is thy voice, and thy countenance is comely."*

b. Hebrews 12:1 – "*Wherefore seeing we also are compassed about with so great a cloud of witnesses, let us lay aside every weight, and the sin which doth so easily beset us, and let us run with patience the race that is set before us,*"

c. I Corinthians 9:24 – "*Know ye not that they which run in a race run all, but one receiveth the prize? So run, that ye may obtain.*"

d. Reveals to us the principle of levels in God, our life being a journey, step by step up the ladder.

   1) II Corinthians 3:18 – "*But we all, with open face beholding as in a glass the glory of the Lord, are changed into the same image from glory to glory, even as by the Spirit of the Lord.*"
   2) Romans 1:17 – "*For therein is the righteousness of God revealed from faith to faith: as it is written, The just shall live by faith.*"
   3) Psalms 84:7 – "*They go from strength to strength, every one of them in Zion appeareth before God.*"
   4) Proverbs 4:18 – "*But the path of the just is as the shining light, that shineth more and more unto the perfect day.*"
   5) Isaiah 28:13 – "*But the word of the LORD was unto them precept upon precept, precept upon precept; line upon line, line upon line; here a little, and there a little; that they might go, and fall backward, and be broken, and snared, and taken.*"
   6) Jeremiah 48:11 – "*Moab hath been at ease from his youth, and he hath settled on his lees, and hath not been emptied from vessel to vessel, neither hath he gone into captivity: therefore his taste remained in him, and his scent is not changed.*"
   7) Exodus 23:30 – "*By little and little I will drive them out from before thee, until thou be increased, and inherit the land.*"
   8) Psalms 115:14 – "The LORD shall increase you more and more…"
   9) Job 17:9 – "*The righteous also shall hold on his way, and he that hath clean hands shall be stronger and stronger.*"

D. Isaiah 6:1-8 – "*[1]In the year that king Uzziah died I saw also the Lord sitting upon a throne, high and lifted up, and his train filled the temple. [2]Above it stood the seraphims: each one had six wings; with twain he covered his face, and with twain he covered his feet, and with twain he did fly. [3]And one cried unto another, and said, Holy, holy, holy, is the LORD of hosts: the whole earth is full of his glory. [4]And the posts of the door moved at the voice of him that cried, and the house was filled with smoke. [5]Then said I, Woe is me! for I am undone; because I am a man of unclean lips, and I dwell in the midst of a people of unclean lips: for mine eyes have seen the King, the LORD of hosts. [6]Then flew one of the seraphims unto me, having a live coal in his hand, which he had taken with the tongs from off the altar: [7]And he laid it upon my mouth, and said, Lo, this hath touched thy lips; and thine iniquity is taken away, and thy sin purged. [8]Also I heard the voice of the Lord, saying, Whom shall I send, and who will go for us? Then said I, Here am I; send me.*"

1. This was Isaiah vision of heaven – The doors move at the praises of God's seraphims. "Seraphims" in Hebrew means "burning ones".
2. This is the door at the end of the ladder, stairs, etc.
3. When we've reached it, we will have finished the race
4. Similar passage – Revelation 4:6-9

E. Mark 11:2-11 – "*[2]And saith unto them, Go your way into the village over against you: and as soon as ye be entered into it, ye shall find a colt tied, whereon never man sat; loose him, and bring him. [3]And if any man say unto you, Why do ye this? say ye that the Lord hath need of him; and straightway he will send him hither. [4]And they went their way, and found the colt tied by the door without in a place where two ways met; and they loose him. [5]And certain of them that stood there said unto them, What do ye, loosing the colt? [6]And they said unto them even as Jesus had commanded: and they let them go. [7]And they brought the colt to Jesus, and cast their garments on him; and he sat upon him. [8]And many spread their garments in the way: and others cut down branches off the trees, and strawed them in the way. [9]And they that went before, and they that followed, cried, saying, Hosanna; Blessed is he that cometh in the name of the Lord: [10]Blessed be the kingdom of our father David, that cometh in the name of the Lord: Hosanna in the highest. [11]And Jesus entered into Jerusalem, and into the temple: and when he had looked round about upon all things, and now the eventide was come, he went out unto Bethany with the twelve."*

1. Once again we see this symbolically of Jesus' second coming.
2. The little colt represents the true "sons of God" in the last days.

3. Verse 2

   a. This colt is tied. He is yoked to the Lord (Matthew 11:28-29)
   b. No man has ever sat on this colt. This simply means no man would ever be allowed to control, master, or break this colt. This colt was born to carry only one burden, the Lord Jesus!

4. Verse 4

   a. Tied by the <u>door</u> – that heavenly portal!
   b. Without – outside normal religion
   c. Two ways met – this speaks of the final decision of this colt company to give all to Jesus.

F. Matthew 25:1-13 – "*[1]Then shall the kingdom of heaven be likened unto ten virgins, which took their lamps, and went forth to meet the bridegroom. [2]And five of them were wise, and five were foolish. [3]They that were foolish took their lamps, and took no oil with them: [4]But the wise took oil in their vessels with their lamps. [5]While the bridegroom tarried, they all slumbered and slept. [6]And at midnight there was a cry made, Behold, the bridegroom cometh; go ye out to meet him. [7]Then all those virgins arose, and trimmed their lamps. [8]And the foolish said unto the wise, Give us of your oil; for our lamps are gone out. [9]But the wise answered, saying, Not so; lest there be not enough for us and you: but go ye rather to them that sell, and buy for yourselves. [10]And while they went to buy, the bridegroom came; and they that were ready went in with him to the marriage: and <u>the door was shut</u>. [11]Afterward came also the other virgins, saying, Lord, Lord, open to us. [12]But he answered and said, Verily I say unto you, I know you not. [13]Watch therefore, for ye know neither the day nor the hour wherein the Son of man cometh.*"

1. Verse 10 – the wise virgins were ready and went through the door into the marriage chamber. In other words, they had finished the race and had reached the top of the ladder.
2. The foolish believers who were unprepared weren't allowed entrance because they hadn't prepared themselves properly. They hadn't paid the price (bought oil)

3. Luke 13:23-30 – "*[23]Then said one unto him, Lord, are there few that be saved? And he said unto them, [24]Strive to enter in at the strait gate: for many, I say unto you, will seek to enter in, and shall not be able. [25]When once the master of the house is risen up, and hath shut to the door, and ye begin to stand without, and to knock at the door, saying, Lord, Lord, open unto us; and he shall answer and say unto you, I know you not whence ye are: [26]Then shall ye begin to say, We have eaten and drunk in thy presence, and thou hast taught in our streets. [27]But he shall say, I tell you, I know you not whence ye are; depart from me, all ye workers of iniquity. [28]There shall be weeping and gnashing of teeth...*"

   a. Verse 25 – once again, those who were not ready or had not gone on into an intimate relationship with the Lord were barred entrance through the door.
   b. Even though they did the following, it still wasn't enough: 1) Eaten in His presence – tasted the Word of God; 2) Drunk in His presence – They had enjoyed the benefits of God's glorious presence but made no effort to have an intimate relationship with Him.

c. There will be intense regret and weeping and gnashing of teeth once it dawns on those believers what they could have had, what all men are called to, but yet they didn't pay the price.

G. Revelation 4:1-11 – "[1]*After this I looked, and, behold, a door was opened in heaven: and the first voice which I heard was as it were of a trumpet talking with me; which said, Come up hither, and I will shew thee things which must be hereafter.* [2]*And immediately I was in the spirit: and, behold, a throne was set in heaven, and one sat on the throne.* [3]*And he that sat was to look upon like a jasper and a sardine stone: and there was a rainbow round about the throne, in sight like unto an emerald.* [4]*And round about the throne were four and twenty seats: and upon the seats I saw four and twenty elders sitting, clothed in white raiment; and they had on their heads crowns of gold.* [5]*And out of the throne proceeded lightnings and thunderings and voices: and there were seven lamps of fire burning before the throne, which are the seven Spirits of God.* [6]*And before the throne there was a sea of glass like unto crystal: and in the midst of the throne, and round about the throne, were four beasts full of eyes before and behind.* [7]*And the first beast was like a lion, and the second beast like a calf, and the third beast had a face as a man, and the fourth beast was like a flying eagle.* [8]*And the four beasts had each of them six wings about him; and they were full of eyes within: and they rest not day and night, saying, Holy, holy, holy, Lord God Almighty, which was, and is, and is to come.* [9]*And when those beasts give glory and honour and thanks to him that sat on the throne, who liveth for ever and ever,* [10]*The four and twenty elders fall down before him that sat on the throne, and worship him that liveth for ever and ever, and cast their crowns before the throne, saying,* [11]*Thou art worthy, O Lord, to receive glory and honour and power: for thou hast created all things, and for thy pleasure they are and were created.*"

1. In Revelation 3:21-22, Jesus had just finished speaking the promises to those who would overcome. He had also just wrapped up His rebuke of the church of Laodicea, which by the way is symbolic of the last church before the coming of the Lord.
2. Verse 1 – "*After this…*", referring to Jesus promises to those who overcame, "*…a door was opened in heaven…*". This signifies that the overcomers had reached the top of the ladder and had finished their race and had come through every level in God. Unto them, the door was opened and they are now in the throne room.

H. Ezekiel 47:1-14 – "[1]*Afterward he brought me again unto the door of the house; and, behold, waters issued out from under the threshold of the house eastward: for the forefront of the house stood toward the east, and the waters came down from under from the right side of the house, at the south side of the altar.* [2]*Then brought he me out of the way of the gate northward, and led me about the way without unto the utter gate by the way that looketh eastward; and, behold, there ran out waters on the right side.* [3]*And when the man that had the line in his hand went forth eastward, he measured a thousand cubits, and he brought me through the waters; the waters were to the ancles.* [4]*Again he measured a thousand, and brought me through the waters; the waters were to the knees. Again he measured a thousand, and brought me through; the waters were to the loins.* [5]*Afterward he measured a thousand; and it was a river that I could not pass over: for the waters were risen, waters to swim in, a river that could not be passed over…*"

1. Verse 1 – The door once again is God's door. Out from under it flows the glory of the last days church.
2. Verse 3-5 – Levels of growth until perfection and the overwhelming glory of God flows like a river out of it. Everywhere the river reaches gets healed.

3. Principle of the river of God flowing out of the saints in the last days:

   a. John 7:38 – "*He that believeth on me, as the scripture hath said, out of his belly shall flow rivers of living water.*"
   b. Psalms 46:4 – "*There is a river, the streams whereof shall make glad the city of God, the holy place of the tabernacles of the most High.*"

c. Revelation 22:1-2 – "[1]*And he shewed me a pure river of water of life, clear as crystal, proceeding out of the throne of God and of the Lamb.* [2]*In the midst of the street of it, and on either side of the river, was there the tree of life, which bare twelve manner of fruits, and yielded her fruit every month: and the leaves of the tree were for the healing of the nations."*

d. Isaiah 43:19-21 – "[19]*Behold, I will do a new thing; now it shall spring forth; shall ye not know it? I will even make a way in the wilderness, and rivers in the desert.* [20]*The beast of the field shall honour me, the dragons and the owls: because I give waters in the wilderness, and rivers in the desert, to give drink to my people, my chosen.* [21]*This people have I formed for myself; they shall shew forth my praise."*

e. Job 28:10 – "*He cutteth out rivers among the rocks; and his eye seeth every precious thing."*

f. Joel 3:14-18 – "[14]*Multitudes, multitudes in the valley of decision: for the day of the LORD is near in the valley of decision.* [15]*The sun and the moon shall be darkened, and the stars shall withdraw their shining.* [16]*The LORD also shall roar out of Zion, and utter his voice from Jerusalem; and the heavens and the earth shall shake: but the LORD will be the hope of his people, and the strength of the children of Israel.* [17]*So shall ye know that I am the LORD your God dwelling in Zion, my holy mountain: then shall Jerusalem be holy, and there shall no strangers pass through her any more.* [18]*And it shall come to pass in that day, that the mountains shall drop down new wine, and the hills shall flow with milk, and all the rivers of Judah shall flow with waters, and a fountain shall come forth of the house of the LORD, and shall water the valley of Shittim."*

g. Zechariah 13:1 – "*In that day there shall be a fountain opened to the house of David and to the inhabitants of Jerusalem for sin and for uncleanness."*

h. Song of Solomon 4:12-16 – "[12]*A garden inclosed is my sister, my spouse; a spring shut up, a fountain sealed.* [13]*Thy plants are an orchard of pomegranates, with pleasant fruits; camphire, with spikenard,* [14]*Spikenard and saffron; calamus and cinnamon, with all trees of frankincense; myrrh and aloes, with all the chief spices:* [15]*A fountain of gardens, a well of living waters, and streams from Lebanon.* [16]*Awake, O north wind; and come, thou south; blow upon my garden, that the spices thereof may flow out. Let my beloved come into his garden, and eat his pleasant fruits."*

i. Isaiah 33:20-24 – "[20]*Look upon Zion, the city of our solemnities: thine eyes shall see Jerusalem a quiet habitation, a tabernacle that shall not be taken down; not one of the stakes thereof shall ever be removed, neither shall any of the cords thereof be broken.* [21]*But there the glorious LORD will be unto us a place of broad rivers and streams; wherein shall go no galley with oars, neither shall gallant ship pass thereby.* [22]*For the LORD is our judge, the LORD is our lawgiver, the LORD is our king; he will save us.* [23]*Thy tacklings are loosed; they could not well strengthen their mast, they could not spread the sail: then is the prey of a great spoil divided; the lame take the prey.* [24]*And the inhabitant shall not say, I am sick: the people that dwell therein shall be forgiven their iniquity."*

j. Matthew 24:37-38 – "[37]*But as the days of Noe were, so shall also the coming of the Son of man be.* [38]*For as in the days that were before the flood they were eating and drinking, marrying and giving in marriage, until the day that Noe entered into the ark,"* (Genesis 6:17) – In the last days it will be a river of glory. A blessing to the remnant (Noah and his son's family), but it will be judgment to those who have not paid the price.

k. II Samuel 23:13-17 – David's mighty men heard Him sigh in his tent, then went and brought forth the water of the well of Bethlehem. They went in the jeopardy of their lives. David then poured the water on the ground which is a type of the last great outpouring of God's glory

l. Judges 15:14-20 – Samson's jawbone of an ass

m. Haggai 2:7 – The glory is the river, "*And I will shake all nations, and the desire of all nations shall come: and I will fill this house with glory, saith the LORD of hosts."*

I. John 10:7-16 – "[7]*Then said Jesus unto them again, Verily, verily, I say unto you, <u>I am the door of the sheep</u>.* [8]*All that ever came before me are thieves and robbers: but the sheep did not hear them.* [9]*I am the door: by me if any man enter in, he shall be saved, and shall go in and out, and find pasture.* [10]*The thief* *cometh not, but for to steal, and to kill, and to destroy: I am come that they might have life, and that they might have it more abundantly. [11]I am the good shepherd: the good shepherd giveth his life for the sheep. [12]But he that is an hireling, and not the shepherd, whose own the sheep are not, seeth the wolf coming, and leaveth the sheep, and fleeth: and the wolf catcheth them, and scattereth the sheep. [13]The hireling fleeth, because he is an hireling, and careth not for the sheep. [14]I am the good shepherd, and know my sheep, and am known of mine. [15]As the Father knoweth me, even so know I the Father: and I lay down my life for the sheep. [16]And other sheep I have, which are not of this fold: them also I must bring, and they shall hear my voice; and there shall be one fold, and one shepherd."* – Jesus literally is the door into salvation and into all that is Godly.

1. John 10:1-5 – "*[1]Verily, verily, I say unto you, He that entereth not by the door into the sheepfold, but climbeth up some other way, the same is a thief and a robber. [2]But he that entereth in by the door is the shepherd of the sheep. [3]To him the porter openeth; and the sheep hear his voice: and he calleth his own sheep by name, and leadeth them out. [4]And when he putteth forth his own sheep, he goeth before them, and the sheep follow him: for they know his voice. [5]And a stranger will they not follow, but will flee from him: for they know not the voice of strangers.*"
2. Revelation 3:7-8 – "*[7]And to the angel of the church in Philadelphia write; These things saith he that is holy, he that is true, he that hath the key of David, he that openeth, and no man shutteth; and shutteth, and no man openeth; [8]I know thy works: behold, I have set before thee an open door, and no man can shut it: for thou hast a little strength, and hast kept my word, and hast not denied my name.*" (Psalms 78:23 – "*Though he had commanded the clouds from above, and <u>opened the doors of heaven</u>*")

J. Psalms 24:3-10 – "*[3]Who shall ascend into the hill of the LORD? or who shall stand in his holy place? [4]He that hath clean hands, and a pure heart; who hath not lifted up his soul unto vanity, nor sworn deceitfully. [5]He shall receive the blessing from the LORD, and righteousness from the God of his salvation. [6]This is the generation of them that seek him, that seek thy face, O Jacob. Selah. [7]Lift up your head, O ye gates; and be ye lift up, ye everlasting doors; and the King of glory shall come in. [8]Who is this King of glory? The LORD strong and mighty, the LORD mighty in battle. [9]Lift up your heads, O ye gates; even lift them up, ye everlasting doors; and the King of glory shall come in. [10]Who is this King of glory? The LORD of hosts, he is the King of glory. Selah.*"

1. David begins by asking, "*Who shall ascend into the hill of the Lord?*"
2. Four things are mentioned in response to this questions – four in Scripture is the number for creation or the new creation man.
3. Those who do these things receive blessing from the Lord

4. Verse 6 – I believe this verse is speaking of the last days generation of sons

   a. Psalms 102:18, "*This shall be written for the generation to come: and the people which shall be created shall praise the LORD*")
   b. Isaiah 65:18 – "*But be ye glad and rejoice for ever in that which I create: for, behold, I create Jerusalem a rejoicing, and her people a joy.*"

5. Verse 7-10 – The door of heaven is an "*everlasting door*". This is the gate of heaven. All that goes to God, goes through there and all that comes from the Lord Jesus comes from there. Jesus returns through that door after having been the "son of man" who died and gave Himself for the world but has been raised up and now is the "*King of glory*".

K. Psalms 100:4 – "*Enter into his gates with thanksgiving, and into his courts with praise: be thankful unto him, and bless his name.*" – We must always remember He is the door. This passage tells us how to get in and that praise is the beginning.

1. Isaiah 60:15-19 – "*...but thou shalt call thy walls Salvation, and thy gates Praise...*"

2. Isaiah 6:3-4 – "[3]*And one cried unto another, and said, Holy, holy, holy, is the LORD of hosts: the whole earth is full of his glory.* [4]*And the posts of the door moved at the voice of him that cried, and the house was filled with smoke.*"
3. Psalms 95:1-2 – We won't enter into the seventh day if we're not worshippers or live in rebellion – "[1]*O come, let us sing unto the LORD: let us make a joyful noise to the rock of our salvation.* [2]*Let us come before his presence with thanksgiving, and make a joyful noise unto him with psalms...*[6]*O come, let us worship and bow down: let us kneel before the LORD our maker.* [7]*For he is our God; and we are the people of his pasture, and the sheep of his hand. To day if ye will hear his voice...*[11]*Unto whom I sware in my wrath that they should not enter into my rest.*"
4. Jeremiah 7:1-2 – "[1]*The word that came to Jeremiah from the LORD, saying,* [2]*Stand in the gate of the LORD's house, and proclaim there this word, and say, Hear the word of the LORD, all ye of Judah, that enter in at these gates to worship the LORD.*"

III. Some Other Notable Doors Of God Found In Scripture

A. Hosea 2:14-20 – "[14]*Therefore, behold, I will allure her, and bring her into the wilderness, and speak comfortably unto her.* [15]*And I will give her her vineyards from thence, and the valley of Achor for <u>a door of hope</u>: and she shall sing there, as in the days of her youth, and as in the day when she came up out of the land of Egypt.* [16]*And it shall be at that day, saith the LORD, that thou shalt call me Ishi; and shalt call me no more Baali.* [17]*For I will take away the names of Baalim out of her mouth, and they shall no more be remembered by their name.* [18]*And in that day will I make a covenant for them with the beasts of the field, and with the fowls of heaven, and with the creeping things of the ground: and I will break the bow and the sword and the battle out of the earth, and will make them to lie down safely.* [19]*And I will betroth thee unto me for ever; yea, I will betroth thee unto me in righteousness, and in judgment, and in lovingkindness, and in mercies.*[20]*I will even betroth thee unto me in faithfulness: and thou shalt know the LORD.*" Achor means "trouble". Trouble is the door of hope to bring us to brideship.

B. Mark 1:32-34 – "[32]*And at even, when the sun did set, they brought unto him all that were diseased, and them that were possessed with devils.* [33]*<u>And all the city was gathered together at the door.</u>* [34]*And he healed many that were sick of divers diseases, and cast out many devils; and suffered not the devils to speak, because they knew him.*"

C. II Samuel 23:15-16 – "[15]*And David longed, and said, Oh that one would give me drink of the water of the <u>well of Bethlehem</u>, <u>which is by the gate</u>!* [16]*And the three mighty men brake through the host of the Philistines, and drew water out of the well of Bethlehem, that was by the gate, and took it, and brought it to David: nevertheless he would not drink thereof, but poured it out unto the LORD.*"

1. I Chronicles 11:17-18 – "[17]*And David longed, and said, Oh that one would give me drink of the water of the well of Bethlehem, that is at the gate!* [18]*And the three brake through the host of the Philistines, and drew water out of the well of Bethlehem, that was by the gate, and took it, and brought it to David: but David would not drink of it, but poured it out to the LORD,*"
2. These three mighty men speak of the remnant in the last days who are so close to the king that they hear Him sighing, longing to drink the water from the well of Bethlehem, "*which is by the gate!*"
3. Bethlehem means "house of bread" – a type of the Word of God

4. The revealed Word of God is by heaven's gate or door. We must break through the hosts of our enemies to see and know the true revelation of the Lord.

   a. Proverbs 1:21 – Speaking of Wisdom here, "*She crieth in the chief place of concourse, in the openings of the gates: in the city she uttereth her words, saying,*"
   b. Proverbs 8:3 – "*She crieth at the gates, at the entry of the city, at the coming in at the doors.*"
   c. Luke 11:49 – "*Therefore also said the wisdom of God, I will send them prophets and apostles, and some of them they shall slay and persecute:*"

D. Colossians 4:3 – "*Withal praying also for us, that God would open unto us a* <u>*door of utterance*</u>*, to speak the mystery of Christ, for which I am also in bonds:*"

E. I Corinthians 16:9 – "*For* <u>*a great door and effectual*</u> *is opened unto me, and* <u>*there are many adversaries*</u>*.*"

F. Acts 14:27 – "*And when they were come, and had gathered the church together, they rehearsed all that God had done with them, and how he had opened the* <u>*door of faith unto the Gentiles*</u>*.*"

G. Psalms 118:19-20 – "[19]*Open to me the* <u>*gates of righteousness*</u>*: I will go into them, and I will praise the LORD:* [20]*This gate of the LORD, into which the righteous shall enter.*" (Isaiah 26:2)

H. Matthew 7:13-14 – "[13]*Enter ye in at the strait gate: for wide is the gate, and broad is the way, that leadeth to destruction, and many there be which go in thereat:* [14]*Because strait is the gate, and narrow is the way, which leadeth unto life, and few there be that find it.*" (Luke 13:24-28)

I. Psalms 87:2 – "*The LORD loveth* <u>*the gates of Zion*</u> *more than all the dwellings of Jacob.*"

J. Hebrews 13:12-13 – "[12]*Wherefore Jesus also, that he might sanctify the people with his own blood, suffered without the gate.* [13]*Let us go forth therefore unto him without the camp, bearing his reproach.*" – Jesus suffered outside the gate and camp

K. II Samuel 11:9 – "*But Uriah slept at the door of the king's house with all the servants of his lord, and went not down to his house.*" – He is an example of true faithfulness; Uriah in Hebrew means – "flame of Jehovah, Jehovah is light, the Lord my light"

L. Exodus 12:7 – "*And they shall take of the blood, and strike it on the two side posts and on the upper door post of the houses, wherein they shall eat it.*"

M. Exodus 29:4 – "*And Aaron and his sons thou shalt bring unto the door of the tabernacle of the congregation, and shalt wash them with water.*" – Aaron and sons washed and sanctified at the door of the tabernacle.

N. Exodus 29:42 – "*This shall be a* <u>*continual burnt offering*</u> *throughout your generations* <u>*at the door of the tabernacle*</u> *of the congregation before the LORD: where I will meet you, to speak there unto thee.*"

O. Deuteronomy 11:20 – "*And thou shalt write them upon the door posts of thine house, and upon thy gates:*" – God's Words were to be written on the doorposts and gats of the houses of His people.

P. Acts 3:2-7 – "[2]*And a certain man lame from his mother's womb was carried, whom they laid daily at the gate of the temple which is called Beautiful, to ask alms of them that entered into the temple;* [3]*Who seeing Peter and John about to go into the temple asked an alms.* [4]*And Peter, fastening his eyes upon him with John, said, Look on us.* [5]*And he gave heed unto them, expecting to receive something of them.* [6]*Then Peter said, Silver and gold have I none; but such as I have give I thee: In the name of Jesus Christ of Nazareth rise up and walk.* [7]*And he took him by the right hand, and lifted him up: and immediately his feet and ancle bones received strength.*"

Q. Revelation 3:20 – Jesus is standing and knocking on the door of the Laodicean church, "*Behold, I stand at the door, and knock: if any man hear my voice, and open the door, I will come in to him, and will sup with him, and he with me.*"

R. Revelation 22:14 – "*Blessed are they that do his commandments, that they may have right to the tree of life, and may enter in through the gates into the city.*" (Genesis 3:23 – entrance of paradise guarded by Cherubims and a flaming sword).

IV. Doorkeepers In The House Of The Lord

A. Psalms 84:10 – "*For a day in thy courts is better than a thousand.* <u>*I had rather be a doorkeeper*</u> *in the house of my God, than to dwell in the tents of wickedness.*"

1. Other translations: "*I have chosen rather to be at the threshold in the house of my God*", "*a gatekeeper*", "*I would rather be a doorman of the Temple of God than live in palaces...*", "*It is better to be a doorkeeper in the House of my God*", "*I would rather stand at the gate of the House...*"
2. Definition for doorkeeper in Hebrew, *caphaph* – to snatch away, terminate, to wait at the threshold; this is the only time this word is found in Scripture.

B. II Chronicles 23:19 – *"And he set the porters at the gates of the house of the LORD, that none which was unclean in any thing should enter in."*

1. Porters at the gate of God's House
2. So that nothing unclean should enter in
3. Definitions for porters

   a. Hebrew, *shower'* – a janitor
   b. Greek, *thuroros* – a watcher, a gatewarden; it comes from the root word, *thura* – a portal or entrance

4. Other translations: *"gatekeepers, so that no one should enter in who was in anyway unclean"*, *"and the unclean in anything doth not go in"*, *"He assigned security guards at the gates of God's Temple so that no one who was unprepared could enter"*, *"The guards at the temple gates kept out everything that was not consecrated and all unauthorized personnel"*,

C. Mark 13:34-37 – *"34For the Son of man is as a man taking a far journey, who left his house, and gave authority to his servants, and to every man his work, and commanded the porter to watch. 35Watch ye therefore: for ye know not when the master of the house cometh, at even, or at midnight, or at the cockcrowing, or in the morning: 36Lest coming suddenly he find you sleeping. 37And what I say unto you I say unto all, Watch."*

1. Porters have authority
2. Porters have a special work to do and that is to watch
3. Greek for watch, *gregoreuo* – to keep awake, be vigilant, to watch; it comes from the root word, *egeiro* – to waken, to rouse from sleep, to cause people to get up from sitting or lying down, to awaken from disease, death, inactivity, obscurity, or non existence, to make to rise up.
4. Other translations: *"He gives orders to the doorkeeper to be constantly alert and on the watch"*, *"to stay on alert"*, *"gatekeeper to watch for His return"*

5. Principles of watching

   a. Habakkuk 2:1 – *"I will stand upon my watch, and set me upon the tower, and will watch to see what he will say unto me, and what I shall answer when I am reproved."*
   b. Matthew 26:41 – *"Watch and pray, that ye enter not into temptation: the spirit indeed is willing, but the flesh is weak."*
   c. Luke 2:8 – *"And there were in the same country shepherds abiding in the field, keeping watch over their flock by night."*
   d. Luke 21:36 – *"Watch ye therefore, and pray always, that ye may be accounted worthy to escape all these things that shall come to pass, and to stand before the Son of man."*
   e. I Corinthians 16:13 – *"Watch ye, stand fast in the faith, quit you like men, be strong."*
   f. I Thessalonians 5:6-9 – *"6Therefore let us not sleep, as do others; but let us watch and be sober. 7For they that sleep sleep in the night; and they that be drunken are drunken in the night. 8But let us, who are of the day, be sober, putting on the breastplate of faith and love; and for an helmet, the hope of salvation. 9For God hath not appointed us to wrath, but to obtain salvation by our Lord Jesus Christ,"*
   g. II Timothy 4:5 – *"But watch thou in all things, endure afflictions, do the work of an evangelist, make full proof of thy ministry."*
   h. Psalms 102:6-7 – *"6I am like a pelican of the wilderness: I am like an owl of the desert. 7I watch, and am as a sparrow alone upon the house top."*

D. John 10:3 – *"To him the porter openeth; and the sheep hear his voice: and he calleth his own sheep by name, and leadeth them out."* – Doorkeepers job is to bring Jesus in

E. I Chronicles 15:23-24 – "*[23]And Berechiah and Elkanah were doorkeepers for the ark. [24]And Shebaniah, and Jehoshaphat, and Nethaneel, and Amasai, and Zechariah, and Benaiah, and Eliezer, the priests, did blow with the trumpets before the ark of God: and Obed-edom and Jehiah were doorkeepers for the ark.*"

1. The doorkeepers and the definitions of their names in Hebrew:

   a. Berechiah – whom Jehovah has blessed, blessing of the Lord, bending the knee
   b. Elkanah – God has redeemed, possession of God, God hath created; it comes from a root word that means – to possess, to acquire
   c. Obed-edom – serving Edom, servant of Edom, a laborer of the earth; Edom in Hebrew means – red, red earth.
   d. Jehiah – He lives of the Lord, by the mercy of the Lord, Jehovah who lives, God is living

F. Nehemiah 11:19 – "*Moreover the porters, Akkub, Talmon, and their brethren that kept the gates, were an hundred seventy and two.*"

1. Akkub – cunning, artful, to come from behind, subtle, to take by the heal
2. Talmon – injurious oppression, oppressed intensely, outcast

G. Isaiah 22:15-24 – "*[15]Thus saith the Lord GOD of hosts, Go, get thee unto this treasurer, even unto Shebna, which is over the house, and say, [16]What hast thou here? and whom hast thou here, that thou hast hewed thee out a sepulchre here, as he that heweth him out a sepulchre on high, and that graveth an habitation for himself in a rock? [17]Behold, the LORD will carry thee away with a mighty captivity, and will surely cover thee. [18]He will surely violently turn and toss thee like a ball into a large country: there shalt thou die, and there the chariots of thy glory shall be the shame of thy lord's house. [19]And I will drive thee from thy station, and from thy state shall he pull thee down. [20]And it shall come to pass in that day, that I will call my servant Eliakim the son of Hilkiah: [21]And I will clothe him with thy robe, and strengthen him with thy girdle, and I will commit thy government into his hand: and he shall be a father to the inhabitants of Jerusalem, and to the house of Judah. [22]And the key of the house of David will I lay upon his shoulder; so he shall open, and none shall shut; and he shall shut, and none shall open. [23]And I will fasten him as a nail in a sure place; and he shall be for a glorious throne to his father's house. [24]And they shall hang upon him all the glory of his father's house, the offspring and the issue, all vessels of small quantity, from the vessels of cups, even to all the vessels of flagons.*"

1. Shebna – who built, who rests himself, youthfulness
2. Eliakim – whom God sets up, whom God causes to stand and be established, God will raise up
3. Revelation 3:7 – "*And to the angel of the church in Philadelphia write; These things saith he that is holy, he that is true, he that hath the key of David, he that openeth, and no man shutteth; and shutteth, and no man openeth;*"
4. Matthew 16:13-19 – "*[13]When Jesus came into the coasts of Caesarea Philippi, he asked his disciples, saying, Whom do men say that I the Son of man am? [14]And they said, Some say that thou art John the Baptist: some, Elias; and others, Jeremias, or one of the prophets. [15]He saith unto them, But whom say ye that I am? [16]And Simon Peter answered and said, Thou art the Christ, the Son of the living God. [17]And Jesus answered and said unto him, Blessed art thou, Simon Barjona: for flesh and blood hath not revealed it unto thee, but my Father which is in heaven. [18]And I say also unto thee, That thou art Peter, and upon this rock I will build my church; and the gates of hell shall not prevail against it. [19]And I will give unto thee the keys of the kingdom of heaven: and whatsoever thou shalt bind on earth shall be bound in heaven: and whatsoever thou shalt loose on earth shall be loosed in heaven.*" – Keys to the Kingdom of Heaven

H. Ezekiel 44:15-30 – Sons of Zadok

1. They shall come near the Lord

2. They minister to Him and stand before Him
3. They shall enter sanctuary
4. They shall come near to His table (table of showbread)
5. They shall keep His charge

6. Verses 17-18 – *"And it shall come to pass, that when they enter in at the gates of the inner court, they shall be clothed with linen garments; and no wool shall come upon them, whiles they minister in the gates of the inner court, and within. 18They shall have linen bonnets upon their heads, and shall have linen breeches upon their loins; they shall not gird themselves with any thing that causeth sweat."*

   a. Clothed in linen garments – Revelation 19:7-9, righteousness of the saints
   b. No wool – no sweating, dead works
   c. Linen bonnets – mind of Christ
   d. Linen breeches – only produce that which is of God and not after the flesh
   e. Nothing to cause sweat – religious dead works, the Law, Adam's curse

I. I Chronicles 15:18 – *"And with them their brethren of the second degree, Zechariah, Ben, and Jaaziel, and Shemiramoth, and Jehiel, and Unni, Eliab, and Benaiah, and Maaseiah, and Mattithiah, and Elipheleh, and Mikneiah, and Obed-edom, and Jeiel, the porters."* – List of porters and the meaning of their name

   1. Zechariah – Jehovah remembers, Jehovah is renowned son
   2. Ben – son, edification of the family
   3. Jaaziel – He is comforted of God, whom God strengthens
   4. Shemiramoth – Most exalted name, fame of the highest, height of the heavens
   5. Jehiel – God lives, he lives of God, by the mercy of God, Jah shall save alive
   6. Unni – afflicted of the Lord, answering is with Jehovah
   7. Eliab – afflicted of the Lord, answering is with Jehovah
   8. Benaiah – whom Jehovah has built, built up of the Lord, Jehovah is intelligent
   9. Maaseiah – refuge of the Lord, work of Jehovah, Jehovah is a refuge; root – shelter, hope
   10. Mattithiah – gift of the Lord
   11. Elipheleh – God distinguishes him, God makes him eminent, distinguished, my God set thou apart
   12. Mikneiah – possession of Jehovah, Jehovah is jealous
   13. Obed-edom – serving Edom, servant of Edom, laborer of the earth; Edom – red, red earth
   14. Jeiel – hidden of God, treasure of God, God snatches away

J. I Chronicles 16:37-38 – *"37So he left there before the ark of the covenant of the LORD Asaph and his brethren, to minister before the ark continually, as every day's work required: 38And Obed-edom with their brethren, threescore and eight; Obed-edom also the son of Jeduthun and Hosah to be porters:"* – Hosah in Hebrew – place of refuge, fleeing to Jehovah, to trust in God

K. Nehemiah 10:28-29, 39 – *"28And the rest of the people, the priests, the Levites, the porters, the singers, the Nethinims, and all they that had separated themselves from the people of the lands unto the law of God, their wives, their sons, and their daughters, every one having knowledge, and having understanding; 29They clave to their brethren, their nobles, and entered into a curse, and into an oath, to walk in God's law, which was given by Moses the servant of God, and to observe and do all the commandments of the LORD our Lord, and his judgments and his statutes…39For the children of Israel and the children of Levi shall bring the offering of the corn, of the new wine, and the oil, unto the chambers, where are the vessels of the sanctuary, and the priests that minister, and the porters, and the singers: and we will not forsake the house of our God."*

L. I Chronicles 9:17-27

Lesson 9

Understanding Types and Symbols

I. The Figurative Language of the Bible

A. Pictures In Word – The Bible was written to us to share God's thoughts and heart. But, God's thoughts are too wonderful for us human beings to fully understand. To help us, God many times in the Scriptures draws for us "pictures in words," so we can see more clearly the spiritual truths of His thoughts and heart.

1. Hosea 7:8 – *"Ephraim, he hath mixed himself among the people; Ephraim is a cake not turned."*(KJV)
"What wonder Ephraim should throw in his lot with the Gentile: No better than a griddle-cake in Ephraim, baked only on one side." (KNOX)
2. Psalm 18:2 – *"The Lord is my rock, and my fortress, and my deliverer; my God, my strength, in whom I will trust; my buckler, and the horn of my salvation, and my high tower."* (KJV)
"The Lord is my firm foundation, my fort and my liberator; my God, my trustworthy defense, my protector, my strong deliverer and my place of retreat." (HAR)
3. Deuteronomy 32:3 – *"My doctrine shall drop as the rain, my speech shall distil as the dew, as the small rain upon the tender herb, and as the showers upon the grass:..."* (KJV)
"May my instruction soak in like the rain" (NAB)
"Let my speech distil as the dew." (Rhm)
"...like mists on the green growth." (Mof)
"As the mist on the fresh grass" (AAT)
"Like droplets on the grass..." (Tor)
"...and light rain on the turf." (Jerus)
4. Psalm 119:05 – *"Thy word is a lamp unto my feet, and a light unto my path."* (KJV)
5. I Peter 1:24 – *"For all flesh is as grass, and all the glory of man as the flower of grass. The grass withereth, and the flower thereof falleth away."* (KJV)
"All mankind is like herbage and all their beauty like it's flowers." (Wey)
"...All earthly like is but grass, and all its splendor like the flower of the field."(NEB)
"The herbage dries up and it's flowers drop off." (Wey)
"The grass dries up. The flowers drop off." (Wms)
6. John 1:29 – *"The next day John seeth Jesus Coming unto him, and saith, Behold the Lamb of God, which taketh away the sin of the world."* (KJV)
"...who is to take away..." (Wey)
"...who is to remove..." (Gspd)
"...who takes and bears away the sin of the world." (Mon)
7. Joshua 1:3 – *"Every place that the sole of your foot shall tread upon, that have I given unto you, as I said unto Moses."* (KJV)
"Every foot of ground you tread I assign to you, as I promised Moses." (Mof)
"As I promised Moses, I will deliver to you." (NAB)
"...my promise to Moses holds good." (Knox)
8. I Thessalonians 2:7 – *"But we were gentle among you, even as a nurse cherisheth her children."* (KJV)
"On the contrary I showed myself among you as gentle as a mother when she tenderly nurses her own children." (Mon)
9. Nahum 1:3 – *"The Lord is slow to anger, and great in power, and will not at all acquit the wicked: the Lord hath his way in the whirlwind and in the storm, and the clouds are the dust of his feet."* (KJV)
"... and the Lord never leaves the guilty unpunished." (ABPS)
"In hurricane and in tempest is his path, and clouds are the dust at this feet." (NAB)
"He shows his power in the terrors of the cyclones and raging storms: clouds are billowing dust beneath his feet!" (Tay)

10. Job 12:2 – *"No doubt but ye are the people, and wisdom shall die with you."* (KJV)
"Strange, that you alone should have the gift of reason, that when you die, wisdom must die too! (Knox)
"Yes, I realize you know everything! All wisdom will die with you!" (Tay)

B. Many of the things God intends for us to know can only be explained to us in such picture language
C. God describes heavenly things by using natural things

1. Romans 1:20 – *"For the invisible things of him from the creation of the world are clearly seen, being understood by the things that are made, even his eternal power and Godhead; so that they are without excuse."*
2. I Corinthians 15:46 – *"Howbeit that was not first which is spiritual, but that which is natural; and afterward that which is spiritual."*
3. Psalms 19:1-3 – *"[1]The heavens declare the glory of God; and the firmament sheweth his handywork. [2]Day unto day uttereth speech, and night unto night sheweth knowledge. [3]There is no speech nor language, where their voice is not heard."*
4. Matthew 13:1-7 – Jesus teaching in parables – *"The same day went Jesus out of the house, and sat by the sea side. And great multitudes were gathered together unto him, so that he went into a ship, and sat; and the whole multitude stood on the shore. And he spake many things unto them in parables, saying, Behold, a sower went forth to sow..."*
5. Hebrews 8:5 – *"Who serve unto the example and shadow of heavenly things as Moses was admonished of God when he was about to make the tabernacle: for, See, saith he, that thou make all things according to the pattern shewed to thee in the mount."*
6. I Chronicles 28:12 – *"And the pattern of all that he had by the spirit, of the courts of the house of the Lord, and of all the chambers round about, of the treasuries of the house of God, and of the treasuries of the dedicated things."*
7. II Corinthians 12:2,4 – *"I knew a man in Christ about fourteen years ago, (whether out of the body, I cannot tell: God knoweth;) such an one caught up to the third heaven...How that he was caught up into paradise, and heard unspeakable words, which it is not lawful for a man to utter."*

D. Figurative language is used to hide deep truth; Figurative language may hide the truth, as well as make it clear. It hides it from the unbelieving, and pierces and makes it clear to those who seek to know the mind of God.

1. Mark 4:11-12 – *"And he said unto them, Unto you it is given to know the mystery of the kingdom of God; but unto them that are without, all these things are done in parables: That seeing they may see, and not perceive; and hearing they may hear, and not understand; lest at any time they should be converted, and their sins should be forgiven them."*
2. Matthew 11:25-26 – *"At that time Jesus answered and said, I thank thee, O Father, Lord of heaven and earth, because thou has hid these things from the wise and prudent, and has revealed them unto babes. Even so, Father, for so it seemed good in thy sight."*
3. II Corinthians 4:3 – *"But if our gospel be hid, it is hid to them that are lost:"*
4. Proverbs 1:5-6 – *"A wise man will hear, and will increase learning; and a man of understanding shall attain unto wise counsels: To understand a proverb, and the interpretation; the words of the wise, and their dark sayings."*
5. I Corinthians 4:1 – *"Let a man so account of us, as of the ministers of Christ, and stewards of the mysteries of God."* The Greek word for "mystery" is "musterion", which means that which is known by the initiated.

The way to understand the hidden truth of the Lord is to be born again and filled with the Spirit, and to have a love for speaking the Scriptures.

II. How To Determine If Figurative Language Is Used.

A. Principles to determine if figurative language is used

1. Decide first whether the word or passage under consideration is being used by the Spirit as a type
2. Not all objects are types
3. Read the passage in context
4. Compare with other passages

   a. I Corinthians 2:13 – *"Which things also we speak, not in the words which man's wisdom teacheth, but which the Holy Ghost teacheth; comparing spiritual things with spiritual."*

   "And we tell and explain this mystery in words not taught by human learning." (Nor)
   "And we speak of these gifts, not in language taught by human philosophy." (TCNT)
   "...in the very words given us by the Holy Spirit." (Tay)
   "Explaining spiritual things to spiritual men." (Con)
   "Matching what is spiritual with what is spiritual" (Knox)

5. Search the Scriptures

   a. II Timothy 2:15 – *"Study to shew thyself approved unto God, a workman that needeth not to be ashamed, rightly dividing the word of truth."*

   "Earnestly seek to commend yourself to God." (Wey)
   "Do yourself to present yourself to God as one approved." (RSV)
   "Aim first at winning God's approval." (Knox)
   "a workman with no reason to be ashamed." (TCNT)
   "...who does not need to be ashamed of this work." (Knox)
   "ever cutting a straight path for the message of the truth." (Mon)
   "Skillfully handling the Word..." (Rhm)
   "...because of his straightforward dealing with the word..." (Wey)

   b. Isaiah 34:16 – *"Seek ye out of the book of the Lord, and read: no one of these shall fail, none shall want her mate: for my mouth it hath commanded, and his spirit it hath gathered them."*
   "Turn back, when the time comes, to this record of divine prophecy, and read it afresh: you shall learn, then that none of these signs are lacking, none waited for the coming of the next." (Knox)
   "...for with his own mouth he has ordered it and with his own breath he has brought them together." (NEB)

   c. II Peter 1:20 – *"Knowing this first, that no prophecy of the Scripture is of any private interpretation."*

   "...understanding this, at the outset, that no prophetic scripture." (Mof)
   "But above all, remember that no prophesy in Scripture." (Wey)
   "can be understood through one's own powers." (Gspd)
   "allows a man to interpret it by himself." (Mof)
   "is a matter of one's own interpretation." (NASB)
   "was ever thought up by the prophet himself." (Tay)

   d. Matthew 18:16 – *"But if he will not hear thee, then take with thee one or two more, that in the mouth of two or three witnesses every word may be established."*

   "But if he refused to listen, call in one or two other people." (Rieu)
   "That every word may be confirmed by the evidence of two or three witnesses." (RSV)

1) II Corinthians 13:1 – *"This is the third time I am coming to you. In the mouth of two or three witnesses shall every word be established."* Other translation, *"This will be my third visit to you. Any charge must be sustained by the evidence of two or three witnesses."* (Gspd)

6. When it is obvious that the thing being spoken of is pointing to something else, or there is a witness that there is something more, then you have a type.
7. The Holy Spirit our teacher may by spirit of revelation, tell you what the object or type means.
8. Don't force the Word to say something it is not saying. If there is no peace or grace as you're reading or studying, or no witness then simple leave it alone. Let the Word explain itself. Let the Word say what it wants, not what you want. This is how we get into error, trying to make the Word say more than it has said.
9. See whether this type is referred to anywhere else in Scripture.
10. How was the type first used in Scripture? The first time you find anything in the Bible, determine a great deal about that thing or principle. It is called the "law of first reference." There in seed form is usually all the truth about that principle hidden within it. For instance take Genesis 1-3 the story of creation.
11. In the context of the passage is it obvious that in symbolic form God is speaking on end-time truth. As you go through the passage or study, all of it must be true to the symbolic point or truth it is revealing.

Finally, let's remember the Bible is rich with symbolic and typical language, far more than most people realize. Hopefully, this book will help you to understand the great depth of God's Word and the richness of every passage.

Lesson 10

The Significance Of The Metals Used In The Tabernacle

Metals Used In The Tabernacle

I. A Look At The Different Metals Found In The Tabernacle

A. **Brass** – Brass speaks to us of judgment and mixture. It's amazing how brass was the most used metal in the outer court, because the outer court relates to our *initial salvation* as well as *judgment for our sin*.

1. Brass's use in the tabernacle: Exodus 27:2-6; 10-11, 17, 19

"[2]And thou shalt make the horns of it upon the four corners thereof: his horns shall be of the same: and thou shalt overlay it with brass. [3]And thou shalt make his pans to receive his ashes, and his shovels, and his basons, and his fleshhooks, and his firepans: all the vessels thereof thou shalt make of brass. [4]And thou shalt make for it a grate of network of brass; and upon the net shalt thou make four brasen rings in the four corners thereof. [5]And thou shalt put it under the compass of the altar beneath, that the net may be even to the midst of the altar. [6]And thou shalt make staves for the altar, staves of shittim wood, and overlay them with brass...[10]And the twenty pillars thereof and their twenty sockets shall be of brass; the hooks of the pillars and their fillets shall be of silver. [11]And likewise for the north side in length there shall be hangings of an hundred cubits long, and his twenty pillars and their twenty sockets of brass; the hooks of the pillars and their fillets of silver...[17]All the pillars round about the court shall be filleted with silver; their hooks shall be of silver, and their sockets of brass...[19]All the vessels of the tabernacle in all the service thereof, and all the pins thereof, and all the pins of the court, shall be of brass."

a. The furniture in the outer court was made of brass.
b. The pillars that caused the tabernacle to stand were in sockets of brass.
c. The pillars themselves were made of brass.
d. All the vessels in the service of the outer court were made of brass.

2. Why we believe brass is a symbol of judgment

a. First, it is used in the outer court in particular. The brazen altar was made up of brass over wood. Wood in Scripture represents humanity. Therefore brass over wood represents judgment on humanity particularly in the respect that Jesus became the Son of man (humanity) to receive that judgment. This is where our sin is judged and put away.
b. Secondly, the brass laver speaks of the ongoing judgment of the Word of God working to wash us in our daily lives which is called the process called sanctification.
c. Numbers 21:4-9 – The serpent made of brass to signify the judgment of God upon their sin

d. Judges 16:20-21 – Bound in fetters of brass; Samson was under the judgment of the Lord
e. II Kings 25:4-7 – Notice this king who had been allowed to surrender and had not obeyed the word of the Lord, now was captured and in giving judgment to him the king of Babylon had had him bound in fetters of brass.
f. Deuteronomy 28:15, 23 – One of the judgments for not hearkening and doing the Word of the Lord was that the heavens would be brass over them. In other words, this represents having no direct communication with the Lord.
g. Numbers 16:36-40 – The brass censers that belonged to the men that the Lord had just destroyed by fire, once again speaks to us of judgment.

3. The ministry of judgment and brass in our lives is brought about by the Holy Spirit.

a. Isaiah 4:4 – "*When the Lord shall have washed away the filth of the daughters of Zion, and shall have purged the blood of Jerusalem from the midst thereof by the spirit of judgment, and by the spirit of burning.*"
b. John 16:7-9 – "[7]*Nevertheless I tell you the truth; It is expedient for you that I go away: for if I go not away, the Comforter will not come unto you; but if I depart, I will send him unto you.* [8]*And when he is come, he will reprove the world of sin, and of righteousness, and of judgment:* [9]*Of sin, because they believe not on me;*"

Jesus, concerning brass, is typified in the tabernacle as "being" the brass altar. He took upon himself human form (wood) so he could receive the judgment (brass) upon Himself that was intended for all mankind.

B. **Silver**

Silver speaks to us of redemption. Silver also represents our foundation, the atonement, and the character of God in our lives. Although the Holy Place is known for its gold, the Tabernacle itself was founded in sockets of silver. In the outer court we have the brass (judgment for our sin) and in the Holy Place we have silver (redemption). We have moved from judgment to redemption.

1. Silver's use in the tabernacle: Exodus 25:3, 26:19, 21, 25, 32, 27:10-11, 17

"[25:3]*And this is the offering which ye shall take of them; gold, and silver, and brass...*[26:19]*And thou shalt make forty sockets of silver under the twenty boards; two sockets under one board for his two tenons, and two sockets under another board for his two tenons...*[21]*And their forty sockets of silver; two sockets under one board, and two sockets under another board...*[25]*And they shall be eight boards, and their sockets of silver, sixteen sockets; two sockets under one board, and two sockets under another board.* [32]*And thou shalt hang it upon four pillars of shittim wood overlaid with gold: their hooks shall be of gold, upon the four sockets of silver.* [27:10]*And the twenty pillars thereof and their twenty sockets shall be of brass; the hooks of the pillars and their fillets shall be of silver.* [11]*And likewise for the north side in length there shall be hangings of an hundred cubits long, and his twenty pillars and their twenty sockets of brass; the hooks of the pillars and their fillets of silver...*[17]*All the pillars round about the court shall be filleted with silver; their hooks shall be of silver, and their sockets of brass.*"

We see here the specific use of silver was a foundational one. It was used to gird up or to hold up the tabernacle. Comparing this with the fact that silver means redemption, we see that these sockets of silver mean to us that it is our foundation in Jesus Christ, our redemption that will keep us securely standing in Him.

2. Silver as redemption

a. Matthew 27:1-9 (Matthew 26:15) – The price Judas received in order to betray Jesus which brought forth our redemption was 30 pieces of silver (Zechariah 11:12-13). Silver is the price of redemption.

b. Exodus 21:32 – *"If the ox shall push a manservant or a maidservant; he shall give unto their master thirty shekels of silver, and the ox shall be stoned."* – It is also ransom money. It's what is used to pay someone to make everything all right. Jesus was sold for silver, payment to redeem us. This was to make everything all right, to settle the debt. Silver speaks then of the redemptive ministry of Jesus.

3. Silver as redemption and foundation

a. Proverbs 25:11 – *"A word fitly spoken is like apples of gold in pictures of silver."*
b. Psalms 68:13 – *"Though ye have lien among the pots, yet shall ye be as the wings of a dove covered with silver, and her feathers with yellow gold."*

4. Silver as God's characteristics in our life

a. I Corinthians 3:12 – *"Now if any man build upon this foundation gold, silver, precious stones, wood, hay, stubble;"*
b. Ezekiel 16:13 – *"Thus wast thou decked with gold and silver; and thy raiment was of fine linen, and silk, and broidered work; thou didst eat fine flour, and honey, and oil: and thou wast exceeding beautiful, and thou didst prosper into a kingdom."*
c. II Timothy 2:19-21 – *"[19]Nevertheless the foundation of God standeth sure, having this seal, The Lord knoweth them that are his. And, Let every one that nameth the name of Christ depart from iniquity. [20]But in a great house there are not only vessels of gold and of silver, but also of wood and of earth; and some to honour, and some to dishonour. [21]If a man therefore purge himself from these, he shall be a vessel unto honour, sanctified, and meet for the master's use, and prepared unto every good work."*

These scriptures all speak to us of that which God has done in our life after salvation. What characteristics of His have been worked into our lives?

C. **Gold**

The Hebrew word used most for gold is a word that means – to shine or shimmer. Another Hebrew word for gold means carved out. Gold speaks to us of God's divine glory, His deity, and His divine nature worked into us. We begin in the tabernacle in the Outer Court with judgment of our sin. Then we move to the Holy Place, which deals with redemption and then to the Most Holy Place into glory. This is the route of our spiritual progression. We go from judgment in our lives, to redemption, to where He has worked his character (gold) into our lives. From this place we receive our glorified bodies.

1. Gold's use in the tabernacle: Exodus 25:3, 11-13, 17-18, 23-39

a. The Ark, Exodus 25:11-13 – *"[11]And thou shalt overlay it with pure gold, within and without shalt thou overlay it, and shalt make upon it a crown of gold round about. [12]And thou shalt cast four rings of gold for it, and put them in the four corners thereof; and two rings shall be in the one side of it, and two rings in the other side of it. [13]And thou shalt make staves of shittim wood, and overlay them with gold."*

b. Mercy Seat & Cherubims, Exodus 25:17-18 – *"[17]And thou shalt make a mercy seat of pure gold: two cubits and a half shall be the length thereof, and a cubit and a half the breadth thereof. [18]And thou shalt make two cherubims of gold, of beaten work shalt thou make them, in the two ends of the mercy seat."* This represents God's nature, His divine character over mercy. He is a merciful God (Exodus 34:6, Psalms 131:7)

c. Table of Shewbread, Exodus 25:23-30 – *"[23]Thou shalt also make a table of shittim wood: two cubits shall be the length thereof, and a cubit the breadth thereof, and a cubit and a half the height thereof. [24]And thou shalt overlay it with pure gold, and make thereto a crown of gold round about. [25]And thou shalt make unto it a border of an hand breadth round about, and thou shalt make a golden crown to the border thereof round about. [26]And thou shalt make for it four rings of gold, and put the rings in the four corners that are on the four feet thereof. [27]Over against the border shall the rings be for places of the staves to bear the table. [28]And thou shalt make the staves of shittim wood, and overlay them with gold, that the table may be borne with them. [29]And thou shalt make the dishes thereof, and spoons thereof, and covers thereof, and bowls thereof, to cover withal: of pure gold shalt thou make them. [30]And thou shalt set upon the table shewbread before me always."* – This represents God's divine character upon His word, His nature shared as we teach the Word.

d. Candlestick, Exodus 25:31-39, *"[31]And thou shalt make a candlestick of pure gold: of beaten work shall the candlestick be made: his shaft, and his branches, his bowls, his knops, and his flowers, shall be of the same. [32]And six branches shall come out of the sides of it; three branches of the candlestick out of the one side, and three branches of the candlestick out of the other side: [33]Three bowls made like unto almonds, with a knop and a flower in one branch; and three bowls made like almonds in the other branch, with a knop and a flower: so in the six branches that come out of the candlestick. [34]And in the candlestick shall be four bowls made like unto almonds, with their knops and their flowers. [35]And there shall be a knop under two branches of the same, and a knop under two branches of the same, and a knop under two branches of the same, according to the six branches that proceed out of the candlestick. [36]Their knops and their branches shall be of the same: all it shall be one beaten work of pure gold. [37]And thou shalt make the seven lamps thereof: and they shall light the lamps thereof, that they may give light over against it. [38]And the tongs thereof, and the snuffdishes thereof, shall be of pure gold. [39]Of a talent of pure gold shall he make it, with all these vessels..."*

Up to this point, gold represents the holiest uses in the tabernacle, but as you can see once you pass the first veil into the Holy Place, God's glory, His nature begins to take the ascendancy. You will find that gold is used throughout the rest of the tabernacle on the rings, boards, fittings, staves, bars, etc. The key here is God's glory and nature are to be throughout His house.

2. Gold's meaning elsewhere in scripture

a. His Divine Nature

1) We must first note all the uses of gold in the tabernacle and in particular the gold in the Most Holy Place where His presence dwells.
2) Revelation 21:18, 21 – We see here in the New Jerusalem the city is also emphatic in its use of gold. This tells us that wherever God is, there is gold. That is because it represents His nature.
3) Exodus 25:11-13 – This is the ark, which is always symbolic of God's manifest presence. It was overlaid with pure gold within and without. He is within and without. His presence is within and without.
4) Song of Solomon 5:11-15 – In this Old Testament picture of Jesus we see that gold makes up his nature and his person.
5) Revelation 1:13 – In this New Testament appearance of Jesus, we see once again gold being descriptive of Him. This speaks of His nature and person

b. His character worked in us

1) Psalms 45:9 – *"Kings' daughters were among thy honourable women: upon thy right hand did stand the queen in gold of Ophir."* – God's ultimate end for us is His glory. When we enter through the last veil, we enter into fullness. We become true full-

grown sons. At this point we enter into all that God has for us. We have the glory and we no longer fall short of it.

2) Paul the Apostle, Acts 9:3-9 – This is the great story of Paul finding Jesus. This is very important because it represents, I believe, something very significant for the last days both to natural Israel and the Sons of God.

a) I Corinthians 15:8 – *"And last of all he was seen of me also, as of one born out of due time."* Paul says he was one born out of due time. In other words what happened to Paul didn't happen to anyone else in his lifetime. He experienced something that was a type for the end time church as well as the last great move of God upon Israel.

b) I Timothy 1:16 – *"Howbeit for this cause I obtained mercy, that in me first Jesus Christ might shew forth all longsuffering, for a pattern to them which should hereafter believe on him to life everlasting."*

Paul says what happened to him was a ***pattern*** for those who would come after him. What was this ***pattern***? Like Paul, and natural Israel, we will experience a move of the glory of God in a dramatic and awesome fashion. It will knock us off our horses. Priests will be ministering from a glorious position (II Chronicles 5). This move of glory in II Chronicles 5 occurs during the feast of tabernacles, at the dedication of the Temple of Solomon (spiritually speaking this represents the final and last house of God). While we are experiencing this as the sons of God, Israel will be having their last great visitation. This is what God has wanted from the beginning.

II. Threefold nature of our redemption

A. Brass – the outer court – judgment for sin – We move then from the outer court (judgment) into:

B. Silver – inner court or Holy Place – redemption. In the outer court it is God who judges us. When we move into the Holy place we are now out of natural light and into supernatural light. We can now judge ourselves because the Lampstand (type of the Baptism of Holy Ghost, Gifts of the Spirit) shines a light on our lives so we can then take care of what ever the Lord wants. After this point we enter:

C. Gold – Most Holy Place – glory – We move from judgment to redemption to glory. We have gone from judgment over humanity (brass over wood) to redemption (Silver sockets supporting the foundation). Redemption undergirds all that God is doing. We then move to glorification (gold over word or God's glory and divinity over our humanity). This is God's highest for us.

1. We are called to obtain the glory. This is our calling. This has been God's desire for us from the beginning.

a. I Thessalonians 2:12 – *"That ye would walk worthy of God, who hath called you unto his kingdom and glory."*
b. II Thessalonians 2:14 – *"Whereunto he called you by our gospel, to the obtaining of the glory of our Lord Jesus Christ."*
c. Hebrews 2:10 – *"For it became him, for whom are all things, and by whom are all things, in bringing many sons unto glory, to make the captain of their salvation perfect through sufferings."*
d. I Peter 5:10 – *"But the God of all grace, who hath called us unto his eternal glory by Christ Jesus, after that ye have suffered a while, make you perfect, stablish, strengthen, settle you."*
e. II Peter 1:3 – *"...through the knowledge of him that hath called us to glory and virtue"*
f. John 17:22 – *"And the glory which thou gavest me I have given them; that they may be one, even as we are one:"*

g. Zechariah 2:5 – "*For I, saith the LORD, will be unto her a wall of fire round about, and will be the glory in the midst of her.*"

h. Numbers 14:21 – "*But as truly as I live, all the earth shall be filled with the glory of the LORD.*"

i. Isaiah 60:1-3, 7, 13 – "*[1]Arise, shine; for thy light is come, and the glory of the LORD is risen upon thee. [2]For, behold, the darkness shall cover the earth, and gross darkness the people: but the LORD shall arise upon thee, and his glory shall be seen upon thee. [3]And the Gentiles shall come to thy light, and kings to the brightness of thy rising…[7]All the flocks of Kedar shall be gathered together unto thee, the rams of Nebaioth shall minister unto thee: they shall come up with acceptance on mine altar, and I will glorify the house of my glory…[13]The glory of Lebanon shall come unto thee, the fir tree, the pine tree, and the box together, to beautify the place of my sanctuary; and I will make the place of my feet glorious.*"

j. Revelation 21:10-11 – "*[10]And he carried me away in the spirit to a great and high mountain, and shewed me that great city, the holy Jerusalem, descending out of heaven from God, [11]Having the glory of God: and her light was like unto a stone most precious, even like a jasper stone, clear as crystal;*"

k. Psalms 102:16 – "*When the LORD shall build up Zion, he shall appear in his glory.*"

l. Psalms 84:11 – "*For the LORD God is a sun and shield: the LORD will give grace and glory: no good thing will he withhold from them that walk uprightly.*"

m. II Corinthians 3:18 – "*But we all, with open face beholding as in a glass the glory of the Lord, are changed into the same image from glory to glory, even as by the Spirit of the Lord.*"

n. Romans 5:2 – "*By whom also we have access by faith into this grace wherein we stand, and rejoice in hope of the glory of God.*"

o. I Samuel 2:8 – "*He raiseth up the poor out of the dust, and lifteth up the beggar from the dunghill, to set them among princes, and to make them inherit the throne of glory: for the pillars of the earth are the LORD's, and he hath set the world upon them.*"

p. Romans 8:18 – "*For I reckon that the sufferings of this present time are not worthy to be compared with the glory which shall be revealed in us.*"

q. II Corinthians 4:17 – "*For our light affliction, which is but for a moment, worketh for us a far more exceeding and eternal weight of glory;*"

r. Haggai 2:6-9 – "*[6]For thus saith the LORD of hosts; Yet once, it is a little while, and I will shake the heavens, and the earth, and the sea, and the dry land; [7]And I will shake all nations, and the desire of all nations shall come: and I will fill this house with glory, saith the LORD of hosts. [8]The silver is mine, and the gold is mine, saith the LORD of hosts. [9]The glory of this latter house shall be greater than of the former, saith the LORD of hosts: and in this place will I give peace, saith the LORD of hosts.*"

s. Isaiah 4:5 – "*And the LORD will create upon every dwelling place of mount Zion, and upon her assemblies, a cloud and smoke by day, and the shining of a flaming fire by night: for upon all the glory shall be a defence.*"

When we enter through the veil, we will then dwell with He who is all glorious. God speaks of His glory. We will be able to handle, walk in, live in and manifest His divine nature and character. This is His heart's desire. The pieces of furniture and the tabernacle show us the way into His presence. A way into the Holy of Holies. The call of deep crying to deep is calling us to come near. So for you and I we say with the Apostle Paul, "*Let us draw near.*"

Lesson 11

The Significance Of Colors

Proverbs 25:2 says, *"It is the glory of God to conceal a thing: but the honour of kings is to search out a matter."* That God has concealed truth in the symbolic use of created things is obvious. One of the essential helps in understanding the Tabernacle of Moses is seeing that God used natural, material things to symbolize and typify great spiritual truth. Yes, it is true that even colors when searched out have great spiritual meaning and can give us insights into unlocking the deep truths of God's Word. This is particularly helpful in understanding the Tabernacle of Moses, the prophetic books, and the book of Revelation. The proper way of interpreting a symbolic color or material is to examine every time it is used and compare them before coming to a general conclusion. *"In the mouth of two or three witnesses..."* (II Corinthians 13:1) means that something is established as a principle or fact in Scripture when it is seen at least three times. Most of the time, however, the Bible will give its own definition for its symbol in the context of that particular verse. If not, you simply compare with others to get the full understanding, letting the Bible interpret itself.

This is a fascinating and wonderful subject to consider. If one can get a true, Biblical understanding of what colors represent, it can unveil and broaden the revelation of a passage of Scripture, subject or doctrine. Understanding colors and their symbolism is essential to any true Bible student or disciple. All theologians agree that colors almost always represent something other than themselves. So to find out what they symbolize, we must truly search the Scriptures to see if we can find the right revelation for each color mentioned. As you read many commentaries and dictionaries of the Bible, or the few who have actually written about it, you find great disagreement as to what they truly represent. That is why we must let the Bible interpret itself, and not approach it with pre-conceived ideas or personal theories. We must let the Scriptures reveal to us what they mean and nothing else. It is true that some colors have several different types associated with them. We will examine all of these and prove them by the Word. We do not need men's ideas of what a color should represent or symbolize. We just simply need the true Biblical account of each color and then apply this to our study. Understanding color and their symbolism is a great key to help open up the Word to us. Hidden deep within the Word of God is revelation, wanting to be revealed, by the use of colors. Every teacher, pastor, prophet, and student of any kind will derive great benefit as they learn how to apply the key of symbolic colors.

I. Symbolic Colors Used In The Bible and Their Interpretation

A. **Scarlet, Crimson, Red** – Sacrifice, suffering, blood

This color is the color of blood and speaks of blood atonement, sacrifice, and Jesus' sacrificial suffering. The Hebrew word for *scarlet* means maggot or worm. This speaks to us of Jesus who became a worm for us in His sacrifice on the cross (Psalms 22:6, Job 25:6). The Greek word for *scarlet* means a kernel or seed of corn. Jesus became that kernel of wheat that fell into the ground and died for us (John 12:24). The definition of scarlet includes the color crimson. They are one in the same.

1. Exodus 25:4-5 – *"And blue, and purple, and scarlet, and fine linen, and goats' hair, And rams' skins dyed red, and badgers' skins, and shittim wood,"*
2. Numbers 19:2 – *"...that they bring thee a red heifer without spot, wherein is no blemish, and upon which never came yoke:"*
3. Hebrews 9:19 – *"For when Moses had spoken every precept to all the people according to the law, he took the blood of calves and of goats, with water, and scarlet wool, and hyssop, and sprinkled both the book, and all the people,"*
4. Joshua 2:18-21 – *"18Behold, when we come into the land, thou shalt bind this line of scarlet thread in the window which thou didst let us down by: and thou shalt bring thy father, and thy mother, and thy brethren, and all thy father's household, home unto thee. 19And it shall be, that whosoever shall go out of the doors of thy house into the street, his blood shall be upon his head, and we will be guiltless: and whosoever shall be with thee in the house, his blood shall be on our head, if any hand be upon him. 20And if thou utter this our business, then we will be quit of thine oath which*

thou hast made us to swear. [21]And she said, According unto your words, so be it. And she sent them away, and they departed: and she bound the scarlet line in the window."

4. Matthew 27:28 – *"And they stripped him, and put on him a scarlet robe."*
5. Leviticus 14:4-5, 49-53 – *"Then shall the priest command to take for him that is to be cleansed two birds alive and clean, and cedar wood, and scarlet, and hyssop..."*
6. Hebrews 9:19-20 – *"[19]For when Moses had spoken every precept to all the people according to the law, he took the blood of calves and of goats, with water, and scarlet wool, and hyssop, and sprinkled both the book, and all the people, [20]Saying, This is the blood of the testament which God hath enjoined unto you."*

7. Blood

   a. Revelation 1:5 – *"And from Jesus Christ, who is the faithful witness...Unto him that loved us, and washed us from our sins in his own blood,"*
   b. Revelation 7:14 – *"...and made them white in the blood of the Lamb."*
   c. Hebrews 9:22 – *"And almost all things are by the law purged with blood; and without shedding of blood is no remission."*
   d. Exodus 12:5-7 – *"Your lamb shall be without blemish...And they shall take of the blood, and strike it on the two side posts and on the upper door post of the houses, wherein they shall eat it."*
   e. Exodus 12:23 – *"For the LORD will pass through to smite the Egyptians; and when he seeth the blood upon the lintel, and on the two side posts, the LORD will pass over the door, and will not suffer the destroyer to come in unto your houses to smite you."*

B. **Blue** – Heaven, all things heavenly

The Hebrew word for blue means deep blue, the color of shellfish. The dictionary definition is – the pure color of a clear sky; the hue between green and violet in the spectrum. As the sky above us is blue, thus the reason for blue defining that which is heavenly. It also represents Jesus' heavenly origin. I Corinthians 15:49 says, *"And as we have borne the image of the earthy, we shall also bear the image of the heavenly"*. The image of the heavenly speaks of Christ's nature.

1. Exodus 25:4 – *"And blue, and purple, and scarlet, and fine linen, and goats' hair,"*
2. Exodus 28:1-5 – The high priest wore an outer garment of solid blue over his white robe. He was the mediator between earthly and heavenly things
3. Numbers 15:37-40 – Israel wore a border of blue on their clothes to encourage them to remember the Lord in heaven, and the commandments that come to them from heaven. This was also to help them remember they had a heavenly walk and they needed to balance their natural life with it.
4. Exodus 24:10 – *"And they saw the God of Israel: and there was under his feet as it were a paved work of a sapphire stone, and as it were the body of heaven in his clearness."* – sapphire is a deep blue
5. Ezekiel 10:1 – *"Then I looked, and, behold, in the firmament that was above the head of the cherubims there appeared over them as it were a sapphire stone..."*
6. Ezekiel 1:26 – *"And above the firmament that was over their heads was the likeness of a throne, as the appearance of a sapphire stone..."*
7. Exodus 26:1, 31-33

C. **White** – Purity, holiness, and righteousness.

Dictionary definition of white is – the color of pure snow; reflecting nearly all the rays of sunlight. White linen was used a lot in the tabernacle and in the priest's garments. Linen in Hebrew means – bleached stuff, white linen.

1. Scriptures for white related to purity

    a. Daniel 12:10 – *"Many shall be purified, and made white, and tried..."*
    b. Isaiah 1:18 – *"Come now, and let us reason together, saith the LORD: though your sins be as scarlet, they shall be as white as snow..."*
    c. Revelation 7:13-14 – *"...What are these which are arrayed in white robes? and whence came they?...These are they which came out of great tribulation, and have washed their robes, and made them white in the blood of the Lamb."*
    d. Psalms 51:7 – *"Purge me with hyssop, and I shall be clean: wash me, and I shall be whiter than snow."*
    e. Revelation 19:7-8, 14
    f. Revelation 1:14
    g. Revelation 20:11

2. Scriptures for white related to holiness

    a. Matthew 17:2 – *"And was transfigured before them: and his face did shine as the sun, and his raiment was white as the light."*
    b. Daniel 7:9 – *"I beheld till the thrones were cast down, and the Ancient of days did sit, whose garment was white as snow..."*
    c. Revelation 20:11 – *"And I saw a great white throne, and him that sat on it, from whose face the earth and the heaven fled away..."*
    d. Song of Solomon 5:10 – *"My beloved is white and ruddy, the chiefest among ten thousand."*
    e. Revelation 1:14 – *"His head and his hairs were white like wool, as white as snow; and his eyes were as a flame of fire;"*
    f. Daniel 11:35 – *"And some of them of understanding shall fall, to try them, and to purge, and to make them white, even to the time of the end: because it is yet for a time appointed."*
    g. Ecclesiastes 9:8 – *"Let thy garments be always white; and let thy head lack no ointment."*

Notice in the above Scriptures as we are purified and tried, we are made white. If you look back at Revelation 19:7-8, you can see that the bride was granted fine linen, clean and white, because she had made herself ready. We are granted whiteness (purity, light) as we allow God to change us and as we make ourselves ready. In Revelation 7:9-14, we find those who were in great tribulation and came out. They attained! They washed their robes and it made them white.

We must let our garments be white. It is up to us. When we are born again, we are made righteous instantaneously in our spirit, but God wants us to be white in our soul and body also. This is the work of sanctification. This is where we must attain.

3. Scriptures for white related to righteousness

    a. Revelation 19:8 – *"And to her was granted that she should be arrayed in fine linen, clean and white: for the fine linen is the righteousness of saints."*
    b. Revelation 19:14 – *"And the armies which were in heaven followed him upon white horses, clothed in fine linen, white and clean."*
    c. Revelation 6:11 – *"And white robes were given unto every one of them..."*
    d. John 20:12 – *"And seeth two angels in white sitting, the one at the head, and the other at the feet, where the body of Jesus had lain."*
    e. Acts 1:10 – *"And while they looked stedfastly toward heaven as he went up, behold, two men stood by them in white apparel;"*
    f. Revelation 15:6 – *"And the seven angels came out of the temple, having the seven plagues, clothed in pure and white linen, and having their breasts girded with golden girdles."* (Matthew 28:2-3) – Angelic beings seem to be described as white and shining. This speaks of the light of God shining through them.

D. **Gold** – God's divine nature or character

1. Exodus 25:11-39
2. Revelation 1:13 – *"And in the midst of the seven candlesticks one like unto the Son of man, clothed with a garment down to the foot, and girt about the paps with a golden girdle."*
3. Revelation 8:3 – *"And another angel came and stood at the altar, having a golden censer; and there was given unto him much incense, that he should offer it with the prayers of all saints upon the golden altar which was before the throne."*
4. Exodus 28:34 – *"A golden bell and a pomegranate, a golden bell and a pomegranate, upon the hem of the robe round about."*
5. Revelation 21:21 – *"And the twelve gates were twelve pearls; every several gate was of one pearl: and the street of the city was pure gold, as it were transparent glass."*
6. Revelation 3:18 – *"I counsel thee to buy of me gold tried in the fire, that thou mayest be rich..."*
7. Song of Solomon 5:11, 14-15 – *"His head is as the most fine gold, his locks are bushy, and black as a raven..."*
8. Psalms 45:9, 13 – *"Kings' daughters were among thy honourable women: upon thy right hand did stand the queen in gold of Ophir...The king's daughter is all glorious within: her clothing is of wrought gold."* – This speaks of God's divine character worked into the bride's life
9. I Peter 1:7 – *"That the trial of your faith, being much more precious than of gold that perisheth, though it be tried with fire, might be found unto praise and honour and glory at the appearing of Jesus Christ:"*

E. **Silver** – Redemption

1. Exodus 25:3 – *"And this is the offering which ye shall take of them; gold, and silver, and brass"*
2. Leviticus 27:3-6, 13 – *"...even thy estimation shall be fifty shekels of silver...But if he will at all redeem it, then he shall add a fifth part thereof unto thy estimation."*
3. Numbers 3:44-51 – *"...And Moses gave the money of them that were redeemed unto Aaron and to his sons, according to the word of the LORD..."*
4. Matthew 26:15 – *"And said unto them, What will ye give me, and I will deliver him unto you? And they covenanted with him for thirty pieces of silver."*
5. Leviticus 5:15-17 – *"If a soul commit a trespass, and sin through ignorance, in the holy things of the LORD; then he shall bring for his trespass unto the LORD a ram without blemish out of the flocks, with thy estimation by shekels of silver..."*
6. Exodus 30:11-16
7. Genesis 44:2 – *"And put my cup, the silver cup, in the sack's mouth of the youngest, and his corn money. And he did according to the word that Joseph had spoken."*

F. **Purple** – Royalty, majesty, wealth

1. Dictionary definition – any color intermediate between red and blue; symbol of imperial, royal or other high rank.
2. This color speaks of kingship and royalty, and the God-man. It speaks of the new creation coming forth in God's people.
3. Other facts: One of original meanings of Canaan (land of our inheritance) means land of purple. In Bible times, purple dye was expensive and was worn only by those of high rank.
4. Judges 8:26 – *"And the weight of the golden earrings that he requested was a thousand and seven hundred shekels of gold; beside ornaments, and collars, and purple raiment that was on the kings of Midian, and beside the chains that were about their camels' necks."*
5. Luke 16:19 – *"There was a certain rich man, which was clothed in purple and fine linen, and fared sumptuously every day:"*
6. Esther 8:15 – *"And Mordecai went out from the presence of the king in royal apparel of blue and white, and with a great crown of gold, and with a garment of fine linen and purple..."* He was now next to the king. Purple is the color worn by kings

7. Song of Solomon 7:5 – "*Thine head upon thee is like Carmel, and the hair of thine head like purple; the king is held in the galleries.*" The bride will wear purple, because she has become royalty. She has had blended the blue of heavenly things and the scarlet of the human, the natural sacrificing and suffering to become purple royalty. The Divine Nature has been worked into her. (Proverbs 31:22)
8. Song of Solomon 3:9-10 – "*King Solomon made himself a chariot of the wood of Lebanon. He made the pillars thereof of silver, the bottom thereof of gold, the covering of it of purple...*"
9. Proverbs 31:22, 25 – "*She maketh herself coverings of tapestry; her clothing is silk and purple...Strength and honour are her clothing...*"
10. John 19:2, 5 – "*And the soldiers platted a crown of thorns, and put it on his head, and they put on him a purple robe...Then came Jesus forth, wearing the crown of thorns, and the purple robe. And Pilate saith unto them, Behold the man!*" Blending blue and scarlet produce purple. Jesus is the greatest example of this. He was Son of God and Son of man.
11. Babylon has this color (Revelation 17:4, 18:12, 16). The purpose is to try to deceive the elect. She is always trying to appear religious. The difference between her (the strange woman, Babylon) and the true church is she has simply put on purple, while the bride has had purple worked into her.

G. **Grey** – Maturity, honor, experience, old age

1. It is the same word in Hebrew that is translated "hoary"
2. Dictionary definition – a color between white and black; a neutral hue
3. Proverbs 20:29 – "*...and the beauty of old men is the gray head.*"
4. Psalms 71:18 – "*Now also when I am old and grayheaded, O God, forsake me not; until I have shewed thy strength unto this generation, and thy power to every one that is to come.*"
5. Proverbs 16:31 – "*The hoary head is a crown of glory...*"
6. Job 15:10 – "*With us are both the grayheaded and very aged men, much elder than thy father.*"
7. Isaiah 46:4 – "*And even to your old age I am he; and even to hoar hairs will I carry you: I have made, and I will bear; even I will carry, and will deliver you.*"
8. Leviticus 19:32 – "*Thou shalt rise up before the hoary head, and honour the face of the old man, and fear thy God: I am the LORD.*"
9. I Samuel 12:1-2

H. **Black** – Darkness, famine, sin or that which is unredeemed in us; it also speaks of God's judgment.

1. Hebrew definition – dusky, to be dim or dark in color; ashy dark colored
2. Dictionary definition – lacking hue or brightness, absorbing light without reflecting any of the rays composing it

3. Scriptures for judgment

    a. Jude 13 – "*Raging waves of the sea, foaming out their own shame; wandering stars, to whom is reserved the blackness of darkness for ever.*"
    b. Jeremiah 4:28 – "*For this shall the earth mourn, and the heavens above be black: because I have spoken it, I have purposed it, and will not repent...*"
    c. Jeremiah 14:2 – "*Judah mourneth, and the gates thereof languish; they are black unto the ground; and the cry of Jerusalem is gone up.*"
    d. Zechariah 6:2, 6 – "*In the first chariot were red horses; and in the second chariot black horses...The black horses which are therein go forth into the north country...*"
    e. Revelation 6:5, 12 – "*And when he had opened the third seal, I heard the third beast say, Come and see. And I beheld, and lo a black horse; and he that sat on him had a pair of balances in his hand...And I beheld when he had opened the sixth seal, and, lo, there was a great earthquake; and the sun became black as sackcloth of hair, and the moon became as blood;*"

f. Nahum 2:10 – *"She is empty, and void, and waste: and the heart melteth, and the knees smite together, and much pain is in all loins, and the faces of them all gather blackness."*
g. Isaiah 50:3 – *"I clothe the heavens with blackness, and I make sackcloth their covering."*
h. Joel 2:6 – *"Before their face the people shall be much pained: all faces shall gather blackness."*

4. Scriptures for darkness or total deception

a. Proverbs 7:9 – *"In the twilight, in the evening, in the black and dark night:"* Here the dark black night speaks of total deception. The Hebrew word means "the little man of the eye, or the pupil or ball". This speaks of the middle of darkness, total deception, being surrounded by it.
b. Jude 8-13 – *"Likewise also these filthy dreamers defile the flesh, despise dominion, and speak evil of dignities...to whom is reserved the blackness of darkness for ever."* These men had reached a place of total darkness and deception. The Greek means gloom, or the shrouding like a cloud; once again, in the middle or covered by darkness and deception.

5. Scripture for sin or that which is unredeemed in us

a. Song of Solomon 1:5-6 – *"I am black, but comely, O ye daughters of Jerusalem, as the tents of Kedar, as the curtains of Solomon. Look not upon me, because I am black, because the sun hath looked upon me..."* The Hebrew word for black here means dusky or dim. This definition helps us understand this better. When we still have unredeemed areas of our life, it doesn't mean we are in total darkness, but the light is dim. There is a mixture of light and darkness at dusk. So then our lives would have a mixture. It is possible to be black but comely. We can still go on with God,until those areas are totally redeemed.

6. Scriptures for famine

a. Revelation 6:5-6 – *"And when he had opened the third seal, I heard the third beast say, Come and see. And I beheld, and lo a black horse; and he that sat on him had a pair of balances in his hand. And I heard a voice in the midst of the four beasts say, A measure of wheat for a penny, and three measures of barley for a penny..."*
b. Lamentations 5:10 – *"Our skin was black like an oven because of the terrible famine."* – The Hebrew word stated here for black means to shrivel.
c. Jeremiah 14:2 – *"Judah mourneth, and the gates thereof languish; they are black unto the ground; and the cry of Jerusalem is gone up."* – The Hebrew word for black here means to be ashy, to mourn
d. Lamentations 4:8 – *"Their visage is blacker than a coal; they are not known in the streets: their skin cleaveth to their bones; it is withered, it is become like a stick."* – The Hebrew word here means to be dark, withholding light
e. Zechariah 6:2, 6

I. **Amber** – The glow of God, the glory of God, the brilliance of His presence, God's fire, the brightness of God.

1. Hebrew word, *Chashmal* – bronze or polished spectrum metal; it is important to note this word is of uncertain derivation.
2. Amber is a brilliant glowing yellow

3. Ezekiel 1:4 – *"And I looked, and, behold, a whirlwind came out of the north, a great cloud, and a fire infolding itself, and a brightness was about it, and out of the midst thereof as the colour of amber, out of the midst of the fire."* – It appears amber is the color of fire. Ezekiel's visions concerning the color amber are all related specifically to the glory of God. It is the color of the glory. Also, Ezekiel's vision as related to the color amber relates more directly to the fire of

God. However, it must be said that the fire of God is tied very heavily to the glory of God to the point where it is hard to discern much difference between the two. Other translations:

"*...out of the midst...a glowing metal...*" ASV
"*...in the midst of the fire...a gleaming bronze...*" RSV

4. Ezekiel 1:27 – "*And I saw as the colour of amber, as the appearance of fire round about within it...I saw as it were the appearance of fire, and it had brightness round about.*" Other translations:

   "*And I saw as it were glowing metal...*" ASV
   "*I saw as it were gleaming bronze...*" RSV
   "*I saw a luster like that of shining metal...*" AAT

5. Ezekiel 8:2 – "*Then I beheld, and lo a likeness as the appearance of fire...as the appearance of brightness, as the colour of amber.*" Other translations:

   "*...appearance of brightness, as it were glowing metal.*" ASV
   "*...brilliant like that of a gleaming metal.*" BER
   "*...like gleaming bronze.*" RSV

J. **Green** – Life, prosperity

1. Hebrew definition – the color of vegetative life
2. Dictionary definition – color of growing foliage, between yellow and blue in the spectrum, full of life and vigor
3. Jeremiah 17:7-8 – "*Blessed is the man that trusteth in the LORD, and whose hope the LORD is. For he shall be as a tree planted by the waters, and that spreadeth out her roots by the river, and shall not see when heat cometh, but her leaf shall be green; and shall not be careful in the year of drought, neither shall cease from yielding fruit.*"
4. Psalms 52:8 – "*But I am like a green olive tree in the house of God...*"
5. Song of Solomon 2:13 – "*The fig tree putteth forth her green figs...*"
6. Psalms 92:14 – Other translation – "*...they shall be full of sap and green*"
7. Psalms 23:2 – "*He maketh me to lie down in green pastures...*"
8. Genesis 1:30 – "*...I have given every green herb for meat...*" (Genesis 9:30)
9. Jeremiah 11:16 – "*The LORD called thy name, A green olive tree, fair, and of goodly fruit...*"
10. Song of Solomon 1:16 – "*Behold, thou art fair, my beloved, yea, pleasant: also our bed is green.*"

Lesson 12

The Study of Numbers

I. The Importance of Numbers

The study of numbers in the Scriptures is both enlightening and deep, as well as fun. Once you understand that most numbers have not only a numerical value but also a revelation behind them, it will change your Bible study forever. Some portions of Scripture could never fully be understood, that is, in their deepest revelation without this key to Bible interpretation. This study, along with an understanding of the colors, names, and objects, man made and natural, will add great meaning and depth to any passage of scripture.

A. Why Study Their Significance? The Bible reveals God to be a God of numbers

1. Psalms 147:4 – "*He telleth the number of the stars; he calleth them all by their names.*" God knows the exact number of stars in the infinite space.
2. Luke 12:6-7 – "[6]*Are not five sparrows sold for two farthings, and not one of them is forgotten before God?* [7]*But even the very hairs of your head are all numbered. Fear not therefore: ye are of more value than many sparrows.*" God knows the number of hairs on the head of every human being that has ever lived. Does that seem like a trivial thing to you? He even counts and knows the number of birds there are.
3. Daniel 5:26 – "*This is the interpretation of the thing: MENE; God hath numbered thy kingdom, and finished it.*" God knows the exact amount of time a kingdom, nation, or dynasty will exist.
4. Job 14:5, 10 – "[5]*Seeing his days are determined, the number of his months are with thee, thou hast appointed his bounds that he cannot pass...*[10]*But man dieth, and wasteth away: yea, man giveth up the ghost, and where is he?*" God knows the number of months a man will live; he has numbered his steps. God has given everything an exact, appointed time.
5. Isaiah 40:12 – "*Who hath measured the waters in the hollow of his hand, and meted out heaven with the span, and comprehended the dust of the earth in a measure, and weighed the mountains in scales, and the hills in a balance?*"

B. God is very specific about how long, short, wide, or deep things are to be. The Tabernacle certainly brings this out. He gives exact dimensions. This is just one example of a multitude, where the Lord gives specific directions and dimensions. For example, in Exodus 30:1-2, God gives the specific dimensions to the altar of incense, "[1]*And thou shalt make an altar to burn incense upon: of shittim wood shalt thou make it.* [2]*A cubit shall be the length thereof, and a cubit the breadth thereof; foursquare shall it be: and two cubits shall be the height thereof: the horns thereof shall be of the same.*"

C. As we search the scriptures, we see that every number has a specific meaning. We understand this as we look at the number throughout the Word of God and compare it with examples of when a certain thing happened a certain number of times. Then, we can come to a conclusion about what they mean as found in the whole Bible.

1. In other words, we see the number seven related to perfection after we do a word study on it.
2. We can also determine that it means perfection by different examples in the scriptures where something happened seven times.
3. Finding a word seven times in one passage also arrives at this.

II. Basic Principles

A. If we will follow certain proper Biblical principles of interpretation, we will never go into error, or extremes, or find ourselves out of balance.

1. All the numbers in the Bible have spiritual significance. A certain number will be our basic foundation
2. Multitudes of these numbers, or doubling and tripling, carry basically the same meaning as the original, only the meaning is intensified.
3. The first use of a number, as found in scripture, will usually give its spiritual meaning. This principle of interpretation is called "*The law of first reference.*"
4. As we search out numbers and their meanings, there should be a consistent definition throughout the Word. As we finish looking at all of the scriptures related to a certain number, we should be able to come away with a general consensus of what that number means by seeing throughout the Word a basic definition.
5. We must remember that a number in a certain passage of scripture may not carry any spiritual significance at all. We must always read the Word in context to ascertain this.
6. Never force a scripture to say something you want it to say. God's Word can defend itself. Error starts when we stretch the Word.
7. Don't go beyond the realm of understanding and balance. You can do this by trying to string numbers together to say what you want them to say. One example of error is using someone's natural address to give spiritual significance. We need to stay in the Scriptures! (Proverbs 11:1) If you need to keep adding, subtracting, multiplying or dividing to achieve a certain definition, leave it alone, you are trying to reason it out with a carnal mind. The Bible is spiritually discerned, not reasoned out. See I Corinthians 2:12-15.
8. The spiritual significance of a number will not always be stated plainly. It may be hidden or concealed, so we must meditate on the passage and allow the Holy Ghost to witness something to us. Another way to bring out true meaning is to compare other passages.
9. We must remember, as we are searching out the meaning of numbers, that we will often find godly and satanic, good and evil, true and false aspects to the numbers.

10. What the Scriptures say about how to search and rightly divide:

    a. Acts 17:11 – "*These were more noble than those in Thessalonica, in that they received the word with all readiness of mind, and searched the scriptures daily, whether those things were so.*" We are to search.

        1) Proverbs 25:2 – "*It is the glory of God to conceal a thing: but the honour of kings is to search out a matter.*"
        2) Psalms 111:2 – "*The works of the LORD are great, sought out of all them that have pleasure therein.*"
        3) Psalms 119:94 – "*I am thine, save me; for I have sought thy precepts.*"
        4) Proverbs 2:1-5

    b. II Timothy 2:15 – "*Study to shew thyself approved unto God, a workman that needeth not to be ashamed, rightly dividing the word of truth.*" We are to rightly divide.
    c. I Thessalonians 5:21 – "*Prove all things; hold fast that which is good.*" Test everything (I John 4:1, Job 34:2-4)
    d. I Corinthians 2:13 – "*Which things also we speak, not in the words which man's wisdom teacheth, but which the Holy Ghost teacheth; <u>comparing spiritual things with spiritual</u>.*"

III. Biblical Numbers And Their Meanings Listed On Next Page

<u>Note</u>: For a complete Scriptural study as to how each specific number and their meanings were determined, please see the book, "Deeper Truth Dictionary Of Bible Types" by Samuel Greene, Ph.D.

List Of Numbers And Their Meaning

Number	Meaning
1	Unity, God, That Which Is First
2	Witness, Division, Separation
3	Godhead, Resurrection
4	Creation, That Which Is Created
5	Grace, Spiritual Ministry
6	Man, Satan
7	Perfection, Completion, Rest
8	New Beginning
9	Finality
10	Law, Government, Completed Cycle
11	Disorder, Disorganization, Confusion
12	Divine Order, Divine Government
13	Rebellion, Backsliding, Sin, Depravity
14	Doubling Of Perfection
15	Rest, Acts Of Grace
16	Fullness
17	Spiritual Order
18	Bondage, Binding
19	Divine Order In Judgment
20	Expectancy
21	Divine Perfection
22	Double Disorder, Confusion
23	Death
24	Priesthood, Heavenly Government
25	Grace Intensified
26	Rebellion Intensified
27	Finality Of What God Does In The Earth
28	Eternal Life
29	Departure
30	Maturity, Preparation For Ministry
31	Offspring, Seed
32	Covenant
33	Promise
34	Birthing Of A Son
35	Hope
36	Enemy
37	Word Of God
38	Slavery
39	Disease
40	Trial, Testing, Probation, Chastening
41	Deception
42	Antichrist
44	Lake Of Fire
45	Inheritance
46	Second Death
48	Dwelling Place
50	Pentecost, Jubilee
56	Seeing The Heavenly
60	Pride
66	Idol Worship
70	Spiritual Order
71	Vengeance
80	Fulfilled Life
90	Rebirth
99	Sealed
100	Fruitfulness, Full Measure
120	End Of All Flesh
130	Appointed Seed
144	The Bride, The Remnant
153	Revival, Sons Of God
200	Insufficiency
300	Faithful Remnant, Deliverance
390	Bearing Iniquity
400	Divine Probation
480	Building Of The Temple
600	Warfare
666	Antichrist
888	Jesus
999	God's Wrath
1000	Perfect Fruitfulness, Rest
1081	The Abyss
1260	Tribulation
144,000	Perfection Of Divine Government

Lesson 13

Materials Used In The Tabernacle

I. Some Significant Materials Used In The Tabernacle

A. **Fine linen** – This corresponds with the teaching on the color white. White speaks of purity, righteousness, and the light of God (Exodus 25:4).

1. Revelation 19:8, 14 – "[8]*And to her was granted that she should be arrayed in fine linen, clean and white: for the fine linen is the righteousness of saints...*[14]*And the armies which were in heaven followed him upon white horses, clothed in fine linen, white and clean.*" The bride was arrayed in fine linen. This speaks of her righteousness and what she has attained to in God
2. Revelation 15:6 – "*And the seven angels came out of the temple, having the seven plagues, clothed in pure and white linen, and having their breasts girded with golden girdles.*" These speak of linen as righteous and light.
3. Exodus 28:1-6, 39-43 – These were the garments of the priests and they speak of righteousness (Verse 43). These garments were worn to cover their nakedness (sin), and spoke of righteousness in that they were able to come into the presence of God.
4. Mark 15:45-46 – Jesus wrapped in fine linen speaks of purity. Linen speaks to us of Jesus, our covering of righteousness.

B. **Goats hair** – These goats were cud-chewing animals with very hairy coats. They were used primarily for milk, butter, cheese and meat, as well as for sacrifice. Their hair was made into containers for wine and water and into clothing. We will consider its sacrificial use. It speaks to us of sin offering, His atonement, and Jesus our scapegoat.

1. Leviticus 16:5-22
2. Hebrews 9:11-15

Jesus was the goat who was killed for our atonement (Isaiah 53:5). He also became the scapegoat in Isaiah 53:8. It carried away all our iniquities (John 1:29). This material speaks to us of Jesus as our covering and His covenant with us. He is responsible for us.

C. **Ram's skin dyed red** – These were the skins of the male sheep tanned with oil and used for outer clothing by shepherds. In the Tabernacle it was used as the exterior clothing.

1. Exodus 25:5 – "*And rams' skins dyed red...*" – This speaks to us of consecration, substitution, atonement and sacrifice. Remember red is the color of scarlet which means sacrifice. Read Numbers 6:17. This material speaks of Jesus as our covering for sin (Psalms 85:2).
2. Exodus 29:1, 15-21, 22, 26 – Consecration
3. Genesis 22:13 – Substitution; here a ram is substituted for Isaac. Jesus was our ram (our substitute).
4. Leviticus 5:14-18 – Atonement
5. Numbers 6:17 – Sacrifice

D. **Badger's skins** – This was probably a goat, because the badger as we know it is not found in Biblical lands. Because so many were needed for covering, it would seem more probable that goats were the animal mentioned here because they were domesticated and available in great numbers. Some believe this was the skin of a seal. This speaks to us of His protection as well as there being no beauty to His sacrifice.

1. His protection – It was used exclusively as a covering to protect. This material speaks to us of Jesus our covering in warfare and trials (Psalm 140:7).

a. Exodus 26:14 – *"And thou shalt make a covering for the tent of rams' skins dyed red, and a covering above of badgers' skins."* (Exodus 36:19, Exodus 39:34)
b. Ezekiel 16:10 – *"I clothed thee also with broidered work, and shod thee with badgers' skin, and I girded thee about with fine linen, and I covered thee with silk."*
c. Exodus 36:19 – *"And he made a covering for the tent of rams' skins dyed red, and a covering of badgers' skins above that."*

2. It was ugly, Isaiah 53:2 – *"For he shall grow up before him as a tender plant, and as a root out of a dry ground: he hath no form nor comeliness; and when we shall see him, there is no beauty that we should desire him."*

E. **Shittim Wood**

It is interesting to note that Shittim (meadow or acacia) was also the name of a place (Numbers 33:49), which was the last place Israel stopped before crossing the Jordan into the Promised Land (Joshua 2:1, 3:1). Shittim represents to us the last effort of our human nature to stop us from going on to fullness. It is a meadow of trees, a nice place to rest, but its purpose is to keep us from crossing the Jordan to receive our inheritance. Our human nature will cry out to stop, to rest, to build a nest, or to stop pressing on (Job 29:18) to the mark of the prize of the high calling of God (Philippians 3:14). It is willing to settle for a meadow of trees. This wood speaks to us of our humanity and the incorruptible humanity of Jesus.

1. Humanity – we've already stated this above but an added picture will be given here.

a. Numbers 25:1 – *"And Israel abode in Shittim, and the people began to commit whoredom with the daughters of Moab."* – Left in Shittim, the people began to commit whoredoms.
b. II Timothy 2:20 – *"But in a great house there are not only vessels of gold and of silver, but also of wood and of earth; and some to honour, and some to dishonour."* Wood speaks of the earthen, fleshy man.
c. I Corinthians 3:12 – *"Now if any man build upon this foundation gold, silver, precious stones, wood, hay, stubble;"* – This speaks of that which is carnal in our life and how it will perish at the judgment. Only manmade things can perish; that which God does is forever.

2. Men are spoken of as trees (wood) in Scripture.

a. Mark 8:24 – *"And he looked up, and said, I see men as trees, walking."*
b. Isaiah 61:3 – *"To appoint unto them that mourn in Zion, to give unto them beauty for ashes, the oil of joy for mourning, the garment of praise for the spirit of heaviness; that they might be called trees of righteousness, the planting of the LORD, that he might be glorified."*
c. Luke 6:43 – *"For a good tree bringeth not forth corrupt fruit; neither doth a corrupt tree bring forth good fruit."*
d. Matthew 3:10 – *"And now also the axe is laid unto the root of the trees: therefore every tree which bringeth not forth good fruit is hewn down, and cast into the fire."*
e. Jeremiah 17:7-8 (Psalms 1:3) – *"[7]Blessed is the man that trusteth in the LORD, and whose hope the LORD is. [8]For he shall be as a tree planted by the waters, and that spreadeth out her roots by the river, and shall not see when heat cometh, but her leaf shall be green; and shall not be careful in the year of drought, neither shall cease from yielding fruit."*

3. Jesus' incorruptible humanity – He is spoken of as a righteous branch. He is human nature that is spotless, without blemish, uncorrupted (Hebrews 4:15, I Peter 2:22, I John 3:5, II Corinthians 5:21).

a. Jeremiah 23:5 – *"Behold, the days come, saith the LORD, that I will raise unto David a righteous Branch, and a King shall reign and prosper, and shall execute judgment and justice in the earth."*

b. Isaiah 11:1-5 – "[1]*And there shall come forth a rod out of the stem of Jesse, and a Branch shall grow out of his roots:* [2]*And the spirit of the LORD shall rest upon him...*"

c. Jeremiah 33:15 – "*In those days, and at that time, will I cause the Branch of righteousness to grow up unto David; and he shall execute judgment and righteousness in the land.*"

d. Zechariah 6:12 – "*And speak unto him, saying, Thus speaketh the LORD of hosts, saying, Behold the man whose name is The BRANCH; and he shall grow up out of his place, and he shall build the temple of the LORD:*"

e. Jesus as the Son of man experienced our humanity but was without sin; He is human nature that is spotless, without blemish, uncorrupted.

1) Hebrews 4:15 – "*For we have not an high priest which cannot be touched with the feeling of our infirmities; but was in all points tempted like as we are, yet without sin.*"
2) I Peter 2:22 – "*Who did no sin, neither was guile found in his mouth:*"
3) I John 3:5 – "*And ye know that he was manifested to take away our sins; and in him is no sin.*"
4) II Corinthians 5:21 – "*For he hath made him to be sin for us, who knew no sin; that we might be made the righteousness of God in him.*"

F. **Oil**

1. Exodus 25:6 – "*Oil for the light...*" Oil is for light – God's anointing is to bring light. Spiritually this means revelation and understanding of God, His Word, and His purposes for His people.

a. Exodus 27:20 – "*And thou shalt command the children of Israel, that they bring thee pure oil olive beaten for the light, to cause the lamp to burn always.*"

b. Exodus 35:14 – "*The candlestick also for the light, and his furniture, and his lamps, with the oil for the light*"

c. Numbers 4:16 – "*And to the office of Eleazar the son of Aaron the priest pertaineth the oil for the light, and the sweet incense, and the daily meat offering, and the anointing oil, and the oversight of all the tabernacle, and of all that therein is, in the sanctuary, and in the vessels thereof.*"

d. Leviticus 24:2 – "*Command the children of Israel, that they bring unto thee pure oil olive beaten for the light, to cause the lamps to burn continually.*"

e. Joel 2:24 – "*And the floors shall be full of wheat, and the fats shall overflow with wine and oil.*"

f. I Samuel 10:1 – "*Then Samuel took a vial of oil, and poured it upon his head, and kissed him, and said, Is it not because the LORD hath anointed thee to be captain over his inheritance?*"

g. I Samuel 16:1, 13 – "[1]*And the LORD said unto Samuel, How long wilt thou mourn for Saul, seeing I have rejected him from reigning over Israel? fill thine horn with oil, and go, I will send thee to Jesse the Bethlehemite: for I have provided me a king among his sons...*[13]*Then Samuel took the horn of oil, and anointed him in the midst of his brethren: and the Spirit of the LORD came upon David from that day forward...*"

h. Ezekiel 16:9-14

2. Hebrew and Greek definitions of oil

a. Hebrew words

1) *Yitshar* – oil as producing light, anointing. It comes from a root word, *tsahar* – to glisten, to press out.
2) *Shemen* – grease, liquid from the olive, richness, often perfumed, fat. It comes from a root word, *shaman* – to shine, to make oily, to wax fat.

b. Greek word, *Elaion* – the olive, the tree or the fruit

3. I believe this speaks of the Holy Ghost, the One that brings light. The Holy Spirit is oil. He is the One that gives us light. As our lamps are burning, the Holy Spirit makes our lamps to shine.

   a. John 16:13 – *"Howbeit when he, the Spirit of truth, is come, he will guide you into all truth: for he shall not speak of himself; but whatsoever he shall hear, that shall he speak: and he will shew you things to come."*
   b. I John 2:27 – *"But the anointing which ye have received of him abideth in you, and ye need not that any man teach you: but as the same anointing teacheth you of all things, and is truth, and is no lie, and even as it hath taught you, ye shall abide in him."*
   c. Joel 2:28 – *"And it shall come to pass afterward, that I will pour out my spirit upon all flesh; and your sons and your daughters shall prophesy, your old men shall dream dreams, your young men shall see visions:"*
   d. John 6:63 – *"It is the spirit that quickeneth; the flesh profiteth nothing: the words that I speak unto you, they are spirit, and they are life."*
   e. Acts 1:8 – *"But ye shall receive power, after that the Holy Ghost is come upon you: and ye shall be witnesses unto me both in Jerusalem, and in all Judaea, and in Samaria, and unto the uttermost part of the earth."*

The Holy Ghost is the oil we need to operate in this life! He gives us understanding, strength, power, etc. We are and should be totally dependent on the Holy Ghost. We need to be filled afresh every day so we can have light, power, strength, and everything essential to make it (Ephesians 5:17-18). Just as the priest had to tend daily to the lamp, we must tend to our soul.

4. Danger of not having oil – There is a grave danger in not allowing the Holy Ghost to come and fill us afresh. It is true that there is only one baptism of the Holy Ghost, but there should be many <u>fillings (Ephesians 5:18)</u>. Every day we should receive a fresh filling and impartation.

   a. Matthew 25:1-14 – *"[1]Then shall the kingdom of heaven be likened unto ten virgins, which took their lamps, and went forth to meet the bridegroom. [2]And five of them were wise, and five were foolish. [3]They that were foolish took their lamps, and took no oil with them: [4]But the wise took oil in their vessels with their lamps..."* – The foolish virgins didn't take or cultivate oil in their lives. They weren't filled on a continual basis with the Holy Ghost. This oil must be **<u>purchased.</u>** You pay the price by going into His Presence and being filled with the Holy Ghost everday. We don't receive this oil by having hands laid on us. Many do not realize that we can spend up the oil we are initially given when filled with the Holy Ghost. (Hebrews 2:1)
   b. Proverbs 21:20 – *"There is treasure to be desired and oil in the dwelling of the wise; but a foolish man spendeth it up."*
   c. Joel 1:10 – *"The field is wasted, the land mourneth; for the corn is wasted: the new wine is dried up, the oil languisheth."* – The light in Israel had grown dim.

The foolish virgins didn't take or cultivate oil in their lives. They weren't filled on a continual basis with the Holy Ghost. This oil must be <u>purchased</u>. You pay the price by going into His Presence and being filled with the Holy Ghost everyday. We don't receive this oil by having hands laid on us. Many do not realize that we can spend up the oil we are initially given when filled with the Holy Ghost (Hebrews 2:1 – *"Therefore we ought to give the more earnest heed to the things which we have heard, lest at any time we should let them slip."*)

5. We are to be filled with the Holy Ghost.

   a. John 7:37-39 – *"[37]In the last day, that great day of the feast, Jesus stood and cried, saying, If any man thirst, let him come unto me, and drink. [38]He that believeth on me, as the scripture hath said, out of his belly shall flow rivers of living water. [39](But this spake he of the Spirit, which they that believe on him should receive: for the Holy Ghost was not yet given; because that Jesus was not yet glorified.)"*

b. Ephesians 5:17-20 – "[17]*Wherefore be ye not unwise, but understanding what the will of the Lord is.* [18]*And be not drunk with wine, wherein is excess; but be filled with the Spirit...*"
c. Acts 1:4, 5, 8, 2:2-4, 10:44-46, 19:2-6
d. Luke 4:1, 14

6. Know the Lord intimately, who is light

   a. James 1:17 – "*Every good gift and every perfect gift is from above, and cometh down from the Father of lights, with whom is no variableness, neither shadow of turning.*"
   b. John 12:46 – "*I am come a light into the world, that whosoever believeth on me should not abide in darkness.*"
   c. I John 1:5 – "*...God is light, and in him is no darkness at all.*"
   d. John 1:4, 9 – "[4]*In him was life; and the life was the light of men...*[9]*That was the true Light, which lighteth every man that cometh into the world.*"
   e. John 8:12 – "*Then spake Jesus again unto them, saying, I am the light of the world: he that followeth me shall not walk in darkness, but shall have the light of life.*"
   f. Psalms 27:1 – "*The LORD is my light and my salvation; whom shall I fear? the LORD is the strength of my life; of whom shall I be afraid?*"
   g. Psalms 89:15 – "*Blessed is the people that know the joyful sound: they shall walk, O LORD, in the light of thy countenance.*"
   h. Psalms 43:3 – "*O send out thy light and thy truth: let them lead me; let them bring me unto thy holy hill, and to thy tabernacles.*"
   i. Proverbs 16:15 – "*In the light of the king's countenance is life; and his favour is as a cloud of the latter rain.*"
   j. Isaiah 2:5 – "*O house of Jacob, come ye, and let us walk in the light of the LORD.*"
   k. Isaiah 60:20 – "*Thy sun shall no more go down; neither shall thy moon withdraw itself: for the LORD shall be thine everlasting light, and the days of thy mourning shall be ended.*"
   l. Micah 7:8 – "*Rejoice not against me, O mine enemy: when I fall, I shall arise; when I sit in darkness, the LORD shall be a light unto me.*"
   m. Isaiah 45:7 – "*I form the light, and create darkness: I make peace, and create evil: I the LORD do all these things.*"

Lesson 14

Sweet Incense

I. **Sweet Incense**, Exodus 25:6 – *"spices...for sweet incense"*

The use of incense in Moses' Tabernacle was partly a sanitary measure. Since the smell of blood, sacrifice and death from many animals permeated the atmosphere, the air would have had to be fumigated. The revelation for us then would be, in the midst of tremendous death, blood, and sacrifice, there will come a beautiful and sweet fragrance. The Hebrew meaning for "sweet" – restful, pleasant a delight and it comes from a root word that means – rest, to settle down

The incense used in worship was to be prepared according to exact specifications, and was to be offered only by the high priest. The Hebrew word for *incense* – fumigation, perfume and it comes from a root word meaning – fumigation in a close place; driving out the occupants; to turn into a fragrance by fire. The obvious revelation for us would be: 1) Worshipping in a close place (intimacy), 2) As we worship and enter in the prior occupants (devils) are driven out, and 3) This worship becomes sweet only as it burns in God's fire (His dealings in our lives)

The use of this formula was banned for private use, and any who violated this prohibition were to be excommunicated from the congregation of Israel. Practically for us, this means our worship to the Lord should be personal, and praise belongs to God alone and to no one else. The penalty of offering bad or strange incense (Exodus 30:9) was severe. In Leviticus 10:1-11 when Aaron's sons, Nadab and Abihu, put incense upon strange fire, they died. Nadab in Hebrew means – willing, one's free will, and it comes from a root word that means to impel oneself. Abihu in Hebrew means – whose father is he. We see this as well in Numbers 16:6-11, 15, 39 with the rebellion of Korah. Other examples of this are found in II Chronicles 26:16-21, Ezekiel 8:5-11, 18, Isaiah 1:10-15 (verse 13), Luke 1:18-20

A. What does this incense represent?

In his first remarks about this incense, God says it is sweet – sweet to Him! This incense was composed of sweet spices, although the truth is most were bitter – bitter to us (but sweet to God). The combination of the spices while being worked into us (spiritual application) may be initially bitter, but the end result will be sweet – these spices worked into a life that will become a sweet perfume to the Lord.

1. Incense as prayer (intercession)

   a. Psalms 141:2 – *"Let my prayer be set forth before thee as incense..."*
   b. Revelation 8:3-4 – *"[3]And another angel came and stood at the altar, having a golden censer; and there was given unto him much incense, that he should offer it with the prayers of all saints upon the golden altar which was before the throne. [4]And the smoke of the incense, which came with the prayers of the saints, ascended up before God out of the angel's hand."*

2. Incense as worship

   a. Malachi 1:11 – *"For from the rising of the sun even unto the going down of the same my name shall be great among the Gentiles; and in every place incense shall be offered unto my name, and a pure offering: for my name shall be great among the heathen, saith the LORD of hosts."*
   b. Proverbs 27:9 – *"Ointment and perfume rejoice the heart: so doth the sweetness of a man's friend by hearty counsel."* The word translated *perfume* is the same word for *incense.*
   c. Psalms 141:2 – *"Let my prayer be set forth before thee as incense; and the lifting up of my hands as the evening sacrifice."*
   d. Revelation 8:3-4 – The angel offers up incense and prayers

B. How it works (or smokes)

Incense was an aromatic substance made up of gums and spices, to be burned. The revelation for us would be then incense would never release a fragrance unless all the ingredients are burned. The fire of God will come upon everything in our lives. We will never truly enter into worship until we have been burned by God's fire.

1. Fire of God

The only way for the spices to flow or to begin to burn incense into a fragrance is 1) the fire of God burning up the dross in our lives, and 2) His dealings in our lives. The bride says in Song of Solomon 4:16, "*Awake, O north wind; and come, thou south; blow upon my garden, that the spices thereof may flow out. Let my beloved come into his garden, and eat his pleasant fruits.*"

a. Malachi 3:2 – "*But who may abide the day of his coming? and who shall stand when he appeareth? for he is like a refiner's fire, and like fullers' soap:*"
b. Zechariah 2:5 – "*For I, saith the LORD, will be unto her a wall of fire round about, and will be the glory in the midst of her.*"
c. Luke 12:49-50 – "*[49]I am come to send fire on the earth; and what will I if it be already kindled? [50]But I have a baptism to be baptized with; and how am I straitened till it be accomplished!*"
d. I Corinthians 3:13 – "*Every man's work shall be made manifest: for the day shall declare it, because it shall be revealed by fire; and the fire shall try every man's work of what sort it is.*"
e. Hebrews 12:29 – "*For our God is a consuming fire.*"
f. Revelation 15:2 – "*And I saw as it were a sea of glass mingled with fire: and them that had gotten the victory over the beast, and over his image, and over his mark, and over the number of his name, stand on the sea of glass, having the harps of God.*"
g. Isaiah 31:9 – "*And he shall pass over to his strong hold for fear, and his princes shall be afraid of the ensign, saith the LORD, whose fire is in Zion, and his furnace in Jerusalem.*"
h. Exodus 3:2 – "*And the angel of the LORD appeared unto him in a flame of fire out of the midst of a bush: and he looked, and, behold, the bush burned with fire, and the bush was not consumed.*"

C. Spiritual Application, Exodus 30:7-10

"*[7]And Aaron shall burn thereon sweet incense every morning: when he dresseth the lamps, he shall burn incense upon it. [8]And when Aaron lighteth the lamps at even, he shall burn incense upon it, a perpetual incense before the LORD throughout your generations. [9]Ye shall offer no strange incense thereon, nor burnt sacrifice, nor meat offering; neither shall ye pour drink offering thereon. [10]And Aaron shall make an atonement upon the horns of it once in a year with the blood of the sin offering of atonements: once in the year shall he make atonement upon it throughout your generations: it is most holy unto the LORD.*"

1. Every morning and every evening we should worship and pray – every day!
2. Perpetual incense

a. Psalms 34:1 – "*I will bless the LORD at all times: his praise shall continually be in my mouth.*" perpetual worship
b. Luke 18:1 – "*And he spake a parable unto them to this end, that men ought always to pray, and not to faint*" – perpetual prayer

3. Principle of morning and evening

a. Joshua 1:8 – "*This book of the law shall not depart out of thy mouth; but thou shalt meditate therein day and night, that thou mayest observe to do according to all that is written therein: for then thou shalt make thy way prosperous, and then thou shalt have good success.*"

b. Psalms 1:2 – *"But his delight is in the law of the LORD; and in his law doth he meditate day and night."*
c. Ecclesiastes 11:6 – *"In the morning sow thy seed, and in the evening withhold not thine hand: for thou knowest not whether shall prosper, either this or that, or whether they both shall be alike good."*
d. Psalms 65:8 – *"They also that dwell in the uttermost parts are afraid at thy tokens: thou makest the outgoings of the morning and evening to rejoice."*
e. Psalms 55:17 – *"Evening, and morning, and at noon, will I pray, and cry aloud: and he shall hear my voice."*
f. Genesis 8:22 – *"While the earth remaineth, seedtime and harvest, and cold and heat, and summer and winter, and day and night shall not cease."*

4. Throughout the generations, we must teach our children to pray and worship and attend to God. We are responsible for our own generation.
5. No strange incense – This is speaking of a mixture in the compound. In the spirit realm it means a mixture. This is a mixture of flesh and religion, a lack of interest, a lack of genuine heart and love in our worship and prayer. These are the impurities.

D. Ingredients to sweet Incense, Exodus 30:34-38

"34And the LORD said unto Moses, Take unto thee sweet spices, stacte, and onycha, and galbanum; these sweet spices with pure frankincense: of each shall there be a like weight: 35And thou shalt make it a perfume, a confection after the art of the apothecary, tempered together, pure and holy: 36And thou shalt beat some of it very small, and put of it before the testimony in the tabernacle of the congregation, where I will meet with thee: it shall be unto you most holy. 37And as for the perfume which thou shalt make, ye shall not make to yourselves according to the composition thereof: it shall be unto thee holy for the LORD. 38Whosoever shall make like unto that, to smell thereto, shall even be cut off from his people."

1. Stacte

A resin believed to be an extract of the stems and branches of the storax tree. This plant flowered in spring. It had highly fragrant white blooms. This produced a rare ointment, most probably myrrh. The Hebrew meaning for "stacte" is to drop or ooze. Myrrh comes from a Hebrew root word meaning bitter. If we are going to break through to become a precious fragrance unto the Lord, we must have some bitter experiences in life. This will cause the precious ointment to ooze out.

2. Onycha

A species of the rockrose like myrrh. It produces the gum ladanum. The resin that exudes from the stems and leaves is spicy, aromatic and fragrant. It was highly valued for its fragrance and medicinal qualities. The Hebrew meaning for this word is to roar or to peel off. God is roaring as the Lion of the Tribe of Judah. And He is peeling off our flesh so that we might have the ingredients to offer – a pure offering in righteousness (Malachi 1:11).

3. Galbanum

An aromic gum resin excreted from the incised lower part of the stem from two Persian plants, part of the Umbelliferae family. It has a pungent, disagreeable odor, but when mixed with the other fragrances, it becomes sweet and retains its fragrance longer. This speaks to us of how our personal ministry, worship, intercession, etc., alone may have a disagreeable odor, but combined with others, the other members of the body of Christ, it becomes a sweet fragrance.

The Hebrew word for galbanum means fat, or richest part. This plant was used in medicine as an antispasmodic. When it is mixed with other fragrant substances it has the effect of increasing the odor, and making it last longer. The revelation to us – Even though we may be rich or full, it is a stench by itself. We need each other to be perfected and to give off a sweet, fragrant smell.

4. Frankincense

A clear yellow resin that flows when an incision is made in the bark of a frankincense tree. When the resin hardens, it forms small yellow tears. Frankincense in Hebrew means whiteness. White speaks of purity. For you and me to have purity, an incision must be made in the bark of our tree. The axe is being laid to the root. God is cutting away our flesh, and although the oil that flows forms into tears, it will bring forth His purity (whiteness) in us.

5. Other facts about these ingredients

a. There were four ingredients – Four is the number in Scripture that means – that which is created, and speaks to us of the new creation man
b. They were all to be the same weight – This speaks of having a proper balance in God

1) Proverbs 11:1 – "*A false balance is abomination to the LORD: but a just weight is his delight.*"
2) Proverbs 20:23 – "*Divers weights are an abomination unto the LORD; and a false balance is not good.*"
3) Proverbs 16:11 – "*A just weight and balance are the LORD's: all the weights of the bag are his work.*"
4) Proverbs 26:7 – "*The legs of the lame are not equal: so is a parable in the mouth of fools*"

c. They were to be tempered together – Tempered in Hebrew means to rub to pieces, to pulverize, to disappear as dust. This means we are losing our identity and taking on His, as well as we are becoming part of a great body, where every joint supplies.
d. Pure and holy – God works purity into all of us.

1) Matthew 5:8 – "*Blessed are the pure in heart: for they shall see God.*"
2) Hebrews 12:14 – "*Follow peace with all men, and holiness, without which no man shall see the Lord:*"
3) II Corinthians 7:1 – "*Having therefore these promises, dearly beloved, let us cleanse ourselves from all filthiness of the flesh and spirit, perfecting holiness in the fear of God.*"
4) Exodus 28:36 – "*And thou shalt make a plate of pure gold, and grave upon it, like the engravings of a signet, HOLINESS TO THE LORD.*"

e. "*beat some of it very small*" – Other translations:

"*...All this thou shalt beat into fine power...*"
"*...crush some of it small...*"
"*...grind some of it fine...*"
"*...you must, pulverize some of it very fine...*"

Lesson 15

The Anointing Oil In The Tabernacle

Every one of us need and should know all about the anointing of God. For God's anointing, which is the essence of God Himself, is the most priceless commodity in the universe. It has been said that "you really can't recognize God's true anointing unless you have some yourself". I know this to be true from some thirty eight years of being a believer and some thirty one years in ministry. Believe me, you know if someone really has it or if they do not! In I John 2:27, it says *"But the anointing which ye have received of him abideth in you, and ye need not that any man teach you: but as the same anointing teacheth you of all things, and is truth, and is no lie, and even as it hath taught you, ye shall abide in him"*. Those who are born again have received God's anointing. Though it may be in seed form, all Christians have some of God's anointing in them. But as we will see later, over our Christian life, we have the ability to receive greater anointings as we grow in His manifest presence, in His authority, etc. David the great king was anointed three different times in His life.

God's anointing has many uses. Exodus 25:6 says "*Oil for the light*", meaning the anointing (the oil) brings revelation and a greater understand of the Scriptures and of God's person as well as the anointing brings us out of darkness. It is used also in the holy calling of ministers, priests, and prophets of God (Exodus 29:7, 21 – *"Then shalt thou take the anointing oil, and pour it upon his head, and anoint him..."*). It is also supposed to be used in bringing God's presence to His tabernacle, or His people (Exodus 30:25 – *"And thou shalt make it an oil of holy ointment, an ointment compound after the art of the apothecary: it shall be an holy anointing oil."*). God's anointing is never to be poured out where there is flesh or anyone who is a stranger to the Gospel (Exodus 30:32-33 – *"Upon man's flesh shall it not be poured, neither shall ye make any other like it, after the composition of it: it is holy, and it shall be holy unto you. Whosoever compoundeth any like it, or whosoever putteth any of it upon a stranger, shall even be cut off from his people."*). God's anointing is made up of specific ingredients that God Himself commanded (Exodus 30:34-35 – *"And the LORD said unto Moses, Take unto thee sweet spices, stacte, and onycha, and galbanum; these sweet spices with pure frankincense: of each shall there be a like weight: And thou shalt make it a perfume, a confection after the art of the apothecary, tempered together, pure and holy"*). All of these specific ingredients hold great revelational truths within them. By understanding the natural ingredients God gave for human anointing oil, it will then give us the spiritual revelation of what God's true anointing is. This natural oil was to be placed upon everything within the Tabernacle of Moses. That Tabernacle and its specific pieces of furniture, which represents not only our way into the holy of holies, but each piece speaks of different places in our walk with God, different dispensations, both ending up at His throne (Exodus 40:9 – *"And thou shalt take the anointing oil, and anoint the tabernacle, and all that is therein, and shalt hallow it, and all the vessels thereof: and it shall be holy"*, Leviticus 8:10 – *"And Moses took the anointing oil, and anointed the tabernacle and all that was therein, and sanctified them"*).

This anointing also speaks of our being sanctified or made holy and that we are consecrated to God (Leviticus 8:12 – *"And he poured of the anointing oil upon Aaron's head, and anointed him, to sanctify him"*, Leviticus 8:30 – *"And Moses took of the anointing oil, and of the blood which was upon the altar, and sprinkled it upon Aaron, and upon his garments, and upon his sons, and upon his sons' garments with him; and sanctified Aaron, and his garments, and his sons, and his sons' garments with him"*). We are also commanded to always have a holy fear and awe of God, and not mix the world and that which is godly (Leviticus 21:12 – *"Neither shall he go out of the sanctuary, nor profane the sanctuary of his God; for the crown of the anointing oil of his God is upon him: I am the LORD"*). And finally, God's anointing is to be used in the breaking of yokes of bondage (Isaiah 10:27 – *"And it shall come to pass in that day, that his burden shall be taken away from off thy shoulder, and his yoke from off thy neck, and the yoke shall be destroyed because of the anointing"*, Isaiah 61:1 – *"The Spirit of the Lord GOD is upon me; because the LORD hath anointed me to preach good tidings unto the meek; he hath sent me to bind up the brokenhearted, to proclaim liberty to the captives, and the opening of the prison to them that are bound"*).

To have God's anointing, whether you be a king, priest, prophet, or any of the five-fold ministers, or just being a born again believer, His anointing marks you as someone very special in God's sight. God has given all believers a taste of His anointing simply because His Spirit lives within them. There is however another dimension to God's anointing which calls someone out for special service to God. God gives His anointing not for vain purposes but to further His Kingdom, promote understanding of His Word, empower His ministers to preach, teach, prophecy, and even to do great miracles that God might be glorified.

His anointing is also called in Psalms 45:7 the "*oil of gladness*". God's holy presence should always bring joy and happiness as recorded in Psalms 16:11 "*Thou wilt shew me the path of life: in thy presence is fulness of joy; at thy right hand there are pleasures for evermore*". God's Word also admonishes us to be very careful about disrespecting, persecuting, or defaming God's anointed ones as found in Psalms 105:15, "*Touch not mine anointed, and do my prophets no harm.*" God's holy anointing is also to be honored, esteemed, and feared. It is certainly never to be taken lightly or misused;because God's anointing, which we could also say is His very essence, His manifest presence upon someone or upon a people is like unto His glory and God's great glory is to be guarded, esteemed, and honored above all else in life.

God's anointing once again is given for holy purposes as seen in Acts 10:38, "*How God anointed Jesus of Nazareth with the Holy Ghost and with power: who went about doing good, and healing all that were oppressed of the devil; for God was with him*". The amazing thing about this verse is the last part, "*for God was with him*". This means to have God's anointing is essentially to have Him in a most powerful and manifested way.

What we will try to accomplish in this particular teaching is to define God's anointing, to see what it is to be used for, and what it isn't to be used for, as well as to cause us to see that this great principle of God's anointing is something we can all run after. By understanding these things, it will certainly once again bring us to a truer, more pure image of God as defined by God Himself in His Word. All of my Christian life has been devoted to be honored by God's anointing so that I could be a "vessel of honor" (II Timothy 2:20-21), to do great things by Him and for Him. To have God's true anointing on your life as a minister of the Gospel means everything to me; not to be used for vain glory or to build one's self up or to draw away disciples after yourself, but to bring this marvelous, holy, and precious anointing of God to His people so to confirm that He is, and that He is always present, always wanting to bless, heal, prosper, deliver and set people free, as well as to confront God's people with the reality of the Divine Presence. I have spent my entire Christian life sitting at the feet of God's true anointed messengers and have seen the impact of what one person with God's true anointing can do. I have fasted, prayed incessantly, studied to show myself approved. I have worshipped with abandon, and sought to live a holy life that God might grant me the privilege of having His anointing. My prayer is that after this lesson, you will want to do the same.

I. Word Definitions for "Oil" in Defining God's Anointing Oil in Scripture

A. Hebrew words

1. *Yitshar* – oil as producing light, anointing; it comes from a root word, *tsahar* – to glisten, to press out oil
2. *Shemen* – grease, liquid from the olive, richness, often perfumed, fat; it comes from a root word, *shaman* – to shine, to make oily, to make fat

B. Greek word, *Elaion* – the olive, the tree or the fruit

II. What Was The Anointing Oil Made of?

A. Scriptures showing the spices

1. Exodus 25:6 – "*Oil for the light, spices for anointing oil, and for sweet incense,*"
2. Exodus 30:22-33 – "*[22]Moreover the LORD spake unto Moses, saying, [23]Take thou also unto thee principal spices, of pure myrrh five hundred shekels, and of sweet cinnamon half so much, even two hundred and fifty shekels, and of sweet calamus two hundred and fifty shekels, [24]And of cassia five hundred shekels, after the shekel of the sanctuary, and of oil olive an hin: [25]And thou shalt make it an oil of holy ointment, an ointment compound after the art of the apothecary: it shall be an holy anointing oil...[31]And thou shalt speak unto the children of Israel, saying, This shall be an holy anointing oil unto me throughout your generations. [32]Upon man's flesh shall it not be poured,*

neither shall ye make any other like it, after the composition of it: it is holy, and it shall be holy unto you. [33]Whosoever compoundeth any like it, or whosoever putteth any of it upon a stranger, shall even be cut off from his people."

The holy anointing oil was composed of four spices mixed in olive oil. All of the spices were imported from somewhere else. Notice there are five ingredients; five is the number of grace.

3. The four spices

   a. **Myrrh** – five hundred shekels or four thousand five hundred drops – five is the Biblical number for grace; One hundred is the number for fruitfulness and full measure: Grace to reach fruitfulness and fullness.
   b. **Sweet Cinnamon** – Two hundred and fifty Shekels or two thousand two hundred and fifty drops – five X fifty = grace to obtain jubilee
   c. **Sweet Calamus** – Two hundred and fifty shekels or two thousand two hundred and fifty drops drops– five X fifty = grace to obtain jubilee
   d. **Cassia** – five hundred shekels or four thousand five hundred drops – five X one hundred = grace to reach fruitfulness or full measure
   e. One shekel is equal to nine drops; nine in Scripture is the number for finality
   f. These spices were mixed in one and a half gallons of olive oil making up the holy anointing oil

B. In-depth definition of the holy anointing oil

1. The Hebrew words for anoint, anointing, anointed

   a. Anoint, *Mashach* – to rub with oil, to paint, to consecrate
   b. Anointed, *Mashiyach* – usually a consecrated person or Messiah (I Samuel 2:10, Psalms 2:2)
   c. Anointing, *Mashchah* – unction

2. Other minor words for anoint, etc. (Hebrew)

   a. *Suk* – to pour out (Deuteronomy 28:40, II Chronicles 28:15, Ruth 3:3, Ezekiel 16:9)
   b. *Balal* – to cause to overflow (Psalms 92:10)
   c. *Dashen* – to be fattened, to anoint to satisfy (Psalms 23:5)
   d. *Shehmen* – grease, richness (Isaiah 10:27)

3. Greek words for anoint, anointed, anointing

   a. *Aleipho* – to be ceremonially anointed, to oil. (Matthew 6:17, mark 16:1, Luke 7:36, John 11:2, John 12:3, Luke 7:38, Mark 6:13, James 5:14)
   b. *Chrio* – to rub (Luke 4:18, Acts 4:27, Acts 10:38, II Corinthians 1:21, Hebrews 1:9)
   c. *Chrisma* – anointing, rubbing in (I John 2:20, I John 2:27)
   d. *Epichrio* – to rub on (John 9:6,11)
   e. *Muridzo* – to anoint for death or burial (Mark 14:8)
   f. *Egchrio* – to rub in (Revelation 3:18)

A good definition out of all these readings would be: To smear, paint, to pour on, to rub on and in with God's Holy Presence

C. By considering each of the 5 ingredients (olive oil plus the 4 spices) of the anointing oil, we can come away with a better understanding of the anointing and what it is all about.

1. **Olive oil** – the oil of the olive can only be produced when the olive is crushed

a. Exodus 30:22-25 – *"...and of oil olive an hin: And thou shalt make it an oil of holy ointment, an ointment compound after the art of the apothecary: it shall be an holy anointing oil."*

b. Genesis 8:11 – *"And the dove came in to him in the evening; and, lo, in her mouth was an olive leaf pluckt off: so Noah knew that the waters were abated from off the earth."* – here it means peace

c. Judges 9:8-9 – *"The trees went forth on a time to anoint a king over them; and they said unto the olive tree, Reign thou over us. But the olive tree said unto them, Should I leave my fatness, wherewith by me they honour God and man, and go to be promoted over the trees?"* – here it causes men to honor God and man and it means God's richness

d. Exodus 27:20 – *"And thou shalt command the children of Israel, that they bring thee pure oil olive beaten for the light, to cause the lamp to burn always."* – it was to be pure and beaten (all mixture removed); pure means no mixture.

Spiritual significance: peace, brings honor to God and men, it is the richness of God; it is pure (holy) and beaten (all mixture removed.) This will cause light (revelation/fire of God) to burn always. It will be bright morning and evening.

e. Matthew 26:36 – *"Then cometh Jesus with them unto a place called Gethsemane, and saith unto the disciples, Sit ye here, while I go and pray yonder."*

The Greek word for Gethsemane means <u>oil press, or olive press</u>. It is only when the olive is pressed that the oil flows out. The anointing will flow through the person who has procured it, the person who has paid the price by allowing himself to be broken, bruised and completely pressed by God. There are <u>Gethsemane's waiting for all of us</u>. Do we really want the anointing?

1) II Corinthians 1:8-10 – *"For we would not, brethren, have you ignorant of our trouble which came to us in Asia, that we <u>were pressed out of measure</u>, above strength, insomuch that we despaired even of life: But we had the sentence of death in ourselves, that we should not trust in ourselves, but in God which raiseth the dead: Who delivered us from so great a death, and doth deliver: in whom we trust that he will yet deliver us;"*

When God sends us a test, it's not to hurt us, but rather it's to allow that which He has done in us to flow out. It's only when we are squeezed that we see the precious thing He's done in us. Remember, you don't have a testimony unless you've passed a test. You're not an overcomer unless you've overcome something.

2) Revelation 3:18 – *"I counsel thee to buy of me <u>gold tried in the fire</u>, that thou mayest be rich; and white raiment, that thou mayest be clothed, and that the shame of thy nakedness do not appear; and anoint thine eyes with eyesalve, that thou mayest see."* – You can only purchase gold (God's divine nature) or obtain it when you are tried in the fire of a circumstance. The gold of His nature doesn't come out until we've been pressed.

a) I Peter 1:7 – *"That the <u>trial of your faith</u>, being <u>much more precious</u> than of gold that perisheth, though <u>it be tried with fire</u>, might be found unto praise and honour and glory at the appearing of Jesus Christ:"*

b) Daniel 12:10 – *"Many shall be purified, and made white, <u>and tried</u>..."*

c) Job 23:10 – *"But he knoweth the way that I take: <u>when he hath tried me</u>, I shall come forth as gold."*

d) Proverbs 17:3 – *"<u>The fining pot is for silver</u>, and the <u>furnace for gold</u>: but the LORD trieth the hearts."*

e) Psalms 45:13 – *"The king's daughter is all glorious within: <u>her clothing is of wrought gold</u>."* – She got gold because she's allowed God to do His process of working into her His nature.

f) Matthew 25:1-10

g) Malachi 3:2-6

The olive oil comes as the olive is crushed. It is the only way to get it, so if we want it, we must be willing to be crushed.

2. **Myrrh**

a. Exodus 30:23 – *"Take thou also unto thee principal spices, of pure myrrh five hundred shekels..."* – Notice that the myrrh was to be pure

b. The Hebrew word for myrrh is *mowr* – distilling in drops, or to drop from;from the Hebrew root word *marar* – to be bitter. – This speaks to us of the bitter experiences we have in this life.

c. What myrrh means:

1) The fragrance of the Lord – Psalms 45:8 – *"All thy garments smell of myrrh, and aloes, and cassia, out of the ivory palaces, whereby they have made thee glad."* – It is part of the ingredients that make up God's fragrance; surely Jesus had some truly bitter experiences

a) Song of Solomon 1:13 – *"A bundle of myrrh is my wellbeloved unto me; he shall lie all night betwixt my breasts."*

b) Song of Solomon 3:6 – *"Who is this that cometh out of the wilderness like pillars of smoke, perfumed with myrrh and frankincense, with all powders of the merchant?"* – Notice what the Bride smells like.

c) Song of Solomon 5:5 – *"I rose up to open to my beloved; and my hands dropped with myrrh, and my fingers with sweet smelling myrrh, upon the handles of the lock."*

All of the above Scriptures speak of an interaction with God and myrrh. We get it by spending time with Him in His presence. Medically speaking, myrrh was used to take out soreness. In the realm of the spirit, there is no greater healing balm, when you are sore from the sin, the world, warfare, etc., than His Holy Presence!

2) Myrrh speaks of bitterness – For us to breakthrough into the precious fragrance of God, there are bitter experiences we must go through. If we want the anointing, of which myrrh is a spice, we will face things in life that will either make us bitter or better.

a) Exodus 15:23-25 – *"And when they came to Marah, they could not drink of the waters of Marah, for they were bitter: therefore the name of it was called Marah. And the people murmured against Moses, saying, What shall we drink? And he cried unto the LORD; and the LORD shewed him a tree, which when he had cast into the waters, the waters were made sweet: there he made for them a statute and an ordinance, and there he proved them,"* – God brings us to these places of testing to prove us. He doesn't bring us to bitter experiences just to torment us, but rather that we might overcome and draw out the sweetness of His fragrance. The bitter experience will always be made sweet if we will just hang in there (Proverb 27:7 – *"...but to the hungry soul every bitter thing is sweet."*)

b) Revelation 10:9 – *"And I went unto the angel, and said unto him, Give me the little book. And he said unto me, Take it, and eat it up; and it shall make thy belly bitter, but it shall be in thy mouth sweet as honey."* – The Word of God is the same – sweet to our mouth and bitter in our belly. As we allow it to do its work, the Word will bring forth the precious character (fragrance) of God in our lives.

c) I Samuel 1:9-28 – *"So Hannah rose up after they had eaten in Shiloh, and after they had drunk. Now Eli the priest sat upon a seat by a post of the temple of the LORD. And she was in bitterness of soul, and prayed unto the LORD, and wept sore. And she vowed a vow, and said, O LORD of hosts, if thou wilt indeed look on the affliction of thine handmaid, and remember me, and not forget thine handmaid, but wilt give unto thine handmaid a man child, then I will give him unto the LORD all the days of his life..."*

We must remember in the bitter places of our Christian life that the tomb is really the womb to experience life, His life, and His precious fragrance. Anointing comes through sacrifice! Remember Jesus was anointed before He died (Mark 14:8), but thank God, He also rose again.

3. **Sweet cinnamon**

a. Exodus 30:23 – *"...and of sweet cinnamon half so much, even two hundred and fifty shekels..."*

b. The Hebrew root word for cinnamon means to erect, also upright rolls of cinnamon bark. – this speaks of God trying to erect something or build something in our lives.

c. Song of Solomon 4:12-15 – *"12A garden inclosed is my sister, my spouse; a spring shut up, a fountain sealed. 13Thy plants are an orchard of pomegranates, with pleasant fruits; camphire, with spikenard, 14Spikenard and saffron; calamus and cinnamon, with all trees of frankincense; myrrh and aloes, with all the chief spices: 15A fountain of gardens, a well of living waters, and streams from Lebanon."* – Fruit in the Bride's life (cinnamon)

Here it speaks of fruit in the life of the Bride. It is speaking of her character. Before God can give us of His precious anointing, He will erect a foundation in our lives. We will have a certain measure of fruit. God is building the image of His Son in our lives. The spices in the garden of Song of Solomon are the nature and fruits of the Holy Spirit. The garden enclosed is His bride. He has enclosed, or separated her to do some very important dealing and erecting within her. He is out to make her into His image. Then He will let those precious spices flow out of her to others.

1) Galatians 5:22-23 – *"But the fruit of the Spirit is love, joy, peace, longsuffering, gentleness, goodness, faith, Meekness, temperance: against such there is no law."*
2) John 15:2-5 – *"Every branch in me that beareth not fruit he taketh away: and every branch that beareth fruit, he purgeth it, that it may bring forth more fruit. Now ye are clean through the word which I have spoken unto you. Abide in me, and I in you. As the branch cannot bear fruit of itself, except it abide in the vine; no more can ye, except ye abide in me. I am the vine, ye are the branches: He that abideth in me, and I in him, the same bringeth forth much fruit: for without me ye can do nothing."*
3) John 15:10 – *"If ye keep my commandments, ye shall abide in my love; even as I have kept my Father's commandments, and abide in his love."*
4) Matthew 7:16, 20 – *"Ye shall know them by their fruits. Do men gather grapes of thorns, or figs of thistles?...Wherefore by their fruits ye shall know them."*

4. **Sweet calamus**

a. Scriptural references for "calamus"

1) Song of Solomon 4:14 – *"Spikenard and saffron; calamus and cinnamon, with all trees of frankincense; myrrh and aloes, with all the chief spices:"*
2) Ezekiel 27:19 – *"Dan also and Javan going to and fro occupied in thy fairs: bright iron, cassia, and calamus, were in thy market."*

Calamus is also translated "sweet cane" in Isaiah 43:24 and Jeremiah 6:20. It is a scented cane that is found among lilies. It is reed-like and is very fragrant when it is bruised. The flower petals used to make perfume must be bruised. The Hebrew root word means to erect or create, to procure (obtain) by purchase. Sweet calamus speaks to us of that which God creates or builds in us, that only comes after a time of bruising or dealing. Notice that the fragrance, sweet calamus, gives only when it is bruised. Notice, also you get this when you pay the price for it.

b. Below are examples of this principle

1) Song of Solomon 4:16 – *"Awake, O north wind; and come, thou south; blow upon my garden, that the spices thereof may flow out. Let my beloved come into his garden, and eat his pleasant fruits."* – The north wind in the scripture speaks of judgment or the dealings of God. Notice the spices do not flow out until a mixture of judgment and peace (the south wind) blows upon this garden.

2) Mark 14:22 – *"And as they did eat, Jesus took bread, and blessed, and brake it, and gave to them, and said, Take, eat: this is my body."*

a) Matthew 14:19 – *"And he commanded the multitude to sit down on the grass, and took the five loaves, and the two fishes, and looking up to heaven, he blessed, and brake, and gave the loaves to his disciples, and the disciples to the multitude."*

We are like that bread He took, blessed, broke, and then gave away. He cannot use us to feed others until we have been blessed (we have grown up in Him, fruit, spices, his blessings, his provision) and then He must break us so that these things He has so freely given to us become His nature within us. Then, only then, can He give us to others.

5. **Cassia**

a. Exodus 30:24 – *"And of cassia five hundred shekels, after the shekel of the sanctuary..."*
b. There are two Hebrew words for cassia: the first means to strip off, to scrape, to purge (Psalm 45:8), and the second means to contract; to bend the body in deference (submission to yielding to, or in courteous regard deferring to another) to stoop, (Exodus 30:24, Ezekiel 27:19) – Once again this ingredient speaks to us of a stripping off, a purging. Also to be bent or broken so that we are humbled by Him into submission.

c. Cassia speaks to us of :

1) The fragrance of the Lord, Psalms 45:8 – *"All thy garments smell of myrrh, and aloes, and cassia, out of the ivory palaces, whereby they have made thee glad."* – His anointing carries a fragrance

2) Of purging and the putting off of the old man; it speaks to us of the stripping off of our old life and nature and of putting on His nature.

a) Malachi 3:3 – *"And he shall sit as a refiner and purifer of silver: and he shall purify the sons of Levi, and purge them as gold and silver, that they may offer unto the LORD an offering in righteousness."* – The words purify and purge in this verse are the same Hebrew word; God is going to purge and purify a people for His name, those that will have God's anointing will allow Him to do this.
b) Isaiah 1:25-26 – *"And I will turn my hand upon thee, and purely purge away thy dross, and take away all thy tin: And I will restore thy judges as at the first, and thy counsellers as at the beginning: afterward thou shalt be called, The city of righteousness, the faithful city."*

c) Titus 2:14 – "*Who gave himself for us, that he might redeem us from all iniquity, and purify unto himself a peculiar people, zealous of good works.*" – the Greek word for purify is the same Greek word that elsewhere is translated purge. He is purifying unto Himself "a peculiar people".
d) John 15:2 – "*Every branch in me that beareth not fruit he taketh away: and every branch that beareth fruit, he purgeth it, that it may bring forth more fruit.*"

3) It speaks of worship and a bended heart, bowed down to Him; the word for worship itself means to fall prostrate, to bend, etc. Psalms 95:6 – "*O come, let us worship and bow down: let us kneel before the LORD our maker.*" – If someone is going to have the anointing, they must be a worshipper; they must love His presence, and they must love Him more than anything else.

4) It also speaks of one who has a broken heart, a bowed heart, it speaks of meekness (teach-ability); If someone is going to have the anointing, he must be teachable, and he must have a humble and broken spirit. His will has been broken and he is now submitted to God

a) Proverbs 5:1 – "*My son, attend unto my wisdom, and bow thine ear to my understanding:*"
b) Proverbs 22:17 – "*Bow down thine ear, and hear the words of the wise, and apply thine heart unto my knowledge.*"
c) Isaiah 66:2 – "*For all those things hath mine hand made, and those things have been, saith the LORD: but to this man will I look, even to him that is poor and of a contrite spirit, and trembleth at my word.*"
d) Isaiah 57:15 – "*For thus saith the high and lofty One that inhabiteth eternity, whose name is Holy; I dwell in the high and holy place, with him also that is of a contrite and humble spirit, to revive the spirit of the humble, and to revive the heart of the contrite ones.*"
e) Psalms 51:17 – "*The sacrifices of God are a broken spirit: a broken and a contrite heart, O God, thou wilt not despise.*" – contrite in Hebrew means crushed

5) The definition for cassia is submission and humility, and this only happens as God purges us (II Corinthians 7:1 – "*Having therefore these promises, dearly beloved, let us cleanse ourselves from all filthiness of the flesh and spirit, perfecting holiness in the fear of God.*")

III. Why We Need the Anointing?

A. It gives revelation and teaches us

1. Exodus 25:6 – "*Oil for the light, spices for anointing oil, and for sweet incense,*" – It takes the anointing to uncover our eyes that we might see into the realm of the supernatural to understand the mysteries of God.

a. Revelation 3:18 – "*...and anoint thine eyes with eyesalve, that thou mayest see.*"
b. John 9:11 – "*He answered and said, A man that is called Jesus made clay, and anointed mine eyes, and said unto me, Go to the pool of Siloam, and wash: and I went and washed, and I received sight.*"
c. I John 2:27 – "*But the anointing which ye have received of him abideth in you, and ye need not that any man teach you: but as the same anointing teacheth you of all things, and is truth, and is no lie, and even as it hath taught you, ye shall abide in him.*"
d. Isaiah 61:1 – "*The Spirit of the Lord GOD is upon me; because the LORD hath anointed me to preach good tidings unto the meek; he hath sent me to bind up the brokenhearted, to*

proclaim liberty to the captives, and the opening of the prison to them that are bound;"

e. Psalms 132:17 – *"There will I make the horn of David to bud: I have ordained a lamp for mine anointed."*

2. The Spirit is the anointing and He only can reveal the deep things of God.

   a. Matthew 16:17 – *"And Jesus answered and said unto him, Blessed art thou, Simon Barjona: for flesh and blood hath not revealed it unto thee, but my Father which is in heaven."*
   b. Luke 2:26 – *"And it was revealed unto him by the Holy Ghost, that he should not see death, before he had seen the Lord's Christ."* (Simeon)
   c. I Corinthians 2:9-12 – *"But as it is written, Eye hath not seen, nor ear heard, neither have entered into the heart of man, the things which God hath prepared for them that love him. But God hath revealed them unto us by his Spirit: for the Spirit searcheth all things, yea, the deep things of God. For what man knoweth the things of a man, save the spirit of man which is in him? even so the things of God knoweth no man, but the Spirit of God. Now we have received, not the spirit of the world, but the spirit which is of God; that we might know the things that are freely given to us of God."* – He is the great teacher (John 14:26)
   d. I John 2:20, 27 – *"But ye have an unction from the Holy One, and ye know all things...But the anointing which ye have received of him abideth in you, and ye need not that any man teach you: but as the same anointing teacheth you of all things, and is truth, and is no lie, and even as it hath taught you, ye shall abide in him."*

3. It delivers us – It is God's anointing that breaks the yoke of bondage and oppression in every life.

   a. Isaiah 10:27 – *"...the yoke shall be destroyed because of the anointing."*
   b. Acts 10:38 – *"How God anointed Jesus of Nazareth with the Holy Ghost and with power: who went about doing good, and healing all that were oppressed of the devil; for God was with him."*
   c. Luke 4:18-19 – *"The Spirit of the Lord is upon me, because he hath anointed me to preach the gospel to the poor; he hath sent me to heal the brokenhearted, to preach deliverance to the captives, and recovering of sight to the blind, to set at liberty them that are bruised, To preach the acceptable year of the Lord."*
   d. Psalms 68:1-3 – *"Let God arise, let his enemies be scattered: let them also that hate him flee before him. As smoke is driven away, so drive them away: as wax melteth before the fire, so let the wicked perish at the presence of God. But let the righteous be glad; let them rejoice before God: yea, let them exceedingly rejoice."*
   e. Psalms 97:1-5 – *"The LORD reigneth; let the earth rejoice; let the multitude of isles be glad thereof. Clouds and darkness are round about him: righteousness and judgment are the habitation of his throne. A fire goeth before him, and burneth up his enemies round about. His lightnings enlightened the world: the earth saw, and trembled. The hills melted like wax at the presence of the LORD, at the presence of the Lord of the whole earth."*
   f. Isaiah 64:1-5 – *"Oh that thou wouldest rend the heavens, that thou wouldest come down, that the mountains might flow down at thy presence, As when the melting fire burneth, the fire causeth the waters to boil, to make thy name known to thine adversaries, that the nations may tremble at thy presence! When thou didst terrible things which we looked not for, thou camest down, the mountains flowed down at thy presence. For since the beginning of the world men have not heard, nor perceived by the ear, neither hath the eye seen, O God, beside thee, what he hath prepared for him that waiteth for him. Thou meetest him that rejoiceth and worketh righteousness, those that remember thee in thy ways: behold, thou art wroth; for we have sinned: in those is continuance, and we shall be saved."*
   g. Psalms 23:5 – *"Thou preparest a table before me in the presence of mine enemies: thou anointest my head with oil; my cup runneth over."*
   h. Zechariah 4:6 – *"Then he answered and spake unto me, saying, This is the word of the LORD*

unto Zerubbabel, saying, Not by might, nor by power, but by my spirit, saith the LORD of hosts."

i. Nahum 1:2-8, 11-14

4. It sanctifies us

   a. Leviticus 8:12 – *"And he poured of the anointing oil upon Aaron's head, and anointed him, to sanctify him."*
   b. Exodus 29:36 – *"And thou shalt offer every day a bullock for a sin offering for atonement: and thou shalt cleanse the altar, when thou hast made an atonement for it, and thou shalt anoint it, to sanctify it."*
   c. Exodus 40:9 – *"And thou shalt take the anointing oil, and anoint the tabernacle, and all that is therein, and shalt hallow it, and all the vessels thereof: and it shall be holy."*

5. A special call to service or minister

   a. Exodus 30:26 – *"And thou shalt anoint the tabernacle of the congregation therewith, and the ark of the testimony,"*
   b. Isaiah 61:1-3 – *"[1]The Spirit of the Lord GOD is upon me; because the LORD hath anointed me to preach good tidings unto the meek; he hath sent me to bind up the brokenhearted, to proclaim liberty to the captives, and the opening of the prison to them that are bound; [2]To proclaim the acceptable year of the LORD, and the day of vengeance of our God; to comfort all that mourn; [3]To appoint unto them that mourn in Zion, to give unto them beauty for ashes, the oil of joy for mourning, the garment of praise for the spirit of heaviness; that they might be called trees of righteousness, the planting of the LORD, that he might be glorified."*
   c. Acts 10:38 – *"How God anointed Jesus of Nazareth with the Holy Ghost and with power: who went about doing good, and healing all that were oppressed of the devil; for God was with him."*
   d. I Samuel 9:16-17 – Saul
   e. I Samuel 16:1, 3, 12 – David
   f. I Kings 1:34-35 – Solomon
   g. I Kings 19:15-16 – Elisha

6. For healing

   a. James 5:14 – *"Is any sick among you? let him call for the elders of the church; and let them pray over him, anointing him with oil in the name of the Lord:"*
   b. Mark 6:13 – *"And they cast out many devils, and anointed with oil many that were sick, and healed them."*

7. For personal sanctification

   a. II Samuel 12:20 – *"Then David arose from the earth, and washed, and anointed himself, and changed his apparel, and came into the house of the LORD, and worshipped: then he came to his own house; and when he required, they set bread before him, and he did eat."*

8. Brings joy and gladness

   a. Psalms 45:7 – *"Thou lovest righteousness, and hatest wickedness: therefore God, thy God, hath anointed thee with the oil of gladness above thy fellows."*
   b. Psalms 23:5 – *"Thou preparest a table before me in the presence of mine enemies: thou anointest my head with oil; my cup runneth over."*

9. To be our inward witness

a. I John 2:20, 27 – *"But ye have an unction from the Holy One, and ye know all things...But the anointing which ye have received of him abideth in you, and ye need not that any man teach you: but as the same anointing teacheth you of all things, and is truth, and is no lie, and even as it hath taught you, ye shall abide in him."*
b. I John 5:10 – *"He that believeth on the Son of God hath the witness in himself: he that believeth not God hath made him a liar; because he believeth not the record that God gave of his Son."*

10. God takes special care for His anointed

a. Psalms 18:50 – *"Great deliverance giveth he to his king; and sheweth mercy to his anointed, to David, and to his seed for evermore."*
b. Psalms 20:6 – *"Now know I that the LORD saveth his anointed; he will hear him from his holy heaven with the saving strength of his right hand."*
c. I Chronicles 16:22 – *"Saying, Touch not mine anointed, and do my prophets no harm."*

11. The anointing brings persecution

a. Psalms 2:2 – *"The kings of the earth set themselves, and the rulers take counsel together, against the LORD, and against his anointed, saying,"*
b. Psalms 89:50-51 – *"Remember, Lord, the reproach of thy servants; how I do bear in my bosom the reproach of all the mighty people; Wherewith thine enemies have reproached, O LORD; wherewith they have reproached the footsteps of thine anointed."*
c. II Samuel 5:17-18 – *"But when the Philistines heard that they had anointed David king over Israel, all the Philistines came up to seek David; and David heard of it, and went down to the hold. The Philistines also came and spread themselves in the valley of Rephaim."*
d. Acts 4:27-31 – *"[27]For of a truth against thy holy child Jesus, whom thou hast anointed, both Herod, and Pontius Pilate, with the Gentiles, and the people of Israel, were gathered together, [28]For to do whatsoever thy hand and thy counsel determined before to be done. [29]And now, Lord, behold their threatenings: and grant unto thy servants, that with all boldness they may speak thy word, [30]By stretching forth thine hand to heal; and that signs and wonders may be done by the name of thy holy child Jesus. [31]And when they had prayed, the place was shaken where they were assembled together; and they were all filled with the Holy Ghost, and they spake the word of God with boldness."*

12. It prepares us to die (soulishly) – Mark 14:3-9 – *"...[8]She hath done what she could: she is come aforehand to anoint my body to the burying."*

13. It renews and refreshes us

a. Psalms 92:10 – *"But my horn shalt thou exalt like the horn of an unicorn: I shall be anointed with fresh oil."*
b. Ezekiel 16:9 – *"Then washed I thee with water; yea, I throughly washed away thy blood from thee, and I anointed thee with oil."*
c. Acts 3:19 – *"Repent ye therefore, and be converted, that your sins may be blotted out, when the times of refreshing shall come from the presence of the Lord;"*
d. Isaiah 28:11-12 – *"For with stammering lips and another tongue will he speak to this people. To whom he said, This is the rest wherewith ye may cause the weary to rest; and this is the refreshing: yet they would not hear."*

14. Oil was the difference in the bride (Matthew 25:1-13)

a. Virgins are all Christians

b. All went forth to meet the Bridegroom (Jesus)
c. Five were wise and five were foolish
d. Wise took no oil in their vessels
e. All had lamps (place in each of us, our soul, that needs the anointing)
f. Some slept (rested in God) and some slumbered (slothful)
g. Midnight comes, the Bridegroom calls
h. All ten heard it and trimmed their lamps
i. The foolish have no oil for their lamps (can't see Him clearly)
j. Oil cannot be given from one to another (only God – II Corinthians 1:21)

k. Oil must be bought; there is a price for God's anointing

   1) Revelation 3:18 – "*I counsel thee to buy of me gold tried in the fire, that thou mayest be rich; and white raiment, that thou mayest be clothed, and that the shame of thy nakedness do not appear; and anoint thine eyes with eyesalve, that thou mayest see.*"
   2) Proverbs 23:23 – "*Buy the truth, and sell it not; also wisdom, and instruction, and understanding.*"
   3) Matthew 13:46 – "*Who, when he had found one pearl of great price, went and sold all that he had, and bought it.*"
   4) Acts 5 1-3 – they kept back part of the price
   5) II Samuel 24:21-24 – "*[21]And Araunah said, Wherefore is my lord the king come to his servant? And David said, To buy the threshingfloor of thee, to build an altar unto the LORD, that the plague may be stayed from the people. [22]And Araunah said unto David, Let my lord the king take and offer up what seemeth good unto him: behold, here be oxen for burnt sacrifice, and threshing instruments and other instruments of the oxen for wood. [23]All these things did Araunah, as a king, give unto the king. And Araunah said unto the king, The LORD thy God accept thee. [24]And the king said unto Araunah, Nay; but I will surely buy it of thee at a price: neither will I offer burnt offerings unto the LORD my God of that which doth cost me nothing. So David bought the threshingfloor and the oxen for fifty shekels of silver.*"

l. The five foolish went to buy, but the Bridegroom came
m. Now is the time to buy oil
n. Without it we will not be ready to be the bride (Revelation 19:7-9)
o. The door was shut to Brideship
p. The foolish cried, "Open to us"
q. Jesus said, "I <u>know</u> you not"
r. We need to be watching, preparing, and buying oil now

Lesson 16

The Outer Court Defined And Revealed

Tabernacle from Outer Court looking in

I. A Symbolic And Natural Look At The Outer Court

A. The description, Exodus 27:9-21

"9And thou shalt make the court of the tabernacle: for the south side southward there shall be hangings for the court of fine twined linen of an hundred cubits long for one side: 10And the twenty pillars thereof and their twenty sockets shall be of brass; the hooks of the pillars and their fillets shall be of silver. 11And likewise for the north side in length there shall be hangings of an hundred cubits long, and his twenty pillars and their twenty sockets of brass; the hooks of the pillars and their fillets of silver. 12And for the breadth of the court on the west side shall be hangings of fifty cubits: their pillars ten, and their sockets ten. 13And the breadth of the court on the east side eastward shall be fifty cubits. 14The hangings of one side of the gate shall be fifteen cubits: their pillars three, and their sockets three. 15And on the other side shall be hangings fifteen cubits: their pillars three, and their sockets three. 16And for the gate of the court shall be an hanging of twenty cubits, of blue, and purple, and scarlet, and fine twined linen, wrought with needlework: and their pillars shall be four, and their sockets four. 17All the pillars round about the court shall be filleted with silver; their hooks shall be of silver, and their sockets of brass. 18The length of the court shall be an hundred cubits, and the breadth fifty every where, and the height five cubits of fine twined linen, and their sockets of brass. 19All the vessels of the tabernacle in all the service thereof, and all the pins thereof, and all the pins of the court, shall be of brass. 20And thou shalt command the children of Israel, that they bring thee pure oil olive beaten for the light, to cause the lamp to burn always. 21In the tabernacle of the congregation without the vail, which is before the testimony, Aaron and his sons shall order it from evening to morning before the LORD: it shall be a statute for ever unto their generations on the behalf of the children of Israel."

1. The court was a space enclosed around the Tabernacle itself, for the use of the priests and Levites in their ministry. It always faced the east.
2. The gate of the court was on the east side.
3. The first encampment was in front or north of Mt. Sinai.
4. This outer court of the tabernacle was 100 cubits long and 50 cubits wide. (150 ft. long and 75 ft. wide)
5. The court was not covered. Only natural light existed here.
6. The outer court speaks of the law age.

B. Materials used and their revelation

1. Fine twined linen – Linen represents righteousness of God, also white meaning purity and innocence. There was no room for any unrighteousness or un-innocent ones. This was God's place. He wanted this holy and righteous covering to surround the tabernacle. God's righteous presence surrounds His people. It also shuts out all sinners.

   a. Revelation 19:8 – *"And to her was granted that she should be arrayed in fine linen, clean and white: for the fine linen is the righteousness of saints."*
   b. Ezekiel 44:17-18 – *"[17]And it shall come to pass, that when they enter in at the gates of the inner court, they shall be clothed with linen garments; and no wool shall come upon them, whiles they minister in the gates of the inner court, and within. [18]They shall have linen bonnets upon their heads, and shall have linen breeches upon their loins; they shall not gird themselves with any thing that causeth sweat."*
   c. Leviticus 16:4 – *"He shall put on the holy linen coat, and he shall have the linen breeches upon his flesh, and shall be girded with a linen girdle, and with the linen mitre shall he be attired: these are holy garments; therefore shall he wash his flesh in water, and so put them on."*
   d. II Chronicles 5:12 – *"Also the Levites which were the singers, all of them of Asaph, of Heman, of Jeduthun, with their sons and their brethren, being arrayed in white linen, having cymbals and psalteries and harps, stood at the east end of the altar, and with them an hundred and twenty priests sounding with trumpets:)"*

2. Sixty pillars around the court

   a. Made of shittim wood
   b. Were probably round
   c. Their diameter was ¼ cubit or about 5 inches
   d. All the same size
   e. Twenty sockets of brass
   f. Hooks and fillets of silver
   g. South side

Of course all of these items find their fulfillment in Jesus as well as for us as His people.

   h. Understanding these by revelation

      1) Sixty is the number for pride. This also represents 60 men on Joseph's side from Adam to Christ
      2) Pillars speak of our foundation
      3) Wood speaks of our humanity
      4) Round represents eternal
      5) 5 inches – Five is the number for grace
      6) Same size represents balance

7) Brass is the color for judgment
8) Silver in scripture represents redemption
9) South speaks of prosperity
10) North speaks of judgment
11) West represents going away from the Lord
12) Fifty cubits speaks of Jubilee
13) Ten cubits speaks of law or Word
14) Fifteen cubits represents rest, acts of grace
15) Three pillars speaks of the Godhead
16) Twenty pillars speaks of expectancy

What does this mean? We humbly come expectantly to God's house, where our pride must be brought low to receive from Him. His foundation is redemption. He judges our soul by His grace, and gives us eternal life and then seeks to bring balance to us as we enter into His dealings of judgment and prosperity. As we start our walk with God, there will be temptations in this outer court with no supernatural light, so the Godhead seeks to bring us to our jubilee, by the Word and acts of grace.

C. The outer court contained two pieces of furniture – two is the number for witness and separation. This is the place where our walk with God begins. Everyone must come this way.

1. Brass Altar – Salvation
2. Laver – Sanctification and holiness

D. The gate of the court, Exodus 27:16 – *"And for the gate of the court shall be an hanging of twenty cubits, of blue, and purple, and scarlet, and fine twined linen, wrought with needlework: and their pillars shall be four, and their sockets four."*

1. Twenty cubits – numbers means expectancy
2. Blue – all things heavenly
3. Purple – royalty
4. Scarlet – suffering
5. Fine twined linen – righteousness worked into our lives by the Holy Spirit.
6. Wrought with needlework – this is the intense and often work, once again, by the Holy Spirit as he takes our old human nature and begins to change it into God's divine nature
7. Pillars – our foundation
8. Silver – our redemption
9. Four – number of creation
10. Brass sockets – judgment

What does all this mean to us spiritually, and what revelation does this gate hold? We as His new creation must be founded solidly in Him. Our foundation is rooted in His redemption, which begins with judgment on our sin. There is no other way to enter in other than to allow God to deal with our sin.

11. Revelation of the gate in Scripture - Entering at this gate will begin our walk with God. There is only one path to God and that's through Jesus.

    a. A gate is like a door; it's an entrance into something, or a door that is shut to us.
    b. Luke 13:24 – *"Strive to enter in at the strait gate: for many, I say unto you, will seek to enter in, and shall not be able."*
    c. Matthew 7:14 – *"Because strait is the gate, and narrow is the way, which leadeth unto life, and few there be that find it."*
    d. Jesus is our gate and our door.

1) John 10:7, 9 – "[7]*Then said Jesus unto them again, Verily, verily, I say unto you, I am the door of the sheep...*[9]*I am the door: by me if any man enter in, he shall be saved, and shall go in and out, and find pasture.*"
2) Proverbs 8:33-35 – "[33]*Hear instruction, and be wise, and refuse it not.* [34]*Blessed is the man that heareth me, watching daily at my gates, waiting at the posts of my doors.* [35]*For whoso findeth me findeth life, and shall obtain favour of the LORD.*"

e. Our walk with God is called many things

1) Matthew 7:14 – it is the narrow way
2) Proverbs 4:18 – path of the just
3) Psalms 16:11, Proverbs 2:19 – path of life
4) Psalms 23:3 – paths of righteousness
5) Psalms 25:10 – paths of mercy and truth
6) Psalms 65:11 – paths drop fatness
7) Jeremiah 6:16 – the old paths wherein is the good way
8) Isaiah 35:8 – highway of holiness
9) Hebrews 12:1 – the race (Ecclesiastes 9:11, I Corinthians 9:24)
10) Philippians 3:14 – "*I press toward the mark for the prize of the high calling of God in Christ Jesus.*" Other translations: "*...I strain to reach the end of the race*", "*...with the goal in view, I press on*"
11) I Kings 19:7 – the journey
12) Job 28:7 – path which no fowl or vulture, or fierce lion or lion's whelps (these are demonic spirits) have not seen, trodden or passed by it.
13) John 14:6 – Jesus is the Way, the Truth, and the Life
14) Psalm 77:19 – path that we don't know (Isaiah 42:16)
15) Psalm 27:11 – a plain path
16) Isaiah 30:21 – walk in the way (Colossians 2:6, Joel 2:7-8)

f. The gate was on the east side – east in scripture speaks of the coming of the Lord.

g. Because this gate represents the beginning of our walk, we must know there is salvation in none other than the Lord Jesus Christ.

1) Acts 4:11-12 – "[11]*This is the stone which was set at nought of you builders, which is become the head of the corner.* [12]*Neither is there salvation in any other: for there is none other name under heaven given among men, whereby we must be saved.*"
2) Acts 2:37-41 – "[37]*Now when they heard this, they were pricked in their heart, and said unto Peter and to the rest of the apostles, Men and brethren, what shall we do?* [38]*Then Peter said unto them, Repent, and be baptized every one of you in the name of Jesus Christ for the remission of sins, and ye shall receive the gift of the Holy Ghost.* [39]*For the promise is unto you, and to your children, and to all that are afar off, even as many as the Lord our God shall call.* [40]*And with many other words did he testify and exhort, saying, Save yourselves from this untoward generation.* [41]*Then they that gladly received his word were baptized: and the same day there were added unto them about three thousand souls.*"
3) John 14:6 – "*Jesus saith unto him, I am the way, the truth, and the life: no man cometh unto the Father, but by me.*"
4) John 10:7-18
5) Ephesians 2:11-22
6) Colossians 1:13-21
7) Hebrews 1:1-3 – "[1]*God, who at sundry times and in divers manners spake in time past unto the fathers by the prophets,* [2]*Hath in these last days spoken unto us by his Son, whom he hath appointed heir of all things, by whom also he made the worlds;* [3]*Who*

being the brightness of his glory, and the express image of his person, and upholding all things by the word of his power, when he had by himself purged our sins, sat down on the right hand of the Majesty on high;"

8) I Timothy 1:15 – *"This is a faithful saying, and worthy of all acceptation, that Christ Jesus came into the world to save sinners; of whom I am chief."*
9) John 6:40, 47-48, 53 – *"And this is the will of him that sent me, that every one which seeth the Son, and believeth on him, may have everlasting life: and I will raise him up at the last day...[47]Verily, verily, I say unto you, He that believeth on me hath everlasting life. [48]I am that bread of life...[53]Then Jesus said unto them, Verily, verily, I say unto you, Except ye eat the flesh of the Son of man, and drink his blood, ye have no life in you."*
10) John 7:37-39 – *"[37]In the last day, that great day of the feast, Jesus stood and cried, saying, If any man thirst, let him come unto me, and drink. [38]He that believeth on me, as the scripture hath said, out of his belly shall flow rivers of living water. [39](But this spake he of the Spirit, which they that believe on him should receive: for the Holy Ghost was not yet given; because that Jesus was not yet glorified.)"*
11) John 3:14-18 – *"[14]And as Moses lifted up the serpent in the wilderness, even so must the Son of man be lifted up: [15]That whosoever believeth in him should not perish, but have eternal life. [16]For God so loved the world, that he gave his only begotten Son, that whosoever believeth in him should not perish, but have everlasting life. [17]For God sent not his Son into the world to condemn the world; but that the world through him might be saved. [18]He that believeth on him is not condemned: but he that believeth not is condemned already, because he hath not believed in the name of the only begotten Son of God."*
12) Matthew 11:28 – *"Come unto me, all ye that labour and are heavy laden, and I will give you rest."*
13) Hebrews 10:5-7 – *"[5]Wherefore when he cometh into the world, he saith, Sacrifice and offering thou wouldest not, but a body hast thou prepared me: [6]In burnt offerings and sacrifices for sin thou hast had no pleasure. [7]Then said I, Lo, I come (in the volume of the book it is written of me,) to do thy will, O God."*
14) Romans 6:23 – *"For the wages of sin is death; but the gift of God is eternal life through Jesus Christ our Lord."*
15) Luke 2:11 – *"For unto you is born this day in the city of David a Saviour, which is Christ the Lord."*
16) Acts 13:38-39 – *"[38]Be it known unto you therefore, men and brethren, that through this man is preached unto you the forgiveness of sins: [39]And by him all that believe are justified from all things, from which ye could not be justified by the law of Moses."*
17) Romans 5:1-2, 8-11 – *"[1]Therefore being justified by faith, we have peace with God through our Lord Jesus Christ: [2]By whom also we have access by faith into this grace wherein we stand, and rejoice in hope of the glory of God...[8]But God commendeth his love toward us, in that, while we were yet sinners, Christ died for us. [9]Much more then, being now justified by his blood, we shall be saved from wrath through him. [10]For if, when we were enemies, we were reconciled to God by the death of his Son, much more, being reconciled, we shall be saved by his life. [11]And not only so, but we also joy in God through our Lord Jesus Christ, by whom we have now received the atonement."*
18) Romans 3:23, 26 – *"For all have sinned, and come short of the glory of God...[26]To declare, I say, at this time his righteousness: that he might be just, and the justifier of him which believeth in Jesus."*
19) John 1:29 – *"The next day John seeth Jesus coming unto him, and saith, Behold the Lamb of God, which taketh away the sin of the world."*
20) I Corinthians 5:7 – *"Purge out therefore the old leaven, that ye may be a new lump, as ye are unleavened. For even Christ our passover is sacrificed for us:"*
21) I Corinthians 1:30 – *"But of him are ye in Christ Jesus, who of God is made unto us wisdom, and righteousness, and sanctification, and redemption:"*

22) I Peter 1:3, 18-19 – "[3]*Blessed be the God and Father of our Lord Jesus Christ, which according to his abundant mercy hath begotten us again unto a lively hope by the resurrection of Jesus Christ from the dead...*[18]*Forasmuch as ye know that ye were not redeemed with corruptible things, as silver and gold, from your vain conversation received by tradition from your fathers;* [19]*But with the precious blood of Christ, as of a lamb without blemish and without spot:*"
23) Colossians 2:6-10 – "[6]*As ye have therefore received Christ Jesus the Lord, so walk ye in him:* [7]*Rooted and built up in him, and stablished in the faith, as ye have been taught, abounding therein with thanksgiving.* [8]*Beware lest any man spoil you through philosophy and vain deceit, after the tradition of men, after the rudiments of the world, and not after Christ.* [9]*For in him dwelleth all the fulness of the Godhead bodily.* [10]*And ye are complete in him, which is the head of all principality and power:*"
24) John 1:1-5, 12-14, 17 – "[1]*In the beginning was the Word, and the Word was with God, and the Word was God.* [2]*The same was in the beginning with God.* [3]*All things were made by him; and without him was not any thing made that was made.* [4]*In him was life; and the life was the light of men.* [5]*And the light shineth in darkness; and the darkness comprehended it not...*[12]*But as many as received him, to them gave he power to become the sons of God, even to them that believe on his name:* [13]*Which were born, not of blood, nor of the will of the flesh, nor of the will of man, but of God.* [14]*And the Word was made flesh, and dwelt among us, (and we beheld his glory, the glory as of the only begotten of the Father,) full of grace and truth...*[17]*For the law was given by Moses, but grace and truth came by Jesus Christ.*"
25) Revelation 5:1-10
26) Matthew 1:21-23 – "[21]*And she shall bring forth a son, and thou shalt call his name JESUS: for he shall save his people from their sins.* [22]*Now all this was done, that it might be fulfilled which was spoken of the Lord by the prophet, saying,* [23]*Behold, a virgin shall be with child, and shall bring forth a son, and they shall call his name Emmanuel, which being interpreted is, God with us.*"

Lesson 17

The Power Of The Atoning Blood

I. A Look At The Blood And Its Power

A. Blood speaks – The word *blood* occurs 447 times in Scripture. Especially frequently in Leviticus, which deals with how we can approach God, and our way into the holiest. In the book of Hebrews, the *blood* is spoken of nearly 100 times, almost always a commentary on Leviticus.

1. Blood contains the essence of human and animal life.
2. The life of our flesh is in (or carried by) the blood.

a. Leviticus 17:11 – *"For the life of the flesh is in the blood: and I have given it to you upon the altar to make an atonement for your souls: for it is the blood that maketh an atonement for the soul."*

When God created man, He molded his body out of the ground. He then breathed into man the breath of life. He somehow breathed into His creation, His own spiritual life and that life was held in the substance we call blood. Blood is not life; it carries life. We humans can only live if this ingredient flows through our veins. Life itself is spiritual, but it must be carried by something natural.

b. I John 5:8 – *"And there are three that bear witness in earth, the spirit, and the water, and the blood: and these three agree in one."* – three witnesses on earth, the water, spirit and blood; The Word by the Holy Spirit is effectual in those who received Him. The blood witnesses to the Father we are now justified. Atonement has been made.

3. Leviticus 17:11-14 – God counts blood as a sacred thing, which He gave to both man and animal. It was forbidden to eat flesh from which the blood had not been removed completely. This was so important to the Lord that the penalty for it was being, "cut off from among his people". This penalty of lost fellowship was very strong.
4. Genesis 4:10 – *"The Lord said, what hast thou done? The voice of thy brother's blood crieth unto me from the ground."* This tells us that the life that was in Abel's blood did not cease after he was murdered. Abel's blood was crying out for vengeance.

a. Hebrews 12:24 – *"...the blood of sprinkling that speaketh better things than that of Abel..."* Abel's blood cried out for justice. Jesus' blood cries out for mercy. This is such a powerful truth, to know that the incorruptible, spotless, pure, and precious blood of Christ Jesus will never stop crying out. Not until this world ends, will it stop crying out to the Father as the Lamb of God for mercy for His creation. The blood is still crying from the mercy seat today because Jesus *"...ever liveth to make intercession for us."*

B. History of blood sacrifices

1. It started way back in the beginning when Adam and Eve sinned

a. Genesis 3:21 – Adam and Eve tried to use fig leaves to cover their nakedness (Verse 7). The King James Version of the Bible uses the word *apron*, which in the Hebrew means, a belt, girdle, armour. It comes from a root word that means to gird on, to be afraid, or to restrain on every side. This was the beginning of religion. Man trying to do only what God can do. Only blood can make atonement for your soul. He made them skins.

1) Leviticus 17:11 – *"For the life of the flesh is in the blood: and I have given it to you upon the altar to make an atonement for your souls: for it is the blood that maketh an atonement for the soul."*

2) Hebrews 9:22 – *"...without shedding of blood is no remission."* – Greek word for remission means – freedom, paid on, forgiveness or release from bondage – it comes from a root that means to send off; Other translations:

"...unless blood is shed, there is no forgiveness to be obtained..."
"...unless blood is poured out, nothing is forgiven..."
"...there is neither release from sin and its guilt nor the remission of the due and merited punishment from sins..."
"...no blood shed, no remission of sin..."

2. Genesis 4:2-4 – Abel, having learned from his Father about sacrificing and himself being a shepherd, offered a lamb and the best parts of the lamb as an offering. The Bible says, *"...God had respect unto Abel and his offering..."* – The Hebrew word for offering means – to apportion, bestow, a donation; Other translations:

"...The Lord looked with favor..."
"...took notice of Abel..."
"...approved of Abel..."
"...the Lord was pleased..."

God respected it because sacrificing and the shedding of blood is a God ordained principle. How sad it is that those who walk and try to please God are persecuted by their brothers. It has been and always will be this way.

3. Genesis 8:20-22

Noah offered these blood sacrifices to the Lord once the ark rested. What the Bible says here is very important, *"...and the Lord smelled a sweet savour: and the Lord said in his heart..."*

This obviously touched God very deeply. After having judged the earth and wiping all of them out, with the exception of Noah and his family, this offering of repentance and thanksgiving caused God to say, *"...neither will I again smite any more every living thing..."* Blood atones and blood changes things. This principle was being established on the earth. If man wanted to repent or bless God, this was the way he should do it.

You might ask why? Remember Jesus is the *"Lamb slain from the foundation of the world..."* (Revelation 13:8) God had already set the precedent, and those that would love Him and walk with Him understood this was His principle. In Genesis 22, when God called upon Abraham to offer Isaac, this principle was further validated. When God saw that Abraham was willing, He poured out His blessing upon him. Hebrews 11:19 tells us Abraham believed God would raise him up from the dead. Now a people is beginning to understand that God requires a sacrifice. He requires that blood be shed. The truth is that God never asks a man to do something that He isn't prepared to do also. He was hinting to the earth that a lamb had already been slain for them.

4. The Passover

a. Exodus 12:1-11 – A lamb for a house

b. Exodus 12:13-14

1) Blood shall be a token
2) When I see the blood
3) I will pass over you

c. Exodus 12:21-24

1) Bunch of hyssop
2) Dip it in the blood
3) Strike the lintel and door post
4) When He seeth the blood
5) The Lord will pass over
6) And will not suffer the destroyer to come into your houses to smite you.

Here we see that the blood not only connects us with God (a blood covenant), but also delivers us from death. The blood brings protection from God to all that have this revelation. He also established this as a feast, a memorial for them to do from then on.

5. Exodus 23:18 – *"Thou shalt not offer the blood of my sacrifice with unleavened bread; neither shall the fat of my sacrifice remain until the morning."*

The Lord is saying here, *"the blood of my sacrifice"*. In other words, God required this shedding of blood. It belongs to Him. What was set in motion here was to be a continual thing throughout Israel's history. God required blood from them, and they would sacrifice animals unto Him.

6. Blood of bulls and goats – Exodus 24:3-8

Moses poured half of the blood, shed from burnt offering, on the altar, and then he sprinkled the people. Israel and God had just made a blood covenant. This was before the Tabernacle had been built. It showed Israel that blood and a sacrifice were required by God. Thus the beginning for the principle of blood sacrifices to the Lord. Blood will be the way. Blood must be shed.

7. Exodus 29:1-3, 10-29 – Cleansing the priests; The blood shed here was to reveal things.

a. *"to hallow them"* – Hallow in Hebrew means – to be or make clean, to sanctify
b. *"Aaron and his sons shall put their hands upon the head of the bullock."* – This was for forgiveness of their sins.

c. Blood was put on

1) The horns of the altar – This speaks of the blood covering the whole earth as well as sanctifying the priests to minister at the altar.
2) The rest of the blood was poured out at the bottom of the altar.

d. Then a ram was brought and Aaron and his sons laid their hands upon the head of the ram.
e. The blood was then sprinkled around and on the altar.
f. The other ram was brought and Aaron and his sons, once again laid their hands on it.
g. The ram was then killed.

h. Blood was to be placed upon the:

1) Tip of the right ear
2) Thumb of right hand
3) Upon the great toe of right foot
4) Then sprinkled upon the altar round about
5) Then a mixture of blood and oil sprinkled on the priests and their garments
6) Then God says they shall be holy

We see that no one can speak or minister for or to Him without blood being shed and placed upon our ear, (to be able to hear from the Lord), on the thumb (to be able to do the work of the Lord), on the toe (to be able to walk with the Lord), and then sprinkled all around the altar (signifying that the altar, or the place they were standing, spiritually speaking, was sanctified). It is not just the blood but blood mixed with oil, (later oil is to be placed on the priests ear, thumb and toe). It takes the blood of Jesus and the anointing of the Holy Ghost to hallow, or make us holy.

8. Exodus 29:36 – This was to happen every day. They offered a bullock for a sin offering for atonement and cleansing. Atonement in Hebrew means – to cover over, to propitiate, to condone, reconcile

9. Atonement for Israel obtained by blood

    a. Leviticus 1:2-5

        1) Israel was to bring of the herd or flock an animal without blemish (symbolically this is speaking of the Lamb of God without spot)
        2) Then they were to put their hands on the head of the animal and kill it. It then made atonement for him. This blood indicated the substitution of the animal's blood for that of the sinner.

10. Joshua 2:4, 9-17, 18 (Joshua 6:23-24)

This is the story of Rahab, the harlot who helped Israel. When Israel came to attack, they promised that neither she nor any of her family would be hurt as long as she placed in the window the piece of <u>scarlet</u> thread. Scarlet is blood red; this is a type of the blood. God spared this lowly harlot because she believed in him. Deliverance truly comes through the blood.

11. I Kings 8:5 – As Solomon was preparing to dedicate the temple, he and all of the children of Israel were sacrificing before the Ark of the Covenant. They were sacrificing sheep and oxen that could not be numbered for multitude. Other translations:

    "*...sacrificing sheep and oxen, so many they could not be numbered or counted.*"

The revelation for us is that at the dedication of God's final house (which Solomon's temple represents), blood will be everywhere. So this tells us that when the last days are fully come, there will be a remembrance of His blood. We come in desperate and needy for blood (Adam). We will go out a people purchased by the precious blood of Christ. A people who will ever be thankful for what our Precious Lord did. Jesus is our one and only saviour. Throughout eternity we will ever be praising Him.

II. The Blood Of the Lamb of God – Though Israel had to do this often, and it only covered their sins, it was pointing to a day when the Messiah would come and redeem them.

    A. John 1:29 – Jesus was the Lamb of God, given to "*...taketh away the sin of the world...*" For Jesus, in one offering, has obtained eternal redemption for us.

        1. Hebrews 9:11-14 – Neither by the blood of bulls and goats and calves, but by His own blood he entered once into the holy place, having obtained eternal redemption for us! How much more shall the blood of Christ, "*...offered himself without spot to God, purge your conscience.*" The blood of animals was now no longer acceptable. Only the one time sacrifice of Jesus, the shedding of His blood is acceptable.

        2. Hebrews 10:1-4

a. The law was a shadow (or a type).
b. Those sacrifices which was offered year by year could never make them perfect.
c. It is not possible for the blood of an animal to take away sins. If so, they would not have been conscious of their sins.

3. Hebrews 10:5-10

   a. God was not interested any more in sacrifice and offerings that were offered by the law.
   b. But he had prepared the body of his own son.
   c. We are sanctified through the offering of the body of Jesus Christ <u>once for all</u>.

4. Hebrews 10:14-22

   a. By one offering he hath perfected for ever them that are sanctified.
   b. This is the new covenant.
   c. Because of Jesus' sacrifice, he will never remember our sins and iniquities any more.
   d. Where remission of these is, there is no more need for sacrifice and offering for sin.
   e. We can now enter boldly into the most holy place by the blood of Jesus.
   f. We can draw near now because our hearts have been sprinkled from an evil conscience by his blood.

5. I Peter 1:19 – The Greek word for *precious* means – valuable, costly, honored and esteemed. It comes from a root that means value, money paid. We have not been redeemed by corruptible things. But with the precious blood of Christ.

   a. I Corinthians 6:20 – We have been bought with a price. The great substitutionary sacrifice of our blessed and wonderful Lord, on the cross is the price for our salvation. It's hard to even read or write this because when we consider His precious blood, it overwhelms us. All we can do is worship and thank Him. So, as Paul says, the way we can thank Him is to glorify God in our lives.
   b. I Corinthians 7:23

6. Joel 3:21 – He has kept His promise to cleanse our blood, with His own blood.

7. Romans 3:23-25

   a. All have sinned and fallen short of His glory.
   b. Being justified freely through the redemption that is in Jesus Christ.

   c. Whom God set forth to be a propitiation.

      1) Propitiation in Greek means an atoning victim. It is translated as "mercy seat" in Hebrews 9:5. He was the atoning victim. His blood stands for the voluntary giving up of His life, by the shedding of His blood in expiatory sacrifice under divine judgment righteously due to us as sinners. He simply took our place.

         a) I John 2:2 – "*He is the propitiation for our sins: and not for ours only, but also for the sins of the whole world.*" Other translations:

            "*...the one who made personal atonement for our sins...*"
            "*...and he is Himself the atoning sacrifice for our sins...*"
            "*...He in his own person, is the atonement for our sins...*"

b) I John 4:10 – *"Herein is love, not that we loved God, but that He loved us, and sent his Son to be the propitiation for our sins."* Other translations:

"…and sending his Son as an atoning sacrifice for our sins…"
"…to make personal atonement…"

8. I Peter 1:2 – *"…sprinkling of the blood of Jesus Christ…"*

9. Matthew 26:28 (I Corinthians 10:16) – This was the last supper. Here He foretold us of His cross, where his blood will be shed for many for the remission of sins.

   a. I Corinthians 11:25-27 – This is why the communion table is so very important. We remember Him there.

10. John 6:53-56

    a. Without symbolically drinking His blood and eating His flesh, we have no life in us.
    b. *"He that eateth my flesh and drinketh my blood, dwelleth in me, and I in him."*

11. Acts 20:28 – The church was purchased by His own blood.
12. Ephesians 1:7 – Redemption through His blood, the forgiveness of sins
13. Ephesians 2:13 – We who were far off are made nigh by the blood of Christ. (Colossians 1:14)
14. Hebrews 13:12, 20 – "[12]Wherefore Jesus also, that he might sanctify the people with his own blood, suffered without the gate…[20]Now the God of peace, that brought again from the dead our Lord Jesus, that great shepherd of the sheep, through the blood of the everlasting covenant,"
15. I John 1:7 – *"…if we walk in light, as he…and the blood of Jesus Christ his Son cleanseth us from all sin."*
16. I John 5:6-8
17. Revelation 1:5 – *"…unto him that loved us and washed us from our sins in his own blood…"*
20. Colossians 1:20 – Peace has come through the blood of Jesus

B. The future of the Blood of Jesus

1. Revelation 19:13 – When the heavens open He is coming again in a vesture dipped in blood on which is written, "King of Kings and Lord of Lords." Truly he has earned these titles as well as the vesture because of his great and marvelous sacrifice.
2. Zechariah 13:1 – In the last days, a fountain will be opened to God's people. The word *fountain* in Hebrew means, something dug, a source of blood, water or tears. I believe that just as we believe the feasts of Passover, Pentecost, and Tabernacles are to be experienced spiritually, so also shall the Day of Atonement. For all those who have struggled against sin, as long as they kept fighting and repenting, the day will come when we, as His people before His coming, will experience deliverance totally from sin (Proverbs 24:16).

3. Revelation 12:9 – *"…And they overcame him* (satan) *by the blood of the Lamb, and by the word of their testimony."* – Other translations:

   "…because of the blood…"
   "…and they conquered him by the blood of the lamb."
   "…they defeated him by the blood of the lamb."
   "…their victory was due to the blood of the lamb."

Lesson 18

The Brazen Altar

The Brazen Altar

I. Exodus 27:1-8, Exodus 38:1-7

Exodus 27:1-8 – "1 *And thou shalt make an altar of shittim wood, five cubits long, and five cubits broad; the*
altar shall be foursquare: and the height thereof shall be three cubits. 2*And thou shalt make the horns of it upon*
the four corners thereof: his horns shall be of the same: and thou shalt overlay it with brass. 3*And thou shalt*
make his pans to receive his ashes, and his shovels, and his basons, and his fleshhooks, and his firepans: all the
vessels thereof thou shalt make of brass. 4*And thou shalt make for it a grate of network of brass; and upon the*
net shalt thou make four brasen rings in the four corners thereof. 5*And thou shalt put it under the compass of the*
altar beneath, that the net may be even to the midst of the altar. 6*And thou shalt make staves for the altar, staves*
of shittim wood, and overlay them with brass. 7*And the staves shall be put into the rings, and the staves shall be*
upon the two sides of the altar, to bear it. 8*Hollow with boards shalt thou make it: as it was shewed thee in the*
mount, so shall they make it."

Exodus 38:1-7 – "1*And he made the altar of burnt offering of shittim wood: five cubits was the length*
thereof, and five cubits the breadth thereof; it was foursquare; and three cubits the height thereof. 2*And he made*
the horns thereof on the four corners of it; the horns thereof were of the same: and he overlaid it with brass. 3*And*
he made all the vessels of the altar, the pots, and the shovels, and the basons, and the fleshhooks, and the
firepans: all the vessels thereof made he of brass. 4*And he made for the altar a brasen grate of network under the*
compass thereof beneath unto the midst of it. 5*And he cast four rings for the four ends of the grate of brass, to be*
places for the staves. 6*And he made the staves of shittim wood, and overlaid them with brass.* 7*And he put the*
staves into the rings on the sides of the altar, to bear it withal; he made the altar hollow with boards."

A. The following ways the Brazen Altar was referred to in Scripture

1. Exodus 27:1 – Alter of Shittim Wood
2. Exodus 30:28 – Altar of Burnt Offering
3. Exodus 38:30 – Brazen Altar
4. Psalms 43:3-4 – Altar of God
5. Exodus 29:36-44 – The Altar
6. Malachi 1:7-8 – The Table of the Lord
7. Leviticus 1:5 – Altar By The Door Of The Tabernacle

B. Hebrew definition of words

1. Altar – to slay or slaughter; it has a distinct reference to the thought of sacrifice
2. Burnt offering – In Hebrew this means, a step, stairs, or ascending, a mount or to be high; this is interesting in that the brazen altar is the first of many steps ascending into God's presence. Without this step there would be no others.

II. Brazen Altar Speaks of the Cross & the Great Sacrifice of our Saviour Jesus, our Precious Lamb of God

A. This, in one sense, is the most important part of the tabernacle due to the fact of its sacrifice; this was Jesus, our Precious Lamb of God

1. I Peter 1:18-19 – "[18]*Forasmuch as ye know that ye were not redeemed with corruptible things, as silver and gold, from your vain conversation received by tradition from your fathers;* [19]*But with the precious blood of Christ, as of a lamb without blemish and without spot:*"
2. Hebrews 7:27 – "*Who needeth not daily, as those high priests, to offer up sacrifice, first for his own sins, and then for the people's: for this he did once, when he offered up himself.*"
3. Hebrews 9:28 – "*So Christ was once offered to bear the sins of many; and unto them that look for him shall he appear the second time without sin unto salvation.*"

B. The Lamb of God (Exodus 12:5 – Leviticus 1:5)

1. Definitions for Lamb

a. Hebrew for Lamb – pushing out, to dominate, old enough to butt
b. Greek for Lamb – lambkin; from a root, a lamb (male) as strong for lifting, to lift, to take up or away, to raise

2. Scripture showing Jesus as the Lamb of God

a. John 1:29 – "*The next day John seeth Jesus coming unto him, and saith, Behold the Lamb of God, which taketh away the sin of the world.*"
b. I Peter 1:18-19 – "[18]*Forasmuch as ye know that ye were not redeemed with corruptible things, as silver and gold, from your vain conversation received by tradition from your fathers;* [19]*But with the precious blood of Christ, as of a lamb without blemish and without spot:*"
c. Acts 8:32 – "*The place of the scripture which he read was this, He was led as a sheep to the slaughter; and like a lamb dumb before his shearer, so opened he not his mouth:*"
d. Isaiah 53:7 – "*He was oppressed, and he was afflicted, yet he opened not his mouth: he is brought as a lamb to the slaughter, and as a sheep before her shearers is dumb, so he openeth not his mouth.*"
e. Revelation 5:6, 8, 12-13 – "[6]*And I beheld, and, lo, in the midst of the throne and of the four beasts, and in the midst of the elders, stood a Lamb as it had been slain, having seven horns and seven eyes, which are the seven Spirits of God sent forth into all the earth...*[8]*And when he had taken the book, the four beasts and four and twenty elders fell down before the Lamb, having every one of them harps, and golden vials full of odours, which are the prayers of saints...*[12]*Saying with a loud voice, Worthy is the Lamb that was slain to receive power, and riches, and wisdom, and strength, and honour, and glory, and blessing.* [13]*And every creature which is in heaven, and on the earth, and under the earth, and such as are in the sea, and all that are in them, heard I saying, Blessing, and honour, and glory, and power, be unto him that sitteth upon the throne, and unto the Lamb for ever and ever.*"
f. Revelation 7:14, 17 – "[14]*And I said unto him, Sir, thou knowest. And he said to me, These are they which came out of great tribulation, and have washed their robes, and made them white in the blood of the Lamb...*[17]*For the Lamb which is in the midst of the throne shall feed them,*

and shall lead them unto living fountains of waters: and God shall wipe away all tears from their eyes."

g. Revelation 12:11 – "*And they overcame him by the blood of the Lamb, and by the word of their testimony; and they loved not their lives unto the death."*
h. Revelation 14:1, 4, 10 – "[1]*And I looked, and, lo, a Lamb stood on the mount Sion, and with him an hundred forty and four thousand, having his Father's name written in their foreheads...*[4]*These are they which were not defiled with women; for they are virgins. These are they which follow the Lamb whithersoever he goeth. These were redeemed from among men, being the firstfruits unto God and to the Lamb...*[10]*The same shall drink of the wine of the wrath of God, which is poured out without mixture into the cup of his indignation; and he shall be tormented with fire and brimstone in the presence of the holy angels, and in the presence of the Lamb"*
i. Revelation 15:3 – "*And they sing the song of Moses the servant of God, and the song of the Lamb, saying, Great and marvellous are thy works, Lord God Almighty; just and true are thy ways, thou King of saints."*
j. Revelation 19:7, 9 – "[7]*Let us be glad and rejoice, and give honour to him: for the marriage of the Lamb is come, and his wife hath made herself ready...*[9]*And he saith unto me, Write, Blessed are they which are called unto the marriage supper of the Lamb. And he saith unto me, These are the true sayings of God."*
k. Revelation 21:22-23 – "[22]*And I saw no temple therein: for the Lord God Almighty and the Lamb are the temple of it.* [23]*And the city had no need of the sun, neither of the moon, to shine in it: for the glory of God did lighten it, and the Lamb is the light thereof."*
l. Revelation 22:1, 3 – "[1]*And he shewed me a pure river of water of life, clear as crystal, proceeding out of the throne of God and of the Lamb...*[3]*And there shall be no more curse: but the throne of God and of the Lamb shall be in it; and his servants shall serve him:"*
m. Revelation 13:8 – "*And all that dwell upon the earth shall worship him, whose names are not written in the book of life of the Lamb slain from the foundation of the world."*
n. Genesis 22:7-8 – "[7]*And Isaac spake unto Abraham his father, and said, My father: and he said, Here am I, my son. And he said, Behold the fire and the wood: but where is the lamb for a burnt offering?* [8]*And Abraham said, My son, God will provide himself a lamb for a burnt offering: so they went both of them together."*

C. Jesus is the fulfillment of the antitype (Lamb)

1. The "Lamb" was to come for 4 things; our faith does not stand on what we do; our faith stands by the blood of Jesus.

   a. Before you were born, provision was made for you, Revelation 13:8 – "*...the Lamb slain from the foundation of the world"* – His sacrifice was for the whole world
   b. Revelation of the grace of God; God never went to self-assured people, Genesis 4:1-5 – Abel had revelation it is not what we can do for God, but we are under grace
   c. A lamb for every house, Exodus 12:3 – "*Speak ye unto all the congregation of Israel, saying, In the tenth day of this month they shall take to them every man a lamb, according to the house of their fathers, a lamb for an house:"*
   d. A lamb was slain for the nation of Israel, John 11:49-51 – "[49]*And one of them, named Caiaphas, being the high priest that same year, said unto them, Ye know nothing at all,* [50]*Nor consider that it is expedient for us, that one man should die for the people, and that the whole nation perish not.* [51]*And this spake he not of himself: but being high priest that year, he prophesied that Jesus should die for that nation;"*

D. Interesting facts on sheep and the spiritual connotation:

1. Sheep are mentioned more than any other animal in the Bible, 750 times – If they are mentioned so often, they must be the most important thing to Him

2. They feed on grass, woods and shrubs – wood speaks of humanity and how we feed upon the things of this earth (Job 5:7, I Corinthians 3:12)
3. Sheep can go long times without water – allow long periods of not being in the presence of God; they have an ability to carry water for a long time (I Kings 19:8); can survive for a long time on the revelation that you already have; have to be able to go through wilderness; have the ability to fast
4. Their fur (coat) provides a covering for people – eventually the saints will prepare a place for the priests (Isaiah 32:2)
5. They are helpless creatures – can not do anything apart from Jesus (Ezekiel 16:8, Matthew 9:36, Psalms 73:27)
6. They depend on shepherds to lead them to water, pasture, and to fight off other beasts everybody should have a shepherd to protect and lead them (Psalms 23:1-3, Zechariah 2:5).
7. Shepherds had to anoint sheep's faces when they would be bitten by snakes – when you are eating of the Word of God you must be careful of false teachers. The only way to do this is the anointing or the witness of the Holy Spirit. (Ecclesiastes 10:8, 18, James 5:14, Proverbs 24:30-31, Proverbs 25:28).
8. Shepherds have a unique relationship to his sheep; he knows each individually; Jesus knows everything about us and He wants an intimate relationship with us (Isaiah 49:1, II Timothy 2:19).
9. Sheep recognize their shepherd's voice; if you know Him, you will know His voice (John 10:3).
10. Sheep are a model of submissiveness; a sheep is an example of how we should do what our shepherd says to do (John 10:4, James 4:7)
11. The have broad, fat tails – this speaks of slothfulness; Eli was fat, sat down and went blind (I Samuel 3:1-2, 4:18); fat can also mean prosperity
12. They were offered in immense numbers in sacrifice – corporate worship; you can expect to make many sacrifices for Jesus; every sheep ultimately will die
13. Sheep are dumb animals – we must have a shepherd to guide us (Isaiah 53:7, Acts 8:32, Psalms 38:13)
14. They travel in herds or flocks (Jeremiah 10:23)
15. They will follow who ever is in front of them, even over a cliff – most Christians move from church to church or not go to church at all; people who follow false doctrine

E. The Brazen Altar and the Cross of Jesus were terrible things to look at. They are a gruesome picture of death and blood

1. Galatians 3:13 – "*Christ hath redeemed us from the curse of the law, being made a curse for us: for it is written, Cursed is every one that hangeth on a tree:*"
2. Deuteronomy 21:22-23 – "[22]*And if a man have committed a sin worthy of death, and he be to be put to death, and thou hang him on a tree:* [23]*His body shall not remain all night upon the tree, but thou shalt in any wise bury him that day; (for he that is hanged is accursed of God;) that thy land be not defiled, which the LORD thy God giveth thee for an inheritance.*"
3. John 3:14 – "*And as Moses lifted up the serpent in the wilderness, even so must the Son of man be lifted up:*"
4. Isaiah 52:14 – "*As many were astonied at thee; his visage was so marred more than any man, and his form more than the sons of men:*"
5. Isaiah 53 speaks of the Lord's death. This death is plural, "deaths", meaning spirit, soul and body.

III. The Brazen Altar

A. Terms to consider

1. Wood – humanity
2. Altar – sacrifice

3. Brass – judgment
4. Offering – Jesus is the antitype (Lamb, bull, goat, ram)
5. Four corners – four corners of the earth
6. Burnt – type of flesh being destroyed
7. Door – entrance, an opening into something
8. Five – grace
9. Three – resurrection and Godhead
10. Four – creation (John 3:16)

B. Other facts about the brass altar

1. Shittim means, meadows of acacia, also promoters of error
2. The fire to light it came from heaven (Leviticus 9:24)
3. It was to never go out (Leviticus 6:12-13)
4. The altar was a scene of perpetual death. Jesus, however, died for sin only once.
5. It is the first piece of furniture; it is the beginning of what God has for us
6. Before God could have anything to do with man, blood needed to be shed (Genesis 3:22)
7. Blood from altar was applied to every other piece of furniture.
8. Had to be put on the mercy seat

C. Wood – Corruptible humanity (Exodus 38:1-8)

1. Numbers 25:1 – *"And Israel abode in Shittim, and the people began to commit whoredom with the daughters of Moab."* – Left in Shittim, these began to commit whoredoms
2. II Timothy 2:20 – *"But in a great house there are not only vessels of gold and of silver, but also of wood and of earth; and some to honour, and some to dishonour."*

3. Wood is an integral part of the Gospel

a. Jesus died on a wooden cross
b. Genesis 22:6-8 – Isaac carried wood for his own sacrifice, which was a type of our Lord's

D. Five cubits long, five cubits broad; the height shall be three cubits, the altar foursquare

1. The number 5

Five is the number that means the grace of God. It is the most prominent number in the whole Tabernacle. Grace dominates in the dwelling God made for Him and His people. If it wasn't for the grace of God, there would be no Tabernacle nor would there be any pieces of furniture that represents His full salvation. God stamped his grace throughout this structure. The number five also represents the five wounds of Jesus on the cross. Look how many times the number 5 is mentioned. There are many more examples; but this is sufficient to let us know God's grace is abundant toward us:

a. Gate was 20 (4x5) x 5 cubits
b. Door to the Holy Place was 10 X 10 (2x5)
c. There were 5 pillars for the door
d. The veil was 10 X 10 (2x5)
e. There were 120 pins (24 X 5)
f. Outer court measured 20 X 5 X 10 X 5 X 5 cubits
g. There were 60 pillars, chapiters, sockets (12 X5)
h. There were 100sockets of silver (20 X 5)
i. Fifteen bars passing through the boards (3 X 5)
j. Ten linen curtains (2 X 5)
k. The Holy Place measured 20 (4 X 5) X 10 (2X5) X 10 (2 X 5) cubits

l. The whole structure measured 30 (6 X 5) X 10 (2X5) X 10 (2 X 5) cubits

2. The number 3

The number 3 in Scripture represents the Godhead and resurrection. This represents the Godhead and its total involvement in the sacrifice of Jesus. God became man to redeem him. He did this by sacrifice. The height of his sacrifice reaches even to the Godhead, which means what ever it takes, this sacrifice is enough. This number also represents the three days and nights of Jesus' atonement. It also represents the resurrection of Jesus.

3. Foursquare (Revelation 21:10-16)

This speaks to us of the sacrifice reaching to the four corners of the earth. Also, the holy Jerusalem or bride, which descends out of heaven, is foursquare. This means that in the eternal tabernacle the altar will still speak (Revelation 15:1-5). Even there we will still be singing the song of the redeemed. Also, the Golden altar, veil, door, and the Most Holy Place were all foursquare.

4. Other facts about the dimensions of this altar

a. This altar was the largest piece of furniture and all the other pieces could fit inside of it. This tells us that all three phases and aspects of our salvation are all carried and fit into the cross. Everything in God comes out of it. It is the most important.
b. The ark was exactly one half the size of the altar

IV. The Horns, Exodus 27:2 – *"And thou shalt make the horns of it upon the four corners thereof: his horns shall be of the same: and thou shalt overlay it with brass."*

A. Horns are typical of power, refuge, salvation, and anointing

1. Salvation

a. Genesis 22:13 – *"And Abraham lifted up his eyes, and looked, and behold behind him a ram caught in a thicket by his horns: and Abraham went and took the ram, and offered him up for a burnt offering in the stead of his son."* The ram was caught in the thicket by its horns. This ram was to be the salvation sacrifice.
b. Luke 1:69 – *"And hath raised up an horn of salvation for us in the house of his servant David;"*
c. Revelation 5:6 – *"And I beheld, and, lo, in the midst of the throne and of the four beasts, and in the midst of the elders, stood a Lamb as it had been slain, having seven horns and seven eyes, which are the seven Spirits of God sent forth into all the earth."* Jesus the lamb with seven horns

2. Power and strength

a. Joshua 7 – The children of Israel blew rams horns at the fall of Jericho.
b. Habakkuk 3:4 – *"And his brightness was as the light; he had horns coming out of his hand: and there was the hiding of his power."* A picture of the Lord in power
c. Revelation 13:1-2 – *"[1]And I stood upon the sand of the sea, and saw a beast rise up out of the sea, having seven heads and ten horns, and upon his horns ten crowns, and upon his heads the name of blasphemy. [2]And the beast which I saw was like unto a leopard, and his feet were as the feet of a bear, and his mouth as the mouth of a lion: and the dragon gave him his power, and his seat, and great authority."* These horns are symbolic of the antichrist kingdom

3. Anointing

a. I Samuel 16:13 – *"Then Samuel took the horn of oil, and anointed him in the midst of his brethren: and the Spirit of the LORD came upon David from that day forward. So Samuel rose up, and went to Ramah."* The anointing of David from a horn of oil, recognizing him as king

B. What was the natural use of these four horns?

These were used to tie the animal that was to be sacrificed, to the altar (Psalm 118:27). They were also sprinkled with blood on the Day of Atonement. They were a place of refuge. (Exodus 21:14)

C. What then is the spiritual truth that these four horns represent?

1. These four horns were to point outward to every part of the world, the four corners. By doing so they spoke to the world of its sin and guilt as well as its need to receive the sacrifice of God's animal to make them free. Jesus is the horn of salvation (Luke 1:68-69)
2. Blood was placed on these horns (Exodus 29:12). This speaks to us of the power of the blood of Jesus. This blood is pointing to the four corners of a lost and dying world.
3. Jesus was the sacrifice bound to the horns of the cross by the love of God
4. These horns were made of wood, which speaks to us of man and his power. They were covered with brass representing judgment. In other words, God has judged the so-called *powerful man*. However, thank God, blood was placed on these horns, which means the blood of Jesus is more powerful than the judgment of God concerning our sin and us.
5. These four horns represent, as stated earlier, power, salvation, strength and anointing.

6. These horns were to be a place of refuge. The cross is a place of refuge for us.

a. I Kings 1:50-53 – Adonijah was caught in sin and fled to the horns of the altar. He wanted a place of refuge from King Solomon. Solomon had mercy on him and gave him a chance to redeem himself. In this situation, "*horns*" represent life and refuge.
b. I Kings 2:28:34 – In this case, horns mean death. Joab found no mercy because he obviously was not repentant of heart. He was killed at the altar. Remember, we cannot fool God. This brazen altar will either be your salvation, if you accept it, or it will be your death, if you refuse it.

D. These horns were overlaid with brass

1. Brass in scripture speaks of judgment

a. Genesis 4:22 – The first mention of brass is found in connection with the family of Cain, upon whom the judgment of God had come.
b. Judges 16:21 – *"But the Philistines took him, and put out his eyes, and brought him down to Gaza, and bound him with fetters of brass; and he did grind in the prison house."* Samson, bound with fetters of brass, was judged by God.
c. Numbers 21:9 – *"And Moses made a serpent of brass, and put it upon a pole, and it came to pass, that if a serpent had bitten any man, when he beheld the serpent of brass, he lived."* The serpent made of brass commemorates the judgment of God upon Israel's sin
d. II Kings 25:4-7 – Zedekiah is bound in fetters of brass, which was the judgment of God for not obeying the Word.
e. Deuteronomy 28:15, 23 – One of the judgments for not hearkening to the Word of the Lord was the heavens would be brass over them, or, there would be no more communication from the Lord.
f. Revelation 1:15 – *"And his feet like unto fine brass, as if they burned in a furnace; and his voice as the sound of many waters."* – Jesus had feet of brass; feet speak of our walk with God. We must begin at His feet. Ultimately we will be like Him, our feet bronze, able to withstand the fire of God as we walk.

2. What brass over wood represents

   a. Brass was the most used metal in the outer court, the reason being, the outer court related to our initial salvation and judgment from sin.

      1) All of the furniture in the outer court was made of brass
      2) The pillars that caused the tabernacle to stand, stood in sockets of brass
      3) The pins were made of brass
      4) All the vessels in the service of the outer court were made of brass

   b. Brass over wood – God's judgment of humanity, and His judgment of Jesus

V. Vessels, Exodus 27:3 – "*And thou shalt make his pans to receive his ashes, and his shovels, and his basons, and his fleshhooks, and his firepans: all the vessels thereof thou shalt make of brass.*" (Exodus 38:3)

A. Hebrew definition of these vessels

1. Pans – to boil up, a pot a thorn, a hook; it is also translated "pots" in Exodus 38:3
2. Shovels – to brush aside, sweep away
3. Basons – a bowl; from a root, to sprinkle
4. Fleshhooks – to draw up
5. Firepans – a pan for live coals; a censer; dissolution, a ruin (in the sense of removal)

B. Natural usages of these vessels

1. The pan/pot was used to carry the ashes outside the camp or tabernacle (Leviticus 6:10-11).
2. The shovels were used to shovel the ashes, for placing the coals into the censers for the golden altar, and for stoking the fire.
3. The basons were to carry the blood, which was to be sprinkled in different places during and after the sacrifice (Exodus 24:5-8). It is also to be poured out at the altar (Leviticus 4:4-7).
4. The fleshhooks were used on the animal to move or to lift pieces of it (I Samuel 2:13-17). The fleshhook had three prongs.
5. The firepans were to carry the live coals from the altar to light the candlestick and cause the incense on the golden altar to burn (Isaiah 6:6).
6. All of the above articles were made of brass.

C. Spiritually defined

1. Pots/Pans

   a. This pot was to pick up the ashes of the consumed sacrifice. This speaks to us of Christ's complete and utter sacrifice (John 19:30).
   b. The brass speaks of judgment. As the ashes were placed into this pot, it is symbolic that judgment had taken its course fully on the sacrifice. God's judgment was satisfied as far as sin was concerned, on the offering of Jesus. Also, the ashes have to be removed or the fire will go out.
   c. Leviticus 6:10-11 – Here the fire (judgment) of God had consumed the burn offering. The priest was to take the ashes to a clean place outside the camp. This obviously speaks of those who took Jesus' body and laid it in a brand new sepulchre (Luke 23:53).

2. Shovels – These shovels placed the coals from the brazen altar into the censers to take them to the golden altar, thus linking the two. Jesus' death gives us the ability to communicate with God (prayer), and to enter His presence and worship Him (worship). Also, the brass shovel speaks

of judgment and the coals of fire, of God's purging, purifying glory. This gives us a double judgment, a double cleansing to prepare us to worship at the golden altar (Isaiah 4:4).

3. Basons – The brass bason carried the blood from the sacrifice to be sprinkled in other parts of the tabernacle. The blood of Jesus has power because it is innocent. All the articles of furniture had to be sprinkled with blood. God's judgment had to be satisfied, as without the shedding of blood, there is no remission of sin. The blood must be carried to every part of our threefold being if we are to be truly sanctified.

4. Fleshhooks

   a. Three-pronged hook made from brass. Three in one: this is indicative of the judgment of the Godhead, Father, Son and Holy Spirit on the sacrifice.
   b. The fleshhook was used to jab into the flesh of the animal and move it to another place or to separate pieces for the priests.
   c. We must eat all of Jesus' sacrifice (Matthew 26:27)
   d. God is going to cut away our flesh – God's judgment (brass) on our flesh

5. Firepans

   a. These firepans carried the coals from the brazen altar to the golden altar. This tells us it is God's cleansing fire and coals that purge us from sin and prepare us to enter into His glory. (Isaiah 6:6-7)
   b. The fire of God that purges (Matthew 3:11) becomes to us His glory (golden altar). The same fire that burns us is the same fire that quickens us and brings us into ever greater dimensions of his glory. To experience God's glory you must experience His judgment. We find out as we go on in Him that they are actually the same (Hebrews 12:29). God's fire can be a blessing or a judgment.

      1) Fire as a judgment, Psalms 11:6 – "*Upon the wicked he shall rain snares, fire and brimstone, and an horrible tempest: this shall be the portion of their cup.*"; Also, fire fell on Sodom and Gomorrah and destroyed it
      2) Fire is a blessing – Malachi 3:3 – "*And he shall sit as a refiner and purifer of silver: and he shall purify the sons of Levi, and purge them as gold and silver, that they may offer unto the LORD an offering in righteousness*"; Also, Isaiah 4:4-6

   c. There was to be a continual fire, Leviticus 6:12-13 – "[12]*And the fire upon the altar shall be burning in it; it shall not be put out: and the priest shall burn wood on it every morning, and lay the burnt offering in order upon it; and he shall burn thereon the fat of the peace offerings.* [13]*The fire shall ever be burning upon the altar; it shall never go out.*"

      1) It was the priest's responsibility to keep the fire stoked.

         a) God's judgment is going to continue until all flesh is consumed
         b) God initially lights this fire (Leviticus 9:24), but it is our responsibility to keep the fire burning. We must stoke the fire (Proverbs 26:20).

            (1) Our responsibility to stir ourselves up (Isaiah 64:7, II Timothy 1:6)
            (2) How do we do this?

               (a) Speaking in tongues – Jude 20
               (b) Acts 20:32 – The Word
               (c) Job 22:23 – Stay in His presence
               (d) Colossians 2:7 – Sitting under teaching

VI. Exodus 27:4-5 – "[4]*And thou shalt make for it a grate of network of brass; and upon the net shalt thou make four brasen rings in the four corners thereof.* [5]*And thou shalt put it under the compass of the altar beneath, that the net may be even to the midst of the altar.*"

A. Grate Network of Brass

1. Natural usage – This altar had a grate or network of interwoven lines of brass. It was positioned in the middle of the altar. It was placed in the center to uphold the body of the sacrifice.

2. Spiritual truth

a. It is an inward decision or an inward working; our hearts are the key to sacrifice.
b. Jesus died between two thieves
c. It was the same height as the mercy seat, which speaks to us of mercy rejoicing over judgment.

B. Four brazen rings

1. Natural usage – These rings were used to help carry the grate and the altar.

2. Spiritual truth:

a. The four rings were in the four corners. This, once again, speaks to us of the Gospel message. It must be carried to the four corners of the earth.
b. These four rings also speak to us of the grace, mercy, love and judgment of God to the earth. In this altar of sacrifice, God revealed that mankind needed to be saved. He needed his sin to be judged, so He provided a sacrifice in His love for us. By accepting the sacrifice of Jesus, He gave us His mercy. By becoming the sacrifice, He gave us His grace.

VII. Staves for the altar, Exodus 27:6-7 – "[6]*And thou shalt make staves for the altar, staves of shittim wood, and overlay them with brass.* [7]*And the staves shall be put into the rings, and the staves shall be upon the two sides of the altar, to bear it.*"

A. Once again the truth of shittim wood (humanity) overlaid with brass (judgment), speaks to us of God judging man for his sin. Also it speaks of judging the incorruptible humanity of our redeemer Jesus.

B. There were two staves; two is the number for witness, division or separation. Spiritually this represents:

1. These two staves were to carry the message of this altar as a witness to the whole earth.
2. To those who refuse this altar of sacrifice will be separated unto punishment, away from God.
3. These two staves also point to the death and resurrection of the Lord
4. It also shows us the need for someone to carry this message.

VIII. Exodus 27:8 – "*Hollow with boards shalt thou make it: as it was shewed thee in the mount, so shall they make it.*"

A. "*Hollow with boards shalt thou make it...*" This altar was to be made hollow.

1. This speaks to us of how Jesus emptied himself (Philippians 2:5-8) of who He was to embrace what we are in order to redeem us.
2. This hollowness also speaks of the openness in the heart of Jesus to heaven (God) and earth (man). He was the perfect intercessor.

3. The hollowness of this piece of furniture made it the largest piece of furniture in the tabernacle. All other pieces of furniture would fit inside of it. This reiterates the fact that everything in God comes out of this initial sacrificial offering.
4. This hollow altar speaks to us of sacrifice and dying to ourselves. It tells us to empty ourselves. We must decrease and He must increase (John 3:30). Death is the way to life.

IX. Other Thoughts On the Brazen Altar

A. The Brazen Altar was mentioned ninth as an article of furniture in the tabernacle – Nine is the number for finality; here at this altar, there comes a finality to sin, to the flesh, to rebellion
B. Whenever the camp moved, each piece of furniture was to be covered. All others were covered with a cloth of blue (heavenly). This Brazen Altar however, was covered with a scarlet covering (Numbers 4:13-14). The color scarlet speaks of sacrifice and suffering.
C. There were no steps to this altar, Exodus 20:26 – "*Neither shalt thou go up by steps unto mine altar, that thy nakedness be not discovered thereon.*" – There are no paths to God other than Jesus.
D. The priests had to be covered and clothed when they ministered at the altar, Exodus 28:40-43 – This tells us that no place was given to the flesh. God is not interested in our flesh. He wants it burned and covered by His nature.
E. This altar is the beginning of holiness of our life, Exodus 29:35-37 – "*Whatsoever toucheth the altar shall be holy.*" This is the beginning of holiness in the life of the believer. His spirit is made holy instantly by God, by virtue of the fact the Lord comes to dwell within him.

Lesson 19

Justification

I. Man Is Born Into Sin and Needs To Be Justified Before God

A. Born into sin

1. Psalms 51:5 – "*Behold, I was shapen in iniquity; and in sin did my mother conceive me.*"
2. Romans 5:12 – "*Wherefore, as by one man sin entered into the world, and death by sin; and so death passed upon all men, for that all have sinned:*"
3. Ephesians 2:1-4 – "[1]*And you hath he quickened, who were dead in trespasses and sins;* [2]*Wherein in time past ye walked according to the course of this world, according to the prince of the power of the air, the spirit that now worketh in the children of disobedience:* [3]*Among whom also we all had our conversation in times past in the lusts of our flesh, fulfilling the desires of the flesh and of the mind; and were by nature the children of wrath, even as others.* [4]*But God, who is rich in mercy, for his great love wherewith he loved us,*"
4. Romans 7:5 – "*For when we were in the flesh, the motions of sins, which were by the law, did work in our members to bring forth fruit unto death.*"

B. All have sinned and need salvation

1. Romans 3:23 – "*For all have sinned, and come short of the glory of God;*"
2. Proverbs 20:9 – "*Who can say, I have made my heart clean, I am pure from my sin?*" (Ecc. 7:20)
3. Psalms 53:3 – "*Every one of them is gone back: they are altogether become filthy; there is none that doeth good, no, not one.*"
4. I Kings 8:46 – "*If they sin against thee, (for there is no man that sinneth not,) and thou be angry with them, and deliver them to the enemy, so that they carry them away captives unto the land of the enemy, far or near;*"
5. Isaiah 53:6 – "*All we like sheep have gone astray; we have turned every one to his own way; and the LORD hath laid on him the iniquity of us all.*"
6. I John 1:8 – "*If we say that we have no sin, we deceive ourselves, and the truth is not in us.*"
7. Isaiah 64:6 – "*But we are all as an unclean thing, and all our righteousnesses are as filthy rags; and we all do fade as a leaf; and our iniquities, like the wind, have taken us away.*"

C. God Wants All Men Saved (Justified)

1. I Timothy 2:4 – "*Who will have all men to be saved, and to come unto the knowledge of the truth.*"
2. Isaiah 45:22 – "*Look unto me, and be ye saved, all the ends of the earth: for I am God, and there is none else.*"
3. Matthew 11:28 – "*Come unto me, all ye that labour and are heavy laden, and I will give you rest.*"
4. Isaiah 1:18 – "*Come now, and let us reason together, saith the LORD: though your sins be as scarlet, they shall be as white as snow; though they be red like crimson, they shall be as wool.*"
5. Revelation 3:20 – "*Behold, I stand at the door, and knock: if any man hear my voice, and open the door, I will come in to him, and will sup with him, and he with me.*"
6. II Corinthians 5:20 – "*Now then we are ambassadors for Christ, as though God did beseech you by us: we pray you in Christ's stead, be ye reconciled to God.*"
7. John 3:15-17 – "[15]*That whosoever believeth in him should not perish, but have eternal life.* [16]*For God so loved the world, that he gave his only begotten Son, that whosoever believeth in him should not perish, but have everlasting life.* [17]*For God sent not his Son into the world to condemn the world; but that the world through him might be saved.*"
8. Acts 2:27 – "*Because thou wilt not leave my soul in hell, neither wilt thou suffer thine Holy One to see corruption.*"

Jesus has paid the price for all the sin of mankind; all they need do is recognize it. God doesn't want anyone to perish or to suffer hell. He knows we were born into sin and needed a Savior. He came to die for us that He might become our salvation! We must receive Jesus to be justified before God.

II. What Does Justification Mean

A. The Greek Word For Justification

1. *Dikaioma* – declaration that a person or thing is righteous; acquittal, to make right, to vindicate
2. Dictionary Definition: "That judicial act of God by which, on the basis of the meritorious work of Christ, imputed to the sinner and received by him through faith, He (God) declares the sinner absolved from his sin, released from its penalty and restored as righteous."
3. It is an act by God to remit and restore one.
4. A good modern definition is that it is just as if you had never sinned.

B. The Essentials Of Justification

There are two basic essentials in the act of justification.

1. It involves:

a. Remission of punishment – This means the believer is declared free of the demands of the law because Jesus satisfied all of them. He will no longer be penalized for sin. The penalty of sin was taken away in the death, burial and resurrection of Jesus. This is more than a pardon, it is a declaration by God that the sinner, though guilty, is now justified and righteous.
b. Restoration to favor and relationship – Having once been out of favor, in sin, a criminal, we are made totally free and clear. Not simply a discharged prisoner. God treats us as if we had never sinned.

C. Jesus has justified us

1. Galatians 3:13 – "*Christ hath redeemed us from the curse of the law, being made a curse for us: for it is written, Cursed is every one that hangeth on a tree:*"
2. II Corinthians 5:21 – "*For he hath made him to be sin for us, who knew no sin; that we might be made the righteousness of God in him.*"
3. Romans 5:8-21 – "*[8]But God commendeth his love toward us, in that, while we were yet sinners, Christ died for us. [9]Much more then, being now justified by his blood, we shall be saved from wrath through him…*"

Lesson 20

Brass Laver

Brass Laver

I. The Brass Laver, Exodus 30:17-21 and Exodus 38:8

Exodus 30:17-21 – "[17]*And the LORD spake unto Moses, saying,* [18]*Thou shalt also make a laver of brass, and his foot also of brass, to wash withal: and thou shalt put it between the tabernacle of the congregation and the altar, and thou shalt put water therein.* [19]*For Aaron and his sons shall wash their hands and their feet thereat:* [20]*When they go into the tabernacle of the congregation, they shall wash with water, that they die not; or when they come near to the altar to minister, to burn offering made by fire unto the LORD:* [21]*So they shall wash their hands and their feet, that they die not: and it shall be a statute for ever to them, even to him and to his seed throughout their generations.*"

Exodus 38:8 – "*And he made the laver of brass, and the foot of it of brass, of the lookingglasses of the women assembling, which assembled at the door of the tabernacle of the congregation.*"

A. First things to note about the laver

1. The laver was sprinkled with blood, anointed with oil (Hebrews 9:2; Exodus 40:11; Lev. 8:11)
2. It was filled with water to the top. It had all the witnesses John spoke of in I John 5:7-8. Aaron and his sons washed their heads and feet here when they went into the tabernacle or when they ministered at the brazen altar. They were told to do this, lest they die. On some occasions the priests had to bathe their entire bodies (Exodus 29:4 and Leviticus 16:4).
3. It was made of looking glasses (polished brass mirrors), which were obtained from the women who assembled by the door of the tabernacle.
4. There is no record of how or if it was covered or how it was carried when the children of Israel would move from camp to camp.
5. The Scriptures do not give us its dimensions or how it really looked.
6. It stood between the Brazen Altar and the Tabernacle.
7. It was highly polished and made of mirrors that reflected the pure, bright light of the sun. It also reflected the image of the priests themselves as they approached.
8. It appeared like a saucer holding a cup; the saucer for the washing of their feet and the cup or upper part for the washing of the hands.
9. God places so much importance on this particular piece of furniture, because He says if Aaron and his sons did not wash here, they would die.

B. What this laver is representative of in general

The laver was made of brass. Here this speaks of God's judgment coming to us through the Word. Water speaks of the washing of the water of the Word. If we are to enter into the deeper things of God (holy place, most holy place), we must be washed, sanctified and we must have received judgment upon our flesh nature. We must be willing to let the Word of God expose us for what we really are. It was a place of judgment, exposure, cleansing and preparation. As a type of the Word it consisted of "milk for babes, bread for children".

1. Water baptism

   a. Matthew 28:19 – "*Go ye therefore, and teach all nations, baptizing them in the name of the Father, and of the Son, and of the Holy Ghost:*"
   b. Mark 16:15-16 – "[15]*And he said unto them, Go ye into all the world, and preach the gospel to every creature.* [16]*He that believeth and is baptized shall be saved; but he that believeth not shall be damned.*"
   c. Acts 2:38 – "*Then Peter said unto them, Repent, and be baptized every one of you in the name of Jesus Christ for the remission of sins, and ye shall receive the gift of the Holy Ghost.*"

2. Sanctification

   a. I Corinthians 1:30 – "*But of him are ye in Christ Jesus, who of God is made unto us wisdom, and righteousness, and sanctification, and redemption:*"
   b. I Thessalonians 4:3-4 – "[3]*For this is the will of God, even your sanctification, that ye should abstain from fornication:* [4]*That every one of you should know how to possess his vessel in sanctification and honour;*"
   c. II Thessalonians 2:13 – "*But we are bound to give thanks alway to God for you, brethren beloved of the Lord, because God hath from the beginning chosen you to salvation through sanctification of the Spirit and belief of the truth:*"
   d. I Peter 1:2 – "*Elect according to the foreknowledge of God the Father, through sanctification of the Spirit, unto obedience and sprinkling of the blood of Jesus Christ: Grace unto you, and peace, be multiplied.*"

3. The washing of the Word of God

   a. Psalms 119:9 – "*Wherewithal shall a young man cleanse his way? by taking heed thereto according to thy word.*"
   b. John 15:3 – "*Now ye are clean through the word which I have spoken unto you.*"
   c. II Corinthians 7:1 – "*Having therefore these promises, dearly beloved, let us cleanse ourselves from all filthiness of the flesh and spirit, perfecting holiness in the fear of God.*"
   d. Ephesians 5:26 – "*That he might sanctify and cleanse it with the washing of water by the word,*"

4. Exposure of the Word of God – The brass mirrors are a type of the Word of God. These mirrors represent the reflection of God's Word exposing and revealing us to ourselves.

   a. James 1:23-25 – "[23]*For if any be a hearer of the word, and not a doer, he is like unto a man beholding his natural face in a glass:* [24]*For he beholdeth himself, and goeth his way, and straightway forgetteth what manner of man he was.* [25]*But whoso looketh into the perfect law of liberty, and continueth therein, he being not a forgetful hearer, but a doer of the work, this man shall be blessed in his deed.*"
   b. II Corinthians 3:18 – "*But we all, with open face beholding as in a glass the glory of the Lord, are changed into the same image from glory to glory, even as by the Spirit of the Lord.*"

c. I Corinthians 13:12 – "*For now we see through a glass, darkly; but then face to face: now I know in part; but then shall I know even as also I am known.*"

5. Intercession

a. Joel 2:17 – "*Let the priests, the ministers of the LORD, weep between the porch and the altar, and let them say, Spare thy people, O LORD, and give not thine heritage to reproach, that the heathen should rule over them: wherefore should they say among the people, Where is their God?*"

b. Lamentations 3:48-51 – "*48Mine eye runneth down with rivers of water for the destruction of the daughter of my people. 49Mine eye trickleth down, and ceaseth not, without any intermission, 50Till the LORD look down, and behold from heaven. 51Mine eye affecteth mine heart because of all the daughters of my city.*"

C. Laver of Brass made from looking glasses

1. We are still in the outer court and still being judged in preparation to enter into the presence of God. All flesh must be dealt with.
2. Looking glass – This mirror is a type of the Word of God (James 1:23-25, II Corinthians 3:18, Hebrews 4:12-13). The word of God is a mirror that shows not only what we are in Jesus but also what we are to become. It also, in the process, will expose to us our own defilement and correct us. When these priests would walk towards this laver, they were looking into a mirror showing what they needed to be cleansed of. What is wonderful is that the same word that exposes (mirror) us is the same word that cleanses us (water). When we see Him in the Word we will always see ourselves for what we really are (Isaiah 6:5, Job 42: 5-6). It is up to us then to take the water and cleanse ourselves.
3. It was made from the looking glasses of the women who assembled by the door of the tabernacle (Exodus 38:8). This speaks to us of how we must be willing to sacrifice vanity in our own life. We must stop looking at ourselves after the natural and allow God to take the instrument of vanity in our own life and make it an instrument to expose us spiritually, as well as to aid in cleansing.
4. God requires women to bring this voluntary offering. It symbolizes them laying down their pride and vanity. The deepest and perhaps strongest part of a woman's nature is to look pretty and to be thought of as beautiful. God wants that crushed in us. At the laver, pride and vanity are dealt with.

a. Women

1) Isaiah 4:1 – "*And in that day seven women shall take hold of one man, saying, We will eat our own bread, and wear our own apparel: only let us be called by thy name, to take away our reproach.*" – In the last days the spirit of the world (pride, vanity) will rise and there will be false submission, rebellion and disregard for authority.
2) I Peter 3:1-6
3) Proverbs 31:30 – "*Favour is deceitful, and beauty is vain: but a woman that feareth the LORD, she shall be praised.*" This is what God would have for his women.
4) Proverbs 31:10 – "*Who can find a virtuous woman? for her price is far above rubies.*"
5) Ecclesiastes 7:26 – "*And I find more bitter than death the woman, whose heart is snares and nets, and her hands as bands: whoso pleaseth God shall escape from her; but the sinner shall be taken by her.*"
6) Isaiah 32:9 – "*Rise up, ye women that are at ease; hear my voice, ye careless daughters; give ear unto my speech.*"

b. Vanity

1) Ecclesiastes 1:2 – *"Vanity of vanities, saith the Preacher, vanity of vanities; all is vanity."*
2) Psalms 39:5-6, 8 – *"[5]Behold, thou hast made my days as an handbreadth; and mine age is as nothing before thee: verily every man at his best state is altogether vanity. Selah. [6]Surely every man walketh in a vain shew: surely they are disquieted in vain: he heapeth up riches, and knoweth not who shall gather them...[11]When thou with rebukes dost correct man for iniquity, thou makest his beauty to consume away like a moth: surely every man is vanity. Selah."*
3) Proverbs 30:8 – *"Remove far from me vanity and lies: give me neither poverty nor riches; feed me with food convenient for me:"*
4) Proverbs 31:30 – *"Favour is deceitful, and beauty is vain: but a woman that feareth the LORD, she shall be praised."*

D. To Wash Withal – If this laver speaks of anything it speaks of cleansing. The water in it is a type also of the Word of God.

1. Washings in Scripture – This laver speaks to us of:

a. Washing of regeneration, Titus 3:5 – *"Not by works of righteousness which we have done, but according to his mercy he saved us, by the washing of regeneration, and renewing of the Holy Ghost;"* When we meet Jesus at the brazen altar we are baptized in His blood but we need to be washed also at salvation.
b. Water Baptism – because this is still an outer court experience it speaks to us of the washing of water baptism.
c. Washing of Cleansing – after salvation and water baptism we need to be cleansed to walk with the Lord.

2. The Word as a cleansing agent – This water is to cleanse and sanctify and perfect the church. The blood saves and redeems us; the water then is to take us into all that God has. The brazen altar, the water and the laver represent the blood.

a. Ephesians 5:26 – *"That he might sanctify and cleanse it with the washing of water by the word"* – The Word is what we take to wash ourselves from our uncleanness. It is the cleansing agent along with the blood in the spirit realm.
b. II Corinthians 7:1 – *"Having therefore these promises, dearly beloved, let us cleanse ourselves from all filthiness of the flesh and spirit, perfecting holiness in the fear of God."*
c. Psalms 119:9-11 – *"[9]Wherewithal shall a young man cleanse his way? by taking heed thereto according to thy word. [10]With my whole heart have I sought thee: O let me not wander from thy commandments. [11]Thy word have I hid in mine heart, that I might not sin against thee."*
d. John 15:3 – *"Now ye are clean through the word which I have spoken unto you."*
e. John 17:17 – *"Sanctify them through thy truth: thy word is truth."*
f. James 1:21 – *"Wherefore lay apart all filthiness and superfluity of naughtiness, and receive with meekness the engrafted word, which is able to save your souls."*

E. Important facts to note

1. The Brazen Altar was square (finished), the Laver was round (continuous).
2. The Altar was made of wood, the Laver of brass (no humanity).
3. The Altar had staves, the Laver didn't (it is not something you carry or move, sanctification is forever).
4. The Altar was covered when they moved, the laver wasn't.
5. The Altar was for blood, the Laver for water (once saved now it's just cleansing).
6. The Altar was for everyone, the Laver for priests (thus the separation of disciples begins).

7. The Laver was for washing away blood – This speaks to us of deliverance from condemnation

a. Psalms 51:14 – "*Deliver me from bloodguiltiness, O God, thou God of my salvation: and my tongue shall sing aloud of thy righteousness.*"
b. Romans 8:1 – "*There is therefore now no condemnation to them which are in Christ Jesus, who walk not after the flesh, but after the Spirit.*"
c. Psalms 66:18-20 – "*[18]If I regard iniquity in my heart, the Lord will not hear me: [19]But verily God hath heard me; he hath attended to the voice of my prayer. [20]Blessed be God, which hath not turned away my prayer, nor his mercy from me.*"
d. John 15:3 – "*Now ye are clean through the word which I have spoken unto you.*"

8. The Altar was for killing, the laver for cleansing and life (John 10:10)
9. There are no specific measurements for the Brass Laver.
10. Of all the pieces of furniture, we have the least information on the laver.
11. Most of what we know is handed down by tradition.
12. It consisted of two parts (a laver and his foot). The number 2 means witness, separation, and division.
13. It is believed that water was taken from the laver to wash the feet (walk) and the hands (works).
14. It was in the outer court still in natural light.
15. It was made of brass (judgment), mirrors (Word of God) and had water in it (cleansing and Holy Spirit); Isaiah 4:4 and John 16:6-12.
16. It had no wood (man cannot cleanse himself). Man must be sanctified by God.

17. The priest was to wash himself – we must judge ourselves

a. I Corinthians 11:31-32 – "*[31]For if we would judge ourselves, we should not be judged. [32]But when we are judged, we are chastened of the Lord, that we should not be condemned with the world.*"
b. I Peter 4:17 – "*For the time is come that judgment must begin at the house of God: and if it first begin at us, what shall the end be of them that obey not the gospel of God?*"

18. The priests were to wash at the laver and then they could wear the holy garments (Exodus 29:4-9); you can't truly minister to the Lord if you haven't been properly cleansed (II Corinthians 7:1)
19. Hebrew word for laver, *Kiyor*, means – pot or pan, washbowl. It was a large pot; it comes from a root word that means – to dig through, a pot or furnace (as if excavated)
20. The Greek word for laver, *loutron*, means – a bath, immersion. The primary verb *louo* means to bathe the whole person. *Loutron* is translated twice in the New Testament as "washing" (Ephesians 5:26 and Titus 3:5).
21. The word "*also*" in verse 17 speaks that this is to be added to our faith.

22. The Laver had a foot upon which it rested, which denotes our foundation in Jesus. All that we will ever do in and for Him stands upon the foundation He (Jesus) has laid.

a. I Corinthians 3:11 – "*For other foundation can no man lay than that is laid, which is Jesus Christ.*"
b. Romans 14:4 – "*Who art thou that judgest another man's servant? to his own master he standeth or falleth. Yea, he shall be holden up: for God is able to make him stand.*"
c. Romans 4:16, 25 – "*[16]Therefore it is of faith, that it might be by grace; to the end the promise might be sure to all the seed; not to that only which is of the law, but to that also which is of the faith of Abraham; who is the father of us all...[25]Who was delivered for our offences, and was raised again for our justification.*"
d. Colossians 1:14-18 – "*[14]In whom we have redemption through his blood, even the forgiveness of sins: [15]Who is the image of the invisible God, the firstborn of every creature: [16]For by him were all things created, that are in heaven, and that are in earth, visible and invisible, whether*

they be thrones, or dominions, or principalities, or powers: all things were created by him, and for him: [17]And he is before all things, and by him all things consist. [18]And he is the head of the body, the church: who is the beginning, the firstborn from the dead; that in all things he might have the preeminence."

e. Psalms 130:3 – "*If thou, LORD, shouldest mark iniquities, O Lord, who shall stand?*"
f. Romans 5:2 – "*By whom also we have access by faith into this grace wherein we stand, and rejoice in hope of the glory of God.*"
g. I Corinthians 15:1 – "*Moreover, brethren, I declare unto you the gospel which I preached unto you, which also ye have received, and wherein ye stand;*"
h. I Peter 5:12 – "*By Silvanus, a faithful brother unto you, as I suppose, I have written briefly, exhorting, and testifying that this is the true grace of God wherein ye stand.*"

23. It doesn't necessarily say this but in Leviticus 1:8-9, 13 it seems the water they used to wash the legs and inwards of the sacrifice was from the laver. The inward parts and legs were washed. The water from the Laver is to cleanse our inward parts.

    a. Psalms 51:6 – "*Behold, thou desirest truth in the inward parts: and in the hidden part thou shalt make me to know wisdom.*"
    b. Jeremiah 31:33 – "*But this shall be the covenant that I will make with the house of Israel; After those days, saith the LORD, I will put my law in their inward parts, and write it in their hearts; and will be their God, and they shall be my people.*"
    c. Proverbs 20:27 – "*The spirit of man is the candle of the LORD, searching all the inward parts of the belly.*"
    d. Proverbs 20:30 – "*The blueness of a wound cleanseth away evil: so do stripes the inward parts of the belly.*"
    e. II Corinthians 4:16 – "*For which cause we faint not; but though our outward man perish, yet the inward man is renewed day by day.*"
    f. I Peter 3:4 – "*But let it be the hidden man of the heart, in that which is not corruptible, even the ornament of a meek and quiet spirit, which is in the sight of God of great price.*"

24. Joel 2:17—weep between the porch and the altar. We fill the Laver with our tears (Luke 7:44)

25. God requires His priests to be holy

    a. Isaiah 52:11 – "*Depart ye, depart ye, go ye out from thence, touch no unclean thing; go ye out of the midst of her; be ye clean, that bear the vessels of the LORD.*"
    b. Psalms 26:6-8 – "*[6]I will wash mine hands in innocency: so will I compass thine altar, O LORD: [7]That I may publish with the voice of thanksgiving, and tell of all thy wondrous works. [8]LORD, I have loved the habitation of thy house, and the place where thine honour dwelleth.*"
    c. Psalms 24:3-5 – "*[3]Who shall ascend into the hill of the LORD? or who shall stand in his holy place? [4]He that hath clean hands, and a pure heart; who hath not lifted up his soul unto vanity, nor sworn deceitfully. [5]He shall receive the blessing from the LORD, and righteousness from the God of his salvation.*"
    d. Hebrews 10:19-22 – "*[19]Having therefore, brethren, boldness to enter into the holiest by the blood of Jesus, [20]By a new and living way, which he hath consecrated for us, through the veil, that is to say, his flesh; [21]And having an high priest over the house of God; [22]Let us draw near with a true heart in full assurance of faith, having our hearts sprinkled from an evil conscience, and our bodies washed with pure water.*"
    e. I Peter 1:22 – "*Seeing ye have purified your souls in obeying the truth through the Spirit unto unfeigned love of the brethren, see that ye love one another with a pure heart fervently:*"

26. The Laver was sprinkled with blood, oil and water, I John 5:8
27. The Laver typifies the Holiness movement brought into the church by John Wesley in the 1700's. The Laver was restored to the church when this happened and it spawned the

Methodists, Nazarenes, and Apostolic Missionary, Alliance denominations. They believed in a second experience called the "*Baptism of the Holy Ghost*" but instead of tongues, they associated it with sanctification. Just as Luther restored the brazen altar with the "reformation" so did God restore sanctification though men like Wesley, George Watson, A. B. Simpson and Andrew Murray.

28. All of the other pieces of furniture in the Tabernacle dealt with God somehow. However, the Laver was specifically for the priests.

F. Priests were to wash themselves, "*that they die not*" – this shows how important it is to God that his priest be clean. They were covered in blood; this was because of sacrifices for sin. They couldn't come into God's presence with other people's sin (blood) on them.

1. Sin brings death – They had to be washed. This is really like the sin unto death.

a. Romans 6:23 – "*For the wages of sin is death...*"
b. Romans 5:12 – "*Wherefore, as by one man sin entered into the world, and death by sin; and so death passed upon all men, for that all have sinned:*"
c. I Corinthians 15:56 – "*The sting of death is sin; and the strength of sin is the law.*"
d. James 1:15 – "*Then when lust hath conceived, it bringeth forth sin: and sin, when it is finished, bringeth forth death.*"
e. Ezekiel 18:14, 20 – "*Now, lo, if he beget a son, that seeth all his father's sins which he hath done, and considereth, and doeth not such like...[20]The soul that sinneth, it shall die. The son shall not bear the iniquity of the father, neither shall the father bear the iniquity of the son: the righteousness of the righteous shall be upon him, and the wickedness of the wicked shall be upon him.*"

2. Examples of those who did die

a. Leviticus 10:1-5 – Nadab and Abihu offered strange fire before the Lord
b. Numbers 3:4

1) Nadab – willing, free will; it comes from a root word that means to impel on oneself.
2) Abihu – he is my father
3) Hebrew word for strange – to turn aside, profane, foreign

c. Acts 5: 1-11 – Ananias & Sapphira

1) Ananias – Jehovah is gracious
2) Sapphira – beautiful, pleasant

d. Saul

1) I Samuel 15:22-35
2) I Samuel 16:1
3) I Samuel 31:6

e. Uzzah, II Samuel 6:1-9

Lesson 21

God's Word: His Cleansing Agent

I. We must see our need to be cleansed

A. Scriptures

1. Matthew 8:3 – *"Be thou clean"*
2. Psalms 51:10 – *"Create in me a clean heart, O God; and renew a right spirit within me."*
3. Isaiah 1:16 – *"Wash you, make you clean; put away the evil of your doings from before mine eyes; cease to do evil..."*
4. Isaiah 66:20 – *"And they shall bring all your brethren for an offering unto the Lord out of all nations upon horses, and in chariots, and in litters, and upon mules, and upon swift beasts, to my holy mountain Jerusalem, saith the Lord, as the children of Israel bring an offering in a clean vessel into the house of the Lord."*
5. Psalms 19:12 – *"Who can understand his errors? cleanse thou me from secret faults."*
6. James 4:8 – *"Draw nigh to God, and he will draw nigh to you. Cleanse your hands, ye sinners; and purify your hearts, ye double minded."*
7. I Thessalonians 4:3-4 – *"For this is the will of God, even your sanctification, that ye should abstain from fornication: That every one of you should know how to possess his vessel in sanctification and honour..."*

II. We wash or cleanse ourselves with the Word

A. Scriptural Examples

1. Ephesians 5:26 – Here Paul says that Christ gave Himself for the church that He might sanctify (make holy) and cleanse it with the washing of water by the Word. This means that just as you cleanse the dirt and grime off your physical body with water, you cleanse the sin and guilt off your soulish man by the Word of God. It is the cleansing agent of the spirit realm. To wash yourself, simply take the Scripture promises and verses that apply to your situation, repent of your sin, then confess and believe the Bible. Let the Scriptures on God's faithfulness calm your fear, etc.

2. II Corinthians 7:1 – Having the promises of God we are able to cleanse ourselves. The Word of God is to us what the laver was to the priests in the Old Testament. When they finished sacrificing animals at the brazen altar, they had to cleanse themselves before they approached the Holy Place. The laver was made of brass mirrors and was filled with water with which they washed away the blood.

   a. We must be cleansed before going into the Holy Place.

      1) Hebrews 10:22 - Water in many places in Scripture speaks of the Word (Ephesians 5:26, John 3:5).
      2) Psalms 24:3-6 – This Scripture is accomplished by taking the Scriptures that apply to your present situation and believing and confessing them, and letting them purge you.

3. Psalms 119:9-11 – How can a young man cleanse his way? – By the Word of God. Notice that the more you hide God's Word in you, the greater your ability to conquer sin. The Word carries with it the power to accomplish what it says (Isaiah 55:11). If we would lay up the Word in our hearts, taking heed to it, cleansing and deliverance would be ours.

   a. John 8:31-33

b. James 1:21 – "*Wherefore lay apart all filthiness and superfluity of naughtiness, and receive with meekness the engrafted word, which is able to save your souls.*"
c. I Peter 1:22 – "*Seeing ye have purified your souls in obeying the truth through the Spirit unto unfeigned love of the brethren, see that ye love one another with a pure heart fervently...*"
d. Proverbs 16:6 – "*By mercy and truth iniquity is purged: and by the fear of the Lord men depart from evil.*"
e. Psalms 119:133 – "*Order my steps in thy word: and let not any iniquity have dominion over me.*"
f. Psalms 17:4 – "*Concerning the works of men, by the word of thy lips I have kept me from the paths of the destroyer.*"

4. John 15:3 – "*Now ye are clean through the word which I have spoken unto you.*" – The Word of God has the ability to cleanse us!
5. John 17:17 – "*Sanctify them through thy truth: thy word is truth.*"

B. A Picture of the Bride

1. Revelation 19:7 & 8
2. Ephesians 5:26 & 27
3. Psalms 45:10-14
4. Song of Solomon 4:7
5. Job 11:13-19
6. Isaiah 4:2-6
7. II Timothy 2:19-21
8. Daniel 12:10

Lesson 22

Sanctification

Sanctification – Greek meaning is to purify or consecrate – separation to God. Sanctification is separation unto God and separation from evil things and ways. Justification is the work of righteousness in our lives, it is a one time work. It deals with the spirit of man. Sanctification is the outworking of justification. It deals with our souls and is concerned with our daily salvation or our allowing what God did in our justification to mature in our souls. In justification, we do very little. In sanctification we must work out and walk out this aspect of salvation. We must allow God to do it, that is purify and cleanse us.

I. I Corinthians 1:30 – *"But of him are ye in Christ Jesus, who of God is made unto us wisdom, and righteousness, and sanctification, and redemption"* – Jesus also is our sanctification. He has given us the wherewithal to become, or in other words, He has prepared the way.

   A. I Thessalonians 5:23 – *"And the very God of peace sanctify you wholly; and I pray God your whole spirit and soul and body be preserved blameless unto the coming of our Lord Jesus Christ."*
   B. Ephesians 5:26 – *"That he might sanctify and cleanse it with the washing of water by the word"*
   C. John 1:12 – *"But as many as received him, to them gave he power to become the sons of God, even to them that believe on his name"*

      1. Ezekiel 11:19-20
      2. Ezekiel 16:6-7, 9-14

II. Sanctification is the will of God

   A. I Thessalonians 4:1-3 – *"[1]Furthermore then we beseech you, brethren, and exhort you by the Lord Jesus, that as ye have received of us how ye ought to walk and to please God, so ye would abound more and more. [2]For ye know what commandments we gave you by the Lord Jesus. [3]For this is the will of God, even your sanctification, that ye should abstain from fornication"* – Sanctification is the will of God. It is yielding our vessels to Him for the glory of God

      1. II Timothy 2:19-22 – *"[19]Nevertheless the foundation of God standeth sure, having this seal, The Lord knoweth them that are his. And, Let every one that nameth the name of Christ depart from iniquity. [20]But in a great house there are not only vessels of gold and of silver, but also of wood and of earth; and some to honour, and some to dishonour. [21]If a man therefore purge himself from these, he shall be a vessel unto honour, sanctified, and meet for the master's use, and prepared unto every good work. [22]Flee also youthful lusts: but follow righteousness, faith, charity, peace, with them that call on the Lord out of a pure heart."*
      2. Proverbs 25:4 – *"Take away the dross from the silver, and there shall come forth a vessel for the finer."*
      3. Exodus 19:10-11 – *"[10]And the LORD said unto Moses, Go unto the people, and sanctify them to day and to morrow, and let them wash their clothes, [11]And be ready against the third day: for the third day the LORD will come down in the sight of all the people upon mount Sinai."* – God has always required sanctification before His people could meet with Him. Sanctification is a process also called overcoming

   B. II Thessalonians 2:13 – *"But we are bound to give thanks alway to God for you, brethren beloved of the Lord, because God hath from the beginning chosen you to salvation through sanctification of the Spirit and belief of the truth"* – God has chosen us to be sanctified. It is His choosing.

      1. Romans 8:28-29 – *"[28]And we know that all things work together for good to them that love God, to them who are the called according to his purpose. [29]For whom he did foreknow, he also did predestinate to be conformed to the image of his Son, that he might be the firstborn among many brethren."*

2. Psalms 17:15 – "*As for me, I will behold thy face in righteousness: I shall be satisfied, when I awake, with thy likeness.*"

III. Salvation Of Our Soul Is Another Definition Of Sanctification

A. I Peter 1:9 – "*Receiving the end of your faith, even the salvation of your souls.*"

1. Luke 21:19 – "*In your patience possess ye your souls.*" – This is speaking of our mind, emotions, etc.

B. It is up to us; what we do with our soul is our business; Our body and spirit belong to God, but our soul is in our hand.

1. I Corinthians 6:20 – "*For ye are bought with a price: therefore glorify God in your body, and in your spirit, which are God's.*"
2. Psalms 119:109 – "*My soul is continually in my hand: yet do I not forget thy law.*"

C. We must commit our soul to Him

1. Psalms 143:8 – "*Cause me to hear thy lovingkindness in the morning; for in thee do I trust: cause me to know the way wherein I should walk; for <u>I lift up my soul unto thee</u>.*"
2. Psalms 25:1 – "*Unto thee, O LORD, do <u>I lift up my soul</u>.*"
3. Lamentations 3:40-41 – "*40Let us search and try our ways, and turn again to the LORD. 41Let us <u>lift up our heart</u> with our hands unto God in the heavens.*"
4. I Peter 4:19 – "*Wherefore let them that suffer according to the will of God <u>commit the keeping of their souls</u> to him in well doing, as unto a faithful Creator.*"
5. Deuteronomy 4:9 – "*Only take heed to thyself, and <u>keep thy soul diligently</u>, lest thou forget the things which thine eyes have seen, and lest they depart from thy heart all the days of thy life: but teach them thy sons, and thy sons' sons;*"
6. Philippians 2:5 – "*Let this mind be in you, which was also in Christ Jesus*"

IV. How Are We Sanctified?

A. Through the Word of God

1. His Word cleanses us

a. John 17:17 – "*Sanctify them through thy truth: thy word is truth.*"
b. Ephesians 5:26 – "*That he might sanctify and cleanse it with the washing of water by the word*"
c. II Corinthians 7:1 – "*Having therefore these promises, dearly beloved, let us cleanse ourselves from all filthiness of the flesh and spirit, perfecting holiness in the fear of God.*"
d. John 15:3 – "*Now ye are clean through the word which I have spoken unto you.*"
e. Psalms 119:9 – "*Wherewithal shall a young man cleanse his way? by taking heed thereto according to thy word.*"

2. His Word makes us free

a. John 8:32 – "*And ye shall know the truth, and the truth shall make you free.*"
b. Proverbs 16:6 – "*By mercy and truth iniquity is purged: and by the fear of the LORD men depart from evil.*"
c. Psalms 119:11 – "*Thy word have I hid in mine heart, that I might not sin against thee.*"

d. I Thessalonians 2:13 – "*For this cause also thank we God without ceasing, because, when ye received the word of God which ye heard of us, ye received it not as the word of men, but as it is in truth, the word of God, which effectually worketh also in you that believe.*"
e. II Corinthians 3:18 – "*But we all, with open face beholding as in a glass the glory of the Lord, are changed into the same image from glory to glory, even as by the Spirit of the Lord.*"
f. James 1:25 – "*But whoso looketh into the perfect law of liberty, and continueth therein, he being not a forgetful hearer, but a doer of the work, this man shall be blessed in his deed.*"
g. Psalms 119:133 – "*Order my steps in thy word: and let not any iniquity have dominion over me.*"

3. His Word restores our soul

a. Psalms 19:7 – "*The law of the LORD is perfect, converting the soul: the testimony of the LORD is sure, making wise the simple.*"
b. James 1:21 – "*Wherefore lay apart all filthiness and superfluity of naughtiness, and receive with meekness the engrafted word, which is able to save your souls.*"
c. Isaiah 55:3 – "*Incline your ear, and come unto me: hear, and your soul shall live; and I will make an everlasting covenant with you, even the sure mercies of David.*"
d. Psalms 119:28 – "*My soul melteth for heaviness: strengthen thou me according unto thy word.*"
e. Psalms 119:49-50 – "[49]*Remember the word unto thy servant, upon which thou hast caused me to hope.* [50]*This is my comfort in my affliction: for thy word hath quickened me.*"

B. We must put off the old man, Ephesians 4:21-24 – "[21]*If so be that ye have heard him, and have been taught by him, as the truth is in Jesus:* [22]*That ye put off concerning the former conversation the old man, which is corrupt according to the deceitful lusts;* [23]*And be renewed in the spirit of your mind;* [24]*And that ye put on the new man, which after God is created in righteousness and true holiness.*"
C. Our minds must be renewed, Romans 12:2 – "*And be not conformed to this world: but be ye transformed by the renewing of your mind, that ye may prove what is that good, and acceptable, and perfect, will of God.*"

D. We must work and walk out our own salvation

1. Philippians 2:12 – "*Wherefore, my beloved, as ye have always obeyed, not as in my presence only, but now much more in my absence, work out your own salvation with fear and trembling.*" – These are the things God requires us to do. No one else can do them for us. And, whether we do them or not determines whether or not we overcame.

a. Reckon ourselves dead to sin, Romans 6:11 – "*Likewise reckon ye also yourselves to be dead indeed unto sin, but alive unto God through Jesus Christ our Lord.*"
b. Judge ourselves, I Corinthians 11:31 – "*For if we would judge ourselves, we should not be judged.*"
c. Cleanse ourselves, II Corinthians 7:1 – "*Having therefore these promises, dearly beloved, let us cleanse ourselves from all filthiness of the flesh and spirit, perfecting holiness in the fear of God*"
d. Mortify self (put to death), Colossians 3:5 – "*Mortify therefore your members which are upon the earth; fornication, uncleanness, inordinate affection, evil concupiscence, and covetousness, which is idolatry:*"
e. Take heed and continue in Word, I Timothy 4:16 – "*Take heed unto thyself, and unto the doctrine; continue in them: for in doing this thou shalt both save thyself, and them that hear thee.*"
f. Purge self, II Timothy 2:21 – "*If a man therefore purge himself from these, he shall be a vessel unto honour, sanctified, and meet for the master's use, and prepared unto every good work.*"

g. Humble self, I Peter 5:6 – "*Humble yourselves therefore under the mighty hand of God, that he may exalt you in due time*"
h. Purify self, I John 3:2-3 – "[2]*Beloved, now are we the sons of God, and it doth not yet appear what we shall be: but we know that, when he shall appear, we shall be like him; for we shall see him as he is.* [3]*And every man that hath this hope in him purifieth himself, even as he is pure.*"
i. Building up yourself, Jude 20 – "*But ye, beloved, building up yourselves on your most holy faith, praying in the Holy Ghost*"

Lesson 23

Water Baptism

I. Water Baptism Is Not Merely A Form Or Meaningless Ceremony. It Is A Definite Experience In The Life Of A Child Of God.

A. Water Baptism

1. Hebrews 6:2 – *"Of the doctrine of baptisms, and of laying on of hands, and of resurrection of the dead, and of eternal judgment."* (Greek) – doctrine of washing
2. Acts 2:38 – *"Then Peter said unto them, Repent, and be baptized every one of you in the name of Jesus Christ for the remission of sins, and ye shall receive the gift of the Holy Ghost."* God's divine plan
3. Meaning of the word "baptize" (Greek) – to dip, to plunge, to immerse. By definition and usage the word means to put into or under water so as to immerse or submerge. We should never make more out of water baptism than it is. Neither, should we belittle it in any way, but we should give it its proper recognition. It is important because Jesus commanded it.

B. Principles of Baptism

1. A test (water) – Throughout the scriptures, water has played an important role in the dealings of God. Water has been used as a test, a proving ground, because it exposes certain things. God has made therefore, water baptism as a test to see if you will do God's will God's way or your way. As we look at these scriptures, we can see water baptism is a test. What is our reaction to it?

a. Exodus 15:22-25 – water of Marah (bitter)

1) Exodus 17:7 – *"And he called the name of the place Massah, and Meribah, because of the chiding of the children of Israel, and because they tempted the LORD, saying, Is the LORD among us, or not?"* – Waters of Meribah (strife)
2) Psalms 81:7 – *"Thou calledst in trouble, and I delivered thee; I answered thee in the secret place of thunder: I proved thee at the waters of Meribah. Selah."*

b. II Kings 5:9-14 – test of pride
c. Judges 7:1-7 (emphasis verse 4) – tried them with water

In many places like communist countries being water baptized is a real test of faith. It is proving ground of whether or not you are serious about your walk with God. In other countries to be immersed in water, not sprinkled, is a real test of faith. For some people it is simply a test of their pride.

2. Old Testament type of water baptism

a. Exodus 14:9-31

1) I Corinthians 10:1-6

a) Just as they were saved out of Egypt – in type as we are. They knew a lamb had been slain (over the post of their doors) and they were delivered from Egypt by the blood of the Lamb that they slew. So, also are we delivered by the blood of the Lamb, Jesus
b) Israel confessed they were slaves, we confer we are sinners; they cried for deliverance – just as we do and both are delivered.

c) They walked through the midst of the sea just as we go into the midst of the water and are baptized (I Corinthians 10:2)

This Old Testament example is a type of our salvation (deliverance from Egypt – lamb slain) and water baptism (passing through the Red Sea).

II. Why Water Baptism Did Not Seem So Unusual To the Jews; Israel as a nation was familiar with the principle of water as a source to cleanse and sanctify. They were use to the term "washings."

A. Washings – As we stated earlier the Greek word for "baptisms" means literally washings.

1. Mark 7:4-5 – "*And when they come from the market, except they wash, they eat not. And many other things there be, which they have received to hold, as the washing of cups, and pots, brasen vessels, and of tables. 5Then the Pharisees and scribes asked him, Why walk not thy disciples according to the tradition of the elders, but eat bread with unwashen hands?*"
2. Hebrews 6:2 – "*Of the doctrine of baptisms, and of laying on of hands, and of resurrection of the dead, and of eternal judgment.*"
3. Hebrews 9:10 – "*Which stood only in meats and drinks, and divers washings, and carnal ordinances, imposed on them until the time of reformation.*"

In each of these scriptures it is the Greek word *baptismos.* Three times translated "washings", and once in Hebrews 6:2 as "baptisms". The Jews, however, took this "washing" literally to mean just that. They did not see that it represented sanctification and cleansing, but nevertheless God restores.

B. Old Testament Washings

1. Laver – Exodus 30: 17-21 – A type of baptism in the Old Testament. Priests washed their hands after killing and offering sacrificed animals on the brazen altar.

a. Brazen altar – speaks of salvation
b. Laver – sanctification and water baptism

2. Consecration of priests

a. Exodus 29:1-9 – (Leviticus 8:6) – Before they were to put clothes on they were washed in water.

1) Bullocks and rams killed – salvation, justification
2) Washing in water – sanctification – water baptism
3) Clothes – garments of righteousness, glorification

3. Purification of uncleanness

a. Numbers 19

1) Leviticus 17:5 – "*To the end that the children of Israel may bring their sacrifices, which they offer in the open field, even that they may bring them unto the LORD, unto the door of the tabernacle of the congregation, unto the priest, and offer them for peace offerings unto the LORD.*"

4. Leviticus 16:26-28 – So, now you see that the Israelites were accustomed to this principle of washing.

III. John's Baptism

A. Matthew 3:1-6

1. John 1:26-33 – There is a distinction between the baptism of John and Christian baptism (Acts 19:1-5). In Acts 19 upon hearing about the Lord Jesus these disciples were rebaptized in the name of Jesus.

John's baptism was a preparatory baptism. Its primary function was to prepare peoples' hearts for the coming of the Messiah. One would repent of his sins and be water baptized, preparing his heart for the time when he would receive Jesus as Saviour and be born again, then water baptized in the name of the Lord. John's baptism then was a baptism of:

a. Repentance
b. Remission of sins
c. Preparation for the Messiah

2. Luke 1:77 – *"To give knowledge of salvation unto his people by the remission of their sins,"*

IV. Jesus' Baptism

A. Matthew 3:13-17 – *"[13]Then cometh Jesus from Galilee to Jordan unto John, to be baptized of him. [14]But John forbad him, saying, I have need to be baptized of thee, and comest thou to me? [15]And Jesus answering said unto him, Suffer it to be so now: for thus it becometh us to fulfil all righteousness. Then he suffered him. [16]And Jesus, when he was baptized, went up straightway out of the water: and, lo, the heavens were opened unto him, and he saw the Spirit of God descending like a dove, and lighting upon him: [17]And lo a voice from heaven, saying, This is my beloved Son, in whom I am well pleased."* – We have to ask ourselves why Jesus was baptized. There was no need for him to repent; he was pure and spotless, without sin. Jesus, himself, gives us the answer.

1. To fulfill all righteousness – The law required all priest to be consecrated when they were around thirty years old.

a. Numbers 4:3 – *"From thirty years old and upward even until fifty years old all that enter into the host, to do the work in the tabernacle of the congregation."*
b. Their consecration consisted of washing and anointing

1) Exodus 29:4-7 – washing
2) Leviticus 8:6-36 – anointing

Jesus, to fulfill all the law, had to comply. The difference comes from the fact he was water baptized from washing and the dove descended upon him for his anointing.

c. Jesus was the Lamb to be slain, Leviticus 1:1-9 – This lamb offered was to be without blemish and its pieces were to be washed in water before being placed upon the altar.
d. He did it to set the example for his disciples of submission and obedience to the Father's will.

1) I Peter 2:21-22 – *"For even hereunto were ye called: because Christ also suffered for us, leaving us an example, that ye should follow his steps:"* [vs22] *"Who did no sin, neither was guile found in his mouth:"*

V. New Testament Examples of Water Baptism

A. Scriptures

1. Matthew 28:19 – *"Go ye therefore, and teach all nations, baptizing them in the name of the Father, and of the Son, and of the Holy Ghost:"*
2. Acts 2:38 – *"Then Peter said unto them, Repent, and be baptized every one of you in the name of Jesus Christ for the remission of sins, and ye shall receive the gift of the Holy Ghost."*
3. Mark 16:16 – *"He that believeth and is baptized shall be saved; but he that believeth not shall be damned."*
4. John 4:1-2
5. Acts 8:12-16
6. Acts 8:35-39
7. Acts 9:15-18
8. Acts 10:44-48
9. Acts 16:30-34
10. Acts 19:1-5

Lesson 24

The Door To The Holy Place

I. The Entrance To The Holy Place, Exodus 26:36-37, 36:37-38

This was to be the entrance way from natural light into supernatural light. The outer court and all it represents was done in sunlight or natural light. Once you step past the Brazen Altar and Brass Laver, you will now be entering into an area where there is only the light that God provides. Man's ability to reason, his intellect, and all of his soulish abilities to understand goes away from him here. The light from the candlestick (Baptism of the Holy Spirit) must be embraced if you are to understand all that the Holy Place offers.

Exodus 26:36-37 – "[36]*And thou shalt make an hanging for the door of the tent, of blue, and purple, and scarlet, and fine twined linen, wrought with needlework.* [37]*And thou shalt make for the hanging five pillars of shittim wood, and overlay them with gold, and their hooks shall be of gold: and thou shalt cast five sockets of brass for them.*"

Exodus 36:37-38 – "[37]*And he made an hanging for the tabernacle door of blue, and purple, and scarlet, and fine twined linen, of needlework;* [38]*And the five pillars of it with their hooks: and he overlaid their chapiters and their fillets with gold: but their five sockets were of brass.*"

A. The door of the tent

1. Hebrew for door – an opening, an entranceway; it comes from a root that means – to open wide, to loosen, to begin, to plow, to carve. From this definition the imagery of the type is fascinating.
2. What this signifies:

    a. An entrance way into greater spiritual realities
    b. Wide enough for all to enter into
    c. Things begin to loosen for us spiritually or our revelation is loosed of the things of God.
    d. Though we are saved, this entranceway is the beginning of the greater realities of God.
    e. Here we begin to plow or to carve out our true revelation of God.

B. Other names for this entrance

1. The hanging for the door of the tent – Exodus 26:36
2. The hanging – Exodus 26:37
3. The hanging for the tabernacle door – Exodus 36:37
4. The door of the tabernacle of the congregation – Leviticus 1:3

C. Facts concerning this door

1. The Holy Place measured 10x10x20 = 2000 cubits; this speaks of the 2000 years of the church age.
2. The Holy Place was reserved specifically for the priests
3. Because this represents the church age, it speaks of the church's priestly ministry

    a. I Peter 2:1-9 – "...[5]*Ye also, as lively stones, are built up a spiritual house, an holy priesthood, to offer up spiritual sacrifices, acceptable to God by Jesus Christ...*[9]*But ye are a chosen generation, a royal priesthood, an holy nation, a peculiar people; that ye should shew forth the praises of him who hath called you out of darkness into his marvellous light:*"
    b. Revelation 1:6 – "*And hath made us kings and priests unto God and his Father; to him be glory and dominion for ever and ever. Amen.*"
    c. Exodus 19:6 – "*And ye shall be unto me a kingdom of priests, and an holy nation. These are the words which thou shalt speak unto the children of Israel.*"

D. Things the door symbolizes:

1. Entrance into the deep things of God
2. Entrance into the Spirit filled life (candlestick)
3. Entrance into true revelation of the Word (shewbread)
4. Entrance into worship in spirit and in truth (golden altar)
5. This door is the passage way into the feast of Pentecost
6. It is the realm of young men, I John 2:13 (outer court – babes and children; holy place – young men; most holy place – aged and fathers)
7. It certainly typifies the 60 fold believer, Matthew 13:23 (outer court – 30 fold; holy place – 60 fold; most holy place – 100 fold)
8. This also is the entrance way into "oil for light"; thus the ability to become one of the wise virgins (Matthew 25:1-13)
9. It is the domain of the acceptable will of God, Romans 12:2 (outer court – good; holy place – acceptable; most holy place – perfect will)

10. The colors of the "hanging"; all of these speak of our entry into these experientially

    a. blue – heavenly
    b. purple – royalty
    c. scarlet – suffering

11. Fine twined linen, wrought with needlework – this speaks of our righteousness being worked into us (Revelation 19:8). The Holy Spirit will now take what God has done in our human spirit and work it (wrought) into our soulish nature. Notice, it is done with needlework – it is a delicate operation (Proverbs 29:21).

12. Five pillars of shittim wood overlaid with gold

    a. Gold represents God's character
    b. Five represents grace
    c. Wood represents humanity
    d. Grace is making us into pillars of God's character over our humanity

13. Five sockets of brass

    a. Five represents grace
    b. Brass represents judgment
    c. This speaks to us of His ongoing work of judgment in our lives. This, of course, is tempered with His mercy and grace.

        1) Proverbs 16:6 – *"By mercy and truth iniquity is purged: and by the fear of the LORD men depart from evil."*
        2) Psalms 101:1 – *"I will sing of mercy and judgment: unto thee, O LORD, will I sing."*
        3) Psalms 103:8 – *"The LORD is merciful and gracious, slow to anger, and plenteous in mercy."*
        4) Proverbs 3:3 – *"Let not mercy and truth forsake thee: bind them about thy neck; write them upon the table of thine heart:"*
        5) Proverbs 20:28 – *"Mercy and truth preserve the king: and his throne is upholden by mercy."*
        6) James 2:13 – *"For he shall have judgment without mercy, that hath shewed no mercy; and mercy rejoiceth against judgment."*

7) Psalms 25:10 – *"All the paths of the LORD are mercy and truth unto such as keep his covenant and his testimonies."*
8) Psalms 61:7 – *"He shall abide before God for ever: O prepare mercy and truth, which may preserve him."*
9) Psalms 85:10 – *"Mercy and truth are met together; righteousness and peace have kissed each other."*
10) Psalms 98:3 – *"He hath remembered his mercy and his truth toward the house of Israel: all the ends of the earth have seen the salvation of our God."*

E. Jesus is the door

1. John 10:7-9 – *"[7]Then said Jesus unto them again, Verily, verily, I say unto you, I am the door of the sheep. [8]All that ever came before me are thieves and robbers: but the sheep did not hear them. [9]I am the door: by me if any man enter in, he shall be saved, and shall go in and out, and find pasture."* – Jesus is and will always be the only entranceway into all that is, belongs to, or is revealed by God and about God.

a. Acts 4:12 – *"Neither is there salvation in any other: for there is none other name under heaven given among men, whereby we must be saved."*
b. John 14:6 – *"Jesus saith unto him, I am the way, the truth, and the life: no man cometh unto the Father, but by me."*
c. I Timothy 2:5 – *"For there is one God, and one mediator between God and men, the man Christ Jesus;"*
d. Hebrews 1:2-3 – *"[2]Hath in these last days spoken unto us by his Son, whom he hath appointed heir of all things, by whom also he made the worlds; [3]Who being the brightness of his glory, and the express image of his person, and upholding all things by the word of his power, when he had by himself purged our sins, sat down on the right hand of the Majesty on high;"*

II. Other Doors In Scripture

A. The door into all things spiritually

1. Revelation 4:1 – *"After this I looked, and, behold, a door was opened in heaven: and the first voice which I heard was as it were of a trumpet talking with me; which said, Come up hither, and I will shew thee things which must be hereafter."*
2. Revelation 3:8 – *"I know thy works: behold, I have set before thee an open door, and no man can shut it: for thou hast a little strength, and hast kept my word, and hast not denied my name."*
3. Matthew 25:10 – *"And while they went to buy, the bridegroom came; and they that were ready went in with him to the marriage: and the door was shut."*
4. Isaiah 6:4 – *"And the posts of the door moved at the voice of him that cried, and the house was filled with smoke."*
5. Psalms 24:7, 9 – *"[7]Lift up your head, O ye gates; and be ye lift up, ye everlasting doors; and the King of glory shall come in…[9]Lift up your heads, O ye gates; even lift them up, ye everlasting doors; and the King of glory shall come in."*
6. Proverbs 8:34-35 – *"[34]Blessed is the man that heareth me, watching daily at my gates, waiting at the posts of my doors. [35]For whoso findeth me findeth life, and shall obtain favour of the LORD."*

B. Door of hope, Hosea 2:15 – *"And I will give her her vineyards from thence, and the valley of Achor for a door of hope: and she shall sing there, as in the days of her youth, and as in the day when she came up out of the land of Egypt."* Achor means "trouble". God will use our valley of trouble as a door of hope in our life.

C. Door of decision (where two ways meet)

1. Mark 11:4 – "*And they went their way, and found the colt tied by the door without in a place where two ways met; and they loose him.*"
2. Revelation 3:20 – "*Behold, I stand at the door, and knock: if any man hear my voice, and open the door, I will come in to him, and will sup with him, and he with me.*"

D. Door of our hearts

1. Song of Solomon 5:4 – "*My beloved put in his hand by the hole of the door, and my bowels were moved for him.*"
2. Revelation 3:20 – "*Behold, I stand at the door, and knock: if any man hear my voice, and open the door, I will come in to him, and will sup with him, and he with me.*"

E. A doorkeeper to God's house

1. Psalms 84:10 – "*For a day in thy courts is better than a thousand. I had rather be a doorkeeper in the house of my God, than to dwell in the tents of wickedness.*"
2. I Samuel 3:15 – "*And Samuel lay until the morning, and opened the doors of the house of the LORD. And Samuel feared to shew Eli the vision.*"
3. Ezekiel 47:1 – "*Afterward he brought me again unto the door of the house; and, behold, waters issued out from under the threshold of the house eastward: for the forefront of the house stood toward the east, and the waters came down from under from the right side of the house, at the south side of the altar.*"

F. Door of expectancy, Genesis 18:1-3 – "[1]*And the LORD appeared unto him in the plains of Mamre: and he sat in the tent door in the heat of the day;* [2]*And he lift up his eyes and looked, and, lo, three men stood by him: and when he saw them, he ran to meet them from the tent door, and bowed himself toward the ground,* [3]*And said, My Lord, if now I have found favour in thy sight, pass not away, I pray thee, from thy servant:*"

G. The blood sprinkled door (salvation, Passover)

1. Exodus 12:22-23 – "[22]*And ye shall take a bunch of hyssop, and dip it in the blood that is in the bason, and strike the lintel and the two side posts with the blood that is in the bason; and none of you shall go out at the door of his house until the morning.* [23]*For the LORD will pass through to smite the Egyptians; and when he seeth the blood upon the lintel, and on the two side posts, the LORD will pass over the door, and will not suffer the destroyer to come in unto your houses to smite you.*"
2. John 10:1-9

H. The door of death

1. Job 38:17 – "*Have the gates of death been opened unto thee? or hast thou seen the doors of the shadow of death?*"
2. Ecclesiastes 12:4 – "*And the doors shall be shut in the streets, when the sound of the grinding is low, and he shall rise up at the voice of the bird, and all the daughters of musick shall be brought low;*"

I. The shut door

1. Genesis 6:6, 16 – "[6]*And it repented the LORD that he had made man on the earth, and it grieved him at his heart...*[16]*A window shalt thou make to the ark, and in a cubit shalt thou finish it above; and the door of the ark shalt thou set in the side thereof; with lower, second, and third stories shalt thou make it.*"

2. Matthew 25:10-11 – "[10]*And while they went to buy, the bridegroom came; and they that were ready went in with him to the marriage: and the door was shut.* [11]*Afterward came also the other virgins, saying, Lord, Lord, open to us.*"
3. Isaiah 26:20 – "*Come, my people, enter thou into thy chambers, and shut thy doors about thee: hide thyself as it were for a little moment, until the indignation be overpast.*"

Lesson 25

Golden Candlestick

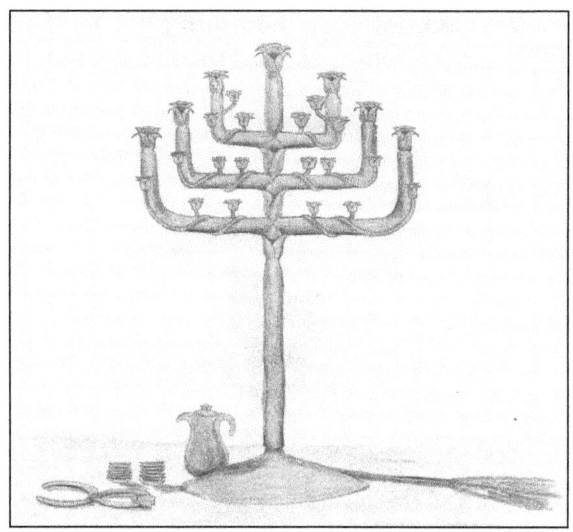

Golden Candlestick

I. Golden Candlestick, Exodus 25:31-40, Exodus 37:17-24, Numbers 4:9, Numbers 8:1-4

Exodus 25:31-40 – "*[31]And thou shalt make a candlestick of pure gold: of beaten work shall the candlestick be made: his shaft, and his branches, his bowls, his knops, and his flowers, shall be of the same. [32]And six branches shall come out of the sides of it; three branches of the candlestick out of the one side, and three branches of the candlestick out of the other side: [33]Three bowls made like unto almonds, with a knop and a flower in one branch; and three bowls made like almonds in the other branch, with a knop and a flower: so in the six branches that come out of the candlestick. [34]And in the candlestick shall be four bowls made like unto almonds, with their knops and their flowers. [35]And there shall be a knop under two branches of the same, and a knop under two branches of the same, and a knop under two branches of the same, according to the six branches that proceed out of the candlestick. [36]Their knops and their branches shall be of the same: all it shall be one beaten work of pure gold. [37]And thou shalt make the seven lamps thereof: and they shall light the lamps thereof, that they may give light over against it. [38]And the tongs thereof, and the snuffdishes thereof, shall be of pure gold. [39]Of a talent of pure gold shall he make it, with all these vessels. [40]And look that thou make them after their pattern, which was shewed thee in the mount.*"

Exodus 37:17-24 – "*[17]And he made the candlestick of pure gold: of beaten work made he the candlestick; his shaft, and his branch, his bowls, his knops, and his flowers, were of the same: [18]And six branches going out of the sides thereof; three branches of the candlestick out of the one side thereof, and three branches of the candlestick out of the other side thereof: [19]Three bowls made after the fashion of almonds in one branch, a knop and a flower; and three bowls made like almonds in another branch, a knop and a flower: so throughout the six branches going out of the candlestick. [20]And in the candlestick were four bowls made like almonds, his knops, and his flowers: [21]And a knop under two branches of the same, and a knop under two branches of the same, and a knop under two branches of the same, according to the six branches going out of it. [22]Their knops and their branches were of the same: all of it was one beaten work of pure gold. [23]And he made his seven lamps, and his snuffers, and his snuffdishes, of pure gold. [24]Of a talent of pure gold made he it, and all the vessels thereof.*"

Numbers 4:9 – "*And they shall take a cloth of blue, and cover the candlestick of the light, and his lamps, and his tongs, and his snuffdishes, and all the oil vessels thereof, wherewith they minister unto it:*"

Numbers 9:1-4 – "*[1]And the LORD spake unto Moses in the wilderness of Sinai, in the first month of the second year after they were come out of the land of Egypt, saying, [2]Let the children of Israel also keep the passover at his appointed season. [3]In the fourteenth day of this month, at even, ye shall keep it in his appointed season: according to all the rites of it, and according to all the ceremonies thereof, shall ye keep it. [4]And Moses spake unto the children of Israel, that they should keep the passover."*

II. Major Themes It Represents

A. Jesus is our light

1. Psalms 27:1 – "*The LORD is my light and my salvation; whom shall I fear? the LORD is the strength of my life; of whom shall I be afraid?*"
2. Psalms 36:9 – "*For with thee is the fountain of life: in thy light shall we see light.*"
3. John 1:4 – "*In him was life; and the life was the light of men.*"
4. John 8:12 – "*Then spake Jesus again unto them, saying, I am the light of the world: he that followeth me shall not walk in darkness, but shall have the light of life.*"
5. II Timothy 1:10 – "*But is now made manifest by the appearing of our Saviour Jesus Christ, who hath abolished death, and hath brought life and immortality to light through the gospel*"
6. John 9:5 – "*As long as I am in the world, I am the light of the world.*"

B. Revelation of the Word of God

1. Proverbs 6:23 – "*For the commandment is a lamp; and the law is light; and reproofs of instruction are the way of life:*"
2. Psalms 119:105 – "*Thy word is a lamp unto my feet, and a light unto my path.*"
3. Psalms 119:130 – "*The entrance of thy words giveth light; it giveth understanding unto the simple.*"
4. II Corinthians 4:4 – "*In whom the god of this world hath blinded the minds of them which believe not, lest the light of the glorious gospel of Christ, who is the image of God, should shine unto them.*"
5. II Corinthians 3:18 – "*But we all, with open face beholding as in a glass the glory of the Lord, are changed into the same image from glory to glory, even as by the Spirit of the Lord.*"
6. Luke 24:27 – "*And beginning at Moses and all the prophets, he expounded unto them in all the scriptures the things concerning himself.*"
7. Mark 4:11 – "*And he said unto them, Unto you it is given to know the mystery of the kingdom of God: but unto them that are without, all these things are done in parables:*"
8. Deuteronomy 29:29 – "*The secret things belong unto the LORD our God: but those things which are revealed belong unto us and to our children for ever, that we may do all the words of this law.*"
9. I Samuel 3:7 – "*Now Samuel did not yet know the LORD, neither was the word of the LORD yet revealed unto him.*"
10. Proverbs 22:20-21 – "*[20]Have not I written to thee excellent things in counsels and knowledge, [21]That I might make thee know the certainty of the words of truth; that thou mightest answer the words of truth to them that send unto thee?*"

C. The church

1. Revelation 1:20 – "*The mystery of the seven stars which thou sawest in my right hand, and the seven golden candlesticks. The seven stars are the angels of the seven churches: and the seven candlesticks which thou sawest are the seven churches.*"
2. Matthew 5:14-16 – "*[14]Ye are the light of the world. A city that is set on an hill cannot be hid. [15]Neither do men light a candle, and put it under a bushel, but on a candlestick; and it giveth light unto all that are in the house. [16]Let your light so shine before men, that they may see your good works, and glorify your Father which is in heaven.*"
3. Zechariah 4:1-5 – "*[1]And the angel that talked with me came again, and waked me, as a man that is wakened out of his sleep, [2]And said unto me, What seest thou? And I said, I have looked, and behold a candlestick all of gold, with a bowl upon the top of it, and his seven lamps thereon, and seven pipes to the seven lamps, which are upon the top thereof: [3]And two olive trees by it, one upon the right side of the bowl, and the other upon the left side thereof...*"

4. Ephesians 5:13-14 – "*[13]But all things that are reproved are made manifest by the light: for whatsoever doth make manifest is light. [14]Wherefore he saith, Awake thou that sleepest, and arise from the dead, and Christ shall give thee light.*"
5. Philippians 2:15 – "*That ye may be blameless and harmless, the sons of God, without rebuke, in the midst of a crooked and perverse nation, among whom ye shine as lights in the world;*"
6. Isaiah 60:1-5 – "*[1]Arise, shine; for thy light is come, and the glory of the LORD is risen upon thee. [2]For, behold, the darkness shall cover the earth, and gross darkness the people: but the LORD shall arise upon thee, and his glory shall be seen upon thee. [3]And the Gentiles shall come to thy light, and kings to the brightness of thy rising...*"
7. I Peter 2:9 – "*But ye are a chosen generation, a royal priesthood, an holy nation, a peculiar people; that ye should shew forth the praises of him who hath called you out of darkness into his marvellous light:*"
8. II Samuel 23:4 – "*And he shall be as the light of the morning, when the sun riseth, even a morning without clouds; as the tender grass springing out of the earth by clear shining after rain.*"
9. Isaiah 62:1 – "*For Zion's sake will I not hold my peace, and for Jerusalem's sake I will not rest, until the righteousness thereof go forth as brightness, and the salvation thereof as a lamp that burneth.*"

D. The baptism of the Holy Ghost – it is a second experience after salvation; the bowls were filled with oil.

1. John 7:37-39 – "*[37]In the last day, that great day of the feast, Jesus stood and cried, saying, If any man thirst, let him come unto me, and drink. [38]He that believeth on me, as the scripture hath said, out of his belly shall flow rivers of living water. [39](But this spake he of the Spirit, which they that believe on him should receive: for the Holy Ghost was not yet given; because that Jesus was not yet glorified.)*"
2. Acts 1:8 – "*But ye shall receive power, after that the Holy Ghost is come upon you: and ye shall be witnesses unto me both in Jerusalem, and in all Judaea, and in Samaria, and unto the uttermost part of the earth.*"
4. Acts 2:1-13 – "*...[4]And they were all filled with the Holy Ghost, and began to speak with other tongues, as the Spirit gave them utterance...*"
5. Acts 8:14-17 – "*[14]Now when the apostles which were at Jerusalem heard that Samaria had received the word of God, they sent unto them Peter and John: [15]Who, when they were come down, prayed for them, that they might receive the Holy Ghost: [16](For as yet he was fallen upon none of them: only they were baptized in the name of the Lord Jesus.) [17]Then laid they their hands on them, and they received the Holy Ghost.*"
6. Acts 10:44-46 – "*[44]While Peter yet spake these words, the Holy Ghost fell on all them which heard the word. [45]And they of the circumcision which believed were astonished, as many as came with Peter, because that on the Gentiles also was poured out the gift of the Holy Ghost. [46]For they heard them speak with tongues, and magnify God. Then answered Peter,*"
7. Acts 19:2-6 – "*[2]He said unto them, Have ye received the Holy Ghost since ye believed? And they said unto him, We have not so much as heard whether there be any Holy Ghost...[6]And when Paul had laid his hands upon them, the Holy Ghost came on them; and they spake with tongues, and prophesied.*"

8. The Holy Spirit is our teacher (He gives us light)

    a. John 14:26 – "*But the Comforter, which is the Holy Ghost, whom the Father will send in my name, he shall teach you all things, and bring all things to your remembrance, whatsoever I have said unto you.*"
    b. John 16:13 – "*Howbeit when he, the Spirit of truth, is come, he will guide you into all truth: for he shall not speak of himself; but whatsoever he shall hear, that shall he speak: and he will shew you things to come.*"
    c. I John 2:20 – "*But ye have an unction from the Holy One, and ye know all things.*"

d. I John 2:27 – *"But the anointing which ye have received of him abideth in you, and ye need not that any man teach you: but as the same anointing teacheth you of all things, and is truth, and is no lie, and even as it hath taught you, ye shall abide in him."*

e. I Corinthians 2:10 – *"But God hath revealed them unto us by his Spirit: for the Spirit searcheth all things, yea, the deep things of God."*

9. This would also include the gifts and fruits of the Spirit

a. Galatians 5:22-23 – *"[22]But the fruit of the Spirit is love, joy, peace, longsuffering, gentleness, goodness, faith, [22]Meekness, temperance: against such there is no law."*

b. I Corinthians 12:1-11 – *"[1]Now concerning spiritual gifts, brethren, I would not have you ignorant. [2]Ye know that ye were Gentiles, carried away unto these dumb idols, even as ye were led. [3]Wherefore I give you to understand, that no man speaking by the Spirit of God calleth Jesus accursed: and that no man can say that Jesus is the Lord, but by the Holy Ghost. [4]Now there are diversities of gifts, but the same Spirit. [5]And there are differences of administrations, but the same Lord. [6]And there are diversities of operations, but it is the same God which worketh all in all. [7]But the manifestation of the Spirit is given to every man to profit withal. [8]For to one is given by the Spirit the word of wisdom; to another the word of knowledge by the same Spirit; [9]To another faith by the same Spirit; to another the gifts of healing by the same Spirit; [10]To another the working of miracles; to another prophecy; to another discerning of spirits; to another divers kinds of tongues; to another the interpretation of tongues: [11]But all these worketh that one and the selfsame Spirit, dividing to every man severally as he will."*

E. Deeper life

1. Hebrews 6:1-3 – *"[1]Therefore leaving the principles of the doctrine of Christ, let us go on unto perfection; not laying again the foundation of repentance from dead works, and of faith toward God, [2]Of the doctrine of baptisms, and of laying on of hands, and of resurrection of the dead, and of eternal judgment. [3]And this will we do, if God permit."*
2. Proverbs 4:18 – *"But the path of the just is as the shining light, that shineth more and more unto the perfect day."*
3. Matthew 4:4 – *"But he answered and said, It is written, Man shall not live by bread alone, but by every word that proceedeth out of the mouth of God."*
4. Philippians 3:10-15 – *"[10]That I may know him, and the power of his resurrection, and the fellowship of his sufferings, being made conformable unto his death; [11]If by any means I might attain unto the resurrection of the dead. [12]Not as though I had already attained, either were already perfect: but I follow after, if that I may apprehend that for which also I am apprehended of Christ Jesus. [13]Brethren, I count not myself to have apprehended: but this one thing I do, forgetting those things which are behind, and reaching forth unto those things which are before, [14]I press toward the mark for the prize of the high calling of God in Christ Jesus. [15]Let us therefore, as many as be perfect, be thus minded: and if in any thing ye be otherwise minded, God shall reveal even this unto you."*
5. Psalms 42:7 – *"Deep calleth unto deep at the noise of thy waterspouts: all thy waves and thy billows are gone over me."*
6. II Corinthians 12:1-10 – a price for revelation

III. More On The Golden Candlestick and What It Means Symbolically

A. Once again it represents the Holy Spirit, revelation, light, a deeper life, gifts and fruits of the Spirit, and the church.

1. The Hebrew word for candlestick, *menorah* – a chandelier, a lampstand; it comes from a root that means – a yoke (for plowing).
2. The word lamp in Hebrew means – to shine, a lamp or flame, burning lamp or a torch

3. This lampstand represents the Pentecostal movement of the early 1900's (led by Charles Parham, William Seymour from Azusa Street, etc.)
4. It was positioned on the south side of the Holy Place (Exodus 26:35). South always speaks of the blessings of God. This lampstand was and is a blessing.
5. These lights were not candles. This was a lampstand upon which were seven lighted lamps with oil. Candles burn out, but these had to be replenished everyday with oil (Matthew 25:1-13). We are responsible to replenish our own oil. Every person who is saved has a lamp. The oil is the power and anointing of the Holy Ghost.
6. This lampstand is inside in the second dimension (holy place). This is where true discipleship begins.
7. No measurements were given for the lampstand. This means there is no way to calculate the revelation of the Word and blessing of the Holy Spirit that God wants to bring forth.
8. There is no wood in this lampstand. It was made wholly of gold (God's nature)
9. Notice it was also "pure" gold. This means untainted by man, clean, and not corrupt.

10. Gold represents God's nature. The lampstand will work with us through the fire.

    a. Job 23:10 – *"But he knoweth the way that I take: when he hath tried me, I shall come forth as gold."*
    b. Psalms 45:9 – *"Kings' daughters were among thy honourable women: upon thy right hand did stand the queen in gold of Ophir."*
    c. Proverbs 27:21 – *"As the fining pot for silver, and the furnace for gold; so is a man to his praise."* – Gold must be formed in the fire
    d. Revelation 3:18 – *"I counsel thee to buy of me gold tried in the fire, that thou mayest be rich; and white raiment, that thou mayest be clothed, and that the shame of thy nakedness do not appear; and anoint thine eyes with eyesalve, that thou mayest see."*
    e. I Corinthians 3:12 – *"Now if any man build upon this foundation gold, silver, precious stones, wood, hay, stubble;"*
    f. I Peter 1:7 – *"That the trial of your faith, being much more precious than of gold that perisheth, though it be tried with fire, might be found unto praise and honour and glory at the appearing of Jesus Christ:"*

11. "Beaten work" – This means the Holy Spirit will be constantly hammering the Word and His character into our lives. We are being shaped by the Holy Spirit's molding.
12. Exodus 30:7-8 – *"[7]And Aaron shall burn thereon sweet incense every morning: when he dresseth the lamps, he shall burn incense upon it. [8]And when Aaron lighteth the lamps at even, he shall burn incense upon it, a perpetual incense before the LORD throughout your generations."* – Every morning we should burn incense. We are supposed to dress the lamps in the morning. Every one of us is supposed to cultivate a hiding place. In the morning and every evening we must worship God.
13. The candlestick was formed out of one talent of Gold. In our economy that would be millions of dollars.

14. It had a central shaft (type of Jesus) out of which came three branches on each side (6 total – 6 being the number of man) – everything comes out of Jesus.

    a. Colossians 1:17-19 – *"[17]And he is before all things, and by him all things consist. [18]And he is the head of the body, the church: who is the beginning, the firstborn from the dead; that in all things he might have the preeminence. [19]For it pleased the Father that in him should all fulness dwell;"*
    b. John 15:1-3, 5, 7 – *"[1]I am the true vine, and my Father is the husbandman. [2]Every branch in me that beareth not fruit he taketh away: and every branch that beareth fruit, he purgeth it, that it may bring forth more fruit. [3]Now ye are clean through the word which I have spoken unto you…[5]I am the vine, ye are the branches: He that abideth in me, and I in him, the same*

bringeth forth much fruit: for without me ye can do nothing. [7]If ye abide in me, and my words abide in you, ye shall ask what ye will, and it shall be done unto you."

c. Colossians 2:10 – *"And ye are complete in him, which is the head of all principality and power:"*

15. The lampstand being formed out of "one" piece of gold would mean symbolically that God and Pentecost can bring unity.
16. The six branches again would represent man and the seventh shaft, the middle one is Jesus. This means man is to reveal the light of the gospel of Jesus. Also, we are incomplete without Him. Seven brings perfection.

17. The four bowls carried the oil. Four is the number for creation. Therefore, this represents God wanting the new creation man to carry His oil to brighten the world.

    a. Matthew 25:3-8 – *"[3]They that were foolish took their lamps, and took no oil with them: [4]But the wise took oil in their vessels with their lamps. [5]While the bridegroom tarried, they all slumbered and slept. [6]And at midnight there was a cry made, Behold, the bridegroom cometh; go ye out to meet him. [7]Then all those virgins arose, and trimmed their lamps. [8]And the foolish said unto the wise, Give us of your oil; for our lamps are gone out."* – God doesn't want our lamps going out.
    b. Psalms 92:10 – *"But my horn shalt thou exalt like the horn of an unicorn: I shall be anointed with fresh oil."* – God wants to anoint us with fresh oil
    c. Proverbs 21:20 – *"There is treasure to be desired and oil in the dwelling of the wise; but a foolish man spendeth it up."* – God doesn't want our lamps to go out.

18. Bowls like almonds – almonds in Scripture speak to us of resurrection and first fruits. The almond tree is the first tree to awake from winter sleep. This symbolizes that as we are filled with the Holy Ghost, our new creation man awakens to shine in the earth and produce fruit.

    a. Jeremiah 1:11-12 – *"[11]Moreover the word of the LORD came unto me, saying, Jeremiah, what seest thou? And I said, I see a rod of an almond tree. [12]Then said the LORD unto me, Thou hast well seen: for I will hasten my word to perform it."*
    b. Numbers 17:8 – *"And it came to pass, that on the morrow Moses went into the tabernacle of witness; and, behold, the rod of Aaron for the house of Levi was budded, and brought forth buds, and bloomed blossoms, and yielded almonds."*

Lesson 26

The Baptism Of The Holy Ghost & Speaking In Tongues

I. Important Words Related To The Baptism Of The Holy Ghost – All of the words we are about to look at are really definitive as to what happens to us when we are baptized in the Holy Ghost. As well as, what this baptism is all about.

A. **Baptize** – The Greek word means to dip, to plunge, to immerse. By definition and usage the word means to put into or under, so as to immerse or submerge. This then means we are to be immersed, put into, submerge in the presence of God, which is God himself. This is something very radical. It is not a drop, a little, or a sprinkling. This means immersion in His presence. That is the baptism of the Holy Ghost. We are to be immersed in the Holy Ghost

B. **Holy Ghost** – We are literally baptized in the third part of the Godhead. This is the only baptism where we are actually baptized in a part of the Godhead. We actually have a mighty portion of God dwelling with us. His purpose is to bring us into a greater fellowship with him, to enable us to do great works.

C. **Fire** – Acts 2:3, *"And there appeared unto them cloven tongues like as of fire, and it sat upon each of them."* – This is an aspect of the baptism of the Holy Ghost many overlook. This aspect is not the blessing of power and of the presence, but this one is the part of his presence that comes to purge us (Luke 3:17). God's fire is sent to purge and burn away from us all that is in our lives that is not of God.

D. **Power** – Acts 1:8, *"But ye shall receive power, after that the Holy Ghost is come upon you…"* This is the Greek word *"dunamis"* meaning force, miraculous power, and ability. It is where we get the word "dynamite." In other words, when we are baptized in the Holy Ghost, we receive power as we are immersed in God's supernatural miracle force. We now have God's power which makes us able to do his miraculous works.

E. **Witness** – Acts 1:8 – *"…after that the Holy Ghost is come upon you: and ye shall be witnesses…"* Being baptized in the Holy Ghost transforms you into a bold witness for Jesus. Consider the apostles hiding for fear (John 20:10) as well as, denying the Lord (John 16:32; Matthew 26:31-35), and look at them after receiving the baptism of the Holy Ghost in Acts 2-5.

II. The Baptism Of The Holy Ghost is *"the promise of the Father"*

1. Acts 1:4-5 – *"[4]And, being assembled together with them, commanded them that they should not depart from Jerusalem, but wait for <u>the promise of the Father</u>, which, saith he, ye have heard of me. [5]For John truly baptized with water; but ye shall be <u>baptized with the Holy Ghost</u> not many days hence."*

    a. Luke 24:49 – *"And, behold, I send <u>the promise of my Father</u> upon you: but tarry ye in the city of Jerusalem, until ye be endued with power from on high."*

    b. Acts 2:4-5 – *"And they were <u>all filled with the Holy Ghost</u>, and began to speak with other tongues, as the Spirit gave them utterance. [5]And there were dwelling at Jerusalem Jews, devout men, out of every nation under heaven."*

    c. Acts 2:32-39 – *"[32]This Jesus hath God raised up, whereof we all are witnesses. [33]Therefore being by the right hand of God exalted, and having <u>received of the Father the promise of the Holy Ghost</u>, he hath shed forth this, which ye now see and hear. [34]For David is not ascended into the heavens: but he saith himself, The LORD said unto my Lord, Sit thou on my right hand, [35]Until I make thy foes thy footstool. [36]Therefore let all the house of Israel know assuredly, that God hath made that same Jesus, whom ye have crucified, both Lord and Christ. [37]Now when they heard this, they were pricked in their heart, and said unto Peter and to the rest of the apostles, Men and brethren, what shall we do? [38]Then Peter said unto them, Repent, and be baptized every one of you in the name of Jesus Christ for the remission of sins, and ye shall receive the gift of the Holy Ghost. [39]For <u>the promise is unto you</u>, and to your children, and to all that are afar off, even as many as the Lord our God shall call."*

2. Galatians 3:13-14 – "[13]*Christ hath redeemed us from the curse of the law, being made a curse for us: for it is written, Cursed is every one that hangeth on a tree:* [14]*That the blessing of Abraham might come on the Gentiles through Jesus Christ; that we might receive the promise of the Spirit through faith.*" Here it is called the "*promise of the Spirit*". Jesus died on the cross, not only for us to be justified by faith (the blessing of Abraham), but in order that we might receive the promise of the Spirit! Jesus died on the cross so that all of His people can receive this baptism.
3. John 7:37-39 – "[37]*In the last day, that great day of the feast, Jesus stood and cried, saying, If any man thirst, let him come unto me, and drink.* [38]*He that believeth on me, as the scripture hath said, out of his belly shall flow rivers of living water.* [39]*(But this spake he of the Spirit, which they that believe on him should receive: for the Holy Ghost was not yet given; because that Jesus was not yet glorified.)*"
4. Ephesians 1:13-14 – "[13]*In whom ye also trusted, after that ye heard the word of truth, the gospel of your salvation: in whom also after that ye believed, ye were sealed with that holy Spirit of promise,* [14]*Which is the earnest of our inheritance until the redemption of the purchased possession, unto the praise of his glory.*"
5. Joel 2:28-29 – "[28]*And it shall come to pass afterward, that I will pour out my spirit upon all flesh; and your sons and your daughters shall prophesy, your old men shall dream dreams, your young men shall see visions:* [29]*And also upon the servants and upon the handmaids in those days will I pour out my spirit.*"

III. A Few Important Questions And Facts About The Baptism Of The Holy Ghost

A. It is a second experience after salvation.

1. Acts 8:5-17 – Notice, they were born again and water baptized, then the apostles sent Peter and John to pray for them to receive the Holy Ghost.
2. Acts 19: 2-7 – "*...since you believed.*" A definitive passage outlining that the baptism is a separate experience to salvation.
3. Ephesians 1:13 – "*In whom ye also trusted, after that ye heard the word of truth, the gospel of your salvation: in whom also after that ye believed, ye were sealed with that holy Spirit of promise,*"
4. John 7:38-39 – "*He that believeth on me, as the scripture hath said, out of his belly shall flow rivers of living water.* [vs. 39] *(But this spake he of the Spirit, which they that believe on him should receive: for the Holy Ghost was not yet given; because that Jesus was not yet glorified.)*"

   a. I Corinthians 12:13 – "*For by one Spirit are we all baptized into one body, whether we be Jews or Gentiles, whether we be bond or free; and have been all made to drink into one Spirit.*"

5. Luke 10:20 – "*Notwithstanding in this rejoice not, that the spirits are subject unto you; but rather rejoice, because your names are written in heaven.*" – The disciples were already saved on the day of Pentecost, so the baptism then would be a second experience. It happens after we are saved. It can happen immediately or at length after being born again. It is up to the individual
6. Mark 16:17 – "*And these signs shall follow them that believe; In my name shall they cast out devils; they shall speak with new tongues;*" – They that believe these signs follow.

B. Is It For Today Or Has It Passed Away? There is not one passage of scripture that even remotely indicates that it is not for today. Like all of God's promises, it is for today.

1. Acts 2:39 – "*For the promise is unto you, and to your children, and to all that are afar off, even as many as the Lord our God shall call.*"
2. I Corinthians 1:4-8 – The gifts are operable until the coming of the Lord. The baptism enables one to move in the gifts.
3. I Corinthians 13:8-10 – What is this which the Bible calls perfect? That which is perfect is not the Bible, as some Baptists would have us believe, all though it is the inspired Word of God. I

believe Paul is talking about Jesus. He is that which is perfect. If you are going to say tongues have passed away you might as well say knowledge has passed away, but, of course, Paul is not saying this. In I Corinthians 1:4-8 he already has said the gifts will be here in operation until the coming of the Lord. That is when all these things will pass away.

4. It is the will of God that every believer receives it – John 7:38-39, Galatians 3:13-14
5. Acts 10:34 – "*Then Peter opened his mouth, and said, Of a truth I perceive that God is no respecter of persons*:" – What he has done for one he will do for all.
6. II Corinthians 1:20 – "*For all the promises of God in him are yea, and in him Amen, unto the glory of God by us.*" (I Kings 8:56)
7. Hebrews 13:8 – "*Jesus Christ the same yesterday, and to day, and for ever.*"
8. Malachi 3:6 – "*For I am the LORD, I change not; therefore ye sons of Jacob are not consumed.*" – God does not change his mind about what he gives to his people.
9. History records people believing and receiving this baptism ever since the early church.
10. I, myself, have received it. So, no matter what someone's theory may be I have personally disproved it.

C. Tongues Are the Evidence of the Baptism of The Holy Ghost

1. I Corinthians 12:7 – "*But the manifestation of the Spirit is given to every man to profit withal.*" – Every man baptized in the Holy Ghost is given the manifestation of the Spirit. I believe in particular this is speaking about tongues. Evidence in all three baptisms

   a. Baptism of Blood – a clean heart, a changed life
   b. Baptism in Water – a soaking, drenched body
   c. Baptism in Holy Ghost – speaking in tongues

2. Accounts of the baptism of the Holy Ghost and the manifestation of tongues.

   a. Acts 2: 1-5
   b. Acts 10: 43-48
   c. Acts 19: 1-7
   d. Acts 9:17 – "*And Ananias went his way, and entered into the house; and putting his hands on him said, Brother Saul, the Lord, even Jesus, that appeared unto thee in the way as thou camest, hath sent me, that thou mightest receive thy sight, and be filled with the Holy Ghost*". (I Corinthians 14:18) – In Paul's account there is no mention of him speaking in tongues, but that does not mean it did not happen. We find later in I Corinthians 14 that he does speak in tongues. This would confirm to me that he did.
   e. Acts 8:14, 18 – In this account, we notice that Simeon "saw" that through laying on of hands the Holy Ghost was given. What did he see? Let's compare this with Acts 2:33. I believe he saw and heard them speak with tongues. Even if the last two accounts (Acts 9:17 and Acts 8:14, 18) could not be proven, we have three witnesses, which according to the Word, establishers this as principle.

IV. Two Types of Speaking in Tongues – This is where most people get confused!

A. Manifestation of the Spirit (prayer language of tongues)

1. I Corinthians 12:7 – "*But the manifestation of the Spirit is given to every man to profit withal*".
2. I Corinthians 14:2, 28 – "[2]*For he that speaketh in an unknown tongue speaketh not unto men, but unto God: for no man understandeth him; howbeit in the spirit he speaketh mysteries...*[28]*But if there be no interpreter, let him keep silence in the church; and let him speak to himself, and to God.*"

3. I Corinthians 14:14-15 – "*[14]For if I pray in an unknown tongue, my spirit prayeth, but my understanding is unfruitful. [15]What is it then? I will pray with the spirit, and I will pray with the understanding also: I will sing with the spirit, and I will sing with the understanding also.*"
4. I Corinthians 14:4 – "*He that speaketh in an unknown tongue edifieth himself; but he that prophesieth edifieth the church*".

This is the prayer language of the Spirit, which every believer is to use to be edified, built up, pray and worship with. These tongues are simply spoken unto God.

B. The gift of Tongues

1. I Corinthians 12:10, 30 – "*...[10]To another the working of miracles; to another prophecy; to another discerning of spirits; to another divers kinds of tongues; to another the interpretation of tongues...[30]Have all the gifts of healing? do all speak with tongues? do all interpret?*" – This is the supernatural gift of speaking in tongues. It is used to speak to men for God. It, along with the interpretation of tongues, is the same as the gift of prophecy.
2. I Corinthians 14: 21-27 – These are the tongues that must be interpreted. These tongues are meant not to edify the individual, but to edify and build up the church.

C. How Can We Understand This?

1. I Corinthians 12:29–30 – "*Are all apostles? are all prophets? are all teachers? are all workers of miracle"s? Have all the gifts of healing? do all speak with tongues? do all interpret?*" – These verses here bring more confusion than any others. We must rightly divide the Scriptures here.

   a. "*Are all apostles?*"
   b. "*Are all prophets?*"

This is referring to the gifts; both ministry offices and supernatural gifts. Not everyone is called to, or given the ministry offices of an apostle, nor is everyone given the supernatural gift of tongues (which is speaking for God to men, not for private worship and edification). But everyone is called to prophecy, everyone is called to preach, all are to speak with tongues (prayer language) I Corinthians 14:5, 30; I Corinthians 12:7.

V. Scriptural Reasons Why We Should Speak In Tongues

A. Tongues are a sign

1. I Corinthians 14:22 – "*Wherefore tongues are for a sign, not to them that believe, but to them that believe not: but prophesying serveth not for them that believe not, but for them which believe.*"
2. Mark 16:17 – "*And these signs shall follow them that believe; In my name shall they cast out devils; they shall speak with new tongues;*"
3. Isaiah 28:11-12 – "*[11]For with stammering lips and another tongue will he speak to this people. [12]To whom he said, This is the rest wherewith ye may cause the weary to rest; and this is the refreshing: yet they would not hear.*"
4. Acts 2:33 – "*Therefore being by the right hand of God exalted, and having received of the Father the promise of the Holy Ghost, he hath shed forth this, which ye now see and hear.*"

Tongues are a sign to the unbeliever. They are a <u>supernatural</u> sign! To believers tongues are not a sign because everyone <u>should</u> be speaking in tongues. Tongues were commonplace in Paul's day and should be now.

B. It is the will of God

1. I Corinthians 14:37-39 – "*... forbid not to speak with tongues.*"
2. I Corinthians 14:5, 15, 26 – "*...I will pray with the spirit, and I will pray with the understanding also: I will sing with the spirit, and I will sing with the understanding also...*" (I Corinthians 14:14 – "*For if I pray in an unknown tongue, my spirit prayeth...*")
3. John 4:23-24 – "[23]*But the hour cometh, and now is, when the true worshippers shall worship the Father in spirit and in truth: for the Father seeketh such to worship him.* [24]*God is a Spirit: and they that worship him must worship him in spirit and in truth.*"
4. Ephesians 5:17-19 – "[17]*Wherefore be ye not unwise, but understanding what the will of the Lord is.* [18]*And be not drunk with wine, wherein is excess; but be filled with the Spirit;* [19]*Speaking to yourselves in psalms and hymns and spiritual songs, singing and making melody in your heart to the Lord;*"

C. It is profitable

1. I Corinthians 12:7 – "*But the manifestation of the Spirit is given to every man to profit withal.*" – Tongues are profitable because they edify, build and stimulate our faith
2. I Corinthians 14:4 – "*He that speaketh in an unknown tongue edifieth himself...*"
3. Jude 20 – "*But ye, beloved, building up yourselves on your most holy faith, praying in the Holy Ghost,*" The word "*edifieth*" in I Corinthians 14:4 and "*building up*" in Jude 20 are the same Greek root word which means to build upon, housebuilder, and to construct. Speaking in tongues enhances our worship. You might ask "What good does it do to speak in tongues?" The answer is, "How good is it to praise and magnify God?"

    a. Acts 2:11 – "*Cretes and Arabians, we do hear them speak in our tongues the wonderful works of God.*"
    b. Acts 10:46 – "*For they heard them speak with tongues, and magnify God. Then answered Peter,*"
    c. I Corinthians 14:17 – "*For thou verily givest thanks well...*"

D. Speaking in tongues brings rest and refreshing.

1. Isaiah 28:11-12 – "[11]*For with stammering lips and another tongue will he speak to this people.* [12]*To whom he said, This is the rest wherewith ye may cause the weary to rest; and this is the refreshing: yet they would not hear.*"
2. Job 32:18-21 – "[18]*For I am full of matter, the spirit within me constraineth me.* [19]*Behold, my belly is as wine which hath no vent; it is ready to burst like new bottles.* [20]*I will speak, that I may be refreshed: I will open my lips and answer.* [21]*Let me not, I pray you, accept any man's person, neither let me give flattering titles unto man.*"
3. Isaiah 41:18 – "*I will open rivers in high places, and fountains in the midst of the valleys: I will make the wilderness a pool of water, and the dry land springs of water.*"
4. John 7:37-39 – "[37]*In the last day, that great day of the feast, Jesus stood and cried, saying, If any man thirst, let him come unto me, and drink.* [38]*He that believeth on me, as the scripture hath said, out of his belly shall flow rivers of living water.* [39]*(But this spake he of the Spirit, which they that believe on him should receive: for the Holy Ghost was not yet given; because that Jesus was not yet glorified.)*"

E. Speaking in tongues will help us say right things. When you are speaking in tongues, you are doing one of four things.

1. Praying according to the will of God (Romans 8:26-27)
2. Edifying or building yourself up (Jude 20)
3. Giving thanks or worshipping (I Corinthians 14:17)
4. Speaking the mysteries of God (I Corinthians 14:2)

The Greek word of "*mysteries*" is "*musterion*" meaning a secret, a mystery. Among the ancient Greeks, the mysteries were religious rites and ceremonies practiced by secret societies into which anyone who so desired might be received. Those who were initiated into these mysteries became possessors of certain knowledge, which was not imparted to the uninitiated. Here is a quote from Vine's dictionary: "We, then, by speaking in tongues are released into God's divine secrets and can and will possess knowledge those who do not speak in tongues will not have."

F. Prayer

1. Romans 8:26-27 – "*[26]Likewise the Spirit also helpeth our infirmities: for we know not what we should pray for as we ought: but the Spirit itself maketh intercession for us with groanings which cannot be uttered. [27]And he that searcheth the hearts knoweth what is the mind of the Spirit, because he maketh intercession for the saints according to the will of God.*"

    a. We do not always know what to pray, but He does
    b. He helps our weaknesses
    c. Always prays according to the will of God

2. Ephesians 6:18 – "*Praying always with all prayer and supplication in the Spirit, and watching thereunto with all perseverance and supplication for all saints;*" – A part of our spiritual armor.
3. Jude 20 – "*But ye, beloved, building up yourselves on your most holy faith, praying in the Holy Ghost,*"
4. I Corinthians 14:14-15 – "*[14]For if I pray in an unknown tongue, my spirit prayeth, but my understanding is unfruitful. [15]What is it then? I will pray with the spirit, and I will pray with the understanding also: I will sing with the spirit, and I will sing with the understanding also.*" – When we pray in the Spirit we are not limited to our own understanding
5. I Thessalonians 5:17 – "*Pray without ceasing.*" – The only way to pray without ceasing is in tongues.

VI. Questions Concerning Tongues

A. Are They The Least Of The Gifts? The answer to that is simply No. Fundamentalists have tried to make light of speaking in tongues, and have tried to deemphasize their importance by saying that because they are the last gift mentioned in I Corinthians 12:10 they are the least.

1. I Corinthians 12:1-30 – These are not listed in order of importance. All of the gifts are operated by the Spirit and none are of greater importance than the other.
2. What are the best gifts? I Corinthians 12:31 – "*But covet earnestly the best gifts: and yet shew I unto you a more excellent way.*" – These would be whatever the love of God demanded for the moment. If healing is needed, then that would be the best gift, if deliverance, faith, miracles, discernment, etc, then whatever the gift needed at the moment would be the best.
3. If we are going to say tongues are the least simply because it is listed last then what about:

    a. I Corinthians 13:13 – "*And now abideth faith, hope, charity, these three; but the greatest of these is charity.*"
    b. Luke 16:10 – "*He that is faithful in that which is least is faithful also in much: and he that is unjust in the least is unjust also in much.*" – No matter what, God expects faithfulness even in the least gift.
    c. Matthew 19:30 – "*But many that are first shall be last; and the last shall be first.*"
    d. Matthew 20:16 – "*So the last shall be first, and the first last: for many be called, but few chosen.*"
    e. Also, why did God seem to ignore the firstborns and choose the younger brothers?

B. Is Love More Important?

1. I Corinthians 12:31 – "*But covet earnestly the best gifts: and yet shew I unto you a more excellent way.*" The reason Paul says this is that love is to be the motivation for the gifts, not an ambitious desire to be seen of men or any other reason. He purposely put *I Corinthians 13* between chapters 12 and 14 to show us love is why we are to move in the gifts. This says to me if we refuse to move in the gifts, we are not walking in God's love. Contents of I Corinthians 12-14*:*

   1) I Corinthians 12 – lists the gifts
   2) I Corinthians 13 – love, our motivation
   3) I Corinthians 14 – how to operate gifts in a meeting

2. We can have both; I Corinthians 14:1 – "*Follow after charity, and desire spiritual gifts, but rather that ye may prophesy.*"

C. Is Tongues Of The Devil? This is one that religious people or any person who does not want to receive truth says. If it is just too hard for them, or it will cost too much, or their pride resists, or they are simply ignorant of the Scripture, or unwilling to obey God's Word because it is not something they like, or it is not of their tradition, they make it easy on themselves and use this excuse.

1. I Corinthians 12:3 – "*Wherefore I give you to understand, that no man speaking by the Spirit of God calleth Jesus accursed: and that no man can say that Jesus is the Lord, but by the Holy Ghost.*" – There is no way anyone speaking by the Spirit (in tongues) can be of the devil.
2. Matthew 11:15-19 – "*[15]He that hath ears to hear, let him hear. [16]But whereunto shall I liken this generation? It is like unto children sitting in the markets, and calling unto their fellows, [17]And saying, We have piped unto you, and ye have not danced; we have mourned unto you, and ye have not lamented. [18]For John came neither eating nor drinking, and they say, He hath a devil. [19]The Son of man came eating and drinking, and they say, Behold a man gluttonous, and a winebibber, a friend of publicans and sinners. But wisdom is justified of her children.*" – Some people will never choose or receive truth no matter what. They will always try to find a way out.
3. This is blasphemy of the Holy Ghost (attributing the works of God to the devil, Matthew 12:22-34).
4. If tongues are really a manifestation of the devil, then why don't the demon-possessed speak in tongues? Why don't we see people in bars speaking in tongues?

D. Has Tongues Passed Away? The answer is NO. That is simply a theological outlook that does not hold light in the Scriptures.

1. Acts 2:39 – "*For the promise is unto you, and to your children, and to all that are afar off, even as many as the Lord our God shall call.*"
2. I Corinthians 1:4-8 – "*[4]I thank my God always on your behalf, for the grace of God which is given you by Jesus Christ; [5]That in every thing ye are enriched by him, in all utterance, and in all knowledge; [6]Even as the testimony of Christ was confirmed in you: [7]So that ye come behind in no gift; waiting for the coming of our Lord Jesus Christ: [8]Who shall also confirm you unto the end, that ye may be blameless in the day of our Lord Jesus Christ.*"
3. I Corinthians 13:8-10 – "*[8]Charity never faileth: but whether there be prophecies, they shall fail; whether there be tongues, they shall cease; whether there be knowledge, it shall vanish away. [9]For we know in part, and we prophesy in part. [10]But when that which is perfect is come, then that which is in part shall be done away.*" – This speaks of Jesus and His manifested sons.
4. I Corinthians 14:39 – "*Wherefore, brethren, covet to prophesy, and forbid not to speak with tongues.*"
5. Why then do so very many godly people speak in tongues?
6. I Corinthians 14:18 – "*I thank my God, I speak with tongues more than ye all*" – Paul spoke with tongues.

Lesson 27

God's Gifts, Ministries, & Fruits Given To Men

In our ongoing attempt to gain a true Biblical image of God, we now will look at the different, wonderful, and varied gifts God has given to men. We have already seen how much He has done for His people and mankind in general, but now we will take a closer look at some special gifts, ministries, and fruits our great God has given to us, to help perfect us, change us, and make us into the people He wants us to be. All of the things mentioned here, you will see, are great helps to becoming more Christ-like, and ultimately conforming us into His holy image.

There is no greater giver than God Himself. The Scripture says in "*Every good gift and every perfect gift is from above, and cometh down from the Father of lights...*" (James 1:17). Any and all that we ever have will be because God gave it. This is true not only for His people, but also for all creation, for as Scripture also says "*...what hast thou that thou didst not receive? now if thou didst receive it, why dost thou glory, as if thou hadst not received it?*" (I Corinthians 4:7). In this lesson I want us to see not only that God is a giver, the giver of all gifts, the greatest gift being His Son Jesus, but I want us to see some of those gifts and ministries that are special to the body of Christ.

I. Our God is a Giver

A. Scriptural examples

1. James 1:17 – "*Every good gift and every perfect gift is from above, and cometh down from the Father of lights, with whom is no variableness, neither shadow of turning.*"
2. Matthew 7:11 – "*If ye then, being evil, know how to give good gifts unto your children, how much more shall your Father which is in heaven give good things to them that ask him?*"

3. Ecclesiastes 3:13 – "*And also that every man should eat and drink, and enjoy the good of all his labour, it is the gift of God.*"

   a. Ecclesiastes 5:19 – "*Every man also to whom God hath given riches and wealth, and hath given him power to eat thereof, and to take his portion, and to rejoice in his labour; this is the gift of God.*"

4. Deuteronomy 8:18 – "*But thou shalt remember the LORD thy God: for it is he that giveth thee power to get wealth, that he may establish his covenant which he sware unto thy fathers, as it is this day.*"
5. Job 5:8-10 – "*[8]I would seek unto God, and unto God would I commit my cause: [9]Which doeth great things and unsearchable; marvellous things without number: [10]Who giveth rain upon the earth, and sendeth waters upon the fields:*"
6. Psalms 136:25 – "*Who giveth food to all flesh: for his mercy endureth for ever.*"

7. Acts 17:25 – "*Neither is worshipped with men's hands, as though he needed any thing, seeing he giveth to all life, and breath, and all things;*"

   a. Ecclesiastes 8:15 – "*Then I commended mirth, because a man hath no better thing under the sun, than to eat, and to drink, and to be merry: for that shall abide with him of his labour the days of his life, which God giveth him under the sun.*"
   b. Isaiah 42:5 – "*Thus saith God the LORD, he that created the heavens, and stretched them out; he that spread forth the earth, and that which cometh out of it; he that giveth breath unto the people upon it, and spirit to them that walk therein:*"

8. Jeremiah 5:24 – *"Neither say they in their heart, Let us now fear the LORD our God, that giveth rain, both the former and the latter, in his season: he reserveth unto us the appointed weeks of the harvest."*
9. Jeremiah 31:35 – *"Thus saith the LORD, which giveth the sun for a light by day, and the ordinances of the moon and of the stars for a light by night, which divideth the sea when the waves thereof roar; The LORD of hosts is his name:"*
10. I Timothy 6:17 – *"Charge them that are rich in this world, that they be not highminded, nor trust in uncertain riches, but in the living God, who giveth us richly all things to enjoy;"*

B. He gave us Jesus

1. John 3:16 – *"For God so loved the world, that he gave his only begotten Son, that whosoever believeth in him should not perish, but have everlasting life."*
2. John 4:16 – *"Jesus saith unto her, Go, call thy husband, and come hither."*
3. Romans 6:23 – *"For the wages of sin is death; but the gift of God is eternal life through Jesus Christ our Lord."*
4. John 6:32-33 – *"Then Jesus said unto them, Verily, verily, I say unto you, Moses gave you not that bread from heaven; but my Father giveth you the true bread from heaven. For the bread of God is he which cometh down from heaven, and giveth life unto the world."*
5. Romans 5:15-18 – *"[15]But not as the offence, so also is the free gift. For if through the offence of one many be dead, much more the grace of God, and the gift by grace, which is by one man, Jesus Christ, hath abounded unto many. [16]And not as it was by one that sinned, so is the gift: for the judgment was by one to condemnation, but the free gift is of many offences unto justification. [17]For if by one man's offence death reigned by one; much more they which receive abundance of grace and of the gift of righteousness shall reign in life by one, Jesus Christ.) [18]Therefore as by the offence of one judgment came upon all men to condemnation; even so by the righteousness of one the free gift came upon all men unto justification of life."*

C. He sent us the Holy Spirit

1. Luke 11:13 – *"If ye then, being evil, know how to give good gifts unto your children: how much more shall your heavenly Father give the Holy Spirit to them that ask him?"*
2. Acts 2:38 – *"Then Peter said unto them, Repent, and be baptized every one of you in the name of Jesus Christ for the remission of sins, and ye shall receive the gift of the Holy Ghost."*
3. John 3:34 – *"For he whom God hath sent speaketh the words of God: for God giveth not the Spirit by measure unto him."*
4. Hebrews 6:4 – *"For it is impossible for those who were once enlightened, and have tasted of the heavenly gift, and were made partakers of the Holy Ghost,"*
5. Acts 8:14-20 – *"[14]Now when the apostles which were at Jerusalem heard that Samaria had received the word of God, they sent unto them Peter and John: [15]Who, when they were come down, prayed for them, that they might receive the Holy Ghost: [16](For as yet he was fallen upon none of them: only they were baptized in the name of the Lord Jesus.) [17]Then laid they their hands on them, and they received the Holy Ghost. [18]And when Simon saw that through laying on of the apostles' hands the Holy Ghost was given, he offered them money, [19]Saying, Give me also this power, that on whomsoever I lay hands, he may receive the Holy Ghost. [20]But Peter said unto him, Thy money perish with thee, because thou hast thought that the gift of God may be purchased with money."*

6. Acts 10:45 – *"And they of the circumcision which believed were astonished, as many as came with Peter, because that on the Gentiles also was poured out the gift of the Holy Ghost."*

    a. Acts 11:17 – *"Forasmuch then as God gave them the like gift as he did unto us, who believed on the Lord Jesus Christ; what was I, that I could withstand God?"*

D. He gives wisdom

1. Proverbs 2:6 – *"For the LORD giveth wisdom: out of his mouth cometh knowledge and understanding."*
2. Daniel 2:21 – *"And he changeth the times and the seasons: he removeth kings, and setteth up kings: he giveth wisdom unto the wise, and knowledge to them that know understanding:"*
3. James 1:5 – *"If any of you lack wisdom, let him ask of God, that giveth to all men liberally, and upbraideth not; and it shall be given him."*

E. He gives peace

1. John 14:27 – *"Peace I leave with you, my peace I give unto you: not as the world giveth, give I unto you. Let not your heart be troubled, neither let it be afraid."*

F. He gives grace

1. James 4:6 – *"But he giveth more grace. Wherefore he saith, God resisteth the proud, but giveth grace unto the humble."*
2. Proverbs 3:34 – *"Surely he scorneth the scorners: but he giveth grace unto the lowly."*
3. I Peter 5:5 – *"Likewise, ye younger, submit yourselves unto the elder. Yea, all of you be subject one to another, and be clothed with humility: for God resisteth the proud, and giveth grace to the humble."*

G. Salvation is the gift of God, Ephesians 2:8 – *"For by grace are ye saved through faith; and that not of yourselves: it is the gift of God:"*

H. The gift of giving, II Corinthians 9:15 – *"Thanks be unto God for his unspeakable gift."*

I. Celibacy, I Corinthians 7:7 – *"For I would that all men were even as I myself. But every man hath his proper gift of God, one after this manner, and another after that."*

J. Power, Isaiah 40:29 – *"He giveth power to the faint; and to them that have no might he increaseth strength."*

K. Victory, I Corinthians 15:57 – *"But thanks be to God, which giveth us the victory through our Lord Jesus Christ."*

L. Songs, Job 35:10 – *"But none saith, Where is God my maker, who giveth songs in the night;"*

M. He gives us the ability to minister

1. Ephesians 3:7 – *"Whereof I was made a minister, according to the gift of the grace of God given unto me by the effectual working of his power."*
2. Ephesians 4:7 – *"But unto every one of us is given grace according to the measure of the gift of Christ."*
3. I Timothy 4:14 – *"Neglect not the gift that is in thee, which was given thee by prophecy, with the laying on of the hands of the presbytery."*
4. II Timothy 1:6 – *"Wherefore I put thee in remembrance that thou stir up the gift of God, which is in thee by the putting on of my hands."*
5. I Peter 4:10 – *"As every man hath received the gift, even so minister the same one to another, as good stewards of the manifold grace of God."*
6. Daniel 1:4 – *"Children in whom was no blemish, but well favoured, and skilful in all wisdom, and cunning in knowledge, and understanding science, and such as had ability in them to stand in the king's palace, and whom they might teach the learning and the tongue of the Chaldeans."*

II. God's Special Spiritual Gifts

A. In general

1. Psalms 68:18-19 – "[18]*Thou hast ascended on high, thou hast led captivity captive: thou hast received gifts for men; yea, for the rebellious also, that the LORD God might dwell among them.* [19]*Blessed be the Lord, who daily loadeth us with benefits, even the God of our salvation. Selah.*"
2. Hebrews 2:4 – "*God also bearing them witness, both with signs and wonders, and with divers miracles, and gifts of the Holy Ghost, according to his own will?*"
3. Romans 11:29 – "*For the gifts and calling of God are without repentance.*"
4. I Corinthians 12:1, 4-7 – "[1]*Now concerning spiritual gifts, brethren, I would not have you ignorant...*[4]*Now there are diversities of gifts, but the same Spirit.* [5]*And there are differences of administrations, but the same Lord.* [6]*And there are diversities of operations, but it is the same God which worketh all in all.* [7]*But the manifestation of the Spirit is given to every man to profit withal.*"
5. I Corinthians 12:27-31 – "[27]*Now ye are the body of Christ, and members in particular.* [28]*And God hath set some in the church, first apostles, secondarily prophets, thirdly teachers, after that miracles, then gifts of healings, helps, governments, diversities of tongues.* [29]*Are all apostles? are all prophets? are all teachers? are all workers of miracles?* [30]*Have all the gifts of healing? do all speak with tongues? do all interpret?* [31]*But covet earnestly the best gifts: and yet shew I unto you a more excellent way.*"

B. God's special gifts listed

1. Nine gifts of the Spirit, I Corinthians 12:8-10 – "[8]*For to one is given by the Spirit the word of wisdom; to another the word of knowledge by the same Spirit;* [9]*To another faith by the same Spirit; to another the gifts of healing by the same Spirit;* [10]*To another the working of miracles; to another prophecy; to another discerning of spirits; to another divers kinds of tongues; to another the interpretation of tongues:*"

    a. Word of wisdom
    b. Word of knowledge
    c. Gift of faith
    d. Gifts of healing
    e. Gift of working of miracles
    f. Gift of discerning of spirits
    g. Gift of diverse kinds of tongues
    h. Gift of interpretation of tongues
    i. Gift of prophecy

2. Five-fold ministry gifts, Ephesians 4:11-12 – "[11]*And he gave some, apostles; and some, prophets; and some, evangelists; and some, pastors and teachers;*[12]*For the perfecting of the saints, for the work of the ministry, for the edifying of the body of Christ:*"

    a. Apostles
    b. Prophets
    c. Evangelists
    d. Pastors
    e. Teachers

3. Other spiritual gifts, I Corinthians 12:28-31 – "[28]*And God hath set some in the church, first apostles, secondarily prophets, thirdly teachers, after that miracles, then gifts of healings, helps, governments, diversities of tongues.* [29]*Are all apostles? are all prophets? are all teachers? are all workers of miracles?* [30]*Have all the gifts of healing? do all speak with tongues? do all interpret?* [31]*But covet earnestly the best gifts: and yet shew I unto you a more excellent way.*"

    a. Helps
    b. Governments

4. Other ministry gifts, Romans 12:5-8 – "[5]*So we, being many, are one body in Christ, and every one members one of another.* [6]*Having then gifts differing according to the grace that is given to us, whether prophecy, let us prophesy according to the proportion of faith;* [7]*Or ministry, let us wait on our ministering: or he that teacheth, on teaching;* [8]*Or he that exhorteth, on exhortation: he that giveth, let him do it with simplicity; he that ruleth, with diligence; he that sheweth mercy, with cheerfulness.*"

   a. Prophecy
   b. Ministry
   c. Teaching
   d. Exhortation
   e. Giving
   f. Ruling
   g. Showing mercy

5. Seven virtues, II Peter 1:5-7 – "[5]*And beside this, giving all diligence, add to your faith virtue; and to virtue knowledge;* [6]*And to knowledge temperance; and to temperance patience; and to patience godliness;* [7]*And to godliness brotherly kindness; and to brotherly kindness charity.*"

   a. Faith
   b. Knowledge
   c. Temperance
   d. Patience
   e. Godliness
   f. Brotherly kindness
   g. Love

6. Nine fruits of the Spirit, Galatians 5:22-23 – "[22]*But the fruit of the Spirit is love, joy, peace, longsuffering, gentleness, goodness, faith,* [23]*Meekness, temperance: against such there is no law.*"

   a. Love
   b. Joy
   c. Peace
   d. Longsuffering
   e. Gentleness
   f. Goodness
   g. Faith
   h. Meekness
   i. Temperance

7. The gifts of holy armor, Ephesians 6:11-17 – "[11]*Put on the whole armour of God, that ye may be able to stand against the wiles of the devil.* [12]*For we wrestle not against flesh and blood, but against principalities, against powers, against the rulers of the darkness of this world, against spiritual wickedness in high places.* [13]*Wherefore take unto you the whole armour of God, that ye may be able to withstand in the evil day, and having done all, to stand.* [14]*Stand therefore, having your loins girt about with truth, and having on the breastplate of righteousness;* [15]*And your feet shod with the preparation of the gospel of peace;* [16]*Above all, taking the shield of faith, wherewith ye shall be able to quench all the fiery darts of the wicked.* [17]*And take the helmet of salvation, and the sword of the Spirit, which is the word of God:*"

   a. Armor of light, Romans 13:12 – "*The night is far spent, the day is at hand: let us therefore cast off the works of darkness, and let us put on the armour of light.*"
   b. Loins girt about with truth
   c. Breastplate of righteousness

d. Feet shod with preparation of the gospel of peace
e. Shield of faith
f. Helmet of salvation
g. Sword of the Spirit

Lesson 28

Table Of Shewbread

Table Of Shewbread

I. Golden Table of Shewbread – Listed in Scripture:

Exodus 25:23-30, Exodus 37:10-16, 40:22-23, Leviticus 24:5-9, Numbers 4:7

Exodus 25:23-30 – "*23Thou shalt also make a table of shittim wood: two cubits shall be the length thereof, and a cubit the breadth thereof, and a cubit and a half the height thereof. 24And thou shalt overlay it with pure gold, and make thereto a crown of gold round about. 25And thou shalt make unto it a border of an hand breadth round about, and thou shalt make a golden crown to the border thereof round about. 26And thou shalt make for it four rings of gold, and put the rings in the four corners that are on the four feet thereof. 27Over against the border shall the rings be for places of the staves to bear the table. 28And thou shalt make the staves of shittim wood, and overlay them with gold, that the table may be borne with them. 29And thou shalt make the dishes thereof, and spoons thereof, and covers thereof, and bowls thereof, to cover withal: of pure gold shalt thou make them. 30And thou shalt set upon the table shewbread before me alway.*"

Exodus 37:10-16 – "*10And he made the table of shittim wood: two cubits was the length thereof, and a cubit the breadth thereof, and a cubit and a half the height thereof: 11And he overlaid it with pure gold, and made thereunto a crown of gold round about. 12Also he made thereunto a border of an handbreadth round about; and made a crown of gold for the border thereof round about. 13And he cast for it four rings of gold, and put the rings upon the four corners that were in the four feet thereof. 14Over against the border were the rings, the places for the staves to bear the table. 15And he made the staves of shittim wood, and overlaid them with gold, to bear the table. 16And he made the vessels which were upon the table, his dishes, and his spoons, and his bowls, and his covers to cover withal, of pure gold.*"

Exodus 40:22-23 – "*22And he put the table in the tent of the congregation, upon the side of the tabernacle northward, without the vail. 23And he set the bread in order upon it before the LORD; as the LORD had commanded Moses.*"

Leviticus 24:5-9 – "*5And thou shalt take fine flour, and bake twelve cakes thereof: two tenth deals shall be in one cake. 6And thou shalt set them in two rows, six on a row, upon the pure table before the LORD. 7And thou shalt put pure frankincense upon each row, that it may be on the bread for a memorial, even an offering made by fire unto the LORD. 8Every sabbath he shall set it in order before the LORD continually, being taken from the children of Israel by an everlasting covenant. 9And it shall be Aaron's and his sons'; and they shall eat it in the holy place: for it is most holy unto him of the offerings of the LORD made by fire by a perpetual statute.*"

Numbers 4:7 – *"And upon the table of shewbread they shall spread a cloth of blue, and put thereon the dishes, and the spoons, and the bowls, and covers to cover withal: and the continual bread shall be thereon:"*

II. Listed Themes The Table of Shewbread Signifies

A. Jesus is the "Bread of life"

1. John 6:32-34, 41-52 – *"[32]Then Jesus said unto them, Verily, verily, I say unto you, Moses gave you not that bread from heaven; but my Father giveth you the true bread from heaven. [33]For the bread of God is he which cometh down from heaven, and giveth life unto the world. [34]Then said they unto him, Lord, evermore give us this bread."*

B. Communion table

1. I Corinthians 11:23-24 – *"[23]For I have received of the Lord that which also I delivered unto you, That the Lord Jesus the same night in which he was betrayed took bread: [24]And when he had given thanks, he brake it, and said, Take, eat: this is my body, which is broken for you: this do in remembrance of me."*
2. I Corinthians 10:15-21

C. This is the piece of furniture that was restored to the body of Christ during the Charismatic movement where priests are the "living bread". All denominations met here.
D. It speaks of "fellowship". The priests congregated here to eat together.
E. It represents "the living Word", "bread of His face", and "bread of His presence" which speaks of the revealed Word of God. This is eating the Word that God is giving Himself. It is the anointed Word.
F. The table of shewbread speaks of divine order in that there were 12 loaves of bread. Twelve in the Scripture speaks of divine order and government.
G. The table of shewbread represents the partaking of the "divine nature" (eating the bread that comes from heaven). Eating at this table prepared the priests to move on to greater depths of worship and intercession as well as preparing us to be changed into His image (II Corinthians 3:18)

H. It represents "five-fold ministry"

1. Exodus 37:12 – *"Also he made thereunto a border of an handbreadth round about; and made a crown of gold for the border thereof round about."* – the term handbreadth speaks of the five fold ministry.
2. Ephesians 4:11 – *"And he gave some, apostles; and some, prophets; and some, evangelists; and some, pastors and teachers;"*
3. Only priests were allowed to eat here making it clear that the table of shewbread speaks of ministry.

4. In the very terms of the five fold ministry, we can see why it signifies this:

   a. Apostle means "one sent forth". The Hebrew word for "table" comes from a root word that means to send forth, to send out, to send away.
   b. Prophet – The priests were eating living bread or bread of His face. This would also emphasize the proceeding Word spoken forth by prophetic utterance.
   c. Pastor – Obviously eating here gives strength to the pastor to feed his sheep. The Hebrew word for "bread" comes from a root word that means – to feed on, to consume, to battle. At this table the priest would receive truths to feed his sheep to prepare them to battle.
   d. Teacher – True Bible teachers must have revelation. This bread gave them that very thing.
   e. Evangelist – Once again the Hebrew root word for "table" means to send forth. This is the kind of evangelist we need today.

I. Table of provision for spiritual food and healing

1. For food

   a. Matthew 6:11 – "*Give us this day our daily bread.*"
   b. Luke 24:35 – "[35]*And they told what things were done in the way, and how he was known of them in breaking of bread.*"
   c. John 6:33, 48 – "[33]*For the bread of God is he which cometh down from heaven, and giveth life unto the world...*[48]*I am that bread of life.*"
   d. Acts 2:42 – "*And they continued stedfastly in the apostles' doctrine and fellowship, and in breaking of bread, and in prayers.*"
   e. Psalms 132:15 – "*I will abundantly bless her provision: I will satisfy her poor with bread.*"
   f. I Kings 17:6 – "*And the ravens brought him bread and flesh in the morning, and bread and flesh in the evening; and he drank of the brook.*"

2. For healing, Mark 7:27 – "*But Jesus said unto her, Let the children first be filled: for it is not meet to take the children's bread, and to cast it unto the dogs.*"

III. Makeup of the Table

A. Important facts about the table of shewbread

1. The table was made of gold over wood. Wood speaks spiritually of our humanity gold speaks of God's divine nature. Therefore this represents the divine nature over our humanity
2. The number 2 involved with the length of it speaks of witness, separation, division
3. The measurement for this table is similar to the brazen altar, the ark of the covenant, and the mercy seat. Everything in all three dimensions measure up to this standard of height. We must come up to it.
3. Once again there is no depth listed as far as measurement is concerned. There is no ending depth to the revelation of His person (Romans 11:33).
4. It was pure gold; this speaks of God's nature being innocence, precious, and clean
5. It was set on the north side of the Holy Place – north in Scripture represents judgment; even at the table of shewbread, judgment is still going on
6. The candlestick would give the light to reveal and illuminate the bread. This means the Holy Spirit must reveal the Word to us. If the candlestick is not lit (i.e. not filled with the Holy Ghost) you can't see to eat the bread.
7. This table is significant of the Lord Himself as the bread of life, John 6:32-33, 48-51, 53-60
8. This was the first use of the word table in the Scriptures. Table in Hebrew means – a table as spread out or a meal; it comes from a root that means – to send away, to send forth, or to send out.
9. Exodus 25:30 – "*And thou shalt set upon the table shewbread before me alway.*" These great spiritual truths are eternal and live even now. They are changing people in His presence.

B. A look at the word table elsewhere in Scripture:

1. Psalms 23:5 – "*Thou preparest a table before me in the presence of mine enemies: thou anointest my head with oil; my cup runneth over.*"
2. Matthew 26:17-28 – Communion table
3. Song of Solomon 1:12 – "*While the king sitteth at his table, my spikenard sendeth forth the smell thereof.*"
4. Malachi 1:7 – "*Ye offer polluted bread upon mine altar; and ye say, Wherein have we polluted thee? In that ye say, The table of the LORD is contemptible.*"

5. Malachi 1:12 – "*But ye have profaned it, in that ye say, The table of the LORD is polluted; and the fruit thereof, even his meat, is contemptible.*"
6. I Corinthians 10:21 – "*Ye cannot drink the cup of the Lord, and the cup of devils: ye cannot be partakers of the Lord's table, and of the table of devils.*"
7. John 13:22-28 – "*22Then the disciples looked one on another, doubting of whom he spake. 23Now there was leaning on Jesus' bosom one of his disciples, whom Jesus loved. 24Simon Peter therefore beckoned to him, that he should ask who it should be of whom he spake. 25He then lying on Jesus' breast saith unto him, Lord, who is it? 26Jesus answered, He it is, to whom I shall give a sop, when I have dipped it. And when he had dipped the sop, he gave it to Judas Iscariot, the son of Simon. 27And after the sop Satan entered into him. Then said Jesus unto him, That thou doest, do quickly. 28Now no man at the table knew for what intent he spake this unto him.*"

8. Jesus is this table. He is the God-man, gold over wood, which speaks of the divine nature over humanity and we are to eat from this.

   a. John 1:1-3, 14 – "*1In the beginning was the Word, and the Word was with God, and the Word was God. 2The same was in the beginning with God. 3All things were made by him; and without him was not any thing made that was made…14And the Word was made flesh, and dwelt among us, (and we beheld his glory, the glory as of the only begotten of the Father,) full of grace and truth.*"
   b. I Timothy 2:5 – "*For there is one God, and one mediator between God and men, the man Christ Jesus;*"
   c. John 6:53 – "*Then Jesus said unto them, Verily, verily, I say unto you, Except ye eat the flesh of the Son of man, and drink his blood, ye have no life in you.*"

C. Crown of Gold – It had a crown of gold round about the top of the table of shewbread – A look at the word crown in Scripture shows us that crowns must be obtained. They are not just given. The Hebrew word for crown here means – a scattering, a molding around the top; it comes from a root word that means – to diffuse, to squeeze.

   a. Esther 2:17 – "*And the king loved Esther above all the women, and she obtained grace and favour in his sight more than all the virgins; so that he set the royal crown upon her head, and made her queen instead of Vashti.*" – The bride will wear it
   b. Revelation 2:10 – "*Fear none of those things which thou shalt suffer: behold, the devil shall cast some of you into prison, that ye may be tried; and ye shall have tribulation ten days: be thou faithful unto death, and I will give thee a crown of life.*" – Crown for faithfulness
   c. Revelation 12:1 – "*And there appeared a great wonder in heaven; a woman clothed with the sun, and the moon under her feet, and upon her head a crown of twelve stars:*" – Church has it (authority)
   d. I Peter 5:4 – "*And when the chief Shepherd shall appear, ye shall receive a crown of glory that fadeth not away.*" – Crown for leadership
   e. James 1:12 – "*Blessed is the man that endureth temptation: for when he is tried, he shall receive the crown of life, which the Lord hath promised to them that love him.*" – Crown for overcoming temptations
   f. II Timothy 4:8 – "*Henceforth there is laid up for me a crown of righteousness, which the Lord, the righteous judge, shall give me at that day: and not to me only, but unto all them also that love his appearing.*" – Crown for finishing your course
   g. I Corinthians 9:25 – "*And every man that striveth for the mastery is temperate in all things. Now they do it to obtain a corruptible crown; but we an incorruptible.*" – Race to win an incorruptible crown
   h. John 19:2, 5 – "*2And the soldiers platted a crown of thorns, and put it on his head, and they put on him a purple robe…5Then came Jesus forth, wearing the crown of thorns, and the purple robe. And Pilate saith unto them, Behold the man!*" – A crown of thorns

i. Zechariah 9:16 – *"And the LORD their God shall save them in that day as the flock of his people: for they shall be as the stones of a crown, lifted up as an ensign upon his land."* – A crown for the remnant
j. Exodus 29:6 – *"And thou shalt put the mitre upon his head, and put the holy crown upon the mitre."* – High Priest's crown that is anointed
k. Leviticus 21:12 – *"Neither shall he go out of the sanctuary, nor profane the sanctuary of his God; for the crown of the anointing oil of his God is upon him: I am the LORD."* – The crown of anointing
l. Hebrews 2:9 – *"But we see Jesus, who was made a little lower than the angels for the suffering of death, crowned with glory and honour; that he by the grace of God should taste death for every man."* – Crown of honor

D. Other aspects of the table of shewbread

1. *"...border of an handbreath round about..."* – This speaks of a wall of covering for the holy bread
2. *"...four rings of gold..."* – The number 4 in Scripture means creation and the ring symbolizes the covenant. So this emphasizes the covenant for the new creation man.
3. Four corners – this symbolizes the worldwide aspect of the table of shewbread. There are priests all over the world that enter in.
4. Four feet – This speaks of a tremendous foundation underneath this table. Four again means creation and feet symbolize our walk. This then would mean that these priests could walk in the truth and take these truths to all of God's creation.

5. The staves – wood overlaid with gold; this symbolizes several things:

   a. Jesus – incorruptible humanity covered in the divine nature
   b. Our corrupt humanity being changed or overlaid with God's glory, his divine nature

6. These staves bear the table

   a. God needs priests to carry this table, to bear it to the ends of the earth
   b. The two staves also speak of balance

      1) Proverbs 11:1 – *"A false balance is abomination to the LORD: but a just weight is his delight."*
      2) Proverbs 16:11 – *"A just weight and balance are the LORD's: all the weights of the bag are his work."*
      3) Proverbs 20:23 – *"Divers weights are an abomination unto the LORD; and a false balance is not good."*
      4) Daniel 5:27 – *"TEKEL; Thou art weighed in the balances, and art found wanting."*

   c. It also symbolizes the balance between fellowship and a balanced word.

7. Dishes of pure gold – These dishes, spoons, and covers are the vessels of the Lord. These divine dishes were used for holding the bread. You must be clean to carry this Word. You must have the divine nature (gold) to carry the Word.

   a. Isaiah 52:11 – *"Depart ye, depart ye, go ye out from thence, touch no unclean thing; go ye out of the midst of her; be ye clean, that bear the vessels of the LORD."*

8. Spoons – These spoons were hollow vessels of gold with incense in them. There were 12 of them. 12 in Scripture represents divine order and government. This represent then, to worship God effectively, we must be emptied of ourselves (hollow) then we can worship (incense) in spirit and in truth.

9. Covers and bowls – These covers and bowls contained strong wine, which was poured out before the Lord (Numbers 28:7). This speaks of His people made up now of His divine nature (gold) pouring out wine (joy) as well as this is typical of the Lord's blood being poured out to the world. It also shows us that we must live a poured out divine life.

E. The shewbread, Leviticus 24:5-9, Numbers 4:7

1. The Hebrew word for Shewbread literally means "bread of His presence" or "bread of faces". The root word for bread again means "to feed on, to consume, to battle". The Hebrew word for "face" is also translated "presence" and means "the face (as the part that turns)" and comes from a root word that means "to face, to turn, to appear, to look". This signifies He is with us as we behold Him in His Word, not only teaching and confirming but also sealing it into us.

   a. Luke 24:28-32 – "*...[32]And they said one to another, Did not our heart burn within us, while he talked with us by the way, and while he opened to us the scriptures?*" Jesus and the two disciples on the road to Emmaus
   b. Matthew 14:14-22 – Feeding of the five thousand
   c. Luke 22:19 – "*And he took bread, and gave thanks, and brake it, and gave unto them, saying, This is my body which is given for you: this do in remembrance of me.*"

2. This was bread, living bread – this is a type of the Word that God's face was looking at; shewbread is the living, present, proceeding revelational truth that is given only to the priests

   a. II Corinthians 4:6 – "*For God, who commanded the light to shine out of darkness, hath shined in our hearts, to give the light of the knowledge of the glory of God in the face of Jesus Christ.*"
   b. II Peter 1:4 – "*Whereby are given unto us exceeding great and precious promises: that by these ye might be partakers of the divine nature, having escaped the corruption that is in the world through lust.*"
   c. Revelation 22:4 – "*And they shall see his face; and his name shall be in their foreheads.*"
   d. II Peter 1:12 – "*Wherefore I will not be negligent to put you always in remembrance of these things, though ye know them, and be established in the present truth.*"

3. Bread of order or arrangement (this is also from the Hebrew word) – This is revelation from the Word that causes His people to come into order

   a. II Chronicles 13:11-13 – "*[11]And they burn unto the LORD every morning and every evening burnt sacrifices and sweet incense: the shewbread also set they in order upon the pure table; and the candlestick of gold with the lamps thereof, to burn every evening: for we keep the charge of the LORD our God; but ye have forsaken him. [12]And, behold, God himself is with us for our captain...*"
   b. I Corinthians 11:34 – "*And if any man hunger, let him eat at home; that ye come not together unto condemnation. And the rest will I set in order when I come.*"
   c. Ephesians 4:11-16

4. Continual Bread

   a. Numbers 4:7 – "*And upon the table of shewbread they shall spread a cloth of blue, and put thereon the dishes, and the spoons, and the bowls, and covers to cover withal: and the continual bread shall be thereon:*"
   b. II Chronicles 2:4-5 – "*[4]Behold, I build an house to the name of the LORD my God, to dedicate it to him, and to burn before him sweet incense, and for the continual shewbread, and for the burnt offerings morning and evening, on the sabbaths, and on the new moons, and on the solemn easts of the LORD our God. This is an ordinance for ever to Israel. [5]And the house which I build is great: for great is our God above all gods.*"

c. Leviticus 24:8 – "*Every sabbath he shall set it in order before the LORD continually, being taken from the children of Israel by an everlasting covenant.*"
d. Matthew 6:11 – "*Give us this day our daily bread.*"

e. Principle of day and night – This is the age defying, unchanging aspect of the Word of God

1) Joshua 1:8 – "*This book of the law shall not depart out of thy mouth; but thou shalt meditate therein day and night, that thou mayest observe to do according to all that is written therein: for then thou shalt make thy way prosperous, and then thou shalt have good success.*"
2) Psalms 1:3 – "*And he shall be like a tree planted by the rivers of water, that bringeth forth his fruit in his season; his leaf also shall not wither; and whatsoever he doeth shall prosper.*"
3) John 8:31-32 – "*[31]Then said Jesus to those Jews which believed on him, If ye continue in my word, then are ye my disciples indeed; [32]And ye shall know the truth, and the truth shall make you free.*"
4) Isaiah 50:4 – "*The Lord GOD hath given me the tongue of the learned, that I should know how to speak a word in season to him that is weary: he wakeneth morning by morning, he wakeneth mine ear to hear as the learned.*"
5) Proverbs 8:33-35 – "*[33]Hear instruction, and be wise, and refuse it not. [34]Blessed is the man that heareth me, watching daily at my gates, waiting at the posts of my doors. [35]For whoso findeth me findeth life, and shall obtain favour of the LORD.*"

5. "*fine flour*" – Flour begins as a whole kernel of wheat. In order to use it, it must be crushed to powder. This symbolized that this bread will crush you. Your revelation will be married to your situation. This speaks to us of the crushing of Jesus as well as all that we go through. Also, it says it was fine flour. This speaks of Jesus' sinless and perfect humanity. There was nothing rough or out of place in Him.
6. "*and bake*" – This speaks of the operation of the fire of God burning and shaping these truths to fit our lives. Sometimes we must wait while the Word is baking within us.
7. "*twelve cakes*" – All twelve tribes were represented. All of God's people are welcome, Romans 12:5 – "*So we, being many, are one body in Christ, and every one members one of another.*" It also speaks of divine government and order because of the number 12. Notice there were two rows of six, one for Jewish believers, and one for Gentile believers.
8. Those twelve loaves were equal in size, weight, and material representing a balanced Word; this means the teaching of "His face" will bring greater understanding and order. We are to be measured by God's standards. God wants us to grow into His person, Ephesians 3:19 – "*And to know the love of Christ, which passeth knowledge, that ye might be filled with all the fulness of God.*"
9. "*two tenth deals shall be in one cake*" – This speaks to us a double portion received as you eat the bread.
10. "*...Set them in two rows. Six upon the table...*" – The cakes are rather large so they probably were piled on top of one another representing Jews and Gentiles living peaceably. The number six in Scripture represents man. God will restore, heal, and sanctify man.
11. "*...And thou shalt put pure frankincense upon each row*" – pure frankincense was put on the bread. Frankincense is a pungent gum resin obtained from 3 species of the genus Boswellia, a tree (Song of Solomon 4:14) native only to South Arabia (Isaiah 60:6, Jeremiah 6:20) and Somaliland. The bark is peeled back a few inches and the resinous sap exudes, forming globules or lumps called "tears". Frankincense was one of the most highly valued of all ancient incense gums, and the limited source of supply made it very costly and one of the most lucrative items in the great land and sea caravans that came from the East. The gum has a fragrant, balsamic odor and was used alone or with other materials for incense. It was one of the ingredients of the holy incense to be used only in Israel's tabernacle (Exodus 30:34) and was placed on the meal offering of first fruits (Leviticus 2:5-16) and on the shewbread (Leviticus 24:7). Later it was

also used as an element in cosmetics and perfume (Song of Solomon 3:6). Frankincense was extensively used throughout the Greco-Roman world as incense and was also used medically, although there is no mention of this in Scripture. Its primary use among the Jews was in worship. Frankincense in Hebrew means whiteness. It speaks of purity, innocence and represents worship in spirit and in truth.

12. "*...that it may be on the bread for a memorial...*" – This speaks of the communion table (Luke 22:19-20 – "*...this do in remembrance of me...*")
13. "*...even an offering made by fire unto the LORD...*" – This speaks of the bread being baked fully (Hosea 7:8). Cake in Hebrew means – punctured; it is from a room that means – to bore, wound, to profane or break.
14. "*Every sabbath he shall set it in order before the LORD continually...*" It was to be set in order on the Sabbath. New loaves were given or changed every Sabbath. This speaks to us of new bread and a new priesthood (a fresh word and a royal priesthood – I Peter 2:9)
15. Leviticus 24:9 – "*And it shall be Aaron's and his sons'; and they shall eat it in the holy place: for it is most holy unto him of the offerings of the LORD made by fire by a perpetual statute.*" – Once again, only priests could eat it as well as set it in order. It was to be eaten in the Holy Place where the lampstand's light shone upon it.
16. It is most holy of all the offerings. It was also to be a perpetual state. It is holy bread (type of the Word) and God appreciates it more than all other offerings made by fire. Why? They can finally begin to see Him, His ways, and His heart.

17. Numbers 4:7-8 – "[7]*And upon the table of shewbread they shall spread a cloth of blue, and put thereon the dishes, and the spoons, and the bowls, and covers to cover withal: and the continual bread shall be thereon:* [8]*And they shall spread upon them a cloth of scarlet, and cover the same with a covering of badgers' skins, and shall put in the staves thereof.*"

    a. Exodus 25:30 – "*And thou shalt set upon the table shewbread before me alway.*" – It is continual (always) bread. There will never be a lack of this bread
    b. Continual bread – Somehow, in the Spirit realm this is happening now

IV. The Difference Between Shewbread and Manna

A. Manna was supernatural bread for the multitudes (Exodus 16:14-36, Numbers 11:1-9). Everyone ate manna. Below are principles about manna:

1. It was round – this speaks of eternity and God's provision for the world
2. Came during the night – this speaks of hard times
3. Given from heaven – God's bread from heaven
4. It was small – it could be missed
5. It was white – innocence
6. First ground, then beaten, and then baked – dealings of God; crushing
7. It tasted of fresh oil
8. It tasted like honey – sweetness
9. Twice as much was gathered on the 6th day – prophetically we are living in the 6th day now; no manna fell on the 7th day; the 6th day there was a double portion
10. No manna fell on the 7th day – this speaks to us of the millennial reign
11. This is the daily bread Jesus spoke of.
12. It was for the multitudes
13. It would breed worms and stink if kept
14. If not gathered early, it was melted by the sun; God expects us to gather early (II Corinthians 6:2 – "*...behold, now is the accepted time; behold, now is the day of salvation.*")
15. Manna was bread to sustain
16. Manna was despised (Numbers 11:4-6)

B. Shewbread was bread in the holy place to be eaten only be priests.

1. The shewbread was prepared on the 6th day.
2. The same day Israel was gathering twice as much, the shewbread was being prepared to be eaten on the 7th and Sabbath day
3. It was also double portion bread (2 omers of flour, 2 crowns of gold, 2 rows of bread)

4. Eaten only by priests; this is bread for true disciples; we are to be priests of God

    a. I Peter 2:9 – "*But ye are a chosen generation, a royal priesthood, an holy nation, a peculiar people; that ye should shew forth the praises of him who hath called you out of darkness into his marvellous light:*"
    b. Revelation 1:6 – "*And hath made us kings and priests unto God and his Father; to him be glory and dominion for ever and ever. Amen.*"
    c. Revelation 5:10 – "*And hast made us unto our God kings and priests: and we shall reign on the earth.*"

5. It had to be eaten in the holy place; can't eat shewbread until filled with the Holy Ghost; it is a place where revelation is flowing.
6. Only worshippers can eat this bread; David ate the shewbread (I Samuel 21:6, Matthew 12:1-4)
7. It was made of fine ground flour which speaks of testings, trials, etc. (John 12:24, 27)
8. It had to be baked (Hosea 7:8) – speaks of the furnace of affliction (Isaiah 48:10), dealings of God, and principle of revelation being married to situation
9. Sprinkled with pure frankincense (Leviticus 24:7); frankincense means white and speaks of worship.
10. When moved, a cloth of blue was spread over it (Numbers 4:7) – blue speaks of everything heavenly.

Lesson 29

Eating the Word

I. Take and Eat.

A. Revelation 10:8-11 – "[8]*And the voice which I heard from heaven spake unto me again, and said, Go and take the little book which is open in the hand of the angel which standeth upon the sea and upon the earth.* [9]*And I went unto the angel, and said unto him, Give me the little book. And he said unto me, Take it, and eat it up; and it shall make thy belly bitter, but it shall be in thy mouth sweet as honey.* [10]*And I took the little book out of the angel's hand, and ate it up; and it was in my mouth sweet as honey: and as soon as I had eaten it, my belly was bitter.* [11]*And he said unto me, Thou must prophesy again before many peoples, and nations, and tongues, and kings.*"

1. Principles to consider (Revelation 10:8)

a. Voice from heaven.
b. Go and take. It's a command.
c. Little book – The Bible is not so hard to understand after all, it may seem monstrous, but it's a little book.
d. Open in the Greek means to open up, root up severely; to open a door or gate. God will open the revelation to those who search for it.
e. Hand of the Angel (Messenger)

The Greek word *angel* means messenger. This could just as easily be a teacher or preacher of the Scriptures. We must come to the hand of man. This is humbling, but it's God's way, He gives the revelation to men, who in turn give it to others.

1) Ecclesiastes 12:11 – "*The words of the wise are as goads, and as nails fastened by the masters of assemblies, which are given from one shepherd.*"
2) II Timothy 2:2 – "*And the things that thou hast heard of me among many witnesses, the same commit thou to faithful men, who shall be able to teach others also.*"

Notice this messenger in Revelation 10 is standing on the sea (types of many peoples) and the earth (where we live). Also he has dominion on the earth.

2. Revelation 10:9

a. I went – We must go to the messenger ourselves.
b. Give me – In other words teach me, feed me.
c. Take it – It's the responsibility of those who teach to be <u>prepared</u> to give. Also not to hoard or keep it to themselves. It was given to them to give away.
d. Eat it up – The Greek word for eat here means to devour; to eat down. God wants us to devour the Scriptures.

1) Jeremiah 15:16-17 – Once we find His Word, we must eat it.

a) Principles to consider.

(1) It brings joy.
(2) We recognize our calling.
(3) It separates us.

2) Ezekiel 2:8-10, 3:1-4

a) Notice the results.

(1) Only the rebellious don't eat.
(2) God will send a teacher.
(3) It will be opened to us.
(4) Written within and without.

This speaks of the letter of the law (without) that is the natural interpretation. That which is within is the Spirit of the Word, revelation. We must dig for it (Proverbs 25:2)

(5) Notice once we eat (Ezekiel 3:1) we are able to speak to others (vs 4).
(6) Fill thy bowels (vs 3) – The Hebrew meaning of bowels reads satisfy yourself.

3. Isaiah 55:1-3

a. You can't purchase this with money; it is bought another way, with love.
b. So much of our labor is not for spiritual things (especially the Word) and ultimately these things never satisfy.
c. Eat what is good. Also, it is a never ending source of strength.
d. If we do incline our ear, our soul shall live, that is our carnal soulish man will change.
e. Belly bitter – This is as it is digested and worked out in our lives. It's sweet when we hear it, but when we try to walk it out, live it, that's when we see this truth come alive

1) Proverbs 23:23 – Once we heard the Word, it's sweet and anointed, but as we proceed to buy that truth and make it operative in our life, we are met with bitter circumstances to see that we do it, and then walk in it.

2) We are not just to hear but to do.

a) Romans 2:13
b) James 1:22
c) Matthew 7:24

3) We need to be hungry.

a) Matthew 5:6
b) Psalms 107:9
c) Psalms 146:7
d) Philemon 4:12-13
e) I Kings 19:5-8
f) Ruth 2:14-15
g) Song of Solomon 5:1
h) Isaiah 65:9-14
i) II Samuel 9:7-8
j) Nehemiah 9:15

4. Revelation 10:10

a. It's our responsibility and initiative to take the Word out of the messenger's hand and devour it.
b. Ate it up

1) We are admonished in Scripture to eat the Word.

a) I Peter 2:2-3 – milk is to be eaten
b) Hebrews 5:12-14 – strong meat is to be eaten
c) Exodus 16:4, 13-16 – bread is to be eaten

2) There is spiritual food.

a) I Corinthians 10:3-4 – This is simply a type of the spiritual food we get as we eat His Word. Natural food for the physical keeps us alive and healthy. Our spirit man must be fed to remain healthy and alive.
b) Exodus 25:30 Bread of His presence
c) John 4:32
d) Ezekiel 42:13
e) Psalms 78:25
f) What do you think we will be eating at the marriage supper of the Lamb, roast beef? No, we will be eating the deep things of Him.
g) John 6:48-51, 53-58 – We are not eating His actual flesh, but His life, His substance, His presence, His Word.

5. Revelation 10:11 – Thou must prophesy; if we will fill ourselves full of the Word, we will prophesy. It is a supernatural response.

B. Future Blessings to Eat.

1. Revelation 2:7 – The tree of life (a type of Jesus). Those who overcome will be given special ability to receive great revelation of our King, unknown to others.
2. Revelation 2:17 – Once again to the overcomer is reserved special revelation that God will only commit to those who have eaten here on earth. Hidden manna speaks of the great mysteries never before revealed.
3. Isaiah 65:13 – God's promise is to that remnant who serve Him here on this earth, while others are hungry, they <u>shall</u> eat.

Lesson 30

Golden Altar Of Incense

The Golden Altar

I. Golden Altar Of Incense, Exodus 30:1-10

"1And thou shalt make an altar to burn incense upon: of shittim wood shalt thou make it. 2A cubit shall be the length thereof, and a cubit the breadth thereof; foursquare shall it be: and two cubits shall be the height thereof: the horns thereof shall be of the same. 3And thou shalt overlay it with pure gold, the top thereof, and the sides thereof round about, and the horns thereof; and thou shalt make unto it a crown of gold round about. 4And two golden rings shalt thou make to it under the crown of it, by the two corners thereof, upon the two sides of it shalt thou make it; and they shall be for places for the staves to bear it withal. 5And thou shalt make the staves of shittim wood, and overlay them with gold. 6And thou shalt put it before the vail that is by the ark of the testimony, before the mercy seat that is over the testimony, where I will meet with thee. 7And Aaron shall burn thereon sweet incense every morning: when he dresseth the lamps, he shall burn incense upon it. 8And when Aaron lighteth the lamps at even, he shall burn incense upon it, a perpetual incense before the LORD throughout your generations. 9Ye shall offer no strange incense thereon, nor burnt sacrifice, nor meat offering; neither shall ye pour drink offering thereon. 10And Aaron shall make an atonement upon the horns of it once in a year with the blood of the sin offering of atonements: once in the year shall he make atonement upon it throughout your generations: it is most holy unto the LORD."

A. Aspects of this altar

1. It was the only piece of furniture that ministers to God. Every other piece of furniture was for our benefit.
2. The smoke from the incense found its way to God. This made God and man aware of an existing fellowship between them.
3. Leviticus 16:12-13 – "*12And he shall take a censer full of burning coals of fire from off the altar before the LORD, and his hands full of sweet incense beaten small, and bring it within the vail: 13And he shall put the incense upon the fire before the LORD, that the cloud of the incense may cover the mercy seat that is upon the testimony, that he die not:*" – Brass and golden altar were connected – without salvation you cannot go in and become a worshipper.
4. This altar is smaller than the brazen altar.

5. Defining all of the sanctifications that must come forth before we can worship at this altar.

   a. Brass altar – judgment on our sin
   b. Brass laver – washings, water, sanctification and cleansing

c. Candlestick – learning to see in the Spirit realm, baptism of the Holy Ghost and His gifts and fruits, revelation
d. Shewbread – bread of His presence, a living revealed Word that we must eat, present truths; by eating this holy bread, we become what we eat (Him)
e. Golden altar of incense – divine nature (gold) over our humanity (wood); it is now the glory of God that now descends upon you. It speaks of His divine glorious nature over our humanity. This is the place of pure worship and intercession ministered by a true priesthood.

6. It is the fifth piece of furniture coming from the front to back of the tabernacle (our access to God). By grace, we will be able to worship there.
7. God will only accept incense that He has so minutely prescribed
8. God also only accepts people (priests) who approach Him that come through Jesus. The fire from the golden altar was taken from the fire from the brazen altar. This speaks to us saying everything we will ever do or become will be based upon the rock of our salvation Jesus.
9. It was exclusively for burning incense. There was no blood sacrifice. This was done once (Hebrews 10:9-12). There is no longer a need for animal sacrifice; a body He has prepared (Hebrews 10:5). During the "Law Age" (outer court), blood was needed. The "Church Age" (holy place – 2000 years) began with the sacrifice of Jesus. The "Ages of Ages" (most holy place) will begin at the beginning of the millennium as well as after.
10. This altar was sprinkled annually seven times with blood. On the day of atonement, it was also anointed with fresh oil.

11. Only Aaron (the High Priest) and his seeds (the priests) could minister at this altar. For us, this means Jesus, our High Priest, and His seed, which is you and me. We are allowed to worship at this golden altar. Hallelujah!

    a. James 1:18 – *"Of his own will begat he us with the word of truth, that we should be a kind of firstfruits of his creatures."*
    b. I Peter 1:23 – *"Being born again, not of corruptible seed, but of incorruptible, by the word of God, which liveth and abideth for ever."*
    c. Isaiah 53:10 – *"Yet it pleased the LORD to bruise him; he hath put him to grief: when thou shalt make his soul an offering for sin, he shall see his seed, he shall prolong his days, and the pleasure of the LORD shall prosper in his hand."*
    d. Psalms 22:30-31 – *"30A seed shall serve him; it shall be accounted to the Lord for a generation. 31They shall come, and shall declare his righteousness unto a people that shall be born, that he hath done this."*

12. Sprinkling of blood and oil on this altar also speaks of no matter how much we mature in God, we must remember that it is the blood that enables us. The power that the blood has when it is dealt with properly is the only thing that enables us. The oil poured out upon the altar speaks of the great Holy Ghost watching over us breaking all our bondages if we let Him.

    a. Isaiah 10:27 – *"And it shall come to pass in that day, that his burden shall be taken away from off thy shoulder, and his yoke from off thy neck, and the yoke shall be destroyed because of the anointing."* – We can lean on those horns until our deliverance comes and it WILL come! We have a refuge of blood and oil at the golden altar.

13. The golden altar was the most sacred piece of furniture in the entire tabernacle. Only the ark of the covenant (which speaks of God's manifest presence) is more sacred.

II. Exodus 30:1-10, Verse by Verse analysis

A. Verse 1 – *"And thou shalt make an altar to burn incense upon: of shittim wood shalt thou make it."*

1. They had to make it. Men build altars; God does not. It is a place we prepare.

   a. Psalms 132:5 – *"Until I find out a place for the LORD, an habitation for the mighty God of Jacob."*
   b. Exodus 15:2 – *"The LORD is my strength and song, and he is become my salvation: he is my God, and I will prepare him an habitation; my father's God, and I will exalt him."*

2. The golden altar was to be used for worship and intercession; the word "*incense*" in the Hebrew comes from a root word that means – a close place where the fumigation drives out the occupants, to smoke.

   a. It was used for prayers and worship.

      1) Prayer, Psalms 141:2 – *"Let my prayer be set forth before thee as incense; and the lifting up of my hands as the evening sacrifice."*
      2) Worship, Revelation 8:3-5 – *"[3]And another angel came and stood at the altar, having a golden censer; and there was given unto him much incense, that he should offer it with the prayers of all saints upon the golden altar which was before the throne. [4]And the smoke of the incense, which came with the prayers of the saints, ascended up before God out of the angel's hand. [5]And the angel took the censer, and filled it with fire of the altar, and cast it into the earth: and there were voices, and thunderings, and lightnings, and an earthquake."*

   b. It had to be made of certain spices. *(See chapter on "Sweet Incense")*
   c. It was made of wood; this speaks of our humanity and the humanity of Jesus.

3. It was positioned as the last piece of furniture before the veil leading to the most holy place; below are some of its names used in Scripture:

   a. Altar of incense – Exodus 30:27, 31:8
   b. Altar of gold – Exodus 35:15, 37:25
   c. Golden altar – Exodus 39:8, 40:26
   d. Golden altar which is before the throne – Revelation 8:3-5
   e. The altar before the Lord – Leviticus 16:12, 18
   f. Altar to burn incense – Exodus 30:1
   g. Altar of sweet incense – Leviticus 4:7

4. Incense begins with man's making and then as it burns it belongs to God

B. Verse 2 – *"A cubit shall be the length thereof, and a cubit the breadth thereof; foursquare shall it be: and two cubits shall be the height thereof: the horns thereof shall be of the same."*

1. The altar was the highest piece of all the furniture.
2. It was foursquare – four is the number in Scripture for creation; therefore, foursquare signifies the whole world could worship there if they became true priests; any of God's creation that went on with the Lord could partake of it.

3. It had four horns on its corners. Horns in Scripture always speak of power and authority, anointing, and strength.

   a. Habakkuk 3:4 – *"And his brightness was as the light; he had horns coming out of his hand: and there was the hiding of his power."*

b. Matthew 28:18-20 – "[18]*And Jesus came and spake unto them, saying, All power is given unto me in heaven and in earth.* [19]*Go ye therefore, and teach all nations, baptizing them in the name of the Father, and of the Son, and of the Holy Ghost:* [20]*Teaching them to observe all things whatsoever I have commanded you: and, lo, I am with you alway, even unto the end of the world. Amen.*"

c. I Samuel 16:1 – "*And the LORD said unto Samuel, How long wilt thou mourn for Saul, seeing I have rejected him from reigning over Israel? fill thine horn with oil, and go, I will send thee to Jesse the Bethlehemite: for I have provided me a king among his sons.*"

d. Psalms 92:10 – "*But my horn shalt thou exalt like the horn of an unicorn: I shall be anointed with fresh oil.*"

C. Verse 3 – "*And thou shalt overlay it with pure gold, the top thereof, and the sides thereof round about, and the horns thereof; and thou shalt make unto it a crown of gold round about.*"

1. It was overlaid with pure gold – this speaks of God's divine nature overlaying or overcoming man's humanity.
2. It contained a crown of pure gold round about – the table of shewbread and the ark of the covenant had crowns as well. These speak of things that we must attain to. No crown is simply given. It must be obtained. From the brass altar to the candlestick it is all about us being redeemed. From the table of showbread on, we make choices that will determine our own destiny.

D. Verses 4-5 – "[4]*And two golden rings shalt thou make to it under the crown of it, by the two corners thereof, upon the two sides of it shalt thou make it; and they shall be for places for the staves to bear it withal.* [5]*And thou shalt make the staves of shittim wood, and overlay them with gold.*"

1. Two golden rings – as Levites carried it, it would swing acting as a huge censer that functions even in transit; this speaks of a continual sacrifice of praise

   a. Psalms 34:1-3 – "[1]*I will bless the LORD at all times: his praise shall continually be in my mouth.* [2]*My soul shall make her boast in the LORD: the humble shall hear thereof, and be glad.* [3]*O magnify the LORD with me, and let us exalt his name together.*"

   b. Hebrews 13:15 – "*By him therefore let us offer the sacrifice of praise to God continually, that is, the fruit of our lips giving thanks to his name.*"

2. The golden rings also signify God's eternal and unending covenant with us.
3. Staves were made of wood which once again speaks of our humanity and Christ's humanity.
4. Staves overlaid with gold – it is only by His divine nature that we could ever handle bearing the golden altar to the world (somebody has to).

E. Verse 6 –"*And thou shalt put it before the vail that is by the ark of the testimony, before the mercy seat that is over the testimony, where I will meet with thee.*"

1. It was placed as the last piece of furniture before the veil, by the ark, and before the mercy seat

2. I believe we are here, spiritually speaking, in God's timetable right now. This speaks of the last piece of furniture added to the body of Christ to prepare us to go into the most holy place:

   a. Brass altar – Reformation, restored at the end of the dark ages
   b. Brass laver – Holiness Movement, 1800's
   c. Lampstand – Pentecostal Movement, early 1900's
   d. Table of shewbread – Latter Rain (1940's), Healing Revival (1950–1960's), and Charismatic Movement (late 1960's thru somewhere around 1980)
   e. Golden altar of incense – Restoration of worship in Spirit and in truth, late 1970's until now

f. Veil, mercy seat, and ark – manifestation of the son's of God, coming of the Lord; this could mean that very soon the breakthrough into the glory may happen

F. Verses 7-8 – "[7]*And Aaron shall burn thereon sweet incense every morning: when he dresseth the lamps, he shall burn incense upon it.* [8]*And when Aaron lighteth the lamps at even, he shall burn incense upon it, a perpetual incense before the LORD throughout your generations.*"

1. Incense to be burned every morning and every evening as lampstand was dressed and lit
2. "*...a perpetual incense...*" – God is raising up a people who will worship Him continually; He is preparing them for beyond the veil

G. Verse 9 – "*Ye shall offer no strange incense thereon, nor burnt sacrifice, nor meat offering; neither shall ye pour drink offering thereon.*"

1. No need for burnt sacrifice; the Lamb took care of that.
2. No need for meal offerings nor drink offerings; these things were applied elsewhere. This is God's house. He and He alone can do whatever He wants and anything He pleases.

3. "*strange incense*"

a. Leviticus 10:1-4 – Story of Nadab and Abihu, the sons of Aaron, offering strange fire before the Lord; they knew better than to do it; fire of God destroyed them

1) Nadab in Hebrew – volunteer, willing, liberal, impelling oneself
2) Abihu in Hebrew – He (God) is my father, whose father is he.

b. Exodus 30:37-38 – "[37]*And as for the perfume which thou shalt make, ye shall not make to yourselves according to the composition thereof: it shall be unto thee holy for the LORD.* [38]*Whosoever shall make like unto that, to smell thereto, shall even be cut off from his people.*"

1) No one was allowed to change the ingredients of the incense.
2) It is a holy thing.
3) Death is the result.

c. God wants true worship (incense), John 4:23-24 – "[23]*But the hour cometh, and now is, when the true worshippers shall worship the Father in spirit and in truth: for the Father seeketh such to worship him.* [24]*God is a Spirit: and they that worship him must worship him in spirit and in truth.*"
d. There is a due order to everything God does.
e. It is not to be used for selfish purposes.
f. Hebrew for "*strange*" here in Exodus 30:9 is *zuwr* – to turn aside (especially for lodging), foreign, profane, to come from another place, to commit adultery (spiritual adultery)
g. The principle of strange or alien gods or things – God never allowed or sanctioned anything strange, that is anything not birthed in Him or in His Word. Nothing brought in from Babylon or any other nation or tribe was to be assimilated into the tabernacle for holy worship.

h. Beware of strangers and what they bring

1) Leviticus 22:25 – "*Neither from a stranger's hand shall ye offer the bread of your God of any of these; because their corruption is in them, and blemishes be in them: they shall not be accepted for you.*"

2) Ezekiel 44:9 – "*Thus saith the Lord GOD; No stranger, uncircumcised in heart, nor uncircumcised in flesh, shall enter into my sanctuary, of any stranger that is among the children of Israel.*"
3) Proverbs 2:16 – "*To deliver thee from the strange woman, even from the stranger which flattereth with her words;*"
4) Proverbs 5:10 – "*Lest strangers be filled with thy wealth; and thy labours be in the house of a stranger;*"
5) Proverbs 6:1 – "*My son, if thou be surety for thy friend, if thou hast stricken thy hand with a stranger,*"

i. Strange gods

1) Genesis 35:2 – "*Then Jacob said unto his household, and to all that were with him, Put away the strange gods that are among you, and be clean, and change your garments:*"
2) Deuteronomy 32:12, 16 – "*[12]So the LORD alone did lead him, and there was no strange god with him...[16]They provoked him to jealousy with strange gods, with abominations provoked they him to anger.*"
3) Joshua 24:20, 23 – "*[20]If ye forsake the LORD, and serve strange gods, then he will turn and do you hurt, and consume you, after that he hath done you good...[23]Now therefore put away, said he, the strange gods which are among you, and incline your heart unto the LORD God of Israel.*"
4) I Samuel 7:3 – "*And Samuel spake unto all the house of Israel, saying, If ye do return unto the LORD with all your hearts, then put away the strange gods and Ashtaroth from among you, and prepare your hearts unto the LORD, and serve him only: and he will deliver you out of the hand of the Philistines.*"
5) Nehemiah 13:27 – "*Shall we then hearken unto you to do all this great evil, to transgress against our God in marrying strange wives?*"
6) Psalms 137:4 – "*How shall we sing the LORD's song in a strange land?*" – This is Babylon
7) Zephaniah 1:8 – "*And it shall come to pass in the day of the LORD's sacrifice, that I will punish the princes, and the king's children, and all such as are clothed with strange apparel.*" – Strange apparel
8) Hebrews 13:9 – "*Be not carried about with divers and strange doctrines. For it is a good thing that the heart be established with grace; not with meats, which have not profited them that have been occupied therein.*" – Strange doctrines
9) Psalms 81:9 – "*There shall no strange god be in thee; neither shalt thou worship any strange god.*"

j. Strange woman

1) Proverbs 5:3 – "*For the lips of a strange woman drop as an honeycomb, and her mouth is smoother than oil:*"
2) Proverbs 5:20 – "*And why wilt thou, my son, be ravished with a strange woman, and embrace the bosom of a stranger?*"
3) Proverbs 6:24 – "*To keep thee from the evil woman, from the flattery of the tongue of a strange woman.*"
4) Proverbs 7:5 – "*That they may keep thee from the strange woman, from the stranger which flattereth with her words.*"
5) Jeremiah 2:21 – "*Yet I had planted thee a noble vine, wholly a right seed: how then art thou turned into the degenerate plant of a strange vine unto me?*"
6) Jeremiah 8:19 – "*Behold the voice of the cry of the daughter of my people because of them that dwell in a far country: Is not the LORD in Zion? is not her king in her? Why have they provoked me to anger with their graven images, and with strange vanities?*"
7) Numbers 16:1-7, 32-35

II. Ingredients for sweet incense – *see "Sweet Incense" chapter*

Lesson 31

The Presence Of God

When referring to God's holy presence in Scripture, it most often represents the word "face." Therefore His presence means God's face is looking at us and watching us. He is turned toward us. In the beginning, God and man fellowshipped together continually. Man walked with God "in the cool of the day." God's presence was well known to him and there was a tremendous love relationship and sharing between God and man. But when mankind fell, they hid themselves from the presence of the Lord (Genesis 3:8). This broke God's heart because He cried to Adam, "*Where art thou?*" (Genesis 3:9). Because of sin, man could not face being in God's presence so he hid himself among the trees of the garden. This is what happens to us when we sin. We cannot bear being in God's presence, so we hide amongst the trees. Trees speak of word, or humanity or the flesh. We hide among our flesh rather than face God's holy presence. Man was eventually driven out of God's immediate presence because of this.

God's precious presence is like His glory. It is the essence of Himself. It is Him personally being near us. This is an awesome privilege for mankind: that God, the ruler of the universe, would stoop so low as to be with us inferior ones; but yet this is His heart. He created us for this purpose that we might dwell together with Him, and have a loving, wonderful relationship with Him. His presence is something that can be felt. It is a tangible thing. We know when it is there and when it is not. There are two aspects to God's presence, one is His omnipresence which is everywhere, because God fills all things, and second there is what we call His manifest presence. This is not the general omnipresence that is everywhere at all times, but it is when He personally comes and draws near to us. What a blessing this is. It is what we were born for and it is His desire. In Exodus 33:14 we read, "*And he said, My presence shall go with thee, and I will give thee rest.*" To the true sons of God, they can't imagine being without it. David cries in Psalms 51:11, "*Cast me not away from thy presence; and take not thy holy spirit from me.*" Moses said in Exodus 33:15-16, "*If thy presence go not with me, carry us not up hence. For wherein shall it be known here that I and thy people have found grace in thy sight? is it not in that thou goest with us? so shall we be separated, I and thy people, from all the people that are upon the face of the earth.*" What Moses is saying is that God's presence is what separates us from everyone else. It is what makes us different. Without it, we are like everyone else. It is a privilege to have it, but we must honor it and Him and never take it for granted. We are talking about God's divine and holy essence. To have it is glorious. To not have it is beyond awful. We are created to be with Him and enjoy His presence. Now that mankind in general has been separated from it, only God's people have the right and privilege to enjoy it. We are told how to enter into it, and that is by singing, and worshipping with thanksgiving (Psalms 100:2, Psalms 95:2). We are also told in Psalms 16:11, "*in thy presence is fulness of joy.*" So we will now look into the Scriptures to define His presence and also how to enter into it, enjoy it, and keep it in our lives. We will also exhaustively look at every aspect of His presence found in Holy Scripture.

I. Word Definitions for Presence

A. Hebrew words

1. *Paniym* – The face, the part that turns, a turning of the face; It comes from a root, *panah* – to turn, to face, appear, to look

This means, when we are talking about the presence of God or when we feel and sense His presence, He has turned His face to look at us. This word is used 2126 times. This word is translated: *face, his countenance, through them, before me, toward, before, my face, in the sight, shewbread, the forefront of, my presence, thy presence, open, in the presence, out of your sight, with thee, from the presence, in my sight, to meet him, his person, he hath compassed, thy face, thy favour, in his sight, honourable, prospect, thy person*. The root word is translated 135 times as – *have prepared, they looked, turned, turneth, we turned, I turned, looked, looketh, looking toward, he beholdeth, prepare ye, look back.*

2. *Neged* – A front, before, in the presence of, in the sight of; It comes from a root, *nagad* – to front, stand boldly out opposite. *Neged* is used 23 times.

3. *Ayin* – An eye, a fountain, well, spring, appearance. It is used 887 times

B. Greek words

1. *Enopion* – In the face of, in the sight of, in the presence of. It is used 97 times.
2. *Prosopon* – The visage, the front, towards, an eye, the countenance; It comes from a root, *pros* – forward to, toward. *Prosopon* is used 78 times.
3. *Katenopion* – Directly in front of, right over against, opposite; It comes from a root, *kata* – down in place or time. *Katenopion* is used 5 times.

C. This word is also translated *"from before"* 1137 times, *"face"* 39 times, *"presence"* 76 times, *"sight"* 40 times, *"countenance"* 30 times, *"from"* 27 times, *"person"* 21 times, *"upon"* 20 times, *"of"* 20 times, *"me"* 15 times, *"against"* 17 times, *"him"* 16 times, *"open"* 13 times, *"for"* 13 times, *"toward"* 9 times.

II. A Look In The Scriptures About God's Presence

A. We need to know God's presence

1. Genesis 28:16 – *"And Jacob awaked out of his sleep, and he said, Surely the LORD is in this place; and I knew it not."* – We should and need to know when God's presence is in a place or not. How sad so many people do not even recognize God's presence.
2. Judges 16:20 – *"...And he awoke out of his sleep, and said, I will go out as at other times before, and shake myself. And he wist not that the LORD was departed from him."* – Once again Samson's sin dulled him to knowing the presence.
3. I Samuel 4:21-22 – *"And she named the child I-chabod, saying, The glory is departed from Israel: because the ark of God was taken...And she said, The glory is departed from Israel: for the ark of God is taken."* – I wonder how many Israelites realized the glory was gone. For most of them it was known to them by their circumstances, not revelation.
4. Isaiah 1:3 – *"The ox knoweth his owner, and the ass his master's crib: but Israel doth not know, my people doth not consider."* – This to me is one of the saddest Scriptures. To think that even dumb animals know where their provision and home is, but God's people don't even care or consider this principle.
5. Jeremiah 2:32 – *"Can a maid forget her ornaments, or a bride her attire? Yet my people have forgotten me days without number."* – How long has it been for all of us since we remembered the Lord and put His presence first? How hard it must be for our loving, wonderful Father to know we have forgotten Him days without number.
6. Leviticus 10:1-4 – *"[1]And Nadab and Abihu, the sons of Aaron, took either of them his censer, and put fire therein, and put incense thereon, and offered strange fire before the LORD, which he commanded them not. [2]And there went out fire from the LORD, and devoured them, and they died before the LORD. [3]Then Moses said unto Aaron, This is it that the LORD spake, saying, I will be sanctified in them that come nigh me, and before all the people I will be glorified. And Aaron held his peace. [4]And Moses called Mishael and Elzaphan, the sons of Uzziel the uncle of Aaron, and said unto them, Come near, carry your brethren from before the sanctuary out of the camp."* – These two priests, who were Aaron's sons, should have known better then to come into God's holy presence while bearing strange fire. Strange could mean anything worldly, fleshly, demonic, or that they had not properly cleansed themselves before coming into the holy place.
7. Leviticus 22:3 – *"Say unto them, Whosoever he be of all your seed among your generations, that goeth unto the holy things, which the children of Israel hallow unto the LORD, having his uncleanness upon him, that soul shall be cut off from my presence: I am the LORD."* – It is very important for us as New Testament kings and priests to remember to never come into our God's holy, righteous, and pure presence without making sure our hearts are right, and that we are cleansed from all sin. We must always "fear the Lord" and respect His presence. We cannot and should not ever take it for granted. But we must remember to always honor and respect Him.

8. Deuteronomy 5:7 – "*Thou shalt have none other gods before me.*" – The phrase "before me" here means "presence". Therefore it could read, "*Thou shalt have none other gods in my presence*". We most earnestly should never allow demons, roots of bitterness, or have any other thing or person sitting upon the throne of our hearts. He is a jealous God and will not compete with anyone else. It must be Him alone we worship.
9. I Samuel 3:4-10 – "*...Now Samuel did not yet know the LORD, neither was the word of the LORD yet revealed unto him...And the LORD came, and stood, and called as at other times, Samuel, Samuel. Then Samuel answered, Speak; for thy servant heareth.*" – I wonder how many times the Lord had already called Samuel. It appears that He had done it many times before. This is why the Bible exhorts us to know Him and to search the Scriptures that He might grant us revelation. Also, I wonder how many of God's people are so bound up in religion and have so totally surrendered their lives to earthly representatives of God, that they only know them and not the Lord personally.
10. II Samuel 6:3-9 – "*And they set the ark of God upon a new cart...And David and all the house of Israel played before the LORD...And when they came to Nachon's threshingfloor, Uzzah put forth his hand to the ark of God, and took hold of it; for the oxen shook it. And the anger of the LORD was kindled against Uzzah; and God smote him there for his error; and there he died by the ark of God...And David was afraid of the LORD that day, and said, How shall the ark of the LORD come to me?*" – David like so many of us cry out, "How can I bring God's manifest presence home to me?" People die when they are negligent in their revelation of how to come into God's presence. It is no light matter. David first became angry. I suppose this is our first response as well. It wasn't until David searched the Scriptures that he understood not just anybody can bring God's presence. God's holy presence can only come upon the shoulders of true priests.

11. Zephaniah 1:7 – "*Hold thy peace at the presence of the Lord GOD: for the day of the LORD is at hand...*" – Oh, how we must learn to keep our mouths shut when we come into God's holy presence. We must learn this principle.

    a. Ecclesiastes 5:1-2 – "*Keep thy foot when thou goest to the house of God, and be more ready to hear, than to give the sacrifice of fools: for they consider not that they do evil. Be not rash with thy mouth, and let not thine heart be hasty to utter any thing before God: for God is in heaven, and thou upon earth: therefore let thy words be few.*"

It takes time and experience of going into His presence to learn how to act properly. Paul said "*study to be quiet*" (I Thessalonians 4:11). The less said is always the best plan. We will learn over time when and where and what to say in His presence.

12. Isaiah 45:22 – "*Look unto me, and be ye saved, all the ends of the earth: for I am God, and there is none else.*" – The word "look" here means His presence. We must get a true revelation of how important His presence is for our salvation and deliverance.

    a. Psalms 42:5 – "*Why art thou cast down, O my soul? and why art thou disquieted in me? hope thou in God: for I shall yet praise him for the help of his countenance.*" – The actual Hebrew here at the end of this verse is "*for His presence is salvation*".

B. God wants us to be in His presence and see His face

If we only knew how much God desires to dwell with us intimately, and how much His heart craves to be with us. We must understand that this is why we were created. We were created to have deep intimate fellowship with Him. He loves us so much, but He can't force us to come to Him. It must be in our own hearts. We must be like David who said, "*My soul followeth hard after thee*" (Psalms 63:8). Also in Psalms 27:4, David said "*One thing have I desired of the LORD, that will I seek after; that I may dwell in the house of the LORD all the days of my life, to behold the beauty of the LORD, and to inquire in his temple.*"

1. Exodus 33:14 – *"And he said, My presence shall go with thee, and I will give thee rest."*
2. Psalms 95:1-7 - *"O come, let us sing unto the LORD: let us make a joyful noise to the rock of our salvation. Let us come before his presence with thanksgiving, and make a joyful noise unto him with psalms. For the LORD is a great God, and a great King above all gods...O come, let us worship and bow down...For he is our God; and we are the people of his pasture, and the sheep of his hand..."*
3. Psalms 100:1-3 – *"Make a joyful noise unto the LORD, all ye lands. Serve the LORD with gladness: come before his presence with singing. Know ye that the LORD he is God: it is he that hath made us, and not we ourselves; we are his people, and the sheep of his pasture."*
4. Psalms 140:13 – *"Surely the righteous shall give thanks unto thy name: the upright shall dwell in thy presence."* – The upright love His presence. It is their chief desire. Would to God that we would allow this Word to so permeate us that it eventually consumes us, and that all we would want to do is be near Him and to know His glorious presence for ourselves, because we love Him so much. Amen!
5. Luke 13:26 – *"...We have eaten and drunk in thy presence, and thou hast taught in our streets."* – Don't waste any opportunity when God's presence is available. Take advantage of it, so that we might be chosen.
6. Acts 3:19 – *"Repent ye therefore, and be converted, that your sins may be blotted out, when the times of refreshing shall come from the presence of the Lord;"* – If all we have to do is stay repented up to enjoy His presence, how difficult is that?!
7. Jude 24 – *"Now unto him that is able to keep you from falling, and to present you faultless before the presence of his glory with exceeding joy"* – God so wants us to be in His eternal presence, He makes this promise to us. Not only will He try to keep us from falling, but He wants to present us faultless before His presence. Remember, He is able to do this, and He wants to do it.
8. Psalms 27:8 – *"When thou saidst, Seek ye my face; my heart said unto thee, Thy face, LORD, will I seek."* – God cannot make us seek Him. He can only ask. There must be something in us that drives us to seek His face. The word face here is presence. The Lord desires us to come and know Him freely.
9. Ezekiel 36:9 – *"For, behold, I am for you, and I will turn unto you..."* – Here God says "I am for you", and then promises us His presence. The word "turn" here is the Hebrew word for presence.
10. Exodus 33:11 – *"And the LORD spake unto Moses face to face, as a man speaketh unto his friend..."* – Could this be possible for all of us, God considering those that love Him His friends? He desires face to face communion.
11. Numbers 6:24-26 – *"The LORD bless thee, and keep thee: The LORD make his face shine upon thee, and be gracious unto thee: The LORD lift up his countenance upon thee, and give thee peace."* – This means God wants His face (presence) to shine upon us, and as He lifts up His countenance, peace is the result. This is what waits for us in the presence of God.
12. Genesis 17:1 – *"...the LORD appeared to Abram, and said unto him, I am the Almighty God; walk before me, and be thou perfect."* – The original Hebrew word for before is presence or face. So it should actually read, "walk in my presence" or "walk in my face". The only way we will ever be perfect or complete is to walk before His presence or face. This makes us constantly aware of Him, and will hopefully encourage us not to sin.
13. Exodus 34:6 – *"And the LORD passed by before him, and proclaimed, The LORD, The LORD God, merciful and gracious, longsuffering, and abundant in goodness and truth,"* – God wants us to be in His presence, so we can understand and get to know who He really is, not like the children of Israel who just knew His acts, but like Moses here to know His ways (Psalms 103:7). If we would just spend more time with Him, we would find out that He is first sovereign, the ruler over all. We then would find that He is merciful and gracious. Today, there are still people who think their God is a hard taskmaster, who can't wait to punish them. Only by being in His precious presence will we learn differently. We would then find He is not short tempered, but longsuffering; that He is the ancient of days, the *"husbandman waiteth for the precious fruit of the earth, and hath long patience for it"* (James 5:7). Lastly, we see He is full and overflowing in goodness and truth. This is what knowing His precious presence will do for us.

14. Genesis 32:30 – *"And Jacob called the name of the place Peniel: for I have seen God face to face, and my life is preserved."* – The name Peniel means "face of God" in Hebrew. Once again, we see someone who is in the manifest presence (face) of God and whose life is preserved. In this case, there was a wrestling match between God and Jacob, fighting over Jacob's soul. But look what His presence does for Jacob, it changes his nature from Jacob, meaning supplanter or deceiver, to Israel, meaning champion or prince with God. Yes, it is true that there are times when God's presence is after something in us, but it is for our good and not for evil. If we would desire to see His face and be in His manifest presence, then eventually our character will have to change. Like II Corinthians 3:18 says, *"But we all, with open face beholding as in a glass the glory of the Lord, are changed into the same image from glory to glory, even as by the Spirit of the Lord."*

15. II Samuel 6:12-21

"12And it was told king David, saying, The LORD hath blessed the house of Obed-edom, and all that
pertaineth unto him, because of the ark of God. So David went and brought up the ark of God from the house of
Obed-edom into the city of David with gladness. 13And it was so, that when they that bare the ark of the LORD
had gone six paces, he sacrificed oxen and fatlings. 14And David danced before the LORD with all his might; and
David was girded with a linen ephod. 15So David and all the house of Israel brought up the ark of the LORD with
shouting, and with the sound of the trumpet. 16And as the ark of the LORD came into the city of David, Michal
Saul's daughter looked through a window, and saw king David leaping and dancing before the LORD; and she
despised him in her heart. 17And they brought in the ark of the LORD, and set it in his place, in the midst of the
tabernacle that David had pitched for it: and David offered burnt offerings and peace offerings before the LORD.
18And as soon as David had made an end of offering burnt offerings and peace offerings, he blessed the people in
the name of the LORD of hosts. 19And he dealt among all the people, even among the whole multitude of Israel, as
well to the women as men, to every one a cake of bread, and a good piece of flesh, and a flagon of wine. So all the
people departed every one to his house. 20Then David returned to bless his household. And Michal the daughter of
Saul came out to meet David, and said, How glorious was the king of Israel to day, who uncovered himself to day
in the eyes of the handmaids of his servants, as one of the vain fellows shamelessly uncovereth himself! 21And
David said unto Michal, It was before the LORD..."

16. Psalms 42:7 – *"Deep calleth unto deep at the noise of thy waterspouts: all thy waves and thy billows are gone over me."* – The deepest part of God's heart is always calling to the deepest place in our own being. *"The noise of His waterspouts, all His waves and billows"* speak of His glorious presence drawing us, wooing, to come near and fellowship with Him.

17. Song of Solomon 1:3-4 – *"Because of the savour of thy good ointments thy name is as ointment poured forth, therefore do the virgins love thee. Draw me, we will run after thee: the king hath brought me into his chambers: we will be glad and rejoice in thee, we will remember thy love more than wine: the upright love thee."*

The fragrance of His presence pours forth from His name (character). Because of this, God's bride loves Him. She asks Him to draw her. We must remember we can't even run after God unless He draws us. But as He does and we respond, we end up being glad because in His presence is fullness of joy (Psalms 16:11). What a delight that God would want to be with us.

18. Song of Solomon 2:8-10 – *"The voice of my beloved! behold, he cometh leaping upon the mountains, skipping upon the hills. My beloved is like a roe or a young hart: behold, he standeth behind our wall, he looketh forth at the windows, shewing himself through the lattice. My beloved spake, and said unto me, Rise up, my love, my fair one, and come away."*

This is such an eye opening look at how our God can't wait to be with us, and how excited He is at the prospect. He tries so hard to get our attention, just like any lover would do. But finally He speaks, and calls unto us to rise up and come away with Him. He wants us to leave behind all the worldly pursuits and pressures and simply spend time with Him. And if we do, He promises to cause us to forget our troubles and worries, as we bask in Him presence.

19. Song of Solomon 5:1 – *"I am come into my garden, my sister, my spouse: I have gathered my myrrh with my spice; I have eaten my honeycomb with my honey; I have drunk my wine with my milk: eat, O friends; drink, yea, drink abundantly, O beloved."*

Once again the Lord has come to visit us and draw us with His presence. He comes with revelation from the Word and the wine of the Holy Ghost, and invites us to drink and eat abundantly of it because we are His beloved! Do any of us really understand? Do any of us really comprehend just how much He loves us and desires to be with us? Oh, what a privilege!

20. Song of Solomon 7:10 – *"I am my beloved's, and his desire is toward me."*

    a. Song of Solomon 2:16 – *"My beloved is mine, and I am his: he feedeth among the lilies."*
    b. Song of Solomon 6:3 – *"I am my beloved's, and my beloved is mine: he feedeth among the lilies."*

These three verses show the growth in the bride. She starts out in chapter 2 by being selfish, but then by chapter 6, it begins to be all about Him. Then finally in chapter 7, she realizes that it is His desire towards her that has made her fall in love with Him. Oh, how He longs to be with us and "feed among the lilies"and enjoy us as His bride-to-be.

21. Song of Solomon 2:3-6 – *"As the apple tree among the trees of the wood, so is my beloved among the sons. I sat down under his shadow with great delight, and his fruit was sweet to my taste. He brought me to the banqueting house, and his banner over me was love. Stay me with flagons, comfort me with apples: for I am sick of love. His left hand is under my head, and his right hand doth embrace me."* – Could there be any greater example of His drawing presence of love?!
22. Song of Solomon 2:14 – *"O my dove, that art in the clefts of the rock, in the secret places of the stairs, let me see thy countenance, let me hear thy voice; for sweet is thy voice, and thy countenance is comely."* – Oh, how He wants to be with us in the secret place of His presence, to see our face, and to hear our voice. What greater love us there than this?!
23. Song of Solomon 3:9-11 – *"King Solomon made himself a chariot of the wood of Lebanon. He made the pillars thereof of silver, the bottom thereof of gold, the covering of it of purple, the midst thereof being paved with love, for the daughters of Jerusalem. Go forth, O ye daughters of Zion, and behold king Solomon with the crown wherewith his mother crowned him in the day of his espousals, and in the day of the gladness of his heart."*
24. Song of Solomon 4:8-16 – *"Come with me from Lebanon, my spouse, with me from Lebanon...Thou hast ravished my heart, my sister, my spouse; thou hast ravished my heart with one of thine eyes, with one chain of thy neck. How fair is thy love, my sister, my spouse! how much better is thy love than wine! and the smell of thine ointments than all spices..."*
25. Psalms 45:10-16 – *"Hearken, O daughter, and consider, and incline thine ear; forget also thine own people, and thy father's house; So shall the king greatly desire thy beauty: for he is thy Lord; and worship thou him..."* – If this passage describes His great desire for us, His overwhelming love for us, and His desire for us to be in His presence, then I can't think of anything written that is more powerful. He longs to draw us with His holy presence. All we have to do is answer and respond to receive all His great benefits that come from being with Him and in His glorious presence.
26. Psalms 46:10-11 – *"Be still, and know that I am God...The LORD of hosts is with us; the God of Jacob is our refuge."*

II. Understanding the Presence of God

A. What is in this presence?

1. **It brings rest** – Exodus 33:14 – *"And he said, My presence shall go with thee, and I will give thee rest."*
2. **It separates us from the world** – Exodus 33:15-16 – *"And he said unto him, If thy presence go not with me, carry us not up hence. For wherein shall it be known here that I and thy people have found grace in thy sight? is it not in that thou goest with us? so shall we be separated, I and thy people, from all the people that are upon the face of the earth."*
3. **Glory and honour** – I Chronicles 16:27 – *"Glory and honour are in his presence; strength and gladness are in his place."*

4. **Exposure and awe** – Job 23:13-16 – *"But he is in one mind, and who can turn him? and what his soul desireth, even that he doeth. For he performeth the thing that is appointed for me: and many such things are with him. Therefore am I troubled at his presence: when I consider, I am afraid of him. For God maketh my heart soft, and the Almighty troubleth me:"*

    a. Jeremiah 5:22 – *"Fear ye not me? saith the LORD: will ye not tremble at my presence, which have placed the sand for the bound of the sea by a perpetual decree, that it cannot pass it: and though the waves thereof toss themselves, yet can they not prevail; though they roar, yet can they not pass over it?"*

5. **Fullness of joy** – Psalms 16:11 – *"Thou wilt shew me the path of life: in thy presence is fulness of joy; at thy right hand there are pleasures for evermore."*
6. **Anointed words and judgment** – Psalms 17:2 – *"Let my sentence come forth from thy presence; let thine eyes behold the things that are equal."*
7. **He hides us in His presence** – Psalms 31:20 – *"Thou shalt hide them in the secret of thy presence from the pride of man: thou shalt keep them secretly in a pavilion from the strife of tongues."*

8. **The earth (humanity) shakes, the heavens are opened, and mountains are ruined** – Psalms 68:7-9 – *"...The earth shook, the heavens also dropped at the presence of God: even Sinai itself was moved at the presence of God..."*

    a. Isaiah 64:1-3 – *"Oh that thou wouldest rend the heavens, that thou wouldest come down, that the mountains might flow down at thy presence, As when the melting fire burneth, the fire causeth the waters to boil, to make thy name known to thine adversaries, that the nations may tremble at thy presence! When thou didst terrible things which we looked not for, thou camest down, the mountains flowed down at thy presence."*

9. **Hills and Mountains (obstacles in our lives) melt and move** – Psalms 97:4-5 – *"...The hills melted like wax at the presence of the LORD, at the presence of the Lord of the whole earth."*

    a. Ezekiel 38:20 – *"So that the fishes of the sea, and the fowls of the heaven, and the beasts of the field, and all creeping things that creep upon the earth, and all the men that are upon the face of the earth, shall shake at my presence, and the mountains shall be thrown down, and the steep places shall fall, and every wall shall fall to the ground."*
    b. Psalms 9:3 – *"When mine enemies are turned back, they shall fall and perish at thy presence."*

10. **The world trembles** – Psalms 114:7 – *"Tremble, thou earth, at the presence of the Lord, at the presence of the God of Jacob;"*

    a. Nahum 1:2-8 – *"...The mountains quake at him, and the hills melt, and the earth is burned at his presence, yea, the world, and all that dwell therein..."*

11. **His presence will follow us wherever we go** – Psalms 139:7-13 – "[7]*Whither shall I go from thy spirit? or whither shall I flee from thy presence?* [8]*If I ascend up into heaven, thou art there: if I make my bed in hell, behold, thou art there.* [9]*If I take the wings of the morning, and dwell in the uttermost parts of the sea;* [10]*Even there shall thy hand lead me, and thy right hand shall hold me.* [11]*If I say, Surely the darkness shall cover me; even the night shall be light about me.* [12]*Yea, the darkness hideth not from thee; but the night shineth as the day: the darkness and the light are both alike to thee.* [13]*For thou hast possessed my reins: thou hast covered me in my mother's womb.*"
12. **The idols of Egypt (the flesh) are moved** – Isaiah 19:1 – "*The burden of Egypt. Behold, the LORD rideth upon a swift cloud, and shall come into Egypt: and the idols of Egypt shall be moved at his presence, and the heart of Egypt shall melt in the midst of it.*"
13. **Angels attend to God's presence and help us** – Isaiah 63:9 – "*In all their affliction he was afflicted, and the angel of his presence saved them: in his love and in his pity he redeemed them; and he bare them, and carried them all the days of old.*"
14. **Times of refreshing** – Acts 3:19 – "*Repent ye therefore, and be converted, that your sins may be blotted out, when the times of refreshing shall come from the presence of the Lord;*"
15. **God will not allow flesh to glory in His presence** – I Corinthians 1:29 – "*That no flesh should glory in his presence.*"

III. Facts About His Presence

A. What is "His presence"?

1. Glory – II Corinthians 3:18 – "*But we all, with open face beholding as in a glass the glory of the Lord, are changed into the same image from glory to glory, even as by the Spirit of the Lord.*"
2. Beauty – Psalms 90:16-17 – "*Let thy work appear unto thy servants, and thy glory unto their children. And let the beauty of the LORD our God be upon us: and establish thou the work of our hands upon us...*"
3. Enabling power – Exodus 33:14 – "*And he said, My presence shall go with thee, and I will give thee rest.*"

B. What cuts His presence off?

1. Genesis 3:8 – "*And they heard the voice of the LORD God walking in the garden in the cool of the day: and Adam and his wife hid themselves from the presence of the LORD God amongst the trees of the garden.*"
2. Genesis 4:16 – "*And Cain went out from the presence of the LORD, and dwelt in the land of Nod, on the east of Eden.*"
3. Isaiah 59:2 – "*But your iniquities have separated between you and your God, and your sins have hid his face from you, that he will not hear.*"
4. Psalms 51:11 – "*Cast me not away from thy presence; and take not thy holy spirit from me.*"
5. Psalms 140:13 – "*Surely the righteous shall give thanks unto thy name: the upright shall dwell in thy presence.*"

C. The devil cannot take His presence.

1. Psalms 9:3 – "*When mine enemies are turned back, they shall fall and perish at thy presence.*"
2. Psalms 31:20 – "*Thou shalt hide them in the secret of thy presence from the pride of man: thou shalt keep them secretly in a pavilion from the strife of tongues.*"
3. Psalms 68:2 – "*As smoke is driven away, so drive them away: as wax melteth before the fire, so let the wicked perish at the presence of God.*"

D. We are to go after Him.

1. Psalms 42:1 – "*As the hart panteth after the water brooks, so panteth my soul after thee, O God.*"
2. Psalms 27:4 – "*One thing have I desired of the LORD, that will I seek after; that I may dwell in the house of the LORD all the days of my life, to behold the beauty of the LORD, and to inquire in his temple.*"
3. Isaiah 55:5 – "*Behold, thou shalt call a nation that thou knowest not, and nations that knew not thee shall run unto thee because of the LORD thy God, and for the Holy One of Israel; for he hath glorified thee.*"

E. How do we go after Him?

1. Hebrews 11:6 – "*But without faith it is impossible to please him: for he that cometh to God must believe that he is, and that he is a rewarder of them that diligently seek him.*"
2. Hebrews 4:16 – "*Let us therefore come boldly unto the throne of grace, that we may obtain mercy, and find grace to help in time of need.*"
3. Psalms 100:2 – "*Serve the LORD with gladness: come before his presence with singing.*"
4. I Corinthians 1:29 – "*That no flesh should glory in his presence.*"
5. Song of Solomon 1:3 – "*Because of the savour of thy good ointments thy name is as ointment poured forth, therefore do the virgins love thee.*"

F. Our assurance

1. Isaiah 64:5 – "*Thou meetest him that rejoiceth and worketh righteousness...*"
2. Song of Solomon 4:10-11 – "*How fair is thy love, my sister, my spouse! How much better is thy love than wine! and the smell of thine ointments than all spices! Thy lips, O my spouse, drop as the honeycomb...*"
3. James 4:8 – "*Draw nigh to God, and he will draw nigh to you...*"

G. Afterwards, we all get together in His presence.

1. Song of Solomon 1:4 – "*Draw me, we will run after thee: the king hath brought me into his chambers: we will be glad and rejoice in thee, we will remember thy love more than wine: the upright love thee.*"

H. Man's nature is to flee from His presence rather than embrace it.

1. Psalms 139:7 – "*Whither shall I go from thy spirit? or whither shall I flee from thy presence?*"
2. Jonah 1:3, 10 – "*But Jonah rose up to flee unto Tarshish from the presence of the LORD...Then were the men exceedingly afraid, and said unto him, Why hast thou done this? For the men knew that he fled from the presence of the LORD, because he had told them.*"
3. Genesis 3:8 – "*And they heard the voice of the LORD God walking in the garden in the cool of the day: and Adam and his wife hid themselves from the presence of the LORD God amongst the trees of the garden.*"
4. Genesis 4:14, 16 – "*Behold, thou hast driven me out this day from the face of the earth; and from thy face shall I be hid; and I shall be a fugitive and a vagabond in the earth; and it shall come to pass, that every one that findeth me shall slay me...And Cain went out from the presence of the LORD, and dwelt in the land of Nod, on the east of Eden.*"
5. Exodus 3:6 – "*Moreover he said, I am the God of thy father, the God of Abraham, the God of Isaac, and the God of Jacob. And Moses hid his face; for he was afraid to look upon God.*"

I. His presence should be everything to us.

1. Psalms 51:11 – "*Cast me not away from thy presence; and take not thy holy spirit from me.*"
2. Psalms 17:2 – "*Let my sentence come forth from thy presence...*"

Lesson 32

Tabernacle Truths In Worship

I. Worship: The Last Great Move Before The Coming Of The Lord And Steps To His Presence

A. The Tabernacle – Three Compartments

1. The Outer Court, Exodus 27:9-19 – All was of brass, which speaks of judgment. This part of the tabernacle is where man's needs are met.

a. Brazen Altar – The brazen altar was made of wood (signifying man) and was overlaid with brass (judgment). This is where the burnt offerings were sacrificed. It is the place of substitution, the place where sin is forgiven. For the New Testament Christian, it is the Cross.

b. The Laver, Exodus 30:17-21 – The laver was made of brass mirrors. It held water for the priests to come and wash themselves before entering into the Holy Place. The laver speaks to us of sanctification, cleansing, baptism in water and the Word of God working in our lives (James 1:23-25). The laver is necessary for every believer if he is to be changed and mature. We must all be water baptized, we must all yield to the Word of God, we must all submit to the Holy Spirit if we want to go into the Holy Place.

2. The Holy Place – Once we leave the Outer Court, we leave the place of our needs being met and we enter into the place of meeting His needs. Everything here is made of gold, speaking of divinity. This is God's place.

a. The Lampstand, Exodus 25:31-40 – In particular, the lampstand speaks of the baptism in the Holy Ghost. All those who desire to know God intimately, who hunger for the supernatural, who cry out for revelation, will come out of man's light into God's light. Many refuse to enter here because they are no longer in control.

b. The Table of Shewbread, Exodus 25:23-30 – The table was made of gold overlaying wood. It was to hold the twelve loaves of bread (the bread of His presence). It is where the High Priest was to eat before the Lord. The table speaks to us of divine order, the number twelve in the Bible representing divine government., It also speaks of revelational teaching (the bread) and fellowship (where they ate together).

c. The Golden Altar, Exodus 30:1-10 –It was wood overlaid with gold. It was the last piece of furniture before the veil. Sweet incense was to burn there perpetually. It speaks to us of praise and intercession.

3. The Most Holy Place – This is the place of His glory, His throne, and His holiness.

a. The Ark, Exodus 25:10-16 – The ark was made of wood overlaid with pure gold. It had a length and breadth but no measurement of height is given. Two cherubim of gold came out from the ends of the Mercy Seat. The Mercy Seat was placed above the ark and the Lord said he would always meet and commune with us from the Mercy Seat. We can always find Him at the Mercy Seat. Here mercy rejoices over judgment. The law was in the ark, but the Mercy Seat was placed over it.

B. God's Final Coronation: Worship – This is found by looking at the different moves of God and seeing what God restored to the church with each move.

1. Brazen Altar: Substitution sacrifice – Martin Luther

2. Laver: Cleansing and Word – John and Charles Wesley
3. Lampstand: Holy Ghost and Gifts – Pentecostal Movement
4. Table of Shewbread: Teaching and Fellowship – Charismatic Movement
5. Golden Altar: Worship and Intercession – The Bride
6. Veil: Ark of Covenant – God's Presence

Lesson 33

The Veil Into The Most Holy Place

The Veil Into The Most Holy Place

I. The Veil, Exodus 26:31-33

Exodus 26:31-33 – "*31And thou shalt make a vail of blue, and purple, and scarlet, and fine twined linen of cunning work: with cherubims shall it be made: 32And thou shalt hang it upon four pillars of shittim wood overlaid with gold: their hooks shall be of gold, upon the four sockets of silver. 33And thou shalt hang up the vail under the taches, that thou mayest bring in thither within the vail the ark of the testimony: and the vail shall divide unto you between the holy place and the most holy.*"

This is the last entrance. It is the entrance into everything God. The only thing you will find after passing through this veil is Him. It is the entrance into all that is holy, glorious, heavenly, and all that is God.

A. Word definitions

1. Hebrew for veil (*vail in KJV*), *poreketh* – a separating, a sacred screen; it stems from another word, *perek* – to break apart, fracture, or severity.
2. Greek for veil, *katapetasma* – something spread thoroughly, the door screen, that which is spread out

B. Other names for this veil

1. It is spelled *vail* in many places, Exodus 26:31
2. The second vail, Hebrews 9:3
3. The covering vail, Numbers 4:5 – The vail was used to cover the ark when the camp was on the move.
4. The vail of the covering, Exodus 35:12, 39:34, 40:21
5. The vail of the testimony, Leviticus 24:3
6. The vail of the sanctuary, Leviticus 4:6

C. Some facts about this veil

1. Only the High Priest could enter through the veil once a year on the day of atonement
2. It measures 10 cubits high and 10 cubits wide.

3. There were four pillars upholding this veil which were made of wood overlaid with gold. The pillars were set in silver sockets. The veil was to be hung from gold hooks connected to the pillars.
4. It was made of blue, purple, scarlet, and fine twined linen.
5. It was made of cunning work – Hebrew word for cunning, *chashab* – to plait, to weave, to plot
6. With cherubims shall it be made – just as the fine linen curtains had inwrought cherubims, so this veil, separating the most holy place from the rest of the sanctuary had them; once again, we find them guarding the glory, guarding the manifest presence of God. Especially here, since this is the last threshold into all that is God.
7. It was to hang upon the four pillars of shittim wood.
8. It was to divide between the holy place and the most holy place.

II. The Spiritual Significance Of This Veil

A. The typology defined

1. The colors and material

a. Blue – everything heavenly; Jesus the Lord from heaven
b. Purple – royalty and authority; Jesus the King of Kings
c. Scarlet – sacrifice, suffering; Jesus the suffering Lamb of God
d. Linen – purity, holiness, righteousness; Jesus our righteousness (Jehovah Tsidkenu)
e. Fine, twined – this speaks of the delicate working of the righteousness of God into our lives by the Lord Jesus.

2. Cherubims – The cherubims mentioned here are inwrought within this veil. They are there to make sure nobody gets through that is not ready. Cherubims are there to guard Him and His glory, just like the entrance to the garden (Genesis 3:24), protecting the way to the tree of life, who is Jesus Himself.

3. Four pillars of wood overlaid with gold

a. Four is the number for creation
b. Pillars – that which is foundational or that which holds things up; the four gospels, the Word made flesh; this also speaks of the gospel message to the whole world (creation)
c. Wood overlaid with gold always speaks of God's divine character over humanity
d. Upon four sockets of silver – silver always speaks of redemption; redemption for all of creation.

In other words, those in creation who have God's character completely covering their old man are the only ones that may pass through this last entrance. All of this is founded upon their redemption. Jesus, the great redeemer, is their foundation.

4. They shall hang up the veil – this covering veil covers heaven and earth
5. The veil shall divide, measure 10 square

a. This veil was meant to hide the glory of God from unapproved men.
b. The number 10 in Scripture speaks of the law (10 commandments), which in this case speaks of how the Word of God separates. Only those walking in the Word could ever enter in.
c. This veil also speaks of the physical body of Jesus, the in between point between God and man. Because of His broken body, we can enter in.

1) Hebrews 10:19-22 – "[19]*Having therefore, brethren, boldness to enter into the holiest by the blood of Jesus,* [20]*By a new and living way, which he hath consecrated for us, through the veil, that is to say, his flesh;* [21]*And having an high priest over the house of God;* [22]*Let us draw near with a true heart in full assurance of faith, having our hearts sprinkled from an evil conscience, and our bodies washed with pure water."*
2) Ephesians 2:13-19
3) Matthew 27:51 – *"And, behold, the veil of the temple was rent in twain from the top to the bottom; and the earth did quake, and the rocks rent;"*
4) I Timothy 2:5 – *"For there is one God, and one mediator between God and men, the man Christ Jesus;"*
5) John 10:7-9 – "[7]*Then said Jesus unto them again, Verily, verily, I say unto you, I am the door of the sheep.* [8]*All that ever came before me are thieves and robbers: but the sheep did not hear them.* [9]*I am the door: by me if any man enter in, he shall be saved, and shall go in and out, and find pasture."*
6) Acts 4:12 – *"Neither is there salvation in any other: for there is none other name under heaven given among men, whereby we must be saved."*
7) John 14:6 – *"Jesus saith unto him, I am the way, the truth, and the life: no man cometh unto the Father, but by me."*

That which was perverted by man has been removed by the sacrifice of God's Son. No more separation. No more "keep out" sign. No more dividing curtain between us and the Father, all because of this wonderful, precious, compassionate, loving, humble, and great Son of Man and Son of God. Jesus, oh how we owe Him everything. Oh how glorious is the grace of God. We had no way. No one could open the door, the veil, and the sealed book (Revelation 5:1-10). Only one could and did it. This is why His name is exalted above all. Revelation 5 tells us the only one who could do it was the Lamb of God. I hope we read this chapter from now on with great reverence and fall down like everyone else in heaven giving Him the greatest glory, the greatest respect, the greatest worship, our total devotion, and all of our allegiance.

B. Through Jesus, we now have access

1. Ephesians 2:13-19 – "[13]*But now in Christ Jesus ye who sometimes were far off are made nigh by the blood of Christ.* [14]*For he is our peace, who hath made both one, and hath broken down the middle wall of partition between us;* [15]*Having abolished in his flesh the enmity, even the law of commandments contained in ordinances; for to make in himself of twain one new man, so making peace;* [16]*And that he might reconcile both unto God in one body by the cross, having slain the enmity thereby:* [17]*And came and preached peace to you which were afar off, and to them that were nigh.* [18]*For through him we both have access by one Spirit unto the Father.* [19]*Now therefore ye are no more strangers and foreigners, but fellowcitizens with the saints, and of the household of God;"*
2. Ephesians 3:11-21 – "[11]*According to the eternal purpose which he purposed in Christ Jesus our Lord:* [12]*In whom we have boldness and access with confidence by the faith of him..."*
3. Ephesians 2:10 – *"For we are his workmanship, created in Christ Jesus unto good works, which God hath before ordained that we should walk in them."*
4. Ephesians 1:6-11 – "[6]*To the praise of the glory of his grace, wherein he hath made us accepted in the beloved..."*
5. Galatians 2:20-21 – "[20]*I am crucified with Christ: nevertheless I live; yet not I, but Christ liveth in me: and the life which I now live in the flesh I live by the faith of the Son of God, who loved me, and gave himself for me.* [21]*I do not frustrate the grace of God: for if righteousness come by the law, then Christ is dead in vain."*
6. Galatians 3:13-14 – "[13]*Christ hath redeemed us from the curse of the law, being made a curse for us: for it is written, Cursed is every one that hangeth on a tree:* [14]*That the blessing of Abraham might come on the Gentiles through Jesus Christ; that we might receive the promise of the Spirit through faith."*
7. Galatians 3:22-29

8. II Corinthians 5:17-21 – "*...[21]For he hath made him to be sin for us, who knew no sin; that we might be made the righteousness of God in him.*"
9. II Corinthians 4:6 – "*For God, who commanded the light to shine out of darkness, hath shined in our hearts, to give the light of the knowledge of the glory of God in the face of Jesus Christ.*"
10. I Corinthians 1:30 – "*But of him are ye in Christ Jesus, who of God is made unto us wisdom, and righteousness, and sanctification, and redemption:*"
11. Romans 5:1-2 – "*Therefore being justified by faith, we have peace with God through our Lord Jesus Christ: [2]By whom also we have access by faith into this grace wherein we stand, and rejoice in hope of the glory of God.*"
12. Romans 6:23 – "*For the wages of sin is death; but the gift of God is eternal life through Jesus Christ our Lord.*"
13. Romans 3:20-26 – "*[20]Therefore by the deeds of the law there shall no flesh be justified in his sight: for by the law is the knowledge of sin. [21]But now the righteousness of God without the law is manifested, being witnessed by the law and the prophets; [22]Even the righteousness of God which is by faith of Jesus Christ unto all and upon all them that believe: for there is no difference: [23]For all have sinned, and come short of the glory of God; [24]Being justified freely by his grace through the redemption that is in Christ Jesus: [25]Whom God hath set forth to be a propitiation through faith in his blood, to declare his righteousness for the remission of sins that are past, through the forbearance of God; [26]To declare, I say, at this time his righteousness: that he might be just, and the justifier of him which believeth in Jesus.*"
15. Philippians 2:5-11
16. Colossians 1:12-22
17. Titus 3:4-7 – "*[4]But after that the kindness and love of God our Saviour toward man appeared, [5]Not by works of righteousness which we have done, but according to his mercy he saved us, by the washing of regeneration, and renewing of the Holy Ghost; [6]Which he shed on us abundantly through Jesus Christ our Saviour; [7]That being justified by his grace, we should be made heirs according to the hope of eternal life.*"
18. Hebrews 2:7-15
19. Hebrews 8:3-6 – "*[3]For every high priest is ordained to offer gifts and sacrifices: wherefore it is of necessity that this man have somewhat also to offer. [4]For if he were on earth, he should not be a priest, seeing that there are priests that offer gifts according to the law: [5]Who serve unto the example and shadow of heavenly things, as Moses was admonished of God when he was about to make the tabernacle: for, See, saith he, that thou make all things according to the pattern shewed to thee in the mount. [6]But now hath he obtained a more excellent ministry, by how much also he is the mediator of a better covenant, which was established upon better promises.*"
20. Hebrews 9:11-15, 28 – "*[11]But Christ being come an high priest of good things to come, by a greater and more perfect tabernacle, not made with hands, that is to say, not of this building; [12]Neither by the blood of goats and calves, but by his own blood he entered in once into the holy place, having obtained eternal redemption for us. [13]For if the blood of bulls and of goats, and the ashes of an heifer sprinkling the unclean, sanctifieth to the purifying of the flesh: [14]How much more shall the blood of Christ, who through the eternal Spirit offered himself without spot to God, purge your conscience from dead works to serve the living God? [15]And for this cause he is the mediator of the new testament, that by means of death, for the redemption of the transgressions that were under the first testament, they which are called might receive the promise of eternal inheritance...*"
21. Hebrews 10:4-21 – "*...[19]Having therefore, brethren, boldness to enter into the holiest by the blood of Jesus,*"
22. Hebrews 13:12, 20
23. I Peter 1:18-21 – "*[18]Forasmuch as ye know that ye were not redeemed with corruptible things, as silver and gold, from your vain conversation received by tradition from your fathers; [19]But with the precious blood of Christ, as of a lamb without blemish and without spot: [20]Who verily was foreordained before the foundation of the world, but was manifest in these last times for you, [21]Who by him do believe in God, that raised him up from the dead, and gave him glory; that your faith and hope might be in God.*"

24. I Peter 2:21-25 – "[21]*For even hereunto were ye called: because Christ also suffered for us, leaving us an example, that ye should follow his steps...*"
25. I John 2:2, 5:11-15
26. Revelation 1:5-6

Oh, how great and marvelous the grace, mercy, and love of our great God and our Saviour Jesus Christ. We, who were once denied, afar off, and blocked out, are now made right by the blood of Jesus. Thanks be unto God for His unspeakable gift. How marvelous are the unsearchable riches of Christ.

C. Other aspects of this veil to consider and things it represents to us

1. This veil leads us into the fullness of God.
2. It represents entrance into the feast of Tabernacles.
3. It is the dwelling place of Fathers – I John 2:14
4. The perfect will of God – Romans 12:2
5. It is the entrance into our inheritance.
6. It is the place for the 100fold believers.
7. It is our entrance into true holiness and godliness.
8. The rent veil symbolized the way into the holiest has been provided.

D. Some thoughts to consider

1. The veil being torn speaks to us that now true revelation can be seen (Proverbs 25:2, II Corinthians 3:13-18).
2. The veil that has covered all humanity is now lifted. They have the ability now to see God (Isaiah 25:6-9).
3. That which has been hidden is now revealed.

   a. Until now, things have been hidden or kept secret.

      1) Isaiah 45:15 – "*Verily thou art a God that hidest thyself, O God of Israel, the Saviour.*"
      2) Psalms 13:1 – "*How long wilt thou forget me, O LORD? for ever? how long wilt thou hide thy face from me?*"
      3) Job 26:9 – "*He holdeth back the face of his throne, and spreadeth his cloud upon it.*"
      4) Job 23:9 – "*On the left hand, where he doth work, but I cannot behold him: he hideth himself on the right hand, that I cannot see him:*"
      5) I Corinthians 2:7 – "*But we speak the wisdom of God in a mystery, even the hidden wisdom, which God ordained before the world unto our glory:*"
      6) Habakkuk 3:4 – "*And his brightness was as the light; he had horns coming out of his hand: and there was the hiding of his power.*"
      7) Ephesians 3:3-5 – "[3]*How that by revelation he made known unto me the mystery; (as I wrote afore in few words,* [4]*Whereby, when ye read, ye may understand my knowledge in the mystery of Christ)* [5]*Which in other ages was not made known unto the sons of men, as it is now revealed unto his holy apostles and prophets by the Spirit;*"
      8) Romans 16:25 – "*Now to him that is of power to stablish you according to my gospel, and the preaching of Jesus Christ, according to the revelation of the mystery, which was kept secret since the world began,*"
      9) Deuteronomy 29:29 – "*The secret things belong unto the LORD our God: but those things which are revealed belong unto us and to our children for ever, that we may do all the words of this law.*"
      10) Colossians 1:26 – "*Even the mystery which hath been hid from ages and from generations, but now is made manifest to his saints:*"

11) I Timothy 3:16 – "*And without controversy great is the mystery of godliness: God was manifest in the flesh, justified in the Spirit, seen of angels, preached unto the Gentiles, believed on in the world, received up into glory.*"

b. Now because the veil is rent, revelation has exploded

1) Revelation 10:7 – "*But in the days of the voice of the seventh angel, when he shall begin to sound, the mystery of God should be finished, as he hath declared to his servants the prophets.*"
2) Mark 4:4 – "*And it came to pass, as he sowed, some fell by the way side, and the fowls of the air came and devoured it up.*"
3) Revelation 2:17 – "*He that hath an ear, let him hear what the Spirit saith unto the churches; To him that overcometh will I give to eat of the hidden manna, and will give him a white stone, and in the stone a new name written, which no man knoweth saving he that receiveth it.*"
4) I Corinthians 2:9-10 – "[9]*But as it is written, Eye hath not seen, nor ear heard, neither have entered into the heart of man, the things which God hath prepared for them that love him.* [10]*But God hath revealed them unto us by his Spirit: for the Spirit searcheth all things, yea, the deep things of God.*"
5) Isaiah 45:3 – "*And I will give thee the treasures of darkness, and hidden riches of secret places, that thou mayest know that I, the LORD, which call thee by thy name, am the God of Israel.*"
6) Psalms 51:6 – "*Behold, thou desirest truth in the inward parts: and in the hidden part thou shalt make me to know wisdom.*"
7) Ezekiel 39:29 – "*Neither will I hide my face any more from them: for I have poured out my spirit upon the house of Israel, saith the Lord GOD.*"
8) Isaiah 54:8 – "*In a little wrath I hid my face from thee for a moment; but with everlasting kindness will I have mercy on thee, saith the LORD thy Redeemer.*"
9) Ephesians 1:9 – "*Having made known unto us the mystery of his will, according to his good pleasure which he hath purposed in himself:*"
10) Ephesians 3:5, 8-11 – "[5]*Which in other ages was not made known unto the sons of men, as it is now revealed unto his holy apostles and prophets by the Spirit...*[8]*Unto me, who am less than the least of all saints, is this grace given, that I should preach among the Gentiles the unsearchable riches of Christ;* [9]*And to make all men see what is the fellowship of the mystery, which from the beginning of the world hath been hid in God, who created all things by Jesus Christ:* [10]*To the intent that now unto the principalities and powers in heavenly places might be known by the church the manifold wisdom of God,* [11]*According to the eternal purpose which he purposed in Christ Jesus our Lord:*"
11) Romans 1:19-20 – "[19]*Because that which may be known of God is manifest in them; for God hath shewed it unto them.* [20]*For the invisible things of him from the creation of the world are clearly seen, being understood by the things that are made, even his eternal power and Godhead; so that they are without excuse:*"
12) Romans 16:25-26 – "[25]*Now to him that is of power to stablish you according to my gospel, and the preaching of Jesus Christ, according to the revelation of the mystery, which was kept secret since the world began,* [26]*But now is made manifest, and by the scriptures of the prophets, according to the commandment of the everlasting God, made known to all nations for the obedience of faith:*"
13) Deuteronomy 29:29 – "*The secret things belong unto the LORD our God: but those things which are revealed belong unto us and to our children for ever, that we may do all the words of this law.*"
14) Colossians 1:26-27 – "[26]*Even the mystery which hath been hid from ages and from generations, but now is made manifest to his saints:* [27]*To whom God would make known what is the riches of the glory of this mystery among the Gentiles; which is Christ in you, the hope of glory:*"

15) Psalms 25:14 – *"The secret of the LORD is with them that fear him; and he will shew them his covenant."*
16) Amos 3:7 – *"Surely the Lord GOD will do nothing, but he revealeth his secret unto his servants the prophets."*
17) I Corinthians 4:1 – *"Let a man so account of us, as of the ministers of Christ, and stewards of the mysteries of God."*
18) Proverbs 22:20-21 – *"[20]Have not I written to thee excellent things in counsels and knowledge, [21]That I might make thee know the certainty of the words of truth; that thou mightest answer the words of truth to them that send unto thee?"*
19) Proverbs 3:32 – *"For the froward is abomination to the LORD: but his secret is with the righteous."*
20) Daniel 2:28-29, 47 – *"[28]But there is a God in heaven that revealeth secrets, and maketh known to the king Nebuchadnezzar what shall be in the latter days. Thy dream, and the visions of thy head upon thy bed, are these; [29]As for thee, O king, thy thoughts came into thy mind upon thy bed, what should come to pass hereafter: and he that revealeth secrets maketh known to thee what shall come to pass...[47]The king answered unto Daniel, and said, Of a truth it is, that your God is a God of gods, and a Lord of kings, and a revealer of secrets, seeing thou couldest reveal this secret."*

c. Remember the veil was rent by God and not man and only when Christ died (Matthew 27:46-53, Luke 23:44-46).
d. It was rent from top to bottom.
e. God now no longer needs to hide or keep secret Himself or His glory.

Lesson 34
Ark Of The Covenant

The Ark Of The Covenant

This ark is symbolic of the manifest presence of God, therefore it is a type of His nature. The ark and the glory of God seem to be inseparable. The only time when the ark is unattached to God's glory is when Hophni and Phineas were the unholy priests of God and they lost the ark in battle. The response of everyone after this loss was "Ichabod", which means "no glory". When the ark is not there, there is no glory. In this case, it was because of the sins of Eli and his sons. The other time is when David tried to bring the ark to Jerusalem, but didn't do it after the "due order" and someone ended up dying because they were ignorant of how to treat the ark, or in truth God's manifest presence. So David removed it.

This ark means so much to us as His people. It is the token of our covenant with God, in that if we walk uprightly with Him, we will always have Him near. To us New Testament believers that ark is no longer relevant in the natural, but speaks of a spiritual symbolic meaning of God's manifest presence going with us and living in us. Begin to think of the ark as personal to you and your walk with God. If you and I would practice the presence of God continually, we would come to know Him intimately, knowing He is always there within us, always there reminding us of His covenant that is unbreakable and incorruptible. It represents His indwelling presence.

To truly understand God's ark, we must have a revelation that it is the most important type of God's glory in the tabernacle, as well as in the entire Old Testament. Other than the "cloud of glory", the other main type is found in the "ark of the covenant". This was the ark over-shadowed by two glorious cherubims that consisted of a box that had resting upon it the mercy seat in the most holy place. This is where God's glory would come and manifest itself to Moses and the priests who were allowed access into the most holy place. God's Shekinah glory would come down in between the two guarding cherubims and rest just above the mercy seat. From this place of visitation, God would speak and commune with Moses. When it would appear all Israel would know it. This was the most sacred of all places. Only those that God allowed (the high priest) would be privileged to be close to it. It is the place where God chose to dwell in the midst of His people. And whenever the ark was taken to any battle sight, both all of Israel and their enemies would know "God had come" to help, rescue and protect His people. The enemies of God feared the ark, because of what it represented, which was God himself.

To truly have an understanding of the glory of God, we must have an understanding of the ark of the covenant. And to that end, we will now consider the ark in the tabernacle and what it represented to Israel and also to us as His people. We will see how it was made, of what it was made, and its significance to God's people. As we behold the beauty of this precious type of the glory of God it will enhance our own worship experience.

I. General Information

A. Important truths about the ark – Exodus 25:10-22, Deuteronomy 10:1-8

1. There were three different arks in the Scripture. All of them carried the same revelation. They were preserving something, saving something, protecting something for a future fulfillment.

a. Noah's ark

1) Genesis 6:13-22; 7:15-18; 8:13 – Preserved a remnant from judgment and death; they were to replenish the earth; made of gopher wood; pitched within and without.
2) I Peter 3:20 – "*Which sometime were disobedient, when once the longsuffering of God waited in the days of Noah, while the ark was a preparing, wherein few, that is, eight souls were saved by water.*"

b. Moses' ark, Exodus 2:3-6 – This ark was made of reeds pitched within and without; preserved Moses from certain death (Exodus 1:22); he was to ultimately be Israel's deliverer. The Hebrew word for both of these arks was *tebah*, or a box.

c. Ark of the Covenant in the Tabernacle of Moses

1) The Hebrew word for this ark was *arown*, or a chest. This comes from a root that means to pluck or to gather.
2) In Genesis 50:26, it refers to the coffin of Joseph.
3) In II Kings 12:10-11, it is referred to as a money chest (II Chronicles 24:6-11).
4) Jeremiah 3:16 – Jeremiah speaks of a day when there will be no more ark (Revelation 21:22-25). We do see it during the Tribulation days (Revelation 11:18-19, 12:1-5).

5) What was preserved in this ark? (Hebrews 9:4)

a) Tables of the law
b) Golden pot of manna
c) Aaron's rod that budded

2. The ark was placed in the Holy of Holies (Exodus 26:34) on the earthen floor.

a. This tells us that the truths contained in this ark will be experienced in the earth.
b. It also speaks of this ark being revealed during the 1000-year reign of Christ on this earth.
c. It speaks of the glory of God filling the earth – Obviously, these passages speak of its preservation until the time appointed.

1) Numbers 14:21 – "*But as truly as I live, all the earth shall be filled with the glory of the LORD.*"
2) Habakkuk 2:14 – "*For the earth shall be filled with the knowledge of the glory of the LORD, as the waters cover the sea.*"

3. It was an oblong shaped box. It measured 2 ½ cubits in length, 1 ½ cubits in width, and 1 ½ cubits high.

a. It was not necessarily a beautiful box. God's glory needs no help in being beautiful. So much of everything God does is like this.

1) Jesus was born in a manger.

2) No pleasure in the legs of man (Psalms 147:10)

b. It was the exact height of the table of showbread and the brazen grate on the brass altar.

4. Once again it revealed the two natures in man: wood and gold (humanity and divinity). There was, however, no wood (flesh) seen in this box. It was covered in gold within and without. This speaks to us of two things:

   a. This is the Godhead in action.

      1) Jesus the wood – Humanity, Son of Man, Our crucified Savior
      2) Inlayed gold, the Holy Spirit – sanctified who dwells within and makes us whole.
      3) Outward covering of gold – finisher of our faith, our great Creator putting on the final touches of perfection.

   b. This speaks to us of our own threefold being

      1) Our spirit – Jesus washed in blood
      2) Our soul – Holy Spirit sanctified
      3) Our body – Ultimately glorified

5. Three pieces of furniture had crowns – These speak of things that we must attain to. No crown is simply given. It must be obtained. From the brass altar to the candlestick, it is all about us being redeemed. From the table of showbread on, we make choices that will determine our own destiny.

   a. Ark (Exodus 25:11)
   b. Golden altar (Exodus 30:3)
   c. Table of showbread (Exodus 25:24-25)

6. Titles given to this ark

   a. Ark of the testimony – Exodus 25:22
   b. Ark of the covenant of the Lord – Numbers 10:33
   c. Ark of the Lord God – I Kings 2:26
   d. Ark of the Lord of all the earth – Joshua 3:13
   e. Ark of God – I Samuel 3:3
   f. The Holy Ark – II Chronicles 35:3
   g. Ark of Thy Strengthen – Psalms 132:8
   h. Ark of the covenant of God – Judges 20:27
   i. Ark of the covenant – Joshua 3:6
   j. Ark of the Lord – Joshua 4:11
   k. Ark of the God of Israel – I Samuel 5:7
   l. Ark of shittim wood – Exodus 25:10

7. This ark would eventually prove to be the most important piece of furniture in the tabernacle.

8. It is the only piece of furniture to inhabit three different sanctuaries – Ultimately His presence is the only endurable thing we can ever have.

   a. Tabernacle of Moses – Exodus 25:10
   b. Tabernacle of David – I Chronicles 16:1
   c. Solomon's Temple – I Kings 8:1-11

9. When it is placed finally in Solomon's Temple, the staves are drawn out. It has come to its final place (I Kings 8:8).
10. It was placed in a temple of stones, (I Kings 6:7) built by Solomon. We are the temple in which it was placed.

    a. I Peter 2:5 – *"Ye also, as lively stones, are built up a spiritual house, an holy priesthood, to offer up spiritual sacrifices, acceptable to God by Jesus Christ."*
    b. Ephesians 2:19-22 – *"19Now therefore ye are no more strangers and foreigners, but fellowcitizens with the saints, and of the household of God; 20And are built upon the foundation of the apostles and prophets, Jesus Christ himself being the chief corner stone; 21In whom all the building fitly framed together groweth unto an holy temple in the Lord: 22In whom ye also are builded together for an habitation of God through the Spirit."*
    c. Psalms 102:13-16 – *"13Thou shalt arise, and have mercy upon Zion: for the time to favour her, yea, the set time, is come. 14For thy servants take pleasure in her stones, and favour the dust thereof. 15So the heathen shall fear the name of the LORD, and all the kings of the earth thy glory. 16When the LORD shall build up Zion, he shall appear in his glory."*

11. When it is finally placed or put to rest in Solomon's Temple, certain items were missing (I Kings 8:9, II Chronicles 5:7-10).

    a. No Aaron's rod – There is no longer a need for the five-fold ministry. Remember it was used, (the rod) to determine the true priesthood. The church is mature (Ephesians 4:11-13).
    b. No manna – The overcomers will have eaten this manna (Revelation 2:17); remember the foundation of this temple was dedicated during the Feast of Tabernacles (I Kings 8:2).

12. The ark was the chief and most sacred of all the furniture of the Tabernacle. Every other piece was subordinate to it. It ultimately was where everything else was directed.

13. It consisted of eight things. Eight is the number of new beginnings.

    a. Ark
    b. Mercy Seat
    c. Cherubims
    d. Glory Cloud
    e. Tablets of Stone
    f. Aaron's Rod
    g. Golden Pot of Manna
    h. Staves

14. The Hebrew word for corners (Exodus 25:12) should be translated feet. It had four feet. This number four represents creation. When the ark was in transit, it was elevated higher than all other pieces.

    a. This represents to us that God wants His manifest presence to be preeminent.
    b. It should be what we see first. No man or his glory, but only the glory of God.

15. It was the first piece of furniture mentioned by God, (showing its great and uppermost position in His heart, Exodus 25:10). Remember, this was to be made after the pattern in heaven (Exodus 25:9, Hebrews 8:1-5).

16. It was covered in transit with a cloth of blue. Blue represents all things heavenly.

17. The four feet, (four corners) also represent:

a. Four Gospels
b. The Gospel of the Kingdom (sonship) going to the world (Matthew 24:14)

18. The ark was made to be carried by four priests (Exodus 25:13-14). This speaks to us of:

    a. Plurality of ministry
    b. The staves kept the ark balanced – This means a balanced message on the glory.
    c. The wood overlaid with gold staves – Once again this brings out tremendous truth of our old human corrupt nature being completely taken over by the divine.

19. What the ark of God represents on the Earth

    a. The throne of God
    b. The manifest presence of God
    c. The manifest presence in His people
    d. The glory of God

20. Just as in Genesis 1:1, *"In the beginning God..."*, God starting with the ark truly represents Himself more than anything. What does this mean? He must be first in time and place in the order of things.

21. It was upon this piece of furniture the high priest sprinkled the blood of atonement once a year.

    a. Leviticus 16
    b. Hebrews 9:7

22. It was from this piece of furniture, God's audible voice was heard speaking to Moses and Aaron. This signifies to us our inner man is where God speaks to us.
23. It is the place of glory; it is the place God dwells (Psalms 80:1).
24. This ark also speaks of the place heaven and earth meet.
25. When the ark was in transit, (Numbers 4:4-6) the covering over the Tabernacle was on it, the covering of badger's skin.

    a. What these items represent:

        1) The Three-fold God
        2) That which comes from heaven isn't necessarily beautiful on earth.
        3) For us to get to the presence of God as we move on in God, we must search, seek and run after Him to find Him.

            a) Proverbs 25:2
            b) Song of Solomon 3:2

II. The Ark, Symbol of the Manifest Presence of God

A. I Samuel 4:1-7, 11, 19-22 – The ark and the glory were synonymous.

B. I Samuel 5:1-10

1. Hebrew for *Ashdod* – I will spoil
2. Hebrew for *Dagon* – Fish god
3. Head (government) and hands (works) were cut off; Dagon bows before the ark
4. Verse 7 – The ark and God were synonymous.

5. Verses 8 and 9 – The ark judges them.
6. Verse 10 – Once again God himself is associated with the ark.

C. I Samuel 6:19-21 – God is associated with the ark.
D. I Samuel 7:1-2 – In Hebrew both Abinadab and Eleazar mean, father of the willing giver. Here the ark remained twenty years.
E. II Samuel 6:1-10 – You can only bring up the manifest presence of God on the shoulders of true priests. You cannot touch the glory, or you will die.
F. II Samuel 6:10-12 – The Lord blessed Obededom. He who has the glory is supremely blessed, both he and his household.
G. I Chronicles 15:1-3, 13-16 – David realized his error and saw that only the Levites were capable and chosen of the Lord to bear the ark.

H. I Chronicles 15:22-25

1. There were the Levites chosen to bring up the ark.

a. In Hebrew *Berechiah* means – Jehovah has blessed, and bending the knee.
b. In Hebrew *Elkanah* means – Possession of God, God has redeemed.
c. In Hebrew *Jehiah* means – He lives of the Lord, God is living, and mercy of Jehovah.
d. In Hebrew *Obededom* means – servant of the earth.

I. II Samuel 6:12-23

1. David's reply to Michal was that he was dancing "*...before the Lord* (the ark)."
2. Wherever the ark is there is great rejoicing.

J. Numbers 10:33-36

1. Three days journey (typical of our Lord's death and resurrection)
2. The ark went before them to search out a resting place.

K. Numbers 14:40-45 – Without the ark (manifest presence) invariably God's people lose in battle.

L. Joshua 3:3-13

This is the great story of how the ark went before the people on the shoulders of the priest during the swelling of the Jordan, and the Jordan rolled back for the people. Following this, the ark (manifest presence) moved into the Promised Land.

M. Ark built by Moses was eventually placed in Shiloh (Joshua 18:1)

The ark remained there until Samuel's time. It was lost until David went and retrieved it. Then it was placed in the Temple of Solomon (II Chronicles 5:7-8), until the last we hear of it in the Old Testament in II Chronicles 35:3 and Jeremiah 3:16, where it speaks of a time when the ark shall be no more.

Lesson 35

The Contents Of The Ark

The Contents Of The Ark

I. Contents Of The Ark, Hebrews 9:4, Exodus 16:32-36 and Numbers 11:4-9

Hebrews 9:4 – "*Which had the golden censer, and the ark of the covenant overlaid round about with gold, wherein was the golden pot that had manna, and Aaron's rod that budded, and the tables of the covenant;*"

Exodus 16:32-36 – "*32And Moses said, This is the thing which the LORD commandeth, Fill an omer of it to be kept for your generations; that they may see the bread wherewith I have fed you in the wilderness, when I brought you forth from the land of Egypt. 33And Moses said unto Aaron, Take a pot, and put an omer full of manna therein, and lay it up before the LORD, to be kept for your generations. 34As the LORD commanded Moses, so Aaron laid it up before the Testimony, to be kept. 35And the children of Israel did eat manna forty years, until they came to a land inhabited; they did eat manna, until they came unto the borders of the land of Canaan. 36Now an omer is the tenth part of an ephah.*"

Numbers 11:4-9 – "*...7And the manna was as coriander seed, and the colour thereof as the colour of bdellium. 8And the people went about, and gathered it, and ground it in mills, or beat it in a mortar, and baked it in pans, and made cakes of it: and the taste of it was as the taste of fresh oil. 9And when the dew fell upon the camp in the night, the manna fell upon it.*"

A. History of manna

1. This is the food God provided for Israel 40 years. The number 40 means trial and testing.
2. The word manna literally means – "What is it?" (Exodus 16:15 – "*And when the children of Israel saw it, they said one to another, It is manna: for they wist not what it was. And Moses said unto them, This is the bread which the LORD hath given you to eat.*) – You may never know how His Word is going to come. It will come in the most unexpected place.
3. Psalm 78:25 – Angels food
4. It came every morning with the dew.
5. It's small, meaning nothing elaborate to us.
6. It was round. This speaks to us of the eternal Word.
7. Every man or woman (numbers were different according to how many in your household); one in each household responsible for word
8. It was a perfect provision.
9. It was not to be left until the next morning. It is only meant for that day; Matthew 6:11 – "*Give us this day our daily bread*"
10. If you tried to hold on to it, it would breed worms and stink.

11. On the sixth day you were supposed to gather twice as much (Double portion); on the seventh day, you rested.
12. It was like coriander seed.
13. It was white, speaking of innocent and pure.
14. It tasted like wafers made with honey.
15. It had to be gathered by them. It is imperative that we don't live in another man's revelation.
16. Ground it or beat it; this speaks of the dealings of God, or "revelation is married to situation."
17. It tasted like oil drenched by dew. This speaks of the Word sent to try to make Israel all she could have been.
18. It was gathered in such a way there was no surplus or lack.

B. Golden pot of manna, Exodus 16:32-35

1. John 6:32 – Jesus is our manna (Philippians 4:19, Matthew 6:11)
2. Reserved for overcomers – Revelation 2:17
3. The overcomer will press beyond the veil and eat this hidden manna.
4. It contained only one Omar, just enough for one man (The many membered Sons of God.)
5. Only 100fold believers could experience it. They had to press beyond the other two dimensions. Now in the third day they are entitled to eat hidden manna. This manna is being preserved, waiting for someone to eat it.
6. Once the children of Israel entered into the Promised Land, the manna ceased (Joshua 5:11-12); It symbolized when we enter into our inheritance, God has a surprise for us.
7. This golden pot was also a memorial of Israel's disobedience (Exodus 16:1-10, Exodus 21:5-6).
8. It was kept for the generations to come, for his people to remember His faithfulness in spite of Israel's differences.
9. It was also "laid up before the Lord." This was bread cooking underneath the mercy seat for a long time. This was truly hidden, unrevealed revelation; reserved only for His overcomers.

C. Aaron's Rod that Budded

1. It speaks of Christ's resurrection.
2. The rod budded into an almond plant, which is a first fruit plant. This refers to us two things, Jesus and the out-resurrecting people.
3. The rod budded in the morning. Morning always speaks of resurrection.
4. This truly speaks of God's choice for leadership; true leadership blossoms.
5. Remember also, it was in the ark (manifest presence) under the mercy seat, sat on by the glory. This is what all leaders should look for in their own ministry:

    a. God's choice
    b. Living in His manifest presence
    c. Mercy rejoicing over judgment
    d. Drenching in glory

6. When you consider a rod in Scripture, who comes to mind?

    a. A scepter of authority – Genesis 49:10
    b. A shepherds rod – govern to flock – Psalm 23:4
    c. Rod of the manchild – Revelation 12:5, Revelation 2:26-27
    d. A rod of correction – Proverbs 13:24, Proverbs 22:15, Proverbs 23:13,14
    e. It is an emblem of God's chosen priesthood.
    f. It speaks of a chosen priesthood (I Peter 2:4).
    g. Out of 12 rods comes one bearing fruit.

7. Numbers 17:8 – *"And it came to pass, that on the morrow Moses went into the tabernacle of witness; and, behold, the rod of Aaron for the house of Levi was budded, and brought forth buds, and bloomed blossoms, and yielded almonds."* – budded, bloomed blossoms, yielded almonds

    a. Hebrew meaning of almond tree: wakeful, hastening, to hasten; to be alert, sleepless, watching – Proverbs 8:34
    b. Native of Syria and Palestine; its blossoms are of a very pale pink color, and appear before the leaves. The Hebrew name, "wakeful hastening" is given to it on account of it's putting forth its blossoms so early, generally February, and sometimes as early as January.
    c. Aaron's rod yielded almonds
    d. Moses was directed to make certain parts of the candlestick for the ark of carved work "like unto almonds" (Exodus 25:33-34).
    e. A type of "first fruits"; since it is the first to blossom, then also it will bear fruit first.
    f. Aaron's rod yielded almonds, flowers, and buds (the word yielded means "weaned". This could be referring to bringing to maturity). Each branch of the lampstand has an almond, a flower and a bud.

Lesson 36

The Mercy Seat

The mercy seat was in the most holy place. It rested above the ark of God which contained the tables of the law, Aaron's rod that budded, and the golden pot of manna. We see here in type several things. First we see a true picture of the Godhead, Jesus the mercy seat, the Holy Spirit as the cherubims guarding God's glory and God the Father as the Shekinah Glory of God resting between the cherubims and upon the mercy seat. Secondly, that the mercy seat is situated above and over the tablets of the law tells us mercy always triumphs over judgment, or as the Bible says over and over again, as in Proverbs 16:6, "*By mercy and truth iniquity is purged: and by the fear of the LORD men depart from evil.*" Thirdly, that when we enter into God's holy presence we always find Him resting upon mercy. Psalms 145:9 "*The LORD is good to all: and his tender mercies are over all his works.*"

The very first thing God defines Himself is merciful, as in Exodus 34:6-7, "[6]*And the LORD passed by before him, and proclaimed, The LORD, The LORD God, merciful and gracious, longsuffering, and abundant in goodness and truth,*[7]*Keeping mercy for thousands, forgiving iniquity and transgression and sin, and that will by no means clear the guilty; visiting the iniquity of the fathers upon the children, and upon the children's children, unto the third and to the fourth generation.*" This is after Moses had pleaded with Him to know Him intimately to show him His glory. We need no other evidence that our God is a merciful God, but after an exhaustive look throughout Scripture, this is confirmed solidly. He is not just merciful, He is mercy personified! Jesus, because of His great and marvelous atoning sacrifice, has become our mercy seat. It was Jesus who became the sacrificed lamb, the scapegoat, our own personal burnt offering to atone for us and our sin as well as the sin of the whole world. The very word itself "mercy seat" speaks of the one who is the atoning victim, the one who has made reconciliation for us. Literally He, Jesus, has become our own personal mercy seat! This is so important for us to know and believe and walk in because of our Adamic nature and its tendency towards sin. Because He has become our mercy seat, we can live above condemnation and blood guiltiness and rejoice that our God is merciful. To the true disciple who is doing his best to walk with God we can now know with certainty that our God will always meet us in mercy. We need never to run from Him or be afraid to come to Him in our hour of need. He will always be there as our precious, living, atoning mercy seat. No wonder the Scriptures declare in Hebrews 4:16, "*Let us therefore come boldly unto the throne of grace, that we may obtain mercy, and find grace to help in time of need.*" So rejoice and rest forever sure in your heart, Jesus has become our mercy seat!

I. The Mercy Seat

A. Word Meanings

1. Greek, *Hilasterion* – Propitiation, an atoning victim, expiatory thing, to make reconciliation for, to atone for. This is the same word translated propitiation in the New Testament. Jesus is our propitiation. He literally is our mercy seat.

a. Romans 3:24-25 – "*Being justified freely by his grace through the redemption that is in Christ Jesus: Whom God hath set forth to be a propitiation through faith in his blood, to declare his righteousness for the remission of sins that are past, through the forbearance of God;*"
b. I John 2:2 – "*And he is the propitiation for our sins: and not for ours only, but also for the sins of the whole world.*"
c. I John 4:10 – "*Herein is love, not that we loved God, but that he loved us, and sent his Son to be the propitiation for our sins.*" Jesus has become to the New Testament child of God their very own mercy seat. The veil was rent (His flesh) and now we can enter in because of His blood.

2. Hebrew, *Kapporeth* – A lid; it comes from a root, *kapher* – To cover, to expiate, to cancel, to make atonement for

B. Defining the mercy seat

1. Exodus 26:34 – *"And thou shalt put the mercy seat upon the ark of the testimony in the most holy place."* – The mercy seat was on top of the ark

   a. Ark – Symbolic of the manifest presence of God
   b. The ark contained the ten commandments, golden pot of manna, and Aarons rod that budded (Hebrews 9:4).

This speaks to us of God's mercy being over His manifest presence. In other words wherever He is, so is His mercy. It also speaks that mercy is over the law (ten commandments), always over His revealed Word (Golden pot of manna), and that His mercy reigns over the ones He chooses.

2. Exodus 30:6 – *"...before the mercy seat that is over the testimony, where I will meet with thee."* – This speaks to us that God will always meet with us in mercy.
3. Hebrews 9:5 – *"And over it the cherubims of glory shadowing the mercy seat..."* – This speaks to us of those who guard the glory (cherubims) overshadowing God's mercy. The glory always rests and overshadows God's mercy.

4. Numbers 7:89 – *"And when Moses was gone into the tabernacle of the congregation to speak with him, then he heard the voice of one speaking unto him from off the mercy seat that was upon the ark of testimony, from between the two cherubims: and he spake unto him."* What this symbolizes

   a. God speaks to His people from the mercy seat.
   b. He speaks to us in the guarded glory through mercy. In everything He says and does, it originates from this place of mercy. Even the ability just to speak with Him is because of mercy.

5. Leviticus 16:2-4 – *"And the LORD said unto Moses, Speak unto Aaron thy brother, that he come not at all times into the holy place within the vail before the mercy seat, which is upon the ark; that he die not: for I will appear in the cloud upon the mercy seat. Thus shall Aaron come into the holy place: with a young bullock for a sin offering, and a ram for a burnt offering. He shall put on the holy linen coat..."* What this symbolizes:

   a. We are not to appear in the manifest presence without our sin being cleansed (sin offering).
   b. There must also be some kind of sacrifice made (burnt offering), either natural or spiritual.
   c. Something or someone must die for us to enter into the mercy seat, once again, either spiritually or soulishly. Something must die within us to appear before His manifest presence. We find ultimately that we must pay the price of sacrifice to see and hear Him in His mercy.
   d. If not, that person will die. As Aaron's sons would later find out, you cannot toy or play with the revealed presence of God.
   e. God's face can be seen only in the glory above mercy.
   f. Also, we should have our garments cleansed and put on the proper priestly garments. We should be clothed in our spiritual garments, the garments of praise, etc. Also, we must have on the linen garment of righteousness which means we have repented of all sin and are demon free, and have cleansed ourselves.

6. Leviticus 16:12-16 – *"[12]And he shall take a censer full of burning coals of fire from off the altar before the LORD, and his hands full of sweet incense beaten small, and bring it within the vail: [13]And he shall put the incense upon the fire before the LORD, that the cloud of the incense may cover the mercy seat that is upon the testimony, that he die not: [14] And he shall take of the blood of the bullock, and sprinkle it with his finger upon the mercy seat eastward; and before the mercy*

seat shall he sprinkle of the blood with his finger seven times. [15]Then shall he kill the goat of the sin offering, that is for the people, and bring his blood within the vail, and do with that blood as he did with the blood of the bullock, and sprinkle it upon the mercy seat, and before the mercy seat: [16]And he shall make an atonement for the holy place, because of the uncleanness of the children of Israel, and because of their transgressions in all their sins: and so shall he do for the tabernacle of the congregation, that remaineth among them in the midst of their uncleanness."

a. Verse 12

   1) Bring sweet incense (worship) beaten small (time taken to worship)
   2) Mix it with holy fire or passion that can only come from being at God's altar. This fire cannot be manufactured, it must be a pure and real zeal, a fire deep from within that yearns for God.

b. Verse 13

   1) As this worship and holy fire ascends, it becomes a pure sweet cloud of worship that covers the mercy seat. Once we see Him and recognize His mercy this shouldn't be hard at all.
   2) We must do this if we are to be in His manifest presence.
   3) If we come in impure or unprepared, we will die.

c. Verse 14 – We must have been washed in the blood, and then remind God that we remember His perfect sacrifice. We have His mercy because He shed His blood.
d. Verse 15 – Confirming that our sins has been atoned for and that we are clean.
e. Verse 16 – When we stand there in God's manifest presence, we are to remember our brothers and sisters who are in sin and uncleansed, and pray for them before the mercy seat. Just as He became the propitiation for our sins, we try and be that to the rest of the body.

7. Exodus 25:17-22 – *"[17]And thou shalt make a mercy seat of pure gold: two cubits and a half shall be the length thereof, and a cubit and a half the breadth thereof. [18]And thou shalt make two cherubims of gold, of beaten work shalt thou make them, in the two ends of the mercy seat. [19]And make one cherub on the one end, and the other cherub on the other end: even of the mercy seat shall ye make the cherubims on the two ends thereof. [20]And the cherubims shall stretch forth their wings on high, covering the mercy seat with their wings, and their faces shall look one to another; toward the mercy seat shall the faces of the cherubims be. [21]And thou shalt put the mercy seat above upon the ark; and in the ark thou shalt put the testimony that I shall give thee. [22]And there I will meet with thee, and I will commune with thee from above the mercy seat, from between the two cherubims which are upon the ark of the testimony, of all things which I will give thee in commandment unto the children of Israel."*

   a. Verse 17

      1) Mercy seat – Made for us to be forgiven, and to have the ability to meet with Him.
      2) Pure – Innocent, clean, virtuous, or holy
      3) Gold – God's divine nature and character
      4) Four cubits total – Four is the number in Scripture for creation or created things. This simply means His mercy is over all His creation, and for those who enter in to the precious Most Holy Place, they are walking in the reality of the "new creation man".
      5) It gives the length and breadth, but not the height or depth of the mercy seat, signifying His mercy is unfathomable. It reaches to the skies (height) and goes to the deepest valley (depth) to help us. Oh how great and unsearchable are the riches of His mercy.

b. Verse 18

1) Two is the number in Scripture for witness and separation. These are His witnesses, and they are that by virtue of being separated from the world, flesh, and the devil.
2) They are a chosen remnant taken from among the rest of the body of Christ (Cherubims).
3) Made of gold – They have God's divine nature and character.
4) Beaten work – Speaks of them being shaped and molded by the dealings of God.

c. Verse 19

1) Cherubims are to guard the glory in Scripture.
2) These have learned all about God's glory, have been changed by it, and also make sure it is protected.
3) However, in guarding it, remember they are grounded (joined to the mercy seat on either side) in His mercy, while they guard the glory.

d. Verse 20

1) Stretch forth their wings on high – These are those who worship in the heavenlies.
2) They form a covering of worship over the mercy seat.
3) Their faces look at one another – They are transparent, and they can look at their brothers right in the eyes, for there is no guile or deceit in them.
4) They are also in unity with their brothers.
5) They shall also both behold the mercy of God, while they look at one another.

e. Verse 21

1) Mercy seat upon the ark – This symbolizes God's manifest presence (ark) is overshadowed by mercy. He promises to meet us at the mercy seat (this is the place where we can always turn to). He will commune with us from a place of mercy
2) Contents in the ark (Hebrews 9:4) – The law, the golden pot of manna, and Aaron's rod that budded. This represents mercy over the law (mercy rejoices over judgment – James 2:13), mercy over God's divine revelation (golden pot), and mercy over God's chosen and fruitful ones (Aaron's rod that budded). Mercy should be a living reality in all true leadership (Aaron's rod). God's mercy reigns over His Word (Golden pot); His hidden manna is laced with mercy.

f. Verse 22

1) God's promise is to always meet us in mercy.
2) It is only because of His great mercy we can have deep communion with Him.
3) God will speak in the last days from a place inside the two cherubim. From there He will utter and give His commandments to His people. Thus, His remnant will be those, out from whom He will speak overshadowed by glory and in mercy.

II. Other Facts About The Mercy Seat

A. The importance of the mercy seat and the revelation thereof

1. It is the place of the revelation of God's Word to His priests
2. It was the place where blood was sprinkled on the Day of Atonement .
3. The mercy seat could not be viewed by everybody, only priests.

4. It was the place where God would appear in the glory. This is where He sits (always in mercy). This is His throne (Psalms 80:1, 99:1, II Samuel 6:2).
5. It was to be a picture or pattern of the heavenly throne.
6. It was intended to be God's dwelling or resting place until a people could be found in whom He would reign and dwell within their hearts; this people is Zion (Ps. 132:13-14)

7. It is interesting that each of the three items found in the ark were associated with rebellion on the part of God's people.

    a. The Law – The making of the golden calf
    b. Aaron's rod – The rebellion led by Korah
    c. Golden post of manna – Israel's complaining in the wilderness.

All three of these items could and should have brought great judgment to Israel, were it not for the mercy seat upon the ark. It was also the place where blood was sprinkled on the Day of Atonement that covered the sins of the people, so that God saw the blood and not their rebellion.

8. The cherubims were not separate from the mercy seat, but they were beaten out of the solid mass of gold, which formed the mercy seat. Thus the cherubims and the mercy seat were one piece. This means that God's remnant (the cherubims, two witnesses, etc) are completely and continually attached to God's mercy and divine nature that holds the glory.
9. The mercy seat differed from all the other pieces of furniture in that no wood (humanity) entered into the composition. It was reserved for God alone. There is to be no sitting down in His presence.

10. An uncovered ark or one without a mercy seat means we would have to stand before the naked law of God. But God in His wisdom hides the law in His manifest presence and covers it with a lid of mercy and His divine character (gold). The mercy seat was to never be severed from the Law. The mercy seat was the lid of the ark. It completed the ark. The two together were considered one piece of furniture

    a. I Samuel 6:19-20 – *"And he smote the men of Beth-shemesh, because they had looked into the ark of the LORD, even he smote of the people fifty thousand and threescore and ten men: and the people lamented, because the LORD had smitten many of the people with a great slaughter. And the men of Beth-shemesh said, Who is able to stand before this holy LORD God? and to whom shall he go up from us?"*

11. Numbers 7:89 – It is the place of precious communion with God; we can only have true communion with God in mercy – *"And when Moses was gone into the tabernacle of the congregation to speak with him, then he heard the voice of one speaking unto him from off the mercy seat that was upon the ark of testimony, from between the two cherubims: and he spake unto him."*

    a. Exodus 25:22 – *"And there I will meet with thee, and I will commune with thee from above the mercy seat, from between the two cherubims which are upon the ark of the testimony, of all things which I will give thee in commandment unto the children of Israel."*

12. At the Brazen altar we start out at a throne of judgment. We end up at a throne of mercy.

III. Word Definitions For Mercy, Mercies, Merciful

A. Hebrew words

1. *Chanan* – To bend or stoop in kindness to an inferior, to bestow favor, to have pity upon, to show graciousness to, to make supplication for
2. *Rachuwn* – Full of compassion
3. *Racham* – To fondle, to love, to have compassion upon, to have pity
4. *Racham* – Compassion, as cherishing the fetus in the womb, tender love, bowels of compassion, great pity.
5. *Kaphar* – To cover, to expiate, to placate or cancel, to appease, to make atonement for, to cleanse, pacify, pardon, to disannul, to purge away, to make reconciliation.
6. *Checed* – Kindness, beauty; It comes from a root word, *chacad* – To bow the neck in courtesy, to be kind.

B. Greek words

1. *Hileos* – Cheerful, propitious, God's graciousness in averting some calamity
2. *Oiktirmon* – Pity; It comes from a root, *oikteiro* – To exercise pity, to have compassion on
3. *Eleemon* – Actively compassionate and merciful; It comes from a root word, *eleeo* – To have compassion by divine grace, to show mercy upon

C. Other words for mercy translated differently in the King James Version

The words lovingkindness and kindness, though translated differently, are the same Hebrew word. You can use these words interchangeably because they mean the same thing. Why the translators chose to translate the same Hebrew word differently, we will never know.

IV. Our God <u>Is</u> <u>Merciful</u>

A. Related Scriptures

1. Exodus 34:5-7 – "[5]*And the LORD descended in the cloud, and stood with him there, and proclaimed the name of the LORD.* [6]*And the LORD passed by before him, and proclaimed, The LORD, The LORD God, merciful and gracious, longsuffering, and abundant in goodness and truth,* [7]*Keeping mercy for thousands, forgiving iniquity and transgression and sin, and that will by no means clear the guilty...*"

a. Other translations of verse 6:

"*...tenderly compassionate...*"
"*...full of compassion and gracious, slow to anger...*"
"*...pitiful and kind, slow to be angry...*"
"*...abounding in steadfast love.*"
"*...rich in kindness, faithful to His promises.*"
"*...plenteous in mercy and truth.*"
"*...ever constant and true.*"
"*...great in mercy and faith.*"

b. Other translations of verse 7:

"*Maintaining constancy to thousands...*"
"*He is true to His promise of mercy a thousand times over...*"
"*...steadfast love for thousands...*"
"*...unto the thousandth generation...*"
"*...for thousands of generations...*"

This Scripture is God proclaiming His great name. Names always reveal character in the Bible. Here He defines His name as merciful. This is how He describes Himself. This merciful God wants us to know His character. It <u>is</u> who He is; it is how He responds; it is how He thinks, believes, and acts. There is a theological term called the law of first reference, and it means the first time a principle appears in the Scriptures, it sets the stage for every other time this principle is found. So we would do well to take heed here, that the first time God defines Himself and His character, He declares Himself merciful.

2. II Corinthians 1:3 – *"Blessed be God, even the Father of our Lord Jesus Christ, the <u>Father of mercies</u>, and the God of all comfort."* – He is the Father, the originator of mercy in the earth. Other translation – *"...the all merciful Father..."*
3. Daniel 9:9 – *"To the Lord our God belong mercies and forgivenesses, though we have rebelled against him;"* Other translations: *"With the Lord our God are tender mercies and forgivenesses...", "To the Lord our God it falls to have mercy and to forgive, for we have been rebels."*
4. Psalms 37:26 – *"He is ever merciful, and lendeth; and his seed is blessed."* – This speaks of His never ending mercy. Other translations: *"He is always compassionate...", "He is continually lending, ever generous...", "All the day long He shareth kindness...",*
5. Ephesians 2:4 – *"But God, who is rich in mercy..."* Other translations: *"Yet God in His abundant compassion...", "How rich God is in mercy..."*
6. Psalms 25:10 – *"All the paths of the LORD are mercy and truth unto such as keep his covenant and his testimonies."* – No matter the path, all of God's paths and ways are filled with mercy unto His people. Other translations: *"All the paths of the Lord are steadfast love and faithfulness...", "All the paths of Jehovah are lovingkindness and truth...", "Kindly and faithfully He ever deals with those...", "The Lord is the essence of mercy and truth...", "All the ways of the Lord are loving and sure...", "Every path He guides us on is fragrant with His lovingkindness and truth..."*
7. Nehemiah 9:17 – *"...but thou art a God ready to pardon, gracious and merciful, slow to anger, and of great kindness, and forsookest them not."* – This tells us God is not only ready but waiting and willing to show mercy. Other translations: *"...God of forgiveness...", "...kind and pitiful...", "...full of compassion...", "...gracious and loving...", "...so kind, so merciful, so patient...", "...abounding in steadfast love...", "...ever constant..."*
8. Nehemiah 9:31 – *"Nevertheless for thy great mercies' sake thou didst not utterly consume them, nor forsake them; for thou art a gracious and merciful God."*
9. Psalms 103:8 – *"The LORD is merciful and gracious, slow to anger, and plenteous in mercy."* – There is no shortage of God's mercy. He has more than enough and then some to give His people. He never runs out of mercy.
10. Psalms 116:5 – *"Gracious is the LORD, and righteous; yea, our God is merciful."*
11. Psalms 117:2 – *"For his merciful kindness is great toward us..."*
12. Jeremiah 3:12 – *"Go and proclaim these words toward the north, and say, Return, thou backsliding Israel, saith the LORD; and I will not cause mine anger to fall upon you: for I am merciful, saith the LORD, and I will not keep anger for ever."* – God doesn't want to stay mad at us. He'd rather show mercy.
13. Joel 2:13 – *"...turn unto the LORD your God: for he is gracious and merciful, slow to anger, and of great kindness..."* (Jonah 4:2)
14. Luke 6:36 – *"Be ye therefore merciful, as your Father also is merciful."*
15. Psalms 89:1 – *"I will sing of the mercies of the LORD for ever: with my mouth will I make known thy faithfulness to all generations."*

16. Psalms 103:4 – *"...who crowneth thee with lovingkindness and tender mercies"* – This is one of the benefits of our salvation.

    a. Psalms 25:6 – *"Remember, O LORD, thy tender mercies and thy lovingkindnesses; for they have been ever of old."*
    b. Psalms 40:11 – *"Withhold not thou thy tender mercies from me, O LORD: let thy lovingkindness and thy truth continually preserve me."*

c. Psalms 69:16 – *"Hear me, O LORD; for thy lovingkindness is good: turn unto me according to the multitude of thy tender mercies."*
d. Psalms 79:8 – *"O remember not against us former iniquities: let thy tender mercies speedily prevent us: for we are brought very low."*
e. Psalms 119:77 – *"Let thy tender mercies come unto me, that I may live: for thy law is my delight."*

17. Psalms 145:9 – *"The LORD is good to all: and his tender mercies are over all his works."*

    a. Psalms 119:156 – *"Great are thy tender mercies, O LORD..."*
    b. Luke 1:78 – *"Through the tender mercy of our God; whereby the dayspring from on high hath visited us,"*

18. Isaiah 54:7-8 – *"For a small moment have I forsaken thee; but with great mercies will I gather thee. In a little wrath I hid my face from thee for a moment; but with everlasting kindness will I have mercy on thee..."*
19. Lamentations 3:22-23 – *"It is of the LORD's mercies that we are not consumed, because his compassions fail not. They are new every morning: great is thy faithfulness."*
20. Psalms 36:5 – *"Thy mercy, O LORD, is in the heavens; and thy faithfulness reacheth unto the clouds."* (Psalms 108:4)
21. Psalms 119:64 – *"The earth, O LORD, is full of thy mercy..."*
22. Psalms 130:7 – *"Let Israel hope in the LORD: for with the LORD there is mercy, and with him is plenteous redemption."*
23. Isaiah 14:1 – *"For the LORD will have mercy on Jacob, and will yet choose Israel, and set them in their own land..."*

24. Proverbs 20:28 – *"Mercy and truth preserve the king: and his throne is upholden by mercy."*

    a. Other translations:

       "...His throne is sustained by mercy."
       "...His throne is founded on kindness."
       "...the seat of His power is based on upright acts."
       "...His throne is established in mercy."

    b. Isaiah 16:5 – *"And in mercy shall the throne be established..."*

25. Hosea 6:6 – *"For I desired mercy, and not sacrifice; and the knowledge of God more than burnt offerings."*
26. Hosea 14:3 – *"...for in thee the fatherless findeth mercy."*
27. Micah 7:18 – *"Who is a God like unto thee, that pardoneth iniquity, and passeth by the transgression of the remnant of his heritage? he retaineth not his anger for ever, because he delighteth in mercy."*
28. James 3:17 – *"But the wisdom that is from above is first pure, then peaceable, gentle, and easy to be intreated, full of mercy and good fruits, without partiality, and without hypocrisy."*
29. James 5:11 – *"...Ye have heard of the patience of Job, and have seen the end of the Lord; that the Lord is very pitiful, and of tender mercy."*
30. Psalms 100:5 – *"For the LORD is good; his mercy is everlasting..."*
31. Isaiah 55:7 – *"Let the wicked forsake his way, and the unrighteous man his thoughts: and let him return unto the LORD, and he will have mercy upon him; and to our God, for he will abundantly pardon."*
32. Luke 1:50 – *"And his mercy is on them that fear him from generation to generation."*
33. Titus 3:5 – *"Not by works of righteousness which we have done, but according to his mercy he saved us, by the washing of regeneration, and renewing of the Holy Ghost"*

34. Hebrews 4:16 – *"Let us therefore come boldly unto the throne of grace, that we may obtain mercy, and find grace to help in time of need."*
35. Hebrews 8:12 – *"For I will be merciful to their unrighteousness, and their sins and their iniquities will I remember no more."*
36. I Peter 1:3 – *"...according to his abundant mercy hath begotten us again unto a lively hope by the resurrection of Jesus Christ..."*

Through all of these Scriptures we see time and time again that our God is a merciful God, and that His mercy is great, abundant, rich, everlasting, tender, and gracious. There is no one like our God! Because of this revelation of His character, we should always be mindful of this in our darkest times, our deepest valleys, or our harrowing wilderness experiences. Man may not forgive and show mercy, but God always does. Bless His glorious, wonderful, and precious name forever!

III. Defining The Mercy Of God

A. Sure mercies

1. Hebrew for sure, *aman* – To build up or support, to foster as a parent or nurse, to be firm or faithful, to morally be true or certain, to guard, to protect.

2. Examples in Scripture of the sure mercies of David

a. Isaiah 55:3 – *"Incline your ear, and come unto me: hear, and your soul shall live; and I will make an everlasting covenant with you, even the sure mercies of David."*
b. Acts 13:34 – *"And as concerning that he raised him up from the dead, now no more to return to corruption, he said on this wise, I will give you the sure mercies of David."*

3. Other passages with this Hebrew word sure

a. Deuteronomy 7:9 – *"Know therefore that the LORD thy God, he is God, the faithful* (Hebrew, *aman) God, which keepeth covenant and mercy with them that love him and keep his commandments to a thousand generations"*
b. I Samuel 25:28 (Abigail – Nabal's wife) – *"...for the LORD will certainly make my lord a sure house; because my lord fighteth the battles of the LORD..."*
c. Psalms 93:5 – *"Thy testimonies are very sure: holiness becometh thine house, O LORD, for ever."*
d. Isaiah 22:20-25 – (Key of David to Eliakim) – *"...And the key of the house of David will I lay upon his shoulder; so he shall open, and none shall shut; and he shall shut, and none shall open. And I will fasten him as a nail in a sure place..."*
e. II Samuel 23:5 – *"Although my house be not so with God; yet he hath made with me an everlasting covenant, ordered in all things, and sure: for this is all my salvation, and all my desire..."*

f. Psalms 89:27-36

"Also I will make him my firstborn, higher than the kings of the earth. My mercy will I keep for him for evermore, and my covenant shall stand fast (Hebrew, *aman) with him. His seed also will I make to endure for ever, and his throne as the days of heaven. If his children forsake my law, and walk not in my judgments; If they break my statutes, and keep not my commandments; Then will I visit their transgression with the rod, and their iniquity with stripes. Nevertheless my lovingkindness will I not utterly take from him, nor suffer my faithfulness to fail. My covenant will I not break, nor alter the thing that is gone out of my lips. Once have I sworn by my holiness that I will not lie unto David. His seed shall endure forever, and his throne as the sun before me."*

4. Lamentations 3:22-25 – "*...It is of the LORD's mercies that we are not consumed, because his compassions fail not. They are new every morning: great is thy faithfulness. The LORD is my portion, saith my soul; therefore will I hope in him. The LORD is good unto them that wait for him...*"

B. Tender mercies

1. Hebrew for tender, *racham* – Compassion in the plural, like cherishing the fetus in the womb.

2. Psalms 25:6 – "*Remember, O LORD, thy tender mercies and thy lovingkindnesses; for they have been ever of old.*"
3. Psalms 40:11 – "*Withhold not thou thy tender mercies from me, O LORD: let thy lovingkindness and thy truth continually preserve me.*"
4. Psalms 51:1 – "*Have mercy upon me, O God, according to thy lovingkindness: according unto the multitude of thy tender mercies blot out my transgressions.*"
5. Psalms 69:16 – "*Hear me, O LORD; for thy lovingkindness is good: turn unto me according to the multitude of thy tender mercies.*"

6. Psalms 77:9-10 – "*Hath God forgotten to be gracious? hath he in anger shut up his tender mercies? Selah. And I said, This is my infirmity: but I will remember the years of the right hand of the most High.*"

   a. Psalms 66:18-20

7. Psalms 79:8 – "*O remember not against us former iniquities: let thy tender mercies speedily prevent us: for we are brought very low.*"
8. Psalms 103:4 – "*...who crowneth thee with lovingkindness and tender mercies;*"
9. Psalms 119:77 – "*Let thy tender mercies come unto me, that I may live: for thy law is my delight.*"
10. Psalms 119:156 – "*Great are thy tender mercies, O LORD: quicken me according to thy judgments*"
11. Psalms 145:9 – "*The LORD is good to all: and his tender mercies are over all his works.*"
12. Luke 1:78 – "*Through the tender mercy of our God; whereby the dayspring from on high hath visited us,*"
13. James 5:11 – "*...Ye have heard of the patience of Job, and have seen the end of the Lord; that the Lord is very pitiful, and of tender mercy.*"

C. Plenteous in mercy

1. Hebrew for plenteous, *rab* – Abundant in size, quantity and quality
2. Psalms 86:5 – "*For thou, Lord, art good, and ready to forgive; and plenteous in mercy unto all them that call upon thee.*"
3. Psalms 86:15 – "*But thou, O Lord, art a God full of compassion, and gracious, longsuffering, and plenteous in mercy and truth.*"
4. Psalms 103:8 – "*The LORD is merciful and gracious, slow to anger, and plenteous in mercy.*"
5. Psalms 130:7 – "*Let Israel hope in the LORD: for with the LORD there is mercy, and with him is plenteous redemption.*"

D. Great mercy

1. Hebrew for great, *rab* – Abundant in size, quantity, and quality

2. Numbers 14:18 – "*The LORD is longsuffering, and of great mercy, forgiving iniquity and transgression...*"

3. I Samuel 12:22 – "*For the LORD will not forsake his people for his great name's sake: because it hath pleased the LORD to make you his people.*"
4. II Samuel 24:14 – "*...let us fall now into the hand of the LORD; for his mercies are great...*"
5. I Kings 3:6 – "*And Solomon said, Thou hast shewed unto thy servant David my father great mercy, according as he walked before thee in truth, and in righteousness, and in uprightness of heart with thee; and thou hast kept for him this great kindness, that thou hast given him a son to sit on his throne, as it is this day.*"
6. Psalms 31:19 – "*Oh how great is thy goodness, which thou hast laid up for them that fear thee...*"
7. Psalms 86:13 – "*For great is thy mercy toward me: and thou hast delivered my soul from the lowest hell.*"
8. Psalms 103:11 – "*For as the heaven is high above the earth, so great is his mercy toward them that fear him.*"
9. Psalms 108:4 – "*For thy mercy is great above the heavens: and thy truth reacheth unto the clouds.*"
10. Psalms 117:2 – "*For his merciful kindness is great toward us...*"
11. Psalms 119:156 – "*Great are thy tender mercies, O LORD: quicken me according to thy judgments*"
12. Psalms 145:8 – "*The LORD is gracious, and full of compassion; slow to anger, and of great mercy.*"
13. Psalms 69:16 – "*Hear me, O LORD; for thy lovingkindness is good: turn unto me according to the multitude of thy tender mercies.*"
14. Isaiah 54:7 – "*For a small moment have I forsaken thee; but with great mercies will I gather thee.*"

E. New every morning

1. Lamentations 3:22-23 – Other translations:

   "*Hope comes with each dawn*"
   "*New things for the mornings*"
   "*His loving kindness begins afresh each day*"

2. Psalms 42:8 – "*Yet the LORD will command his lovingkindness in the daytime, and in the night his song shall be with me...*"
3. Psalms 92:2 – "*To shew forth thy lovingkindness in the morning, and thy faithfulness every night,*"
4. Psalms 143:8 – "*Cause me to hear thy lovingkindness in the morning...*"
5. Isaiah 33:2 – "*O LORD, be gracious unto us; we have waited for thee: be thou their arm every morning, our salvation also in the time of trouble.*"

F. Excellent

1. Hebrew word – valuable; brightness, costly, fat; it comes from a root – to be heavy, rare, valuable

   a. Psalms 36:7 – "*How excellent is thy lovingkindness, O God! therefore the children of men put their trust under the shadow of thy wings.*"
   b. Psalms 17:7 – "*Shew thy marvellous lovingkindness, O thou that savest by thy right hand...*"

G. Forever

1. Psalms 37:26 – "*He is ever merciful, and lendeth; and his seed is blessed.*"
2. Psalms 77:7-11 – He's merciful, we forget
3. Psalms 100:5 – "*For the LORD is good; his mercy is everlasting...*"
4. Psalms 23:6 – "*Surely goodness and mercy shall follow me all the days of my life: and I will dwell in the house of the LORD for ever.*"
5. Psalms 136 – "*...for his mercy endureth for ever...*"
6. I Chronicles 16:34 – "*O give thanks unto the LORD; for he is good; for his mercy endureth for ever.*"

7. II Samuel 7:15 – "*But my mercy shall not depart away from him...*"
8. II Chronicles 5:13
9. II Chronicles 7:3-5

H. Abundant

a. I Peter 1:3 – "*Blessed be the God and Father of our Lord Jesus Christ, which according to his abundant mercy hath begotten us again unto a lively hope by the resurrection of Jesus Christ from the dead,*"

IV. Mercy and Judgment

A. Mercy rejoices over judgment.

1. James 2:13 – Other translations:

"*...mercy triumphs over judgment...*"
"*...mercy glories in the face of judgment...*"
"*...mercy boasteth over judgment...*"

2. Proverbs 20:28 – "*Mercy and truth preserve the king: and his throne is upholden by mercy.*"

B. Other related passages

1. Psalms 25:5-11
2. Psalms 51:1
3. Psalms 145:9

C. Examples of mercy rejoicing over judgment

1. John 8:1-11
2. Jonah 3:10
3. II Samuel 12:13-14
4. Luke 23:39-43
5. I Samuel 25:32-35
6. Jeremiah 30:12-20

IV. Mercy and Truth

A. The combination of these two delivers us from iniquity.

1. Proverbs 16:6 – "*By mercy and truth iniquity is purged: and by the fear of the LORD men depart from evil.*"

2. Psalms 61:7 – "*He shall abide before God for ever: O prepare mercy and truth, which may preserve him.*"

a. Psalms 40:11 – "*Withhold not thou thy tender mercies from me, O LORD: let thy lovingkindness and thy truth continually preserve me.*"

3. Psalms 85:10 – "*Mercy and truth are met together; righteousness and peace have kissed each other.*"
4. Psalms 57:3 – "*...God shall send forth his mercy and his truth.*"

5. Ephesians 4:15 – *"But speaking the truth in love, may grow up into him in all things, which is the head, even Christ:"*
6. Exodus 34:5-8
7. Psalms 25:5-6 – *"Lead me in thy truth, and teach me: for thou art the God of my salvation; on thee do I wait all the day. Remember, O LORD, thy tender mercies and thy lovingkindnesses; for they have been ever of old."*

B. The Lord is a God of mercy and truth.

1. Psalms 86:15 – *"But thou, O Lord, art a God full of compassion, and gracious, longsuffering, and plenteous in mercy and truth."*

    a. Proverbs 20:28 – *"Mercy and truth preserve the king: and his throne is upholden by mercy."*
    b. Psalms 115:1 – *"Not unto us, O LORD, not unto us, but unto thy name give glory, for thy mercy, and for thy truth's sake."*
    c. II Samuel 2:6 – *"And now the LORD shew kindness and truth unto you..."*

C. He wants us to walk in mercy and truth.

    a. Proverbs 3:3 – *"Let not mercy and truth forsake thee: bind them about thy neck; write them upon the table of thine heart:"*
    b. Proverbs 14:22 – *"Do they not err that devise evil? but mercy and truth shall be to them that devise good."*

V. Examples Of God's Mercy

A. Scriptures

1. Ezra 9:9-13
2. Job 33:27-30 – *"He looketh upon men, and if any say, I have sinned, and perverted that which was right, and it profited me not; He will deliver his soul from going into the pit, and his life shall see the light. Lo, all these things worketh God oftentimes with man, To bring back his soul from the pit, to be enlightened with the light of the living."*
3. II Chronicles 36:15 – *"And the LORD God of their fathers sent to them by his messengers, rising up betimes, and sending; because he had compassion on his people, and on his dwelling place:"*
4. Genesis 8:21 – *"And the LORD smelled a sweet savour; and the LORD said in his heart, I will not again curse the ground any more for man's sake; for the imagination of man's heart is evil from his youth; neither will I again smite any more every thing living, as I have done."*
5. Genesis 18:26 – *"And the LORD said, If I find in Sodom fifty righteous within the city, then I will spare all the place for their sakes."*
6. Exodus 15:13 – *"Thou in thy mercy hast led forth the people which thou hast redeemed: thou hast guided them in thy strength unto thy holy habitation."*
7. Exodus 32:14 – *"And the LORD repented of the evil which he thought to do unto his people."*
8. Leviticus 26:41, 45 – *"And that I also have walked contrary unto them, and have brought them into the land of their enemies; if then their uncircumcised hearts be humbled, and they then accept of the punishment of their iniquity...But I will for their sakes remember the covenant of their ancestors, whom I brought forth out of the land of Egypt in the sight of the heathen, that I might be their God: I am the LORD."*
9. Numbers 21:8 – *"And the LORD said unto Moses, Make thee a fiery serpent, and set it upon a pole: and it shall come to pass, that every one that is bitten, when he looketh upon it, shall live."*
10. Deuteronomy 4:37 – *"And because he loved thy fathers, therefore he chose their seed after them, and brought thee out in his sight with his mighty power out of Egypt;"*

11. Judges 2:18 – *"And when the LORD raised them up judges, then the LORD was with the judge, and delivered them out of the hand of their enemies all the days of the judge: for it repented the LORD because of their groanings by reason of them that oppressed them and vexed them."*
12. II Samuel 14:14 – *"For we must needs die, and are as water spilt on the ground, which cannot be gathered up again; neither doth God respect any person: yet doth he devise means, that his banished be not expelled from him."*
13. II Samuel 12:13 – *"And David said unto Nathan, I have sinned against the LORD. And Nathan said unto David, The LORD also hath put away thy sin; thou shalt not die."*
14. II Samuel 24:14-16 – *"And David said unto Gad, I am in a great strait: let us fall now into the hand of the LORD; for his mercies are great: and let me not fall into the hand of man. So the LORD sent a pestilence upon Israel from the morning even to the time appointed: and there died of the people from Dan even to Beer-sheba seventy thousand men. And when the angel stretched out his hand upon Jerusalem to destroy it, the LORD repented him of the evil, and said to the angel that destroyed the people, It is enough: stay now thine hand..."*
15. II Kings 13:23 – *"And the LORD was gracious unto them, and had compassion on them, and had respect unto them, because of his covenant with Abraham, Isaac, and Jacob, and would not destroy them, neither cast he them from his presence as yet."*
16. II Kings 14:26-27 – *"For the LORD saw the affliction of Israel, that it was very bitter: for there was not any shut up, nor any left, nor any helper for Israel. And the LORD said not that he would blot out the name of Israel from under heaven: but he saved them by the hand of Jeroboam the son of Joash."*

VI. We Are To Be Like Him

A. We are to be merciful.

1. Luke 6:36 – *"Be ye therefore merciful, as your Father also is merciful."*
2. Proverbs 31:26 – *"She openeth her mouth with wisdom; and in her tongue is the law of kindness."* – This is speaking of the bride; Malachi 2:5-7, Colossians 3:12-14

3. Micah 6:8 – *"He hath shewed thee, O man, what is good; and what doth the LORD require of thee, but to do justly, and to love mercy, and to walk humbly with thy God?"*

    a. Ephesians 4:32 – *"And be ye kind one to another, tenderhearted, forgiving one another, even as God for Christ's sake hath forgiven you."*
    b. II Peter 1:4-9

4. Zechariah 7:8-9 – *"...Thus speaketh the LORD of hosts, saying, Execute true judgment, and shew mercy and compassions every man to his brother:"*
5. Luke 10:25-36

Lesson 37

The Cherubims Of Gold

The Cherubims Of God

I. Introduction

As with all Biblical subjects, there is a broad difference of opinion as to who the cherubims are. What one must do then is search the scriptures to see what is so (Acts 17:11). God for His glory's sake hides revelation within the Word and it's an honor to *"search it out"* (Proverbs 25:2). He declares if we seek Him we find Him when we *"search for Him with all of our hearts"* (Jeremiah 29:13). So as we give ourselves to study this subject, we can be confident the Lord will teach us.

These marvelous beings seem to always be associated with the glory of God, the throne of God, and guarding and protecting paradise (the way of life) or the place of God's revealed presence. They are always seen in the plural which represents that it is a many-member thing God is doing in the last days. Their ministry is one of flowing together in service to the Lord. This is a new ministry coming forth, a ministry of glory, a Holy Place ministry that is God's Word.

Let us approach this study with an open heart (II Corinthians 3:18), and as we search diligently, we will find the true revelation of the cherubims of glory. And perhaps by seeing who they are, be provoked ourselves to running after and serving the Lord with more passion than ever before.

A. Important facts about cherubims

1. The traditional viewpoint is that they are an order of angels.
2. As you can see here they are joined to each other as well as joined to the mercy seat (Exodus 25:18). Angels cannot be one with Jesus. Only redeemed men can.
3. Perhaps these two cherubims could typify something else:

   a. Song of Solomon 6:13 – *"Return, return, O Shulamite; return, return, that we may look upon thee. What will ye see in the Shulamite? As it were the company of two armies."*
   b. Two Witnesses – Revelation 11
   c. Zechariah 4:3, 11-14 – *"[3]And two olive trees by it, one upon the right side of the bowl, and the other upon the left side thereof...[11]Then answered I, and said unto him, What are these two olive trees upon the right side of the candlestick and upon the left side thereof? [12]And I answered again, and said unto him, What be these two olive branches which through the two golden pipes empty the golden oil out of themselves? [13]And he answered me and said, Knowest thou not what these be? And I said, No, my lord. [14]Then said he, These are the two anointed ones, that stand by the LORD of the whole earth."*
   d. Two companies of Jewish and Gentile believers

e. One for the Old Testament and one for the New Testament guarding forever the glory and the mercy seat, the ark, and all that is in it.
f. Revelation 3:21 – "*To him that overcometh will I grant to sit with me in my throne, even as I also overcame, and am set down with my Father in his throne.*" Overcomers sit with Him on His throne.
g. Ezekiel 10:8 – "*And there appeared in the cherubims the form of a man's hand under their wings.*"

II. Definition of Word (Cherubims)

A. The Hebrew word is of uncertain derivation. Nobody knows for sure what it means. It is possibly from the Hebrew root word

1. *Karah* – Give a feast
2. *Kerub* – Imaginary figure; celestial, as if contending

B. Greek – same as Hebrew

III. Who Are They? There are varying opinions and schools of thought concerning cherubims.

A. They are angelic beings, which is probably most widely held, Hebrews 1:13-14 – "[13]*But to which of the angels said he at any time, Sit on my right hand, until I make thine enemies thy footstool?* [14]*Are they not all ministering spirits, sent forth to minister for them who shall be heirs of salvation?*"
B. They represent the Godhead: Two cherubims representing the Father and the Holy Spirit with the mercy seat in the middle which represents Jesus
C. The third opinion is that the cherubims are symbolic or represent redeemed men out of every nation, etc., who are restored to the image of Christ.

I believe they represent a company within the great Body of Christ, a rank (I Corinthians 15:23) if you will, a remnant who enter into the highest place of worship and glory. Whoever they are, they are completely made of gold, live in the Most Holy Place, and are constantly in the glory of God.

D. Other facts

1. Though different, the cherubims seem to be linked with the seraphims, who are only mentioned once in Isaiah 6:2, 6 (Hebrew for seraphims – "burning ones"). The cherubims have a much fuller revelation in Scripture.

2. The Living Creatures found in Ezekiel and Revelation are the same

a. Ezekiel 1:5 – "*Also out of the midst thereof came the likeness of four living creatures. And this was their appearance; they had the likeness of a man.*"
b. Ezekiel 9:3 – "*And the glory of the God of Israel was gone up from the cherub, whereupon he was, to the threshold of the house. And he called to the man clothed with linen, which had the writer's inkhorn by his side;*"
c. Ezekiel 10
d. Revelation 4:6-9
e. Revelation 5:9-12

3. It seems that their ministry is one of protecting, carrying, providing, being and ministering to:

a. The glory of God
b. The throne of God
c. Their service is rendered mostly to God.

4. Rabbinical tradition assigns the four faces of the cherubims (man, lion, ox, eagle) to the standards of divisions in the camp of Israel.

    a. The lion (Judah) or the east
    b. The ox (Ephraim) or the west – in Ezekiel 10 it is the face of a cherub
    c. The man (Rueben) or the south
    d. The eagle (Dan) or the north

Thus cherubims are the standard that leads the natural Israelites when they traveled. It would speak to us then, that the cherubims with their four faces will lead the heavenly host.

IV. The Cherubims In The Tabernacle Of Moses And The Mercy Seat, Exodus 37:6-9

"6And he made the mercy seat of pure gold: two cubits and a half was the length thereof, and one cubit and a half the breadth thereof. 7And he made two cherubims of gold, beaten out of one piece made he them, on the two ends of the mercy seat; 8One cherub on the end on this side, and another cherub on the other end on that side: out of the mercy seat made he the cherubims on the two ends thereof. 9And the cherubims spread out their wings on high, and covered with their wings over the mercy seat, with their faces one to another; even to the mercy seatward were the faces of the cherubims."

A. In the unfolding revelation of the cherubims, we come now to the mercy seat.

1. The mercy seat was to rest over the Ark of the Covenant. Inside the ark was the golden pot of manna (supernatural provision), the law (the Word) and Aaron's rod that budded (God's authority and choice). This was all to be overlaid with mercy.

B. Exodus 25:17-22 – The cherubims in particular

"17And thou shalt make a mercy seat of pure gold: two cubits and a half shall be the length thereof, and a cubit and a half the breadth thereof. 18And thou shalt make two cherubims of gold, of beaten work shalt thou make them, in the two ends of the mercy seat. 19And make one cherub on the one end, and the other cherub on the other end: even of the mercy seat shall ye make the cherubims on the two ends thereof. 20And the cherubims shall stretch forth their wings on high, covering the mercy seat with their wings, and their faces shall look one to another; toward the mercy seat shall the faces of the cherubims be. 21And thou shalt put the mercy seat above upon the ark; and in the ark thou shalt put the testimony that I shall give thee. 22And there I will meet with thee, and I will commune with thee from above the mercy seat, from between the two cherubims which are upon the ark of the testimony, of all things which I will give thee in commandment unto the children of Israel."

1. "*...Thou shalt make...*" Thus the cherubims were created by men.
2. There were two cherubims; two is the number in Scripture for witness and separation. They are a witness of God's glory. They are separated from the rest of their brethren and separated unto God.
3. Cherubims – Notice they are spoken of in the plural. It is a corporate thing that God is going to do with these cherubims.
4. "*of pure gold*" – These were made of pure gold. This speaks of God's pure and holy divine character. These have His image.

5. "*of beaten work*"

    a. Hebrew for "*beaten work*" – rounded work, molded by hammering out of one piece; it comes from a root word that means – something turned.

1) This speaks to us of God's dealing and shaping in the lives of His people. Hammering them into submission, we are the work on the wheels (Jeremiah 18:3-4).
2) Out of one piece – two in one – unity in our diversity. We all come from the same mold originally.
3) Something turned – Speaks of repentance;
4) God doubles what He does to show it is of Him (Joseph's two dreams, etc.)

6. *"shalt thou make them"* – This says that men have a lot to do with the shaping and forming of character. We help bring and beat the gold for the cherubims.

7. *"two ends of the mercy seat"*

a. These cherubims begin their ministry and end it in mercy.
b. They are also guarding God's glory and mercy (keeping the way of the Tree of Life)
c. Redeemed men who serve in a position of glory – are a witness of the glory and the mercy of God as a covering for the ministry of the Word (Law), authority (Rod), and provision (Manna).

8. *"one cherub on the one end, and the other cherub on the other end"* – This speaks to us, though these cherubims are united, they have their own distinct duty to fulfill – unified but individual in their ministries.

9. *"stretch forth their wings on high"*

a. Isaiah 40:31 – *"But they that wait upon the LORD shall renew their strength; they shall mount up with wings as eagles; they shall run, and not be weary; and they shall walk, and not faint."*
b. These cherubims are able to fly which speaks of translation
c. Mount above circumstances
d. High places of worship

10. *"covering the mercy seat with their wings"* – Once again the picture of guarding the glory, the revealed presence of God

11. *"their faces shall look one to another"*

a. Ministry in unison
b. See their need for each other
c. Proverbs 27:19 – *"As in water face answereth to face, so the heart of man to man."* – These are transparent, showing each other their true hearts.

12. *"toward the mercy seat shall the faces of the cherubims be"*

a. They are always beholding the glory.
b. Their ministry is strictly "Most Holy Place."
c. Keeping the mercy and glory of God always in their perspective (vision).

V. The Cherubims and the Curtains

A. Exodus 26:1-3, Exodus 36:8

Exodus 26:1-3, "[1]*Moreover thou shalt make the tabernacle with ten curtains of fine twined linen, and blue, and purple, and scarlet: with cherubims of cunning work shalt thou make them.* [2]*The length of one curtain shall be eight and twenty cubits, and the breadth of one curtain four cubits: and every one of the curtains shall have one measure. [3]The five curtains shall be coupled together one to another; and other five curtains shall be coupled one to another."*

Exodus 36:8, *"And every wise hearted man among them that wrought the work of the tabernacle made ten curtains of fine twined linen, and blue, and purple, and scarlet: with cherubims of cunning work made he them."*

1. *"thou shalt make"* – Men make the cherubims. Their origin is human
2. Ten – Ten is the number for the law; government; a completed cycle.
3. Curtains – Represents covering, protection from the elements, enhancement of beauty.
4. Fine – Not just any linen but the best
5. Twined – Hebrew – To twist (the Lord will shake everything that can be shaken)
6. Linen – Represents righteousness of the saints (Revelation 19:8)
7. Blue – Heavenly
8. Purple – Royalty
9. Scarlet – Suffering, sacrifice
10. Cunning – Hebrew – to plait, to weave, to plot, to think
11. The length – 28 cubits – Twenty-eight in scripture is the number for eternal life. Their length is eternal.
12. The breadth – 4 cubits – Four is the number for creation. Their ministry covers all creation

13. Coupled together in groups of five – Five is the number for grace and spiritual ministry and two is the number for witness and separation.

    a. They witness by grace
    b. They're separated by grace
    c. They form a covering of grace for the priests and creation.

14. The priests would walk, and fulfill their ministry under these linen curtains – the cherubims watching over, guarding and protecting the true ministry as well as God's glory.

VI. The Cherubims and the Veil

A. Exodus 26:31-33, Exodus 36:35-36

Exodus 26:31-33, *"[31]And thou shalt make a vail of blue, and purple, and scarlet, and fine twined linen of cunning work: with cherubims shall it be made: [32]And thou shalt hang it upon four pillars of shittim wood overlaid with gold: their hooks shall be of gold, upon the four sockets of silver. [33]And thou shalt hang up the vail under the taches, that thou mayest bring in thither within the vail the ark of the testimony: and the vail shall divide unto you between the holy place and the most holy."*

Exodus 36:35-36, *"[35]And he made a vail of blue, and purple, and scarlet, and fine twined linen: with cherubims made he it of cunning work. [36]And he made thereunto four pillars of shittim wood, and overlaid them with gold: their hooks were of gold; and he cast for them four sockets of silver."*

1. The veil was placed between the glory of God and the general priesthood. Only the high priest could go through once a year. The veil was a divider between the Most Holy Place and the Holy Place. Once again the cherubims are found guarding and protecting the glory, the way.
2. Blue – Heavenly
3. Purple – Royalty
4. Scarlet – Suffering, sacrifice
5. Fine twined – The best work
6. Linen – Righteousness of saints

7. Hung upon four pillars of wood (humanity) overlaid with gold (God's character). This divider is hung over all of humanity to separate the precious from the vile. It hangs upon the remnant of creation that has God's holy nature.
8. Four sockets of silver – Creation redeemed (The number four represents creation and silver represents redemption)
9. The veil divides the manifest presence of God from the priests who cannot go in.

Lesson 38

The Cloud of Glory

I. The Cloud Of Glory, Exodus 40: 33-38

After Moses finished the work, the glory came in the form of a cloud. The "Cloud" is the presence of God Himself. It is the glory of God revealed, the presence and power of the Holy Spirit. Just as the cloud was to reveal the rainbow of promise after the flood, so the cloud of God's glory reveals the loving kindness and promises of the Lord to His people. The glorious Holy Spirit is the indwelling presence in the Church. We are to be a habitation of God through the Spirit, temples of the Holy Ghost, "*[19]Now therefore ye are no more strangers and foreigners, but fellowcitizens with the saints, and of the household of God; [20]And are built upon the foundation of the apostles and prophets, Jesus Christ himself being the chief corner stone; [21]In whom all the building fitly framed together groweth unto an holy temple in the Lord: [22]In whom ye also are builded together for an habitation of God through the Spirit*" (Ephesians 2:19-22).

Exodus 40:33-38 – "*[33]And he reared up the court round about the tabernacle and the altar, and set up the hanging of the court gate. So Moses finished the work. [34]Then a cloud covered the tent of the congregation, and the glory of the LORD filled the tabernacle. [35]And Moses was not able to enter into the tent of the congregation, because the cloud abode thereon, and the glory of the LORD filled the tabernacle. [36]And when the cloud was taken up from over the tabernacle, the children of Israel went onward in all their journeys: [37]But if the cloud were not taken up, then they journeyed not till the day that it was taken up. [38]For the cloud of the LORD was upon the tabernacle by day, and fire was on it by night, in the sight of all the house of Israel, throughout all their journeys.*"

A. Defining the Glory Cloud in Scripture

1. The cloud led the Children of Israel – Just as the cloud of God's glory led the Israelites as they left Egypt and began to walk with God, so the Holy Spirit leads and guides every believer as he turns from the world and follows the Lord. The cloud protected them from heat, i.e. tribulation and oppression. The cloud illuminated them at night. The Holy Spirit gives light to the believer and delivers him from the powers of darkness.

   a. Exodus 13:21-22 – "*[21]And the LORD went before them by day in a pillar of a cloud, to lead them the way; and by night in a pillar of fire, to give them light; to go by day and night: [22]He took not away the pillar of the cloud by day, nor the pillar of fire by night, from before the people.*"

   b. Numbers 9:15-23

"*[15]And on the day that the tabernacle was reared up the cloud covered the tabernacle, namely, the tent of the testimony: and at even there was upon the tabernacle as it were the appearance of fire, until the morning. [16]So it was alway: the cloud covered it by day, and the appearance of fire by night. [17]And when the cloud was taken up from the tabernacle, then after that the children of Israel journeyed: and in the place where the cloud abode, there the children of Israel pitched their tents. [18]At the commandment of the LORD the children of Israel journeyed, and at the commandment of the LORD they pitched: as long as the cloud abode upon the tabernacle they rested in their tents. [19]And when the cloud tarried long upon the tabernacle many days, then the children of Israel kept the charge of the LORD, and journeyed not. [20]And so it was, when the cloud was a few days upon the tabernacle; according to the commandment of the LORD they abode in their tents, and according to the commandment of the LORD they journeyed. [21]And so it was, when the cloud abode from even unto the morning, and that the cloud was taken up in the morning, then they journeyed: whether it was by day or by night that the cloud was taken up, they journeyed. [22]Or whether it were two days, or a month, or a year, that the cloud tarried upon the tabernacle, remaining thereon, the children of Israel abode in their tents, and journeyed not: but when it was taken up, they journeyed. [23]At the commandment of the LORD they rested in the tents, and at the commandment of the LORD they journeyed: they kept the charge of the LORD, at the commandment of the LORD by the hand of Moses."*

b. Nehemiah 9:12-19

"[12]Moreover thou leddest them in the day by a cloudy pillar; and in the night by a pillar of fire, to give them light in the way wherein they should go. [13]Thou camest down also upon mount Sinai, and spakest with them from heaven, and gavest them right judgments, and true laws, good statutes and commandments: [14]And madest known unto them thy holy sabbath, and commandedst them precepts, statutes, and laws, by the hand of Moses thy servant: [15]And gavest them bread from heaven for their hunger, and broughtest forth water for them out of the rock for their thirst, and promisedst them that they should go in to possess the land which thou hadst sworn to give them. [16]But they and our fathers dealt proudly, and hardened their necks, and hearkened not to thy commandments, [17]And refused to obey, neither were mindful of thy wonders that thou didst among them; but hardened their necks, and in their rebellion appointed a captain to return to their bondage: but thou art a God ready to pardon, gracious and merciful, slow to anger, and of great kindness, and forsookest them not. [18]Yea, when they had made them a molten calf, and said, This is thy God that brought thee up out of Egypt, and had wrought great provocations; [19]Yet thou in thy manifold mercies forsookest them not in the wilderness: the pillar of the cloud departed not from them by day, to lead them in the way; neither the pillar of fire by night, to shew them light, and the way wherein they should go."

c. Psalms 78:14 – *"In the daytime also he led them with a cloud, and all the night with a light of fire."*
d. Romans 8:14 – *"For as many as are led by the Spirit of God, they are the sons of God."*

2. Cloud of separation – The cloud separated the children of Israel from Pharaoh and his hosts and from the land of Egypt. We are sanctified by the Holy Spirit and delivered from our enemies by the glory.

    a. Exodus 14:19-24

"[19]And the angel of God, which went before the camp of Israel, removed and went behind them; and the pillar of the cloud went from before their face, and stood behind them: [20]And it came between the camp of the Egyptians and the camp of Israel; and it was a cloud and darkness to them, but it gave light by night to these: so that the one came not near the other all the night. [21]And Moses stretched out his hand over the sea; and the LORD caused the sea to go back by a strong east wind all that night, and made the sea dry land, and the waters were divided. [22]And the children of Israel went into the midst of the sea upon the dry ground: and the waters were a wall unto them on their right hand, and on their left. [23]And the Egyptians pursued, and went in after them to the midst of the sea, even all Pharaoh's horses, his chariots, and his horsemen. [24]And it came to pass, that in the morning watch the LORD looked unto the host of the Egyptians through the pillar of fire and of the cloud, and troubled the host of the Egyptians,"

3. Cloud of baptism – Israel was baptized in the cloud and in the sea. It is now the will of God for every believer to be baptized in water and in the Holy Spirit.

    a. I Corinthians 10:1-4 – *"[1]Moreover, brethren, I would not that ye should be ignorant, how that all our fathers were under the cloud, and all passed through the sea; [2]And were all baptized unto Moses in the cloud and in the sea; [3]And did all eat the same spiritual meat; [4]And did all drink the same spiritual drink: for they drank of that spiritual Rock that followed them: and that Rock was Christ."* (Exodus 14:19-24)
    b. Acts 2:38-39 – *"[38]Then Peter said unto them, Repent, and be baptized every one of you in the name of Jesus Christ for the remission of sins, and ye shall receive the gift of the Holy Ghost. [39]For the promise is unto you, and to your children, and to all that are afar off, even as many as the Lord our God shall call."*

4. The cloud and the manna – The cloud appeared with the promise of manna. The Holy Spirit presents and accompanies the Word of God. The Spirit and the Word agree. How we need the Holy Spirit's presence when feeding on the Word of God!

   a. Exodus 16:10-15

"[10]And it came to pass, as Aaron spake unto the whole congregation of the children of Israel, that they looked toward the wilderness, and, behold, the glory of the LORD appeared in the cloud. [11]And the LORD spake unto Moses, saying, [12]I have heard the murmurings of the children of Israel: speak unto them, saying, At even ye shall eat flesh, and in the morning ye shall be filled with bread; and ye shall know that I am the LORD your God. [13]And it came to pass, that at even the quails came up, and covered the camp: and in the morning the dew lay round about the host. [14]And when the dew that lay was gone up, behold, upon the face of the wilderness there lay a small round thing, as small as the hoar frost on the ground. [15]And when the children of Israel saw it, they said one to another, It is manna: for they wist not what it was. And Moses said unto them, This is the bread which the LORD hath given you to eat."

   b. I Corinthians 2:9-12 – *"[9]But as it is written, Eye hath not seen, nor ear heard, neither have entered into the heart of man, the things which God hath prepared for them that love him. [10]But God hath revealed them unto us by his Spirit: for the Spirit searcheth all things, yea, the deep things of God. [11]For what man knoweth the things of a man, save the spirit of man which is in him? even so the things of God knoweth no man, but the Spirit of God. [12]Now we have received, not the spirit of the world, but the spirit which is of God; that we might know the things that are freely given to us of God."*

5. The cloud at Mt. Sinai – What Mt. Sinai was to Israel after their deliverance from Egypt by the Passover, so Pentecost is to the believer after our deliverance from the world by the power of the Blood of the Lamb. The cloud of God's glory is revealed in Pentecost. It is the call to a deeper and more intimate relationship with the Lord

   a. Exodus 19:9, 16-25 – The glory cloud here also represents God's confirmation of one's call to ministry as seen with Moses, *"[9]And the LORD said unto Moses, Lo, I come unto thee in a thick cloud, that the people may hear when I speak with thee, and believe thee for ever. And Moses told the words of the people unto the LORD...[16]And it came to pass on the third day in the morning, that there were thunders and lightnings, and a thick cloud upon the mount, and the voice of the trumpet exceeding loud; so that all the people that was in the camp trembled. [17]And Moses brought forth the people out of the camp to meet with God; and they stood at the nether part of the mount. [18]And mount Sinai was altogether on a smoke, because the LORD descended upon it in fire: and the smoke thereof ascended as the smoke of a furnace, and the whole mount quaked greatly..."*
   b. Exodus 24:15-18 – *"[15]And Moses went up into the mount, and a cloud covered the mount. [16]And the glory of the LORD abode upon mount Sinai, and the cloud covered it six days: and the seventh day he called unto Moses out of the midst of the cloud. [17]And the sight of the glory of the LORD was like devouring fire on the top of the mount in the eyes of the children of Israel. [18]And Moses went into the midst of the cloud, and gat him up into the mount: and Moses was in the mount forty days and forty nights."*
   c. Acts 2:4 – *"And they were all filled with the Holy Ghost, and began to speak with other tongues, as the Spirit gave them utterance."*
   d. II Corinthians 3:2-3, 7-8 – *"[2]Ye are our epistle written in our hearts, known and read of all men: [3]Forasmuch as ye are manifestly declared to be the epistle of Christ ministered by us, written not with ink, but with the Spirit of the living God; not in tables of stone, but in fleshy tables of the heart...[7]But if the ministration of death, written and engraven in stones, was glorious, so that the children of Israel could not stedfastly behold the face of Moses for the glory of his countenance; which glory was to be done away: [8]How shall not the ministration of the spirit be rather glorious?"*

6. The Cloud upon the Mount of Transfiguration – The cloud of God's glory had left the Temple in Jerusalem in the days of Ezekiel because of the sins of Israel. Now, the Lord Jesus, God's only begotten Son and the true Temple of God, had come to the earth to dwell among men. As He prayed on the Mount, He was transfigured and His face shown as the sun. The glory of God shown through the veil of His flesh and the Glory Cloud of God's presence overshadowed Him. God the Father spoke from the cloud and said, "*This is My beloved Son...hear ye Him.*"

   a. Matthew 17:5 – "*While he yet spake, behold, a bright cloud overshadowed them: and behold a voice out of the cloud, which said, This is my beloved Son, in whom I am well pleased; hear ye him.*" (Mark 9:7, Luke 9:34-35)
   b. Ezekiel 9:3, 10:4, 18, 11:23 – "[3]*And the glory of the God of Israel was gone up from the cherub, whereupon he was, to the threshold of the house. And he called to the man clothed with linen, which had the writer's inkhorn by his side...*"
   c. John 1:14 – "*And the Word was made flesh, and dwelt among us, (and we beheld his glory, the glory as of the only begotten of the Father,) full of grace and truth.*"

7. The Cloud proclaimed the Name of the Lord – The Holy Spirit proclaims the Name of the Lord Jesus Christ, the greatest name in heaven and earth. In the cloud, His true character is revealed.

   a. Exodus 34:5-7 – "[5]*And the LORD descended in the cloud, and stood with him there, and proclaimed the name of the LORD.* [6]*And the LORD passed by before him, and proclaimed, The LORD, The LORD God, merciful and gracious, longsuffering, and abundant in goodness and truth...*"
   b. Acts 2:36-38

8. Exodus 33:8-11 – His voice is heard, "[8]*And it came to pass, when Moses went out unto the tabernacle, that all the people rose up, and stood every man at his tent door, and looked after Moses, until he was gone into the tabernacle.* [9]*And it came to pass, as Moses entered into the tabernacle, the cloudy pillar descended, and stood at the door of the tabernacle, and the LORD talked with Moses.* [10]*And all the people saw the cloudy pillar stand at the tabernacle door: and all the people rose up and worshipped, every man in his tent door.* [11]*And the LORD spake unto Moses face to face, as a man speaketh unto his friend...*"

   a. Psalms 99:7 – "*He spake unto them in the cloudy pillar: they kept his testimonies, and the ordinance that he gave them.*"
   b. Ezekiel 1:28 – "*As the appearance of the bow that is in the cloud in the day of rain, so was the appearance of the brightness round about. This was the appearance of the likeness of the glory of the LORD. And when I saw it, I fell upon my face, and I heard a voice of one that spake.*"
   c. Deuteronomy 5:22 – "*These words the LORD spake unto all your assembly in the mount out of the midst of the fire, of the cloud, and of the thick darkness, with a great voice: and he added no more. And he wrote them in two tables of stone, and delivered them unto me.*"
   d. Matthew 17:5 – "*While he yet spake, behold, a bright cloud overshadowed them: and behold a voice out of the cloud, which said, This is my beloved Son, in whom I am well pleased; hear ye him.*"

9. Proverbs 16:15 – It is the latter rain and His favor, "*In the light of the king's countenance is life; and his favour is as a cloud of the latter rain.*"
10. Isaiah 19:1 – Idols and demons leave when it comes, "*The burden of Egypt. Behold, the LORD rideth upon a swift cloud, and shall come into Egypt: and the idols of Egypt shall be moved at his presence, and the heart of Egypt shall melt in the midst of it.*"
11. Job 26:9 – His throne (authority) is in the midst, "*He holdeth back the face of his throne, and spreadeth his cloud upon it.*"

12. II Chronicles 5:14 – All ministry by and to man ceases, *"So that the priests could not stand to minister by reason of the cloud: for the glory of the LORD had filled the house of God."*

13. Exodus 40:38 – Protection from the elements; protection in the night season, *"For the cloud of the LORD was upon the tabernacle by day, and fire was on it by night, in the sight of all the house of Israel, throughout all their journeys."*

    a. Psalms 105:39 – *"He spread a cloud for a covering; and fire to give light in the night."*
    b. Isaiah 4:5 – *"And the LORD will create upon every dwelling place of mount Zion, and upon her assemblies, a cloud and smoke by day, and the shining of a flaming fire by night: for upon all the glory shall be a defence."*

B. Appearances of the Cloud throughout the Scriptures:

1. Numbers 11:24-25 – It appeared when God appointed the seventy elders.
2. Numbers 12:5 – It showed up when Miriam spoke against Moses' wife.
3. Numbers 14:14 – It appeared as Moses pleaded for Israel.
4. Numbers 16:42 – It manifested during Korah's rebellion.
5. II Chronicles 5:13-14 and I Kings 8:10-11 – It fell and filled Solomon's temple during the dedication of the foundation being laid.
6. Ezekiel 1:28; 8:11; 10:3-4 – Ezekiel's visions
7. Luke 2:8-9 – It appeared to the shepherds at the birth of Christ.
8. Matthew 3:16 – It was present at the baptism of Christ.
9. Matthew 27:45 – It was present at the death of Christ.
10. Acts 1:9 – It was there at Christ's ascension.

11. It will appear at His return:

    a. Matthew 24:30 – *"And then shall appear the sign of the Son of man in heaven: and then shall all the tribes of the earth mourn, and they shall see the Son of man coming in the clouds of heaven with power and great glory."*
    b. I Thessalonians 4:17 – *"Then we which are alive and remain shall be caught up together with them in the clouds, to meet the Lord in the air: and so shall we ever be with the Lord."*
    c. Mark 13:26 – *"And then shall they see the Son of man coming in the clouds with great power and glory."*
    d. Luke 21:27 – *"And then shall they see the Son of man coming in a cloud with power and great glory."*
    e. Revelation 1:7 – *"Behold, he cometh with clouds; and every eye shall see him, and they also which pierced him: and all kindreds of the earth shall wail because of him. Even so, Amen."*
    f. Daniel 7:13 – *"I saw in the night visions, and, behold, one like the Son of man came with the clouds of heaven, and came to the Ancient of days, and they brought him near before him."*
    g. Revelation 14:14 – *"And I looked, and behold a white cloud, and upon the cloud one sat like unto the Son of man, having on his head a golden crown, and in his hand a sharp sickle."*

12. Revelation 11:12 – It will appear during the tribulation at the raising up of the two witnesses.
13. Revelation 10:1 – The last days messenger is clothed with it.
14. I Kings 18:44 – We see the cloud rising out of the sea bringing rain.
15. Job 26:9 – His throne is covered by it.
16. Psalm 105:39 – God spreads His cloud over us for a covering.
17. Proverbs 16:15 – The presence of the cloud is His favor.
18. Isaiah 4:5 – It appears upon the dwelling places of Mount Zion.
19. Isaiah 19:1 – God rides upon the cloud.
20. Isaiah 60:8 – It is there as the saints are caught up to God.

C. We are called to obtain the Glory

1. II Thessalonians 2:14 – *"Whereunto he called you by our gospel, to the obtaining of the glory of our Lord Jesus Christ."*
2. Zechariah 2:8 – *"For thus saith the LORD of hosts; After the glory hath he sent me unto the nations which spoiled you: for he that toucheth you toucheth the apple of his eye."*
3. I Peter 5:10 – *"But the God of all grace, who hath called us unto his eternal glory by Christ Jesus, after that ye have suffered a while, make you perfect, stablish, strengthen, settle you."*
4. I Thessalonians 2:12 – *"That ye would walk worthy of God, who hath called you unto his kingdom and glory."*
5. II Corinthians 3:18 – *"But we all, with open face beholding as in a glass the glory of the Lord, are changed into the same image from glory to glory, even as by the Spirit of the Lord."*
6. II Peter 1:3 – *"According as his divine power hath given unto us all things that pertain unto life and godliness, through the knowledge of him that hath called us to glory and virtue:"*
7. Revelation 21:11 – *"Having the glory of God: and her light was like unto a stone most precious, even like a jasper stone, clear as crystal;"*
8. Hebrews 2:10 – *"For it became him, for whom are all things, and by whom are all things, in bringing many sons unto glory, to make the captain of their salvation perfect through sufferings."*
9. I Samuel 2:8 – *"He raiseth up the poor out of the dust, and lifteth up the beggar from the dunghill, to set them among princes, and to make them inherit the throne of glory: for the pillars of the earth are the LORD's, and he hath set the world upon them."*
10. Isaiah 43:7 – *"Even every one that is called by my name: for I have created him for my glory, I have formed him; yea, I have made him."*

D. Some will enter in

1. Exodus 24:15-18 – *"[15]And Moses went up into the mount, and a cloud covered the mount. [16]And the glory of the LORD abode upon mount Sinai, and the cloud covered it six days: and the seventh day he called unto Moses out of the midst of the cloud. [17]And the sight of the glory of the LORD was like devouring fire on the top of the mount in the eyes of the children of Israel. [18]And Moses went into the midst of the cloud, and gat him up into the mount: and Moses was in the mount forty days and forty nights."*
2. Matthew 17:5 – *"While he yet spake, behold, a bright cloud overshadowed them: and behold a voice out of the cloud, which said, This is my beloved Son, in whom I am well pleased; hear ye him."*
3. Isaiah 60:8-10, 13, 19 – *"Who are these that fly as a cloud, and as the doves to their windows? [9]Surely the isles shall wait for me, and the ships of Tarshish first, to bring thy sons from far, their silver and their gold with them, unto the name of the LORD thy God, and to the Holy One of Israel, because he hath glorified thee. [10]And the sons of strangers shall build up thy walls, and their kings shall minister unto thee: for in my wrath I smote thee, but in my favour have I had mercy on thee...[13]The glory of Lebanon shall come unto thee, the fir tree, the pine tree, and the box together, to beautify the place of my sanctuary; and I will make the place of my feet glorious...[19]The sun shall be no more thy light by day; neither for brightness shall the moon give light unto thee: but the LORD shall be unto thee an everlasting light, and thy God thy glory."*
4. Isaiah 4:2-5 – *"[2]In that day shall the branch of the LORD be beautiful and glorious, and the fruit of the earth shall be excellent and comely for them that are escaped of Israel. [3]And it shall come to pass, that he that is left in Zion, and he that remaineth in Jerusalem, shall be called holy, even every one that is written among the living in Jerusalem: [4]When the Lord shall have washed away the filth of the daughters of Zion, and shall have purged the blood of Jerusalem from the midst thereof by the spirit of judgment, and by the spirit of burning. [5]And the LORD will create upon every dwelling place of mount Zion, and upon her assemblies, a cloud and smoke by day, and the shining of a flaming fire by night: for upon all the glory shall be a defence."*
5. II Chronicles 5:10-14 – *"[10]There was nothing in the ark save the two tables which Moses put therein at Horeb, when the LORD made a covenant with the children of Israel, when they came out of Egypt. [11]And it came to pass, when the priests were come out of the holy place: (for all the priests*

that were present were sanctified, and did not then wait by course: [12]Also the Levites which were the singers, all of them of Asaph, of Heman, of Jeduthun, with their sons and their brethren, being arrayed in white linen, having cymbals and psalteries and harps, stood at the east end of the altar, and with them an hundred and twenty priests sounding with trumpets:) [13]It came even to pass, as the trumpeters and singers were as one, to make one sound to be heard in praising and thanking the LORD; and when they lifted up their voice with the trumpets and cymbals and instruments of musick, and praised the LORD, saying, For he is good; for his mercy endureth for ever: that then the house was filled with a cloud, even the house of the LORD; [14]So that the priests could not stand to minister by reason of the cloud: for the glory of the LORD had filled the house of God."

E. Worship brings the glory cloud

1. Isaiah 6:3-4 – "*[3]And one cried unto another, and said, Holy, holy, holy, is the LORD of hosts: the whole earth is full of his glory. [4]And the posts of the door moved at the voice of him that cried, and the house was filled with smoke.*"
2. II Chronicles 5:11-14
3. Psalms 22:3 – "*But thou art holy, O thou that inhabitest the praises of Israel.*"

Lesson 39

The Glory Of God

I believe that the most important commodity in the universe is the glory of God! When we speak of the glory of God, we are really speaking of Him, for the glory of God is the divine essence of Himself. Wherever He is, so is the glory. God and His glory are synonymous. They are one and the same. The glory of God is His divine nature and person. As both the Hebrew and Greek words define it, it is the "weight" of His "divine splendor" and "majesty". This glory was also completely and directly revealed through Jesus Christ, God Himself revealed in human form.

The glory of God is not some ethereal thing. It is a presence that has "weight" (Hebrew word – *kabod*) and it can be felt. To put it simply, you can know when it is there and when it is not. Because of our inability as humans to receive it in its entirety, God reveals it to us in stages, "glory to glory" (II Corinthians 3:18), because it is His very divine nature and presence that is completely holy and pure, full of light and power. To behold it in all of its greatness would simply destroy us. Moses in the Old Testament is the perfect example. His natural face shown brightly because of being in it, so much so that the children of Israel asked him to cover his face because it was too much for them to behold. However, for the New Testament believer who allows God to conform them to His image, to renew their mind allowing the Holy Spirit to sanctify them, set them apart from the world, the flesh and the devil, and who also having already a start by becoming a "partaker of the divine nature", one day will be able to "see His face" and handle all of His glory's weight and splendor. The Scriptures declare "*I will not give my glory unto another*" (Isaiah 48:11), but yet at the same time tells us over and over again we have been called to "obtain His glory" (II Thessalonians 2:14). Therefore we must understand that when He says He won't give His glory to another, it doesn't mean His people won't ultimately enjoy it and receive it. They will have His image, His likeness, His nature, and His character, as the apostle Paul said, "it is no longer I that liveth" (Galatians 2:20), they will not be considered "another." The Jesus in them can handle and receive His glory. So He is actually not giving His glory to another, but to Himself, within His people. There is a great day coming as Isaiah says where we will hear His voice saying, "*Arise, shine; for thy light is come, and the glory of the LORD is risen upon thee*" (Isaiah 60:1), and later "*his glory shall be seen upon thee*" (Isaiah 60:2). This tells us then that there will come a time when we will no longer "fall short of the glory of God." Those who have tasted and seen His glory and have marveled in it's splendor will gladly tell you there is nothing greater or more important. Let us now allow the Holy Scriptures to define for us this great characteristic of our God, ultimately with the hope of eventually receiving of and walking in it. Remember, "*Christ in you, the hope of glory*" (Colossians 1:27).

As we search the Scriptures, we find that the glory of God is a recurring theme. The whole purpose of the tabernacle was so God can come and dwell with His people. It is mentioned over and over again, throughout the Word of God. A true understanding and knowledge of God's glory will bring to us not only a great revelation of Himself and His purpose, but we will see how important, especially in these last days, it is for us to know how our calling and destiny is attached to the glory.

For many people, the glory is an enigma. It's an unknown, unseen, unfelt thing. Some make a mockery of it, some disdain it, and others are simply mystified by it. Others just don't care, or are at best, lukewarm in their attitude toward it. There are many, though, who because of slothfulness or an unwillingness to press into it, are jealous and envious of those who love it and live for it and *have it.*

Nevertheless, for many of us, there is deep within us a great and all consuming longing to be clothed in the glory. We want to worship in it, to live in and by it. Our whole existence revolves around His glory. We can't live without it. To be without the glory is to be completely and utterly naked. There is a growing revelation among God's true sons of their calling to the glory and their ultimate destiny in it. The glory is what we were born for. The reason for our creation was to share in God's glory. Having tasted it and seen it – which really means tasting and seeing Him, there is no going back. Satan's counterfeit "religion" can never compare to it. One moment in the glory can change our lives forever. It seals our fate! We become determined to spend the rest of our earthly lives groaning, desiring, and fighting to stay in it. The Bible says, "*The God of glory thundereth.*" Do you hear the call of the glory? Have you tasted the manifested presence of

God? If you have, then you know what I mean. It will separate us from the world, the flesh, the devil, our friends, and even our families. But, in the end, we know it will be worth it. There is no greater commodity in the universe than the glory of God. Neither is there any greater calling than that of the call to obtain His glory. He has made it so.

So, we undertake this study of the Scriptures so that we can truly understand what it is, who it is, what our calling to it is, and our ultimate destiny in it.

Remember, Proverbs 25:2, "*It is the glory of God to conceal a matter, and the honor of kings to search it out.*" We will search it out exhaustively, and by doing so my earnest prayer is that the prayer of the Apostle Paul will become a reality to our lives. "*That the God of our Lord Jesus Christ, the Father of glory, may give unto you the spirit of wisdom and revelation in the knowledge of him. The eyes of your understanding being that ye may know what is the hope of his calling, and what the riches of the glory of his inheritance in the saints.*" (Ephesians 1:17-18)

I. Why We Should Study The Glory Of God?

A. He is glorious. He is the God of glory. His glory is his divine essence and presence.

1. Isaiah 33:21 – "*But there the glorious LORD will be unto us a place of broad rivers and streams...*"
2. John 17:5 – "*And now, O Father, glorify thou me with thine own self with the glory which I had with thee before the world was.*"
3. Exodus 15:6-7 – "*Thy right hand, O LORD, is become glorious in power: thy right hand, O LORD, hath dashed in pieces the enemy. And in the greatness of thine excellency thou hast overthrown them that rose up against thee...*"
4. Psalms 76:4 – "*Thou art more glorious and excellent than the mountains of prey.*"
5. I Chronicles 16:27 – "*Glory and honour are in his presence; strength and gladness are in his place*"
6. Psalms 24:9-10 – "*Lift up your heads, O ye gates; even lift them up, ye everlasting doors; and the King of glory shall come in. Who is this King of glory? The LORD of hosts, he is the King of glory.*"

B. It's important to Him.

1. Isaiah 42:8 – "*I am the LORD: that is my name: and my glory will I not give to another, neither my praise to graven images.*"
2. Isaiah 48:11 – "*For mine own sake, even for mine own sake, will I do it: for how should my name be polluted? and I will not give my glory unto another.*"
3. Jeremiah 14:21 – "*Do not abhor us, for thy name's sake, do not disgrace the throne of thy glory: remember, break not thy covenant with us.*"
4. I Samuel 4:21 – "*And she named the child I-chabod, saying, The glory is departed from Israel: because the ark of God was taken...*"

C. He wants us to have His glory.

1. John 11:40 – "*Jesus saith unto her, Said I not unto thee, that, if thou wouldest believe, thou shouldest see the glory of God?*"
2. Isaiah 58:8 – "*...the glory of the LORD shall be thy rereward.*"
3. Isaiah 43:7 – "*Even every one that is called by my name: for I have created him for my glory, I have formed him; yea, I have made him.*"
4. Psalms 84:11 – "*For the LORD God is a sun and shield: the LORD will give grace and glory: no good thing will he withhold from them that walk uprightly.*"
5. Psalms 149:5 – "*Let the saints be joyful in glory...*"
6. Isaiah 4:5 – "*And the LORD will create upon every dwelling place of mount Zion, and upon her assemblies, a cloud and smoke by day, and the shining of a flaming fire by night: for upon all the glory shall be a defence.*"

7. Isaiah 60:1-2 – "*Arise, shine; for thy light is come, and the glory of the LORD is risen upon thee. For, behold, the darkness shall cover the earth, and gross darkness the people: but the LORD shall arise upon thee, and his glory shall be seen upon thee.*"
8. II Corinthians 3:7-10, 18 – "*...But we all, with open face beholding as in a glass the glory of the Lord, are changed into the same image from glory to glory, even as by the Spirit of the Lord.*"

D. We are called to obtain the glory.

1. I Thessalonians 2:12 – "*That ye would walk worthy of God, who hath called you unto his kingdom and glory.*"
2. II Thessalonians 2:14 – "*Whereunto he called you by our gospel, to the obtaining of the glory of our Lord Jesus Christ.*"
3. II Peter 1:3 – "*...through the knowledge of him that hath called us to glory and virtue:*"
4. I Peter 5:10 – "*...the God of all grace, who hath called us unto his eternal glory by Christ Jesus...*"

E. His glory should be everything to us.

1. I Corinthians 10:31 – "*Whether therefore ye eat, or drink, or whatsoever ye do, do all to the glory of God.*"
2. Psalms 138:5 – "*Yea, they shall sing in the ways of the LORD: for great is the glory of the LORD.*"
3. Psalms 3:3 – "*But thou, O LORD, art a shield for me; my glory, and the lifter up of mine head.*"

F. We should be longing for it (the glory), for Him.

1. Psalms 63:2 – "*To see thy power and thy glory, so as I have seen thee in the sanctuary.*"
2. Exodus 33:18 – "*And he said, I beseech thee, shew me thy glory.*"
3. John 7:18 – "*...but he that seeketh his glory that sent him, the same is true, and no unrighteousness is in him.*"

G. Our destiny is all wrapped up in it.

1. Psalms 102:16 – "*When the LORD shall build up Zion, he shall appear in his glory.*"
2. Romans 8:30 – "*Moreover whom he did predestinate, them he also called: and whom he called, them he also justified: and whom he justified, them he also glorified.*"
3. Revelation 21:11 – "*Having the glory of God: and her light was like unto a stone most precious, even like a jasper stone, clear as crystal;*"
4. Haggai 2:7, 9 – "*And I will shake all nations, and the desire of all nations shall come: and I will fill this house with glory, saith the LORD of hosts...The glory of this latter house shall be greater than of the former...*"
5. Isaiah 61:3 – "*...that they might be called trees of righteousness, the planting of the LORD, that he might be glorified.*"
6. Isaiah 60:7, 9 – "*...and I will glorify the house of my glory...to bring thy sons from far, their silver and their gold with them, unto the name of the LORD thy God, and to the Holy One of Israel, because he hath glorified thee.*"
7. Psalms 45:13 – "*The king's daughter is all glorious within: her clothing is of wrought gold.*"
8. Ephesians 5:27 – "*That he might present it to himself a glorious church...*"
9. I Samuel 2:8 – "*He raiseth up the poor out of the dust, and lifteth up the beggar from the dunghill, to set them among princes, and to make them inherit the throne of glory...*"
10. I Corinthians 15:49 – "*And as we have borne the image of the earthy, we shall also bear the image of the heavenly.*"
11. Romans 8:18 – "*For I reckon that the sufferings of this present time are not worthy to be compared with the glory which shall be revealed in us.*"
12. II Corinthians 4:17 – "*For our light affliction, which is but for a moment, worketh for us a far more exceeding and eternal weight of glory;*"

13. Philippians 3:21 – "*Who shall change our vile body, that it may be fashioned like unto his glorious body...*"
14. II Thessalonians 1:10 – "*When he shall come to be glorified in his saints, and to be admired in all them that believe (because our testimony among you was believed) in that day.*"

H. One day the whole earth will be covered in His glory.

1. Numbers 14:21 – "*But as truly as I live, all the earth shall be filled with the glory of the LORD.*"
2. Psalms 72:19 – "*And blessed be his glorious name for ever: and let the whole earth be filled with his glory; Amen, and Amen.*"
3. Isaiah 6:3 – "*And one cried unto another, and said, Holy, holy, holy, is the LORD of hosts: the whole earth is full of his glory.*"
4. Habakkuk 2:14 – "*For the earth shall be filled with the knowledge of the glory of the LORD, as the waters cover the sea.*"
5. Isaiah 40:5 – "*And the glory of the LORD shall be revealed, and all flesh shall see it together: for the mouth of the LORD hath spoken it.*"
6. Psalms 102:15 – "*So the heathen shall fear the name of the LORD, and all the kings of the earth thy glory.*"

I. The heavens declare His glory.

1. Psalms 97:6 – "*The heavens declare his righteousness, and all the people see his glory.*"
2. Psalms 19:1 – "*The heavens declare the glory of God; and the firmament sheweth his handywork.*"
3. Zechariah 2:8 – "*For thus saith the LORD of hosts; After the glory hath he sent me unto the nations...*"
4. I Chronicles 16:24 – "*Declare his glory among the heathen; his marvelous works among all nations.*"

J. He is to be glorified.

1. Psalms 145:5 – "*I will speak of the glorious honour of thy majesty, and of thy wondrous works.*"
2. Psalms 66:2 – "*Sing forth the honour of his name: make his praise glorious.*"
3. Psalms 96:8 – "*Give unto the LORD the glory due unto his name: bring an offering, and come into his courts.*"

II. Hebrew Words for Glory and Their Definitions.

A. These are listed in order of importance and the number of times they are found.

1. *Kabawd* means a weight

a. Weight in a good sense. It refers to the great physical weight or quantity of a thing. The word does not simply mean heavy, but a heavy or imposing quantity of things.
b. Imposing presence or position
c. Splendor; quality of being magnificent, glorious, or sumptuous; display of imposing pomp or grandeur.
d. Copiousness; large in quantity or number, abundant supply.
e. Honor, nobility; emphasizing the position of an individual, the respect due it, and the importance of the one being honored.
f. Wealth; significant and positive reputation, as well as one's great quantity and abundance.
g. Reputation; majesty
h. The word glory can also mean; majesty, abundant supply or large in quantity or number.

i. It comes from the root word – *Kabed* which means; to be heavy (in a bad sense – burdensome, severe, dull); (in a good sense – numerous, rich, honorable); to make weighty, to honor. To be very rich.

j. The word *Kabawd* is translated glory (156 times), honor (32 times), glorious (10 times), gloriously (1 time), honorable (1 time). You can see that it means mostly good things; it does however, reveal the two voices of God.

   1) Romans 11:22 – "*Behold therefore the goodness and severity of God…*"
   2) Isaiah 45:7 – "*I form the light, and create darkness: I make peace, and create evil: I the LORD do all these things.*"
   3) Lamb and Lion
   4) Luke 24:50 – Bethany – house of affliction and fruitfulness

2. *Tiphereth* means ornament, beauty, honor; it comes from a root word - *paar* – it means to gleam, to embellish, to boast, to glorify, explain or to make clear oneself, or to shake a tree
3. *Tsbiy*– prominence, splendor, a gazelle as beautiful. It comes from a root word, *tsabah*, which means to amass, to grow turgid, and to array an army against.
4. *Halal* – to be clear (of sound but usually of color), to shine, to make a show, to boast, and to be clamorously foolish. This is obviously one of the main Hebrew words for praise. It means to glory in His name. It also means to praise, celebrate, glory, sing, and boast. It is the source of the word Hallelujah.
5. *Hador* – magnificence, ornament, splendor, or honor.
6. *Shabach*– to address in a loud tone, to pacify by words.
7. *Howd* – grandeur, an imposing form or appearance, splendor, majesty, authority.

III. Greek Words for Glory and Their Definitions

A. These are listed in order of importance and the number of times they are found.

1. *Doxa* – means glory (as very apparent), dignity. Doxa primarily signifies an opinion, an estimate, and hence the honor resulting from a good opinion.
2. *Kauchaoinai* – to boast or glory.
3. *Enduo* – sense of sinking into a garment, to put on, to enter into, to clothes oneself.
4. *Endoxos* – splendid, noble, in glory. It signifies "held in honor" or "high repute".

B. Dictionary definition

1. *Glory* – exalted, praise, honor or distinction bestowed; something that makes one honored or illustrious. Adoring praise or worshipful thanksgiving; resplendent beauty or magnificence; a state of absolute happiness, gratification, contentment; the splendor and bliss of heaven; a surrounding radiance of light represented about the head or whole of a scared being.
2. *Glorify* – to magnify with praise; to treat as more excellent or splendid than would normally be considered.

IV. The glory is the essence of GOD Himself. It is His presence, (In Hebrew, the word for presence is face.) when the presence of GOD is upon us, it means He has turned His face to us. It is the most precious commodity in the universe. Wherever the glory is…GOD is!

A. The GOD of glory – The majesty and purity and greatness of our GOD is the glory of GOD.

1. Acts 7:2 – "*…The GOD of glory…*"
2. Matthew 6:13 – "*…thine is the kingdom, and the power, and the glory…*"
3. I Chronicles 29: 10-14 – "*…thine O Lord is the greatness, and the power, and the glory…*"
4. Psalms 8:1 – "*…thou hast set thy glory above the heavens…*"

5. Psalms 102:15 – "*...heathen shall fear...and all the Kings...thy glory...*"
6. Ephesians 1:17 – "*...the Father of glory...*" (literally, "the Father of glories.)
7. Isaiah 60:19 – "*...thy GOD thy glory...*"
8. Psalms 113:4 – "*...his glory above the heavens...*"
9. I Corinthians 2:8 – "*...the Lord of glory...*"
10. I Peter 4:14 – "*...the Spirit of glory...*"
11. Psalms 29:3 – "*...the GOD of glory thundereth...*"
12. Habakkuk 3:3-6
13. Matthew 16:27 – "*...Son of man shall come in the glory of His father...*"
14. Job 40: 9-10 – "*...deck thyself now with majesty and excellence; and array thyself with glory and beauty.*"

B. As GOD reveals Himself, we see His glory

1. Exodus 33:18 – "*And he said, I beseech thee, shew me thy glory.*" – Moses asks GOD to show him His glory. God's answer then is to define it for us.

a. Exodus 33: 19 – "*...I will make all my goodness pass before thee...*"

The word goodness here is also *tuwb* – it means good in the widest sense, the best, beauty, and gladness. It comes from a root word, *towb* that simply means; to be good in the widest sense; to be joyful, glad, pleasant, lovely, appropriate, precious. If this doesn't describe GOD, I don't know what else could! What he was really telling Moses was "*the real me will be passing by you.*" GOD is goodness personified. All He knows is to be good in the greatest and widest sense. Because He is goodness, it makes the rest of His great characteristics good as well. As he passed by Moses he was saying "*I am completely good and because of it I'm joyful, glad, pleasant, lovely, precious, and I always do what's appropriate.*" No matter what you've heard or been taught, this is who GOD really is, <u>it is His nature</u>.

1) Goodness of GOD – The words glory and goodness could truly then become synonymous.
2) Mark 10:18 – there is none good but one, that is GOD.
3) II Chronicles 6:41 – "*Now therefore arise, O LORD God, into thy resting place, thou, and the ark of thy strength: let thy priests, O LORD God, be clothed with salvation, and let thy saints rejoice in goodness.*" – When GOD is in His resting place, goodness abounds.

4) God's goodness is great

a) Nehemiah 9:25 – "*...and possessed houses full of all goods, wells digged, vineyards, and oliveyards, and fruit trees in abundance: so they did eat, and were filled, and became fat, and delighted themselves in thy great goodness.*"
b) II Samuel 7:28 – "*And now, O Lord GOD, thou art that God, and thy words be true, and thou hast promised this goodness unto thy servant:*"
c) Psalms 21:3-5 – "*...His glory is great in thy salvation...*"
d) Psalms 31:19 – "*Oh how great is thy goodness...*"

5) Psalms 27:13 – "*...the goodness of the Lord in the land of the living...*"
6) Psalms 23:6 – "Surely goodness and mercy shall follow me all the days of my life: and I will dwell in the house of the Lord for ever."
7) Psalms 33:5 – "*...earth is full of the goodness of the Lord.*"
8) Psalms 52:1 – "*...the goodness of GOD endureth continually...*"
9) Psalms 65:4 – "*...satisfied with the goodness of thy house...*"
10) Psalms 68:10 – "*...thou, O God, hast prepared of thy goodness for the poor.*"
11) Psalms 107:8,9 – "*...O that men would praise the Lord for His goodness...*" (Also Psalms 107:15, 21, 31)

12) Psalms 144:2 – "*David calls the Lord 'my goodness...*"
13) Isaiah 63:7 – "*I will mention the lovingkindnesses of the Lord, and the praises of the Lord, according to all that the Lord hath bestowed on us, and the great goodness toward the house of Israel, which he hath bestowed on them according to his mercies, and according to the multitude of his lovingkindnesses.*"
14) Jeremiah 31:12,14 – "*...flow together to the goodness of the Lord...*"
15) Jeremiah 33:9 – "*And it shall be to me a name of joy, a praise and an honour before all the nations of the earth, which shall hear all the good that I do unto them: and they shall fear and tremble for all the goodness and for all the prosperity that I procure unto it.*"
16) Hosea 3:5 – "*...and shall fear the Lord and His goodness in the latter days...*"
17) Zechariah 9:17 – "*For how great is his goodness...*"
18) Romans 2:4 – "*...the goodness of GOD leadeth thee to repentance...*"
19) Romans 11:22 –"*... behold therefore the goodness...*"
20) Galatians 5:22 –"*...fruit of the Spirit is goodness...*" (Ephesians 5:9 – "*...the fruit of the Spirit is in all goodness and righteousness and truth*")
21) II Thessalonians 1:11 – "*...fulfil all the good pleasure of his goodness, and the work of faith with power:*"

b. Exodus 33:19 – "*I will proclaim the name of the Lord before thee*" – Your name reveals your character. God has no problem revealing himself. His name is great, because He is great and good.

1) His great name reveals His person

a) Genesis 14:18-20 – Melchizedek, King of Peace, King of Righteousness
b) Genesis 17:1 – Almighty – I Am EL Shaddai – The All Sufficient, Nurturing, Breasty One
c) Genesis 32:29, 30 – my life is preserved
d) Exodus 3:13-15 – I will be, what I will be

2) His name is synonymous with His presence. God's name and the place of His presence are one and the same.

a) Numbers 6:22-27
b) Nehemiah 1:9 – "*...and will bring them unto the place that I have chosen to set my name there.*"
c) Psalms 20:1 – "*The LORD hear thee in the day of trouble; the name of the God of Jacob defend thee;*"
d) Psalms 54:1 – "*...Save me, O God, by thy name...*"
e) Psalms 74:7 – "*...they have defiled by casting down the dwelling place of thy name to the ground.*"

C. Glory is an attribute of GOD

1. Psalms 24:7 – "*...the King of Glory...*" – He is the King of the GOD of glory.
2. Psalms 29:3 – "*...the GOD of Glory thundereth...*" – Other translations:

"*The Lord fulminates across the waters; the glorious GOD is thundering. The Lord roars over the vast deeps.*"
"*The voice of the Lord is upon the waters; it is the glorious GOD that maketh the thunder. It is the Lord that ruleth the sea.*"

When we speak of the attributes of GOD, especially concerning His glory, we mean that attributes are the characteristics of quality belonging to a person. So when we speak of this particular attribute of GOD, that is

His glory, we mean this characteristic or quality that belongs to GOD as GOD. This is what makes Him who and what He is.

3. Revelation 19:1 – *"...Alleluia; Salvation, and glory, and honour, and power, unto the Lord our God:"*

D. GOD's glory appears – The revelation of GOD's power and characteristics are sometimes accompanied by visible or tangible phenomenon.

V. First and Foremost God's Glory is revealed in Christ Jesus

A. Scriptures

1. II Corinthians 4:6 – *"For God, who commanded the light to shine out of darkness, hath shined in our hearts, to give the light of the knowledge of the glory of God in the face of Jesus Christ."*
2. Hebrews 1:3 – *"Who being the brightness of his glory, and the express image of his person..."*
3. Hebrews 2:7-9 – *"...But we see Jesus, who was made a little lower than the angels for the suffering of death, crowned with glory and honour; that he by the grace of God should taste death for every man."*
4. Hebrews 3:3 – *"For this man was counted worthy of more glory than Moses, inasmuch as he who hath builded the house hath more honour than the house."*
5. James 2:1 – *"My brethren, have not the faith of our Lord Jesus Christ, the Lord of glory, with respect of persons."*
6. Revelation 4:11 – *"Thou art worthy, O Lord, to receive glory and honour and power..."*
7. Luke 4:15 – *"And he taught in their synagogues, being glorified of all."*
8. Psalms 8:3-5 – *"...For thou hast made him a little lower than the angels, and hast crowned him with glory and honour."*
9. John 13:31-32 – *"Therefore, when he was gone out, Jesus said, Now is the Son of man glorified, and God is glorified in him. If God be glorified in him, God shall also glorify him in himself, and shall straightway glorify him."*
10. John 1:14 – *"And the Word was made flesh, and dwelt among us, (and we beheld his glory, the glory as of the only begotten of the Father,) full of grace and truth."*
11. John 2:11 – *"This beginning of miracles did Jesus in Cana of Galilee, and manifested forth his glory; and his disciples believed on him."*
12. Colossians 1:27 – *"To whom God would make known what is the riches of the glory of this mystery among the Gentiles; which is Christ in you, the hope of glory:"*
13. John 17:5 – *"And now, O Father, glorify thou me with thine own self with the glory which I had with thee before the world was."*

VI. There Are Degrees Of Glory

A. Scriptures

1. II Corinthians 3:18 – *"...from glory to glory..."*
2. II Corinthians 3:13 – *"And not as Moses, which put a vail over his face..."* (Exodus 34:29-33)

The more Moses went in the glory, the more his face shone, and he had to wear a veil to cover his face because the children of Israel could not look upon him. This says to me the more you and I grow in the glory, the more time we spend in the glory, in His manifest presence, in His face, we are going to be changed, not so much in outward appearance as Moses, but our souls are being changed into His holy image. (Romans 8:29-30)

3. The principle being changed from glory to glory

a. Jeremiah 48:11 – vessel to vessel
b. Proverbs 4:18 – more and more
c. Romans 1:17 – faith to faith
d. Psalms 84:7 – strength to strength
e. II Corinthians 2:16 – death unto death, life unto life
f. I Corinthians 15:41-57 – as one star differeth from another start in glory
g. II Corinthians 4:16 – renewed day by day
h. Luke 24:36-51 – after the resurrection; Revelation 1:10-16 – 40 years later

Look how much Jesus changed the longer he stayed in the glory. It is imperative for us to keep coming into His revealed presence, and as we do we will be changed and made ready for stepping through the veil.

VII. How God Gets Glory

A. Scriptures

1. Psalms 50:23 – "*Whoso offereth praise glorifieth me...*"
2. Matthew 5:16 – "*Let your light so shine before men, that they may see your good works, and glorify your Father which is in heaven.*"
3. Matthew 9: 8 – "*...when the multitudes saw it, they marveled, and glorified God, which had given such power unto men.*"
4. Matthew 15:30-31 – "*Insomuch that the multitude wondered, when they saw the dumb to speak, the maimed to be whole, the lame to walk, and the blind to see: and they glorified the God of Israel.*"
5. Luke 13:13 – "*...woman with spirit of infirmity...*" *And he laid his hands on her, and immediately she was made straight and glorified God.*"
6. Luke 17:15 – "*... when he saw that he was healed, turned back, and with a loud voice glorified God*"
7. Luke 18:43 – blind man – "*And immediately he received his sight, and followed him, glorifying God...*"
8. John 11:4 – Lazarus - "*...This sickness is not unto death, but for the glory of God...*"
9. John 15:8 – "*Herein is my Father glorified, that ye bear much fruit; so shall ye be my disciples.*"
10. John 21:19 – Peters future death – "*This spake he, signifying by what death he should glorify God.*"
11. Acts 4:21 – Peter and John in prison for healing the lame man at the gate – "*...for all men glorified God for that which was done.*"
12. Acts 11:18 – Peter before Jerusalem council about Gentiles receiving the Holy Ghost – "*When they heard these things, they held their peace, and glorified God, saying...*"
13. Romans 15:9 – "*And that the Gentiles might glorify God for his mercy; as it is written...*"
14. I Corinthians 6:20 – "*For ye are bought with a price: therefore glorify God in your body, and in your spirit, which are God's.*"
15. I Peter 2:12 – "*Having your conversation honest among the Gentiles: that, whereas they speak against you as evildoers, they may by your good works, which they shall behold, glorify God in the day of visitation.*"
16. I Peter 4:14 – persecution – "*If ye be reproached for the name of Christ, happy are ye; for the Spirit of glory and of God resteth upon you: on their part he is evil spoken of, but on your part he is glorified.*"
17. Isaiah 60:21 – "*Thy people also shall be all righteous: they shall inherit the land forever, the branch of my planting, the work of my hands, that I may be glorified.*"
18. Isaiah 61:3 – "*To appoint unto them that mourn in Zion, to give unto them beauty for ashes, the oil of joy for mourning, the garment of praise for the spirit of heaviness; that they might be called trees of righteousness, the planting of the Lord, that he might be glorified.*"
19. Leviticus 10:3 – Nadab and Abihu offering strange fire – "*...this is it that the Lord spoke, saying, I will be sanctified in them that come nigh me, and before all the people I will be glorified...*"

VIII. The Glory Can Depart

A. Scriptural Examples

1. I Samuel 4:21-22 – *"And she named the child Ichabod, saying, The glory is departed from Israel: because the ark of God was taken, and because of her father-in-law and her husband. And she said, The glory is departed from Israel: for the ark of God is taken."*

   a. How did this happen?

      1) I Samuel 2:22-25
      2) I Samuel 2:27-36
      3) I Samuel 3:11-14
      4) I Samuel 4:2-19

2. Habakkuk 2:16 – *"Thou art filled with shame for glory: drink thou also, and let thy foreskin be uncovered: the cup of the Lord's right hand shall be turned unto thee, and shameful spewing shall be on thy glory."*
3. Malachi 2:1-2 – *"And now, O ye priests, this commandment is for you. If ye will not hear, and if ye will not lay it to heart, to give glory unto my name, saith the Lord of hosts, I will even send a curse upon you, and I will curse your blessings: yea, I have cursed them already, because ye do not lay it to heart."*
4. Jeremiah 2:11 – *"Hath a nation changed their gods, which are yet no gods? but my people have changed their glory for that which doth not profit."*
5. Hosea 4:6-7 – *"My people are destroyed for lack of knowledge: because thou hast rejected knowledge, I will also reject thee, that thou shalt be no priest to me: seeing thou hast forgotten the law of thy God, I will also forget thy children. As they were increased, so they sinned against me: therefore will I change their glory into shame."*
6. Romans 1:21-24 – *"Because that, when they knew God, they glorified him not as God, neither were thankful; but became vain in their imaginations, and their foolish heart was darkened. Professing themselves to be wise, they became fools, And changed the glory of the incorruptible God into an image made like to corruptible man, and to birds, and fourfooted beasts, and creeping things. Wherefore God also gave them up to uncleanness through the lusts of their own hearts, to dishonor their own bodies between themselves."*

I suppose one of the most startling revelations to come out of this study on the glory of God is the following absolute paramount truth: that we are called to obtain the glory of God.

This is what we were born for; it is the true reason for our existence. All that God is and has, He is willing and desperately wants to share with His people. However, it must be a people who have been prepared by allowing the dealings of God to purge them and sanctify them. They must have the image of Christ.

Remember how we have considered that God said, "*...I will not give my glory unto another*" (Isaiah 42:8, 48:11). These purged people, however, will not BE "*another,*" because they will have lost their identity in Jesus. In the last days, this great remnant of overcomers will have fought the good fight of faith and prevailed over the world, the flesh, and the devil. They will have done so only because the grace of God helped them and made them to become willing. These overcomers will then manifest forth His glory in the earth: they will shew forth the true nature of God in the last great day of visitation—the last great move of God.

IX. Called To Obtain God's Glory

A. Scriptures

1. I Thessalonians 2:12 – "*That ye would walk worthy of God, who hath called you unto his kingdom and glory*" – Another translation: "*who invites you to share His own kingdom and glory*"

2. II Thessalonians 2:14 – "*Whereunto He called you by our gospel, to the obtaining of the glory of our Lord Jesus Christ*" – Other translations:

   "*so that you may share in the glory of God*"
   "*so that you may possess for your own the splendor of God*"
   "*...to gain the glory of God*"

3. Hebrews 2:10 – "*For it became Him, for whom are all things, and by whom are all things, in bringing many sons unto glory*"
4. Isaiah 43:7 – "*Even everyone that is called by my name: for I have created him for my glory...*" – Another translation: "*...whom I have created and formed and made for my glory*" – Our destiny could not be conveyed more clearly: "*the mystery which hath been hid from ages...Christ IN YOU, the hope of glory*" (Colossians 1:26-27, emphasis added).
5. I Peter 5:10 – "*But the God of all grace, who hath called us unto His eternal glory by Christ Jesus, after that ye have suffered awhile, make you perfect, stablish, strengthen, settle you.*" – We see here that to enter into this calling, we must first allow the dealings of God in our lives, which takes a lifetime.

6. II Peter 1:3 – "*According as His divine power hath given unto us all things that pertain to life and godliness, through the knowledge of Him that hath called us to glory and virtue.*" – Other translations:

   "*who hath called us to His own glory and excellence*"
   "*who hath called us to share His glory and virtue*"
   "*who called us by His own splendor and might*"
   "*have been called to share in God's own excellence and glory*"

This may seem to some too much to believe, but nonetheless the Scriptures are very clear about it.

7. Romans 9:23 – "*And that He might make known the riches of His glory on the vessels of mercy, which He had afore prepared unto glory.*" – God has taken great preparation in the unfolding of His great mystery and purpose. From the beginning we have been called to share in His glory (see Jeremiah 17:12 and I Samuel 2:6-8).
8. Zechariah 2:8 – "*For thus saith the Lord of hosts; After the glory hath He sent me unto the nations...*" – This calling began with Israel who didn't fulfill what God wanted for them. Now it has been passed on to us. We are to go after the glory, and then once we receive it and understand it, we are to take it to the nations.
9. Romans 8:18 and 30 – "*For I reckon that the sufferings of the present time are not worthy to be compared with the glory which shall be revealed in us...Moreover whom He did predestinate, them He also called: and whom He called, them He also justified: and whom He justified, them He also glorified.*" – Our ultimate destiny is to receive the final aspect of our salvation: We have been justified, we are being sanctified, we shall be glorified (II Corinthians 1:10).
10. Ephesians 1:18 – "*The eyes of your understanding being enlightened; that ye may know what is the hope of His calling, and what the riches of the glory of His inheritance in the saints*" – Only by being enlightened can we begin to understand the glory of our inheritance. It is intended for all.
11. Colossians 3:4 – "*When Christ, who is our life, shall appear, then shall ye also appear with Him in glory*" – To those for whom Christ is their life, we must know and believe that when He appears in glory, so shall we be in glory like Him (see also I John 3:2).
12. II Timothy 2:10 – "*Therefore I endure all things for the elects sakes, that they may also obtain the salvation which is in Christ Jesus with eternal glory*" – Once again we see that there is an enduring of sanctification and the dealings of God to obtain this precious glory.

13. I Peter 4:13 – "*But rejoice, inasmuch as ye are partakers of Christ's sufferings; that when His glory shall be revealed, ye may be glad also with exceeding joy.*" – Suffering and glory go hand in hand throughout the Scriptures. No suffering, no glory.
14. Philippians 3:20-21 – "*For our conversation is in heaven; from whence we also look for the Saviour, the Lord Jesus Christ: who shall change our vile body, that it may be fashioned like unto His glorious body, according to the working whereby He is able even to subdue all things unto Himself.*" – Our destiny is to have these old earthly bodies changed and made like unto His new glorious body (see also I Corinthians 15:38-58).
15. II Corinthians 4:17 – "*For our light affliction, which is but for a moment, worketh for us a far more exceeding and eternal weight of glory.*" – There are degrees of glory and according to how much we allow God to sanctify us in this life will determine our degree or weight of glory.
16. II Corinthians 3:18 – "*But we all, with open face beholding as in a glass the glory of the Lord, are changed into the same image from glory to glory, even as by the Spirit of the Lord.*" – It is the ministry of the glass ("glass" = mirror = The Word) and of the Holy Spirit that we are changed into His image from one realm of glory to another.
17. Isaiah 60:1-3, 7 – "*Arise, shine; for thy light is come, and the glory of the Lord is risen upon thee. For, behold, the darkness shall cover the earth, and gross darkness the people: but the Lord shall arise upon thee, and his glory shall be seen upon thee. And the Gentiles shall come to thy light, and kings to the bright of thy rising...and I will glorify the house of my glory.*"
18. Ephesians 3:16 – "*That He would grant you, according to the riches of His glory, to be strengthened with might by His Spirit in the inner man.*" – So we see from all of the above passages of Scripture that we are called to obtain, and receive, and walk in His glory!

X. How to Bring God's Glory and Presence – What Can We Do To Bring God's Presence?

I Chronicles 13:12 – "*And David was afraid of God that day, saying, How shall I bring the ark of God home to me?*" The ark is symbolic of the manifest presence of God.

A. How to bring it home to you personally and corporately

1. I Chronicles 15:2, 12-15 – "*[2]Then David said, None ought to carry the ark of God but the Levites: for them hath the LORD chosen to carry the ark of God, and to minister unto him for ever...[12]And said unto them, Ye are the chief of the fathers of the Levites: sanctify yourselves, both ye and your brethren, that ye may bring up the ark of the LORD God of Israel unto the place that I have prepared for it. [13]For because ye did it not at the first, the LORD our God made a breach upon us, for that we sought him not after the due order. [14]So the priests and the Levites sanctified themselves to bring up the ark of the LORD God of Israel. [15]And the children of the Levites bare the ark of God upon their shoulders with the staves thereon, as Moses commanded according to the word of the LORD.*"

   a. Only true priests are chosen to carry God's presence.
   b. It must be done after the due order.
   c. Priests sanctified themselves to carry the ark.
   d. It must be borne upon the shoulders of the sanctified priests. In other words, they must have the character to carry it.

2. Exodus 33:13-19, Exodus 34:5-8

   a. Amplified translation of Exodus 33:13-19 – "*Now therefore, I pray you, if I have found favor in Your sight, show me now Your way, that I may know You (progressively become more deeply and intimately acquainted with You, perceiving and recognizing and understanding more strongly and clearly) and that I may find favor in Your sight...And the Lord said, My Presence shall go with you...And the Lord said unto Moses, I will do this thing also that you have asked, for you have found favor, loving kindness and mercy in my sight and I know you personally and by name. And Moses said, I beseech You, show me Your glory. And God said, I will make all my goodness pass before you..."*

1) A strong desire to know God intimately
2) A desire for His glory
3) God knows you personally and by name

3. II Chronicles 5:13-14 – *"It came even to pass, as the trumpeters and singers were as one, to make one sound to be heard in praising and thanking the LORD; and when they lifted up their voice with the trumpets and cymbals and instruments of music, and praised the LORD, saying, For he is good; for his mercy endureth for ever: that then the house was filled with a cloud, even the house of the LORD; So that the priests could not stand to minister by reason of the cloud: for the glory of the LORD had filled the house of God."*

   a. Trumpeters and singers were as one, to make one sound.
   b. We must have the revelation that the Lord is good and His mercy endures forever.

4. Isaiah 6:1-4 – *"1 In the year that king Uzziah died I saw also the Lord sitting upon a throne, high and lifted up, and his train filled the temple. 2Above it stood the seraphims: each one had six wings; with twain he covered his face, and with twain he covered his feet, and with twain he did fly. 3And one cried unto another, and said, Holy, holy, holy, is the LORD of hosts: the whole earth is full of his glory. 4And the posts of the door moved at the voice of him that cried, and the house was filled with smoke."*

   a. Our idols must die
   b. Revelation of the Godhead, and that He is holy

5. Isaiah 64:1 – *"Oh that thou wouldest rend the heavens, that thou wouldest come down, that the mountains might flow down at thy presence,"* – Intercession
6. Psalms 100:1-5 – *"1Make a joyful noise unto the LORD, all ye lands. 2Serve the LORD with gladness: come before his presence with singing. 3Know ye that the LORD he is God: it is he that hath made us, and not we ourselves; we are his people, and the sheep of his pasture. 4Enter into his gates with thanksgiving, and into his courts with praise: be thankful unto him, and bless his name. 5For the LORD is good; his mercy is everlasting; and his truth endureth to all generations."* – A joyful noise, singing, knowing He's God and we are His people, thanksgiving, praise, blessing His name
7. Acts 3:19 – *"Repent ye therefore, and be converted, that your sins may be blotted out, when the times of refreshing shall come from the presence of the Lord;"*
8. II Chronicles 6:12-13 – *"And he stood before the altar of the LORD in the presence of all the congregation of Israel, and spread forth his hands: For Solomon had made a brasen scaffold, of five cubits long, and five cubits broad, and three cubits high, and had set it in the midst of the court: and upon it he stood, and kneeled down upon his knees before all the congregation of Israel, and spread forth his hands toward heaven,"*
9. II Corinthians 3:17 – *"Now the Lord is that Spirit: and where the Spirit of the Lord is, there is liberty."* – Liberty

   a. Galatians 5:1 – *"Stand fast therefore in the liberty wherewith Christ hath made us free, and be not entangled again with the yoke of bondage."*
   b. Galatians 2:4 – *"And that because of false brethren unawares brought in, who came in privily to spy out our liberty which we have in Christ Jesus, that they might bring us into bondage:"*

10. II Chronicles 7:1-2 – *"Now when Solomon had made an end of praying, the fire came down from heaven, and consumed the burnt offering and the sacrifices; and the glory of the LORD filled the*

house. And the priests could not enter into the house of the LORD, because the glory of the LORD had filled the LORD's house." – Sacrifice yourself

11. I Peter 2:5 – "*Ye also, as lively stones, are built up a spiritual house, an holy priesthood, to offer up spiritual sacrifices, acceptable to God by Jesus Christ.*" (Jeremiah 33:11, Hebrews 13:15)

Lesson 40

The High Priest Walk Of Worship

The High Priest

I. The High Priests Walk Of Worship

A. Exodus 28:31-35 – "[31]*And thou shalt make the robe of the ephod all of blue.* [32]*And there shall be an hole in the top of it, in the midst thereof: it shall have a binding of woven work round about the hole of it, as it were the hole of an habergeon, that it be not rent.* [33]*And beneath upon the hem of it thou shalt make pomegranates of blue, and of purple, and of scarlet, round about the hem thereof; and bells of gold between them round about:* [34]*A golden bell and a pomegranate, a golden bell and a pomegranate, upon the hem of the robe round about.* [35]*And it shall be upon Aaron to minister: and his sound shall be heard when he goeth in unto the holy place before the LORD, and when he cometh out, that he die not.*"

1. Verse 31

a. Robe – covering
b. Ephod – an apron- like garment worn over the priests robe and under his breastplate.
c. Blue – color that represents all things heavenly

2. Verse 32

a. Hole – for the head (Jesus); hole represents that we must have this head, not our head, to walk as a priest
b. Binding of woven work – This represents work done around the neck. The neck is the foundation that holds the head. Our foundation (neck) must have experienced the dealings of God, years of preparation in the Word and in the glory of God. The greater the foundation, the greater you can build upon it. We need a great woven foundation to support His head if we are to have a walk of worship.
c. Not rent – There can be no cracks in our foundation.

3. Verse 33

a. Hem – where your feet are and feet are always associated with our walk in God
b. Pomegranates – These are symbolic in Scripture of fruitfulness; sweet, juicy, red, full of seeds. This also speaks of the fruit of the spirit, evident in our walk. The symbolism here is

that our walk should be fruitful, sweet, and juicy (the presence), full of testimony of His sacrifice, and full of life.

c. Pomegranates of blue, purple, and scarlet – Our walk of worship should have all these attributes in it:

1) Blue – heavenly
2) Purple – royalty, majesty
3) Scarlet – sacrifice

d. Bells – Bell in Hebrew means a struck bell and it comes from a root word that means to tap or beat regularly, to agitate, to move, to trouble, to impel. The type here is that our walk of worship should make a noise, a regular noise, a sound that will move, or strike a chord, in some. While in others it will agitate or cause them to be troubled. It will definitely bring a reaction of some kind.
e. Gold – Gold in Scripture always speaks of the divine nature. This speaks of heavenly, divine worship, the sound from heaven.

4. Verse 34 – A golden bell and a pomegranate: These two mixing and clanging speak of our walk of worship symbolizing the divine nature mixing with our fruitful, juicy, life filled walk, testifying of His great sacrifice. This is the sound the earth is waiting to hear. This is also the balance God seeks, our talk matching our walk. Our walk is absolutely genuine, one of pure worship.

5. Verse 35

a. This robe is upon us to minister to the Lord
b. This is the only sound that is heard in the Holy Place. It is the sound of our worship walking
c. It also assures us and others that we are alive and not dead

1) Psalms 115:17 – *"The dead praise not the LORD, neither any that go down into silence."*
2) Psalms 88:10 – *"Wilt thou shew wonders to the dead? shall the dead arise and praise thee? Selah."*

II. Worship is to be our walk too.

A. It is a continual worship.

1. Luke 24:53 – *"And were continually in the temple, praising and blessing God. Amen."*
2. Psalms 34:1 – *"I will bless the LORD at all times: his praise shall continually be in my mouth."*
3. Hebrews 13:15 – *"By him therefore let us offer the sacrifice of praise to God continually, that is, the fruit of our lips giving thanks to his name."*
4. Exodus 30:8 – *"And when Aaron lighteth the lamps at even, he shall burn incense upon it, a perpetual incense before the LORD throughout your generations."*
5. II Chronicles 30:21 – *"And the children of Israel that were present at Jerusalem kept the feast of unleavened bread seven days with great gladness: and the Levites and the priests praised the LORD day by day, singing with loud instruments unto the LORD."*
6. Psalms 146:2 – *"While I live will I praise the LORD: I will sing praises unto my God while I have any being."*
7. Psalms 119:164 – *"Seven times a day do I praise thee because of thy righteous judgments."*
8. Psalms 72:15 – *"And he shall live, and to him shall be given of the gold of Sheba: prayer also shall be made for him continually; and daily shall he be praised."*

Lesson 41

The Noise Of The Tabernacle

In this lesson I want to, by the grace of God, with total dependence on the Holy Ghost, and God's exhaustive Word, reveal the principle of the sound of God. I am speaking of the sounds of heaven. Paul stated very clearly in I Corinthians 14:10 *"there are...many kinds of voices in the world, and none of them is without signification."* It is also true that there is a cacophony of sounds coming to us and surrounding us each day. Some sound emanates from satan our adversary, some just come from the world we live in, while other sounds are exploding in our minds. All of these sounds that we are bombarded with each moment of every day have a distinct purpose and have great meaning, either for good or bad. In the midst, however, of these sounds is the most glorious sound in the universe, the sound of our God and the sounds that radiate from His throne. These are the sounds we seek to define and come to hear and know.

"Deep calleth unto deep" Psalms 42:7 says. Are you listening? The Scriptures declare, *"Hear attentively the noise of his voice, and the sound that goeth out of his mouth. He directeth it under the whole heaven...God thundereth marvellously with his voice..."* (Job 37:2-5). Perhaps we need to be a little more attentive. In Job 33:14 it says, *"For God speaketh once, yea twice, yet man perceiveth it not."* Also in Job 36:29, *"Also can any understand the spreadings of the clouds, or the noise of his tabernacle?"* We will find many of these Scriptural passages coming from Job, because in Job 38:1 we find, *"Then the LORD answered Job out of the whirlwind, and said..."* Job needed the whirlwind of God and the voice that came out of it because he had temporarily forgotten who he was. One thing is for sure, God has no problem speaking, for *"the LORD shall cause his glorious voice to be heard..."* (Isaiah 30:30), and *"the LORD's voice crieth unto the city..."* (Micah 6:9). My prayer is that the Lord can use this lesson to help us hear *"the sound of a going in the mulberry trees"* (II Samuel 5:22-24); that we can experience the *"sound of a rushing mighty wind"* (Acts 2:1), and hear *"His voice as the sound of many waters"* (Revelation 1:13-15); most importantly though that we hear *"the sound of an abundance of rain"* (I Kings 8:41-46).

My greatest hope, prayer, and desire is that this lesson liberates you from any bondage brought about by Babylonish, lukewarm churches that seem more selfish and arrogant everyday. We want substance to triumph over style. We don't desire to be in situations where there is so-called worship and the noise is deafening. It is just sounding brass and tinkling cymbals. We desire however the real thing, God's true glorious presence. I pray the Lord instills in every one of us a zeal, a desire, and an unsatisfied heart that longs to know the real Jesus and to hear His sound. For the Word declares in Psalms 89:15, *"Blessed is the people that know the joyful sound: they shall walk, O LORD, in the light of thy countenance."* If this lesson can help you to hear, recognize, and respond to the sound of God, then it has served its purpose. It is important that we don't mistake the voice of God for simply thunder or an angel, but can discern the sound of God (John 12:28-29).

So as we begin, let us start with an unveiled (open) face as it relates to the Scripture and this principle. Let us give liberty to the Holy Ghost to teach, help, and enlighten us so we can for the rest of our lives hear and know God's sound coming out of heaven. Unlike Israel who when they heard His sound and saw His might, sinned and told Moses to go alone to *"the thick darkness where God was"* (Exodus 20:21). No, we will be looking and listening, always knowing that His voice is to be heard above every other voice. At our local churches, we will begin to tell everyone Jesus is in the house because it was *"noised that He was in the house"* (Mark 2:1).

May God open our ears to hear what the Spirit is saying to the church. As we do, we will be lifted to a new level of faith, hope, love, and worship because we hear God's joyful sound. We will be listening Lord. Please help us to hear the sound of God, whether it be the sound of a whirlwind, a blast of the trumpet, a still small voice, a voice of thunder, or a sound of a going in the mulberry trees. We then now not only believe, but promise to draw ever closer to you so that we can hear God's sound!

I. The Noise Of His Tabernacles - Job 36:29 – *"Also can any understand the spreadings of the clouds, or the noise of his tabernacle?"*

A. Other translations: *"or the thunderings of his pavilion"*, *"the thunder that rolls from heaven"*, *"how he speaks in thunder"*, *"or the crashes that come from his canopy"*, *"how he sends thunder from where he lives"*, *"how he thunders from his dwelling place"*

B. Hebrew definitions for Noise, *teshu'ah* – a crashing or loud clamor, crying, shouting, stir; it comes from a root word, *show* – to rush over, a tempest; that brings devastation, storm, destroy, wasteness.

   1. Psalms 50:3 – *"Our God shall come, and shall not keep silence: a fire shall devour before him, and it shall be very tempestuous round about him."* Tempestuous in Hebrew, *sa'ar* – a storm, to shiver, fear

C. Examples in scripture - God's house

   1. Ezra 3:10-13 – foundation laid for the temple
   2. Psalms 33:3 – *"Sing unto him a new song; play skilfully with a loud noise."*
   3. Psalms 66:1-2 – *"Make a joyful noise unto God, all ye lands: vs2 Sing forth the honour of his name: make his praise glorious."*
   4. Psalms 95:1-2 – *"1O come, let us sing unto the LORD: let us make a joyful noise to the rock of our salvation. 2Let us come before his presence with thanksgiving, and make a joyful noise unto him with psalms."*
   5. Psalms 100:1 – *"Make a joyful noise unto the LORD, all ye lands."*
   6. Psalms 84:1-4 – *"1How amiable are thy tabernacles, O Lord of hosts! 2My soul longeth, yea, even fainteth for the courts of the Lord: my heart and my flesh crieth out for the living God. 3Yea, the sparrow hath found an house, and the swallow a nest for herself, where she may lay her young, even thine altars, O Lord of hosts, my King, and my God. 4Blessed are they that dwell in thy house: they will be still praising thee. Selah."*
   7. Jeremiah 33:11 – *"The voice of joy, and the voice of gladness, the voice of the bridegroom, and the voice of the bride, the voice of them that shall say, Praise the LORD of hosts: for the LORD is good; for his mercy endureth for ever: and of them that shall bring the sacrifice of praise into the house of the LORD. For I will cause to return the captivity of the land, as at the first, saith the LORD."*
   8. Numbers 23:21 – *"He hath not beheld iniquity in Jacob, neither hath he seen perverseness in Israel: the LORD his God is with him, and the shout of a king is among them."*
   9. Luke 15:25 – *"Now his elder son was in the field: and as he came and drew nigh to the house, he heard musick and dancing."*
   10. Isaiah 66:5-6 – *"Hear the word of the LORD, ye that tremble at his word; your brethren that hated you, that cast you out for my name's sake, said, Let the LORD be glorified: but he shall appear to your joy, and they shall be ashamed. 6A voice of noise from the city, a voice from the temple, a voice of the LORD that rendereth recompence to his enemies."*
   11. Zechariah 9:12-17 – *"...make a noise as through wine..."*
   12. Mark 2:1 – *"And again he entered into Capernaum, after some days; and it was noised that he was in the house."*
   13. II Chronicles 5:11-14 – *"...one sound, glory fell on God's house..."*
   14. II Chronicles 30:21, 25-27 – Hezekiah restores Passover observance, *"...27priests the Levites arose and blessed the people: and their voice was heard, and their prayer came up to his holy dwelling place, even unto heaven."*
   15. Psalms 66:8 – *"O bless our God, ye people, and make the voice of his praise to be heard:"*
   16. Psalms 47:1-9 – *"...O clap your hands, all ye people; shout unto God with the voice of triumph..."*
   17. Psalms 132:7-9
   18. Isaiah 12:4-6 – In that day – *"Cry out and shout, thou inhabitant of Zion:"*
   19. Joel 3:16 – *"The LORD also shall roar out of Zion, and utter his voice from Jerusalem; and the heavens and the earth shall shake: but the LORD will be the hope of his people, and the strength of the children of Israel."*

20. Amos 3:7-8 – *"Surely the Lord GOD will do nothing, but he revealeth his secret unto his servants the prophets. [8]The lion hath roared, who will not fear? the Lord GOD hath spoken, who can but prophesy?"*
21. Psalms 150:1-6 – *"let everything that hath breath"*
22. Psalms 149:1-9 – *"let them praise"*

D. His noise elsewhere in Scripture:

1. Psalms 42:7 –*"Deep calleth unto deep at the noise of thy waterspouts: all thy waves and thy billows are gone over me."*
2. Revelation 5:8-14
3. Psalms 118:15 – *"The voice of rejoicing and salvation is in the tabernacles of the righteous: the right hand of the LORD doeth valiantly."*
4. Psalms 29:9 – *"The voice of the LORD maketh the hinds to calve, and discovereth the forests: and in his temple doth every one speak of his glory."*
5. Revelation 11:19 – *"And the temple of God was opened in heaven, and there was seen in his temple the ark of his testament: and there were lightnings, and voices, and thunderings, and an earthquake, and great hail."*
6. II Samuel 6:15-17 – *"[15]So David and all the house of Israel brought up the ark of the LORD with shouting, and with the sound of the trumpet..."*
7. Psalms 89:15 – *"Blessed is the people that know the joyful sound: they shall walk, O LORD, in the light of thy countenance."*
8. Ezekiel 10:1-5 – *"...sound heard even to the outer court..."*
9. Psalms 63:1-8 – *"To see thy power and thy glory, so as I have seen thee in the sanctuary."*
10. Isaiah 6:1-5 – *"...[3]And one cried unto another, and said, Holy, holy, holy, is the LORD of hosts: the whole earth is full of his glory. [4]And the posts of the door moved at the voice of him that cried, and the house was filled with smoke..."*

II. The Voice Of The Lord Walking, Genesis 3:8 – *"And they heard the voice of the LORD God walking in the garden in the cool of the day: and Adam and his wife hid themselves from the presence of the LORD God amongst the trees of the garden."*

A. Other translations: *"They heard the sound of the Lord walking in the garden...walking up and down"*, *"when they heard the sound of God strolling in the garden in the evening breeze"*, *"And when they heard the voice of the Lord God walking in paradise in the afternoon air"*

B. Word definitions in Hebrew

1. Voice, *qowl* – to call aloud, a voice or sound
2. Walking, *halak* – to walk literally or figuratively, to rest comfortably with. Elsewhere this same Hebrew word is used:

   a. Genesis 5:22-24 – Enoch walked with God and was not
   b. Genesis 6:9 – *"These are the generations of Noah: Noah was a just man and perfect in his generations, and Noah walked with God."*
   c. Genesis 17:1 – *"And when Abram was ninety years old and nine, the LORD appeared to Abram, and said unto him, I am the Almighty God; walk before me, and be thou perfect."*
   d. Exodus 33:14 – *"And he said, My presence shall go with thee, and I will give thee rest."*

3. Garden, *gan* – a garden as fenced; it comes from the root word, *ganan* – to hedge about, to protect or defend
4. Cool, *ruwach* – wind, breath, a sensible or violent exhalation, life, spirit; it comes from a root word, *ruwach* – to blow, breathe, smell, perceive, anticipate, enjoy. This is the same Hebrew

word translated "*Spirit*" in the Old Testament (example, Genesis 1:2 – "*And the Spirit of God moved upon the face of the waters.*")

5. Eden – pleasure, delight; it comes from a root word meaning – to be soft or pleasant, to live voluptuously, delicate

C. God's Garden is our Soul – He wants to come into our garden

1. Song of Solomon 8:13 – "*Thou that dwellest in the gardens, the companions hearken to thy voice: cause me to hear it.*"
2. Song of Solomon 4:12-16 – "*12A garden inclosed is my sister, my spouse; a spring shut up, a fountain sealed. 13Thy plants are an orchard of pomegranates, with pleasant fruits; camphire, with spikenard, 14Spikenard and saffron; calamus and cinnamon, with all trees of frankincense; myrrh and aloes, with all the chief spices: 15A fountain of gardens, a well of living waters, and streams from Lebanon. 16Awake, O north wind; and come, thou south; blow upon my garden, that the spices thereof may flow out. Let my beloved come into his garden, and eat his pleasant fruits.*"
3. Song of Solomon 5:1-9 – "*I am come into my garden*" – He comes, she rejects
4. Genesis 2:8 – "*And the LORD God planted a garden eastward in Eden; and there he put the man whom he had formed.*"
5. Song of Solomon 6:2-3 – "*2My beloved is gone down into his garden, to the beds of spices, to feed in the gardens, and to gather lilies. 3I am my beloved's, and my beloved is mine: he feedeth among the lilies.*"
6. Song of Solomon 6:8-13 – the Bride's garden

D. He will restore our ability that was lost

1. Isaiah 51:3 – "*For the LORD shall comfort Zion: he will comfort all her waste places; and he will make her wilderness like Eden, and her desert like the garden of the LORD; joy and gladness shall be found therein, thanksgiving, and the voice of melody.*"
2. Jeremiah 31:10-14
3. Ezekiel 36:33-35
4. Joel 2:3 – "*A fire devoureth before them; and behind them a flame burneth: the land is as the garden of Eden before them, and behind them a desolate wilderness; yea, and nothing shall escape them.*"

E. Can We Hear Him?

1. Job 37:2 – "*Hear attentively the noise of his voice, and the sound that goeth out of his mouth.*"
2. Psalms 89:15 – "*Blessed is the people that know the joyful sound: they shall walk, O LORD, in the light of thy countenance.*"
3. Revelation 10:7 – "*But in the days of the voice of the seventh angel, when he shall begin to sound, the mystery of God should be finished, as he hath declared to his servants the prophets.*"
4. Isaiah 46:10 – "*Declaring the end from the beginning, and from ancient times the things that are not yet done, saying, My counsel shall stand, and I will do all my pleasure:*"
5. I Kings 19:11-13
6. Psalms 95:7 – "*For he is our God; and we are the people of his pasture, and the sheep of his hand. To day if ye will hear his voice,*"
7. Proverbs 8:1-10 – wisdom cries out (Proverbs 1:20 – "*Wisdom crieth without; she uttereth her voice in the streets:*")
8. Song of Solomon 2:8-12

III. Sound Of An Abundance Of Rain

A. I Kings 18:41 – "*And Elijah said unto Ahab, Get thee up, eat and drink; for there is a sound of abundance of rain.*"

1. Other translations: "*the sound of the noise of a heavy shower*", "*I hear a mighty rain storm coming*", "*the sound of the rushing of rain*", "*the sound of a heavy rain storm can be heard*", "*the sound of the roar of a heavy shower*", "*I hear the roar of rain approaching*".

    a. Joel 2:23, 28 – "*[23]Be glad then, ye children of Zion, and rejoice in the LORD your God: for he hath given you the former rain moderately, and he will cause to come down for you the rain, the former rain, and the latter rain in the first month...[28]And it shall come to pass afterward, that I will pour out my spirit upon all flesh; and your sons and your daughters shall prophesy, your old men shall dream dreams, your young men shall see visions:*"
    b. Acts 2:1-2 – "*[1]And when the day of Pentecost was fully come, they were all with one accord in one place. [2]And suddenly there came <u>a sound from heaven</u> as of a rushing mighty wind, and it filled all the house where they were sitting.*"
    c. Psalms 42:7 – "*Deep calleth unto deep at the <u>noise of thy waterspouts</u>: all thy waves and thy billows are gone over me.*"
    d. II Samuel 5:22-25 – "*[22]And the Philistines came up yet again, and spread themselves in the valley of Rephaim. [23]And when David inquired of the LORD, he said, Thou shalt not go up; but fetch a compass behind them, and come upon them over against the mulberry trees. [24]And let it be, when thou hearest the sound of a going in the tops of the mulberry trees, that then thou shalt bestir thyself: for then shall the LORD go out before thee, to smite the host of the Philistines. [25]And David did so, as the LORD had commanded him; and smote the Philistines from Geba until thou come to Gazer.*"

B. Story of Elijah – Type of last days prophetic company prophesying God's rain

1. James 5:17-18 – "*[17]Elias was a man subject to like passions as we are, and he prayed earnestly that it might not rain: and it rained not on the earth by the space of three years and six months. [18]And he prayed again, and the heaven gave rain, and the earth brought forth her fruit.*"
2. Psalms 89:15 – "*Blessed is the people that know the joyful sound: they shall walk, O LORD, in the light of thy countenance.*"
2. Revelation 11:3-6
3. Ezekiel 37:1-10
4. I Kings 18:24 – The God that answers by fire.

IV. The Voice Of Thunder, Job 40:9 – "*Hast thou an arm like God? or canst thou thunder with a voice like him?*"

A. Other Translations: "*and can you thunder with a voice like His?*", "*Can you shout as loudly as He?*", "*have you a voice of thunder like His*", "*Can your voice thunder as loud as mine?*"

B. Word definitions of thunder

1. Hebrew words

    a. *Ra'am* – to tumble, be violently agitated, to crash, to irritate with anger, to roar, make to fret, trouble
    b. *Qowl* – to call aloud by voice or sound, to cry out, to proclaim; this is the same Hebrew word translated "*voice*"

2. Greek word, *bronte* – to roar

C. Examples in Scripture of God's thundering voice

1. Job 37:2-5 – "*[2]Hear attentively the noise of his voice, and the sound that goeth out of his mouth. [3]He directeth it under the whole heaven, and his lightning unto the ends of the earth. [4]After it a*

voice roareth: he thundereth with the voice of his excellency; and he will not stay them when his voice is heard. 5God thundereth marvellously with his voice; great things doeth he, which we cannot comprehend."

a. Two kinds of His voice, Revelation 1:13-16 – "*...out of his mouth went a sharp twoedged sword...*" – The two-edged sword represents both the lion and the lamb nature of His voice:

1) God's voice as thunder

a) Hosea 6:5 – "*Therefore have I hewed them by the prophets; I have slain them by the words of my mouth: and thy judgments are as the light that goeth forth.*"
b) II Thessalonians 2:8 – "*And then shall that Wicked be revealed, whom the Lord shall consume with the spirit of his mouth, and shall destroy with the brightness of his coming:*"
c) Revelation 19:15 – "*And out of his mouth goeth a sharp sword, that with it he should smite the nations: and he shall rule them with a rod of iron: and he treadeth the winepress of the fierceness and wrath of Almighty God.*"
d) Psalms 46:6 – "*The heathen raged, the kingdoms were moved: he uttered his voice, the earth melted.*"

2) God's voice as a still small voice

a) I Kings 19:12 – "*And after the earthquake a fire; but the LORD was not in the fire: and after the fire a still small voice.*"
b) Song of Solomon 5:16 – "*His mouth is most sweet: yea, he is altogether lovely. This is my beloved, and this is my friend, O daughters of Jerusalem.*"

3) Examples of both

a) Deuteronomy 32:1-3 – rain or dew
b) Lamentations 3:38 – "*Out of the mouth of the most High proceedeth not evil and good?*"

2. Psalms 29:3-5 – "*3The voice of the LORD is upon the waters: the God of glory thundereth: the LORD is upon many waters. 4The voice of the LORD is powerful; the voice of the LORD is full of majesty. 5The voice of the LORD breaketh the cedars; yea, the LORD breaketh the cedars of Lebanon.*"

a. His voice will get the job done, Isaiah 55:11 – "*So shall my word be that goeth forth out of my mouth: it shall not return unto me void, but it shall accomplish that which I please, and it shall prosper in the thing whereto I sent it.*"

3. Revelation 4:2-5 – Voice from the throne, "*And out of the throne proceeded lightnings and thunderings and voices:* "

a. Revelation 11:19 – "*And the temple of God was opened in heaven, and there was seen in his temple the ark of his testament: and there were lightnings, and voices, and thunderings, and an earthquake, and great hail.*"

4. I Samuel 7:10 – "*And as Samuel was offering up the burnt offering, the Philistines drew near to battle against Israel: but the LORD thundered with a great thunder on that day upon the Philistines, and discomfited them; and they were smitten before Israel.*"

a. II Samuel 22:7-16 – "*...The Lord thundered from heaven, and the most High uttered his voice...*"

5. His voice as seen by those that don't walk with him

    a. Exodus 19:16-20, 20:18-21
    b. John 12:28-30 – some said it thundered

6. Psalms 77:18 – "*The voice of thy thunder was in the heaven: the lightnings lightened the world: the earth trembled and shook.*" – Brings revelation
7. Psalms 81:7 – "*Thou calledst in trouble, and I delivered thee; I answered thee in the secret place of thunder: I proved thee at the waters of Meribah. Selah.*" From His throne (the secret place) He speaks and deliverance comes
8. Revelation 6:1 – "*And I saw when the Lamb opened one of the seals, and I heard, as it were the noise of thunder, one of the four beasts saying, Come and see.*" This is the opening of the seven sealed book – Word of God
9. Revelation 14:2 – "*And I heard a voice from heaven, as the voice of many waters, and as the voice of a great thunder: and I heard the voice of harpers harping with their harps:*" – He speaks and worship ensues (Revelation 4:2; 5-11)
10. Deuteronomy 4:33-39 – He thunders so he can instruct us, and because he loves us.

11. Psalms 68:33 – "*To him that rideth upon the heavens of heavens, which were of old; lo, he doth send out his voice, and that a mighty voice.*" His mighty voice:

    a. Psalms 29:2-10
    b. Isaiah 30:30 – "*And the LORD shall cause his glorious voice to be heard, and shall shew the lighting down of his arm, with the indignation of his anger, and with the flame of a devouring fire, with scattering, and tempest, and hailstones.*"

V. Sound Of A Going, II Samuel 5:22-25 – "[22]*And the Philistines came up yet again, and spread themselves in the valley of Rephaim.* [23]*And when David inquired of the LORD, he said, Thou shalt not go up; but fetch a compass behind them, and come upon them over against the mulberry trees.* [24]*And let it be, when thou hearest <u>the sound of a going</u> in the tops of the mulberry trees, that then thou shalt bestir thyself: for then shall the LORD go out before thee, to smite the host of the Philistines.* [25]*And David did so, as the LORD had commanded him; and smote the Philistines from Geba until thou come to Gazer.*"

A. Other Translations of verse 24:

"The sound of marching"
"In thy hearing the sound of a stepping"
"hear a sound of marching feet"
"the sound of shuffling in the trees, get ready to move, it's a signal, God is going ahead of you to smash the Philistines"
"at the sound of footsteps"
"then you shall act promptly"
"move quickly"

B. Gods Heavenly Army Fights For Us

1. II Kings 7:3-8 – "*...a noise of chariots...*" – Other translations:

"For the Lord had made thy Syrians army hear of chariots and horses, the noise of a great army",
"noise of a great force"
"The Master had made the army hear the sound of horses and a mighty army on the march"
"to hear the clatter of speeding chariots, and the galloping of horses and the sounds of a great army approaching"

a. His Army

1) Job 25:2-3 – "[2]*Dominion and fear are with him, he maketh peace in his high places.* [3]*Is there any number of his armies? and upon whom doth not his light arise?"*
2) Revelation 19:14 – *"And the armies which were in heaven followed him upon white horses, clothed in fine linen, white and clean."*
3) Psalms 24:10 – *"Who is this King of glory? The LORD of hosts, he is the King of glory. Selah."* Hebrew for host, *tsaba* – a mass of persons organized for war, soldiers waiting upon war; Other translations: *"The Lord of heavens armies", "God of the angel armies", "The commander of all of heavens armies"*
4) Psalms 110:3 – *"Thy people shall be willing in the day of thy power, in the beauties of holiness from the womb of the morning: thou hast the dew of thy youth."*

2. II Chronicles 20:1, 4, 18, 22 – *"the LORD set ambushments, and they were smitten*
3. Exodus 14:14-27 – Moses

C. He Fights For Us

1. Deuteronomy 1:30 – *"The LORD your God which goeth before you, he shall fight for you, according to all that he did for you in Egypt before your eyes;"*
2. Deuteronomy 3:22 – *"Ye shall not fear them: for the LORD your God he shall fight for you."*
3. Deuteronomy 20:1-4
4. Psalms 103:20-22
5 Deuteronomy 33:26-27
6. Daniel 4:35 – *"And all the inhabitants of the earth are reputed as nothing: and he doeth according to his will in the army of heaven, and among the inhabitants of the earth: and none can stay his hand, or say unto him, What doest thou?"*

D. Mahanaim, Genesis 32:1-2 – *"And Jacob went on his way, and the angels of God met him.* [vs2] *And when Jacob saw them, he said, This is God's host: and he called the name of that place Mahanaim."*

VI. Discerning God's Sound, Song of Solomon 8:13 – *"Thou that dwellest in the gardens, the companions hearken to thy voice: cause me to hear it."*

A. Discerning the Voice of God

1. I Corinthians 14:10 – *"There are, it may be, so many <u>kinds of voices</u> in the world, and none of them is without signification."*

a. Job 36:29 – *"Also can any understand the spreadings of the clouds, or the noise of his tabernacle?"*
b. Job 37:2 – *"Hear attentively the noise of his voice, and the sound that goeth out of his mouth."*
c. Micah 6:9 – *"The LORD's voice crieth unto the city, and the man of wisdom shall see thy name: hear ye the rod, and who hath appointed it."*
d. Isaiah 45:19 – *"I have not spoken in secret, in a dark place of the earth: I said not unto the seed of Jacob, Seek ye me in vain: I the LORD speak righteousness, I declare things that are right."*
e. Isaiah 30:30 – *"And the LORD shall cause his glorious voice to be heard, and shall shew the lighting down of his arm, with the indignation of his anger, and with the flame of a devouring fire, with scattering, and tempest, and hailstones."*
f. Jeremiah 25:30 – *"Therefore prophesy thou against them all these words, and say unto them, The LORD shall roar from on high, and utter his voice from his holy habitation; he shall*

mightily roar upon his habitation; he shall give a shout, as they that tread the grapes, against all the inhabitants of the earth."

g. Job 40:9- *"Hast thou an arm like God? or canst thou <u>thunder</u> with a voice like him?"*

2. Psalms 89:15 – *"<u>Blessed is the people that know</u> the joyful sound: they shall walk, O LORD, in the light of thy countenance."*

3. Psalms 42:7 – *"<u>Deep calleth unto deep</u> at the noise of thy waterspouts: all thy waves and thy billows are gone over me."*

B. Some Examples in Scripture of Discerning and Not Discerning

1. Didn't Discern

a. Job 33:14 – *"For God speaketh once, yea twice, yet man perceiveth it not."*
b. Amos 8:11 – *"Behold, the days come, saith the Lord GOD, that I will send a famine in the land, not a famine of bread, nor a thirst for water, but of hearing the words of the LORD"*
c. I Corinthians 3:1-11 – *"...could not speak unto you as unto spiritual..."*
d. Hebrews 5:11-14 – *"...dull of hearing..."*

2. Examples in Scripture

a. I Samuel 3:3-11 – Samuel and Eli when the Lord was trying to speak to Samuel
b. Genesis 27:20-28 – *"...22And Jacob went near unto Isaac his father; and he felt him, and said, The voice is Jacob's voice, but the hands are the hands of Esau..."*
c. John 12:29 – *"29The people therefore, that stood by, and heard it, said that it thundered: others said, An angel spake to him."*
d. John 21:1-7 – The disciples didn't discern it was Jesus on the shore.
e. John 20:11-18 – Mary didn't discern it was Jesus at the sepulchre.
f. Luke 24:13 – On the way to Emmaus

C. Hearing His Sound – How We Can

1. John 7:46 – *"The officers answered, <u>Never man spake like this man</u>."*
2. Hebrews 1:2 – *"Hath in these last days <u>spoken unto us by his Son</u>, whom he hath appointed heir of all things, by whom also he made the worlds;"*
3. Joel 2:11 – *"And the LORD shall utter his* voice before his army*: for his camp is very great: for he is strong that executeth his word: for the day of the LORD is great and very terrible; and who can abide it?"*
4. Psalms 108:7 –*"God hath <u>spoken in his holiness</u>; I will rejoice, I will divide Shechem, and mete out the valley of Succoth."*
5. John 6:63 – *"It is the spirit that quickeneth; the flesh profiteth nothing: <u>the words that I speak unto you, they are spirit, and they are life."</u>*
6. II Peter 1:17-18 – *"such a <u>voice from the excellent glory</u>."* – Glory Cloud
7. John 10:27 – *"<u>My sheep hear my voice,</u> and I <u>know them</u>, and they <u>follow me</u>:"*

8. Luke 1:39-44 – babe leaped in her womb – <u>witness of the Spirit</u>

a. I John 2:20-27 – *"But ye have an unction from the Holy One, and ye know all things."*
b. Luke 24:32
c. Genesis 2:7 – *"breathed into his nostrils the breath of life;"*
d. Job 32:8 – *"But there is a spirit in man: and the inspiration of the Almighty giveth them understanding."*

9. Deuteronomy 5:4 – "*The LORD talked with you face to face in the mount out of the midst of the fire,*"
10. Genesis 17:3 – "*And Abram fell on his face: and God talked with him, saying,*"
11. John 18:37 – "*Pilate therefore said unto him, Art thou a king then? Jesus answered, Thou sayest that I am a king. To this end was I born, and for this cause came I into the world, that I should bear witness unto the truth. Every one that is of the truth heareth my voice.*"
12. Revelation 1:10-12 – "*I was in the Spirit on the Lord's day, and heard behind me a great voice, as of a trumpet,*"
13. Revelation 3:20 – "*Behold, I stand at the door, and knock: if any man hear my voice,*"
14. Psalms 85:8 – "*I will hear what God the LORD will speak: for he will speak peace unto his people, and to his saints: but let them not turn again to folly.*"
15. Jeremiah 7:23 – "*But this thing commanded I them, saying, Obey my voice, and I will be your God, and ye shall be my people: and walk ye in all the ways that I have commanded you, that it may be well unto you.*"
16. James 3:17 – "*But the wisdom that is from above is first pure, then peaceable, gentle, and easy to be intreated, full of mercy and good fruits, without partiality, and without hypocrisy.*"
17. Hebrews 12:25 – "*See that ye refuse not him that speaketh. For if they escaped not who refused him that spake on earth, much more shall not we escape, if we turn away from him that speaketh from heaven*"
18. I Kings 19:12-13 – Still Small Voice

VII. Still Small Voice, I Kings 19:11-13 – "*[11]And he said, Go forth, and stand upon the mount before the LORD. And, behold, the LORD passed by, and a great and strong wind rent the mountains, and brake in pieces the rocks before the LORD; but the LORD was not in the wind: and after the wind an earthquake; but the LORD was not in the earthquake: [12]And after the earthquake a fire; but the LORD was not in the fire: and after the fire a still small voice. [13]And it was so, when Elijah heard it, that he wrapped his face in his mantle, and went out, and stood in the entering in of the cave. And, behold, there came a voice unto him, and said, What doest thou here, Elijah?*"

A. Hebrew word definitions for Still

1. *Demamah* – quiet, calm, silence
2. *Menuwchah* – repose or peacefully, consolation, ease, comfortable, quiet, rest
3. *Raphah* – to slacken, to abate, to cease, draw toward evening, fain
4. *Shebeth* – rest, cessation, sit still; it comes from a root, *shabath* – to repose
5. *Yatsob* – to place anything so as to stay, desist from exertion

B. Examples in Scripture

1. Psalms 46:10 – "*Be still, and know that I am God: I will be exalted among the heathen, I will be exalted in the earth.*"
2. There is a time to be still.

a. Ecclesiastes 3:7 – "*A time to rend, and a time to sew; a time to keep silence, and a time to speak;*"
b. Exodus 14:13-14 – "*[13]And Moses said unto the people, Fear ye not, stand still, and see the salvation of the LORD, which he will shew to you to day: for the Egyptians whom ye have seen to day, ye shall see them again no more for ever. [14]The LORD shall fight for you, and ye shall hold your peace.*"
c. I Samuel 9:27 – "*And as they were going down to the end of the city, Samuel said to Saul, Bid the servant pass on before us, (and he passed on,) but stand thou still a while, that I may shew thee the word of God.*"
d. I Samuel 12:7 – "*Now therefore stand still, that I may reason with you before the LORD of all the righteous acts of the LORD, which he did to you and to your fathers.*"

e. Psalms 23:1-3 – "[1]*The LORD is my shepherd; I shall not want.* [2]*He maketh me to lie down in green pastures: he leadeth me beside the still waters.* [3]*He restoreth my soul: he leadeth me in the paths of righteousness for his name's sake.*"

3. Matthew 12:17-21 – "...[19]*He shall not strive, nor cry; neither shall any man hear his voice in the streets...*" – God speaks to our spirits.

    a. Proverbs 20:27 – "*The spirit of man is the candle of the LORD, searching all the inward parts of the belly.*"
    b. I John 5:10 – "*He that believeth on the Son of God hath the witness in himself: he that believeth not God hath made him a liar; because he believeth not the record that God gave of his Son.*"
    c. I Corinthians 6:17 – "*But he that is joined unto the Lord is one spirit.*"
    d. Job 32:8 – "*But there is a spirit in man: and the inspiration of the Almighty giveth them understanding.*"
    e. I Corinthians 2:9-12
    f. Job 36:9 – "*Then he sheweth them their work, and their transgressions that they have exceeded.*"
    g. Job 6:13 – "*Is not my help in me? and is wisdom driven quite from me?*"
    h. I John 2:20 – "*But ye have an unction from the Holy One, and ye know all things.*"
    i. I John 2:27 – "*But the anointing which ye have received of him abideth in you, and ye need not that any man teach you: but as the same anointing teacheth you of all things, and is truth, and is no lie, and even as it hath taught you, ye shall abide in him.*"
    j. Luke 24:32 – "*And they said one to another, Did not our heart burn within us, while he talked with us by the way, and while he opened to us the scriptures?*"
    k. Luke 1:39-44
    l. John 14:23 – "*Jesus answered and said unto him, If a man love me, he will keep my words: and my Father will love him, and we will come unto him, and make our abode with him.*"

4. James 3:17 – "*But the wisdom that is from above is first pure, then peaceable, gentle, and easy to be intreated, full of mercy and good fruits, without partiality, and without hypocrisy.*"

    a. Isaiah 32:17-18 – "*work of righteousness shall be peace;...*"
    b. Isaiah 30:15 – "*For thus saith the Lord GOD, the Holy One of Israel; In returning and rest shall ye be saved; in quietness and in confidence shall be your strength: and ye would not.*"
    c. Proverbs 1:33 – "*But whoso hearkeneth unto me shall dwell safely, and shall be quiet from fear of evil.*"
    d. Ecclesiastes 9:7 – "*Go thy way, eat thy bread with joy, and drink thy wine with a merry heart; for God now accepteth thy works.*"
    e. I Thessalonians 4:11 –"*And that ye study to be quiet, and to do your own business, and to work with your own hands, as we commanded you;*"
    f. James 1:19 – "*Wherefore, my beloved brethren, let every man be swift to hear, slow to speak, slow to wrath:*"
    g. Job 37:2 –"*Hear attentively the noise of his voice, and the sound that goeth out of his mouth.*"
    h. Isaiah 30:7 – "*For the Egyptians shall help in vain, and to no purpose: therefore have I cried concerning this, Their strength is to sit still.*"

VIII. Sound Of A Trumpet, Psalms 47:5 – "*God is gone up with a shout, the LORD with the sound of a trumpet.*"

A. Other Translations: "*God has ascended with a mighty shout. The Lord has ascended with trumpets blaring*", "*God goes up to shouts of acclaim, Adonai to a blast on the shofar*", "*...amid the blaring of ram's horns*", "*There are shouts of joy and the blast of trumpets as the Lord goes up*"

B. Examples in Scripture

1. Hebrews 12:18-24

    a. Exodus 19:16-20
    b. Exodus 20:18-21

2. Joshua 6:1-5, 20 – Walls of Jericho
3. Judges 7:16-22 – Gideons three hundred
4. II Samuel 6:15-18 – *"brought up the ark of the Lord with shouting and with the sound of the trumpet"*
5. Nehemiah 4:16-20 – building the wall, *"when ye hear the sound of the trumpet, resort ye thither unto us: our God shall fight for us"*
6. Joel 2:1 – *"Blow ye the trumpet in Zion, and sound an alarm in my holy mountain: let all the inhabitants of the land tremble: for the day of the LORD cometh, for it is nigh at hand;"*
7. Zechariah 9:12-17 – the Lord God shall blow the trumpet
8. Revelation 1:10-13 – *"I was in the Spirit on the Lord's day, and heard behind me a great voice, as of a trumpet,"*
9. Revelation 4:1 – *"After this I looked, and, behold, a door was opened in heaven: and the first voice which I heard was as it were of a trumpet talking with me; which said, Come up hither, and I will shew thee things which must be hereafter."*
10. Numbers 10:1-6 – blowing an alarm or trumpet for the calling of the assembly, and for the journeys.
11. Numbers 10:9-10 - if ye go to war then shall ye blow an alarm with trumpets
12. I Corinthians 15:51-57 – at the last trumpet call
13. I Thessalonians 4:15-18 – *"Lord himself shall descend from heaven with a shout...and with the trumpet of God"*

IX. Voice Out Of The Whirlwind, Job 38:1 – *"Then the LORD answered Job out of the whirlwind, and said,"*

A. Other translations: *"out of the storm"*, *"out of the storm wind"*, *"and now, finally God answered Job from the eye of a violent storm"*,

    1. Job 40:6 – *"Then answered the LORD unto Job out of the whirlwind, and said,"*

B. Hebrew word definitions for whirlwind

    1. *Ca'ar* – a hurricane, storm, tempest; it comes from the root, *ca' ar* – to rush upon, to toss, tossed with tempest, sore trouble, to scatter with
    2. *Cuwphah* – a hurricane, storm, tempest, Red Sea; it comes from the root, *cuwph* – to snatch away, terminate, consume, have an end to perish utterly.
    3. *Ruwach* – wind, breath; same word translated Spirit

C. Examples of His voice in the whirlwind

    1. Ezekiel 1:3-4; 24-28
    2. Nahum 1:3-7 - the Lord hath His way in the whirlwind
    3. II Samuel 22:11-14 – wings of the wind – thundered from heaven – Most High voice
    4. Isaiah 30:27-31
    5. Psalms 50:3 – *"very tempestuous round about him"*.

        a. Isaiah 29:6 – *"Thou shalt be visited of the LORD of hosts with thunder, and with earthquake, and great noise, with storm and tempest, and the flame of devouring fire."*

D. God's whirlwind - He controls the storm

1. Psalms 107:24-31
2. Psalms 148:8 – "*Fire, and hail; snow, and vapour; stormy wind fulfilling his word:*"

E. He uses the whirlwind to teach us

1. Jonah 1:1-4
2. Song of Solomon 4:16 – "*Awake, O north wind; and come, thou south; blow upon my garden, that the spices thereof may flow out. Let my beloved come into his garden, and eat his pleasant fruits.*"
3. Zechariah 7:8-14 – Dealings of God
4. Mark 4:35-41
5. Hosea 13:1-4
6. Hosea 8:1-14

F. One day like Elijah the whirlwind will carry us to Glory

1. II Kings 2:1; 11
2. Job 37:9 – "*Out of the south cometh the whirlwind: and cold out of the north.*"

G. The remnant and the whirlwind

1. Isaiah 41:10-16 – a new sharp threshing instrument
2. Isaiah 32:2 – "*And a man shall be as an hiding place from the wind, and a covert from the tempest; as rivers of water in a dry place, as the shadow of a great rock in a weary land.*"

H. The whirlwind related to God's judgment on the wicked

1. Isaiah 40:21-25
2. Isaiah 66:12-16
3. Jeremiah 23:19-20
4. Jeremiah 30:23-24

X. Voice Out Of The Excellent Glory – Voice Out Of The Cloud, Exodus 24:15-18 – "*[15]And Moses went up into the mount, and a cloud covered the mount. [16]And the glory of the LORD abode upon mount Sinai, and the cloud covered it six days: and the seventh day he called unto Moses out of the midst of the cloud. [17]And the sight of the glory of the LORD was like devouring fire on the top of the mount in the eyes of the children of Israel. [18]And Moses went into the midst of the cloud, and gat him up into the mount: and Moses was in the mount forty days and forty nights.*"

A. Example in Scripture

1. Exodus 19:9 – "*And the LORD said unto Moses, Lo, I come unto thee in a thick cloud, that the people may hear when I speak with thee, and believe thee for ever. And Moses told the words of the people unto the LORD.*"
2. Exodus 34:5-8 – "*the LORD descended in the cloud, and stood with him there, and proclaimed the name of the LORD.*"
3. Numbers 11:24-25 – "*And the LORD came down in a cloud, and spake unto him,*"
4. Numbers 12:-10 – "*God calls Moses, Miriam and Aaron out of the cloud*"
5. Ezekiel 1:4; 25-28 – "*God speaking out of the cloud of Glory*"
6. Matthew 17:1-5 – [vs.5]"*behold, a bright cloud overshadowed them: and behold a voice out of the cloud, which said, This is my beloved Son, in whom I am well pleased; hear ye him.*"

a. Luke 9:28-36 – they feared as they entered into the cloud

b. II Peter 1:16-18 – *"there came such a voice to him from the excellent glory"*

7. Ezekiel 10:1-7 – *"...[4]Then the glory of the LORD went up from the cherub, and stood over the threshold of the house; and the house was filled with the cloud, and the court was full of the brightness of the LORD's glory. [5]And the sound of the cherubims' wings was heard even to the outer court, as the voice of the Almighty God when he speaketh..."*

B. God's Cloud of Glory

1. Exodus 13:21-22 – *"[21]And the LORD went before them by day in a pillar of a cloud, to lead them the way; and by night in a pillar of fire, to give them light; to go by day and night: [22]He took not away the pillar of the cloud by day, nor the pillar of fire by night, from before the people."* The cloud leads us.
2. The cloud separates us from the world, Exodus 14:19-20; 24
3. It will be there to catch us up at the end times – I Thessalonians 4:17, Isaiah 60:8
4. Revelation 10:1 – last day company clothed with a cloud
5. Sign of him pouring out his glory – I Kings 18:44
6. Psalms 105:39 – *"He spread a cloud for a covering"*
7. Proverbs 16:15 – It is the favour of God.
8. Isaiah 4:5 – It is our defence (Zechariah 2:5 wall of fire).
9. II Chronicles 5:10-13 – sign of the last great move of God
10. Job 26:9 – His throne is coved by it.

C. II Peter 1:17 – *"For he received from God the Father honour and glory, when there came such a voice to him from the excellent glory, This is my beloved Son, in whom I am well pleased."* Other translations:

"and a voice was borne to him by the splendid Majestic Glory in the bright cloud that over shadowed him...", "such an utterance as this was made to him by the Majestic Glory", "we saw it with our own eyes: Jesus resplendent with light from God the Father as the voice of Majestic Glory spoke. This is my Son, marked by my love, the focus of all my delight", "and the voice that come to him from the grandeur of the Sh'khinah saying...", "but we saw the greatness of Jesus with our own eyes. Jesus heard the voice of God, the greatest glory, when he received honor and glory from God the Father. The voice said "This is my Son whom I Love, and I am very pleased with Him.", "when the voice of our Majestic God spoke those word to him", "I was there on the holy mountain when he shone out with honor given him by God his Father; I heard that glorious, majestic voice calling down from heaven, saying, "This is my much-loved Son; I am well pleased with him.", "when such a voice come to him out of the great glory saying...", "out of the wonderous glory..."when the voice come to him from the supreme glory"

1. Excellent in Greek, *megaloprepes*; befitting greatness or magnificence, majestic; this is the only place in Scripture this word is found; it comes from 2 roots words: 1) *megas* – exceedingly great, high, large, loud, mighty, strong, & 2) *prepo* – to tower up, to be suitable or proper, to become comely
2. Job 37:23 – *"Touching the Almighty, we cannot find him out: he is excellent in power, and in judgment, and in plenty of justice: he will not afflict.*
3. Psalms 76:4 – *"Thou art more glorious and excellent than the mountains of prey."*
4. Psalms 148:13 – *"Let them praise the name of the LORD: for his name alone is excellent; his glory is above the earth and heaven."*
5. Psalms 150:2 – *"Praise him for his mighty acts: praise him according to his excellent greatness."*
6. Isaiah 28:29 – *"This also cometh forth from the LORD of hosts, which is wonderful in counsel, and excellent in working."*

XI. Voice From Off The Mercy Seat, Exodus 25:22 – *"And there I will meet with thee, and I will commune with thee from above the mercy seat, from between the two cherubims which are upon the ark of the testimony, of all things which I will give thee in commandment unto the children of Israel."*

A. Commune in Hebrew, *dabar* – to properly arrange words, to speak, answer
B. Other translations: *"I will meet you there and talk to you from above the atonement cover", "I will speak intimately with you", "have spoken with thee from off the mercy seat", "I will meet with you there at set times and speak with you from above the....", "I will come to you, face to face, and make clear to you all the orders I have to give...", "there I will meet with you, and I will tell you from above the mercy seat..."*

C. Other Scriptures showing His voice from the Mercy Seat

1. Numbers 7:89 – *"And when Moses was gone into the tabernacle of the congregation to speak with him, then he heard the voice of one speaking unto him from off the mercy seat that was upon the ark of testimony, from between the two cherubims: and he spake unto him."* Other translations:

"he heard the voice speaking to him from above the mercy seat"
"the voice was coming from between the two gold creatures with wings that were above the..."
"he heard the voice speaking to him from above the throne of mercy on the ark conntaining the words of God's promise..."
"then the voice come to his ears from over the cover which was on the ark of witness."
"he heard the Lord speaking to him from above the lid on the covenant Box"

2 Exodus 33:9 – *"And it came to pass, as Moses entered into the tabernacle, the cloudy pillar descended, and stood at the door of the tabernacle, and the LORD talked with Moses."*

XII. Called By The Audible Voice Of God

A. Moses – Exodus 3:1-5

1. Moses' name literally means "taken out of the water, drawn forth, a son."
2. Backside of the desert for 40 years
3. Comes to Horeb which means desert, desolation, to dry up, to lay waste, to be destroyed
4. True character is formed in the dry places in the wilderness.

a. Psalms 66:12 – *"Thou hast caused men to ride over our heads; we went through fire and through water: but thou broughtest us out into a wealthy place."*
b. Acts 9:16 – *"For I will shew him how great things he must suffer for my name's sake."*
c. Psalms 63:1 – *"O God, thou art my God; early will I seek thee: my soul thirsteth for thee, my flesh longeth for thee in a dry and thirsty land, where no water* is"
d. I Corinthians 10:13 – *"There hath no temptation taken you but such as is common to man: but God is faithful, who will not suffer you to be tempted above that ye are able; but will with the temptation also make a way to escape, that ye may be able to bear it."*

5. The Burning Bush, Exodus 3:2 – *"And the angel of the LORD appeared unto him in a flame of fire out of the midst of a bush: and he looked, and, behold, the bush burned with fire, and the bush was not consumed."*

a. Burned but not consumed
b. Exodus 3:3 – *"And Moses said, I will now turn aside, and see this great sight, why the bush is not burnt."*
c. Exodus 3:4 – *"And when the LORD saw that he turned aside to see, God called unto him out of the midst of the bush, and said, Moses, Moses. And he said, Here am I."*

B. Paul – Acts 9:1-18

1. Paul's name means "little" or "a love slave"
2. Changed from Saul which means "asked for" or "your presence is demanded"
3. Journeying to Damascus which means "moist with blood, sackcloth, activity."
4. Acts 9:4 – Paul heard the voice of God
5. Acts 9:8 - He had to be led to the city because he was blinded by the light.
6. Acts 9:9 – Fasted for 3 days
7. Audible because of the type of ministry he would have, Acts 9:16 – *"For I will shew him how great things he must suffer for my name's sake."*

C. Adam

1. Genesis 1:26-31 – God forms man and gives him dominion
2. Genesis 2 – Man is placed in the garden and given his assignment
3. Genesis 3:6-9 – God calls for Adam
4. God called for Adam not because he didn't know where he was, but because Adam didn't know where he was.

D. Isaiah – Isaiah 6:1-8

1. Isaiah's name means "salvation of the Lord, Jehovah is helper, save thou Jehovah"
2. Isaiah 6:8 – *"Also I heard the voice of the Lord, saying, Whom shall I send, and who will go for us? Then said I, Here am I; send me."*
3. Isaiah heard God after King Uzziah died – Soul ties and idols will keep us from hearing the voice of God.

E. Gideon – Judges 6:11-24

1. Gideon's name means "one who cuts down trees, a cutting down, he that bruises, great warrior."
2. Judges 6:11 – Gideon is in a place where God is threshing him.
3. Judges 6:15 – Gideon's look of faith and confidence

   a. Jeremiah 1:6 – *"Then said I, Ah, Lord GOD! behold, I cannot speak: for I am a child."*
   b. Exodus 4:10-11

F. Abraham – Isaiah 51:2

1. Genesis 12:1 - The calling of God separates.
2. The hardest part of the call of God is that you are called alone.
3. Other times God speaks to Abraham

   a. Genesis 18:1-5
   b. Genesis 22:1-4
   c. Genesis 22:9-18

G. Samuel

1. I Samuel 3:1-15, 19-21
2. The Lord called Samuel many times.

   a. lived in the house of the Lord
   b. served in the temple

c. didn't have an intimate knowledge of the Lord because of leadership
d. God speaks to Samuel and the first thing Samuel does is open the doors of the house (I Samuel 3:15)

XIII. The Sound From Father's House – The Local Church

A. Luke 15:25 – "*Now his elder son was in the field: and as he came and drew nigh to the house, he heard musick and dancing.*" Other translations:

"*he heard music and dancing in the house*"
"*as he came closer to the house he heard the sound of music and dancing*"
"*when he returned home, he heard dance music coming from the house*"
"*the sound of music and dancing comes to his ears*"
"*he drew near the house and heard music played by a number of musicians in concert, and the sound of people dancing a circular dance on the lawn*"

B. Job 36:29 – "*Also can any understand the spreadings of the clouds, or the noise of his tabernacle?*" Other translations:

"*the thunderings of His pavillion*"
"*the noises of His tabernacle*"
"*how He thunders from His dwelling place*"
"*or the thunders of His tent*"
"*the crashings of His pavillion*"

C. Acts 2:1-4 – "[1]*And when the day of Pentecost was fully come, they were all with one accord in one place.* [2]*And suddenly there came a sound from heaven as of a rushing mighty wind, and it filled all the house where they were sitting.* [3]*And there appeared unto them cloven tongues like as of fire, and it sat upon each of them.* [4]*And they were all filled with the Holy Ghost, and began to speak with other tongues, as the Spirit gave them utterance.*" Other translations of verse 2:

"*like the rushing of a violent tempest blast, and it filled the whole house in which they were sitting*"
"*a sound as a bearing violent breath, and it filled all the house where they were sitting*"
"*the sound like the roaring of a mighty wind storm*"
"*it filled the entire house*"
"*it filled the whole building*"
"*filled the house where they were meeting*"
"*a sound like the rushing of a violent wind, and all the house where they were was full of it*"

D. Mark 2:1 – "*And again he entered into Capernaum, after some days; and it was noised that he was in the house.* Other translations:

"*it was heard that He is in the house*"
"*it was reported that He was in the house*"
"*the news went about that He was in the house*"
"*it was understood that He was in the house*"
"*the news spread that He was home*"

E. II Chronicles 5:11-14 – "*...*[14]*So that the priests could not stand to minister by reason of the cloud: for the glory of the LORD had filled the house of God...*" Other translations:

"*by reason of the cloud; for the glory of the Lord had filled the house of God*"
"*for the honour of Jehovah hath filled the house of God*"
"*for the glory of the Lord filled the temple*"

"the Lord's splendor filled God's temple"
"for the house of God was full of the glory of the Lord"

F. Ezra 3:10-13 – "*So that the people could not discern the noise of the shout of joy from the noise of the weeping of the people: for the people shouted with a loud shout, and the noise was heard afar off.*" Other translations:

"and the sound was heard a far off"
"and the noise had been heard unto a distance"
"the sound was heard for away"
"the sound of their voices reverberated for miles around"
"the sound was heard a long way off"
"so loud that it could be heard for miles"

G. Psalms 100:4 – "*Enter into his gates with thanksgiving, and into his courts with praise: be thankful unto him, and bless his name.*" Other translation: "*enter with the password: Thank you! make yourselves at home, talking praise, thank Him worship Him*"
H. Matthew 21:14-16 – "*children crying in the temple, and saying, Hosanna*"
I. Psalms 29:9 – "*The voice of the LORD maketh the hinds to calve, and discovereth the forests: and in his temple doth every one speak of his glory.*" Other translations:

"while in His temple everyone is saying Glory"
"in His temple all cry Glory"
"everyone shouts glory"
"we fall to our knees, we call out Glory"
"in His temple everyone say's Glory to God"
"but in His temple all are praising, Glory, Glory to the Lord"
"in His temple everything say's Glory"

J. Psalms 95:1-3 – "Come *before His presence with thanksgiving, and make a joyful noise*"
K. Psalms 150: 1-6 – "*let them praise Him*"
L. Psalms 66:8 – "*O bless our God, ye people, and make the voice of his praise to be heard:*" Other translations:

"and loudly sing his praises"
"give him a thunderous welcome!"
"loudly proclaim his praises"
"and sound the voice of his praise"
"sound His praise abroad"
"let the voice of his praise be heard"

M. Isaiah 66:6 – "*A voice of noise from the city, a voice from the temple, a voice of the LORD that rendereth recompence to his enemies.*" Other translations:

"hear that noise from the temple"
"what is that terrible noise from the temple"
"a sound from the temple"
"that sound comes from the temple"
"listen to the sound from the temple"

N. Ezekiel 10:3-5 – "[5]*And the sound of the cherubims' wings was heard even to the outer court, as the voice of the Almighty God when he speaketh.*" Other translations:

"was heard as far as the outer court"

"as far away as the outer court"
"and could be heard even in the outer court yard"
"were audible all the way to the outer court"
"could be heard clear out in the outer court"

O. Revelation 11:19 – *"And the temple of God was opened in heaven, and there was seen in his temple the ark of his testament: and there were lightnings, and voices, and thunderings, and an earthquake, and great hail."*

P. Psalms 81:1-5 – *"...[4]For this was a statute for Israel, and a law of the God of Jacob."* Other translations:

"for this was a statue for Israel, and ordinance of the God of Jacob"
"For this is required by the decrees of Israel; it is a regulation of the God of Jacob. He made it a law for Israel"
"this is a rule of the God of Jacob"
"it is the command of the Lord of Jacob"
"this is a law for Israel, a legal decision from the God of Jacob"

Lesson 42

Our Three-Fold Salvation

I. Three-fold Salvation – II Corinthians 1:10 – *"Who delivered us from so great a death, and doth deliver: in whom we trust that he will yet deliver us;"* – Our salvation is complete and uttermost.

A. Salvation Covering Every Part Of Man

1. Spirit – Justification
2. Soul – Sanctification
3. Body – Glorification

The three-fold God created a three-fold man. After man fell, he needed a salvation that covered his entire (three-fold) being.

B. Seeing This In Detail

<u>SPIRIT</u>	<u>SOUL</u>	<u>BODY</u>
Outer Court	Holy Place	Most Holy Place
Past Salvation	Present Salvation	Future Salvation
Justification	Sanctification	Glorification
Passover	Pentecost	Tabernacles
Standing	State	Temple
Delivered	Being Delivered	Will Be Delivered
Penalty Of Sin	Power Of Sin	Presence Of Sin
Perfect	Being Made Perfect	Perfected
Savior	Lord	Husband
Grace	Works	Inheritance
Gift Of God (free)	Must Be Attained	Reward

Our three-fold salvation encompasses that which God has done, is doing and will do for us. The salvation that has taken place is in the realm of our human spirit. It is complete. It is perfect. It is finished and it is eternal. This is the place where we are already overcomers. This is the grace of God. The salvation that is taking place is in the realm of our soul. It involves our works. It is where we are learning to overcome. It is the part of us that desperately needs to be changed into His image! The salvation that is going to take place will be in the realm of our bodies. It is when we will be changed instantly and will receive our eternal, glorified bodies. This will be instant and spontaneous. The degree of change and glory will be determined by how we have allowed God to change our souls into His image.

II. We Have A Complete Salvation

A. Hebrews 7:25 – *"Wherefore he is able also to save them to the uttermost that come unto God by him, seeing he ever liveth to make intercession for them."* – The Greek word for "uttermost" means completely and perfectly.

1. Hebrews 2:3 – *"so great"* – Another translation – *"If we ignore a deliverance so great."*
2. Hebrews 5:9 (Isaiah 45:17, 51:6) – *"everlasting"*
3. II Samuel 23:5 – *"sure"* – The Hebrew word for "sure" means guarded, hedged about, protected.
4. Matthew 26:27 – *"all of it"* – This means there is a lot to this salvation.

B. The salvation you and I have experienced is beyond wonderful, it is glorious – This salvation is not partial in any sense of the word. It is <u>total</u> and <u>complete</u>.

III. Understanding Our Three-fold Salvation

A. God Is Three-fold: Father, Son and Holy Ghost

1. I John 5:7 – "*For there are three that bear record in heaven, the Father, the Word, and the Holy Ghost: and these three are one.*"
2. Matthew 28:19 – "*Go ye therefore, and teach all nations, baptizing them in the name of the Father, and of the Son, and of the Holy Ghost:*"
3. II Corinthians 13:14 – "*The grace of the Lord Jesus Christ, and the love of God, and the communion of the Holy Ghost, be with you all. Amen.*"
4. John 14:16 – "*And I will pray the Father, and he shall give you another Comforter, that he may abide with you for ever;*"

B. Man Is Three-fold: Spirit, Soul and Body

1. I Thessalonians 5:23 – "*And the very God of peace sanctify you wholly; and I pray God your whole spirit and soul and body be preserved blameless unto the coming of our Lord Jesus Christ.*"
2. Hebrews 4:12 – "*For the word of God is quick, and powerful, and sharper than any twoedged sword, piercing even to the dividing asunder of soul and spirit, and of the joints and marrow, and is a discerner of the thoughts and intents of the heart.*"
3. Genesis 2:7 – "*And the LORD God formed man of the dust of the ground, and breathed into his nostrils the breath of life; and man became a living soul.*"
4. Isaiah 53:5 – "*But he was wounded for our transgressions, he was bruised for our iniquities: the chastisement of our peace was upon him; and with his stripes we are healed.*"

C. Salvation Is Three-fold: Justification, Sanctification and Glorification

D. Baptism Is Three-fold.

1. Hebrews 6:2 – "*baptisms*" means plural
2. Types of Baptisms:

   a. Baptism into the Body of Christ – This is the baptism in blood for our human spirit.
   b. Baptism in water for our bodies.
   c. Baptism in the Holy Ghost for our souls.

IV. Aspects Of Three-fold Salvation – When most of us think of salvation, we think of receiving Jesus as Savior. Within that salvation, there is a three-fold out-working; each applying to a different part of man.

A. Justification

This part of our salvation is received immediately upon conversion. It is when the blood of Jesus washes our human spirit clean. Our spirit is then inhabited by the Holy Spirit; our sins are forgiven and we can commune with the Father. We pass from death to life. Our human spirit, from this time on, is incapable of sinning (I John 5:18; Hebrews 12:23). This does not mean we will never sin again. Our souls and our bodies WILL sin, but our spirits are inhabited by God (I John 1:8-10, I John 2:1-2, Romans 7:14-25). If we did not sin, there would be no need for daily repentance.

1. Some simple facts about justification:

   a. It is the salvation that is past (completed).
   b. It delivers us from the penalty of sin.
   c. It takes place in our spirit.
   d. All we have to do is receive it. Works have nothing to do with it. It is received by faith. We are saved simply by the grace of God. It is a free, eternal gift.

e. It secures our place in heaven.

2. Scriptural references

a. Ephesians 2:8 – "*For by grace are ye saved through faith; and that not of yourselves: it is the gift of God*"
b. Titus 3:5-7 – "*5Not by works of righteousness which we have done, but according to his mercy he saved us, by the washing of regeneration, and renewing of the Holy Ghost; 6Which he shed on us abundantly through Jesus Christ our Saviour; 7That being justified by his grace, we should be made heirs according to the hope of eternal life.*"
c. Isaiah 53:5 – "*But he was wounded for our transgressions, he was bruised for our iniquities: the chastisement of our peace was upon him; and with his stripes we are healed.*"
d. II Corinthians 1:10 – "*<u>Who delivered us from so great a death</u>, and doth deliver: in whom we trust that he will yet deliver us;*"

B. Sanctification

Sanctification deals with our being set apart to God in this life. It is the process whereby our souls are being conformed into His image. Sanctification basically takes place in our mind (soul). It is <u>not</u> an instantaneous work. It is a process whereby we yield ourselves DAILY to God. It is the aspect of salvation taking place NOW. It is where we learn to overcome.

1. Simple facts about sanctification:

a. It is our daily salvation.
b. It delivers us from the power of sin.
c. It takes place in our soul (emotions, reasoning, intellect, will, etc.)
d. This is where our works play a big role. We must allow the Holy Spirit to work, yielding our instruments, our members, to Him instead of sin. We must also purge ourselves. God will not hold us accountable for sin prior to salvation, but He will judge us for sin after salvation unless we repent and judge ourselves daily.
e. The measure of glory we will have and what our rewards will be when Jesus returns is determined by how much we have given over to Him in this life.

2. Scripture references:

a. II Corinthians 1:10 – "*Who delivered us from so great a death, <u>and doth deliver</u>: in whom we trust that he will yet deliver us;*"
b. Philippians 2:12-13 – "*12Wherefore, my beloved, as ye have always obeyed, not as in my presence only, but now much more in my absence, work out your own salvation with fear and trembling. 13For it is God which worketh in you both to will and to do of his good pleasure.*"
c. I Timothy 4:16 – "*Take heed unto thyself, and unto the doctrine; continue in them: for in doing this thou shalt both save thyself, and them that hear thee.*"
d. James 1:21 – "*Wherefore lay apart all filthiness and superfluity of naughtiness, and receive with meekness the engrafted word, which is able to save your souls.*"
e. I Chronicles 16:23 – "*Sing unto the LORD, all the earth; shew forth from day to day his salvation.*"
f. Psalms 96:2 – "*Sing unto the LORD, bless his name; shew forth his salvation from day to day.*"

C. Glorification

This aspect of our salvation is referred to in the Scriptures as in the future salvation. It is the final phase of our great and uttermost salvation. It is when our bodies will be redeemed and glorified. The measure of glory is determined by how we let sanctification work in our souls. We will literally shine with God's glory; some as the sun, some as the stars.

1. Simple facts about glorification:

    a. It is the salvation referred to in the future.
    b. It takes place in our bodies.
    c. It will deliver us from the presence of sin.
    d. It is an instantaneous work determined by our growth in the Lord while on earth.

2. Scriptural references:

    a. Philippians 3:21 – "*Who shall change our vile body, that it may be fashioned like unto his glorious body, according to the working whereby he is able even to subdue all things unto himself.*"
    b. I Corinthians 15:40-44 – "[40]*There are also celestial bodies, and bodies terrestrial: but the glory of the celestial is one, and the glory of the terrestrial is another.* [41]*There is one glory of the sun, and another glory of the moon, and another glory of the stars: for one star differeth from another star in glory.* [42]*So also is the resurrection of the dead. It is sown in corruption; it is raised in incorruption:* [43]*It is sown in dishonour; it is raised in glory: it is sown in weakness; it is raised in power:* [44]*It is sown a natural body; it is raised a spiritual body. There is a natural body, and there is a spiritual body.*"
    c. I Corinthians 15:51-53 – "[51]*Behold, I shew you a mystery; We shall not all sleep, but we shall all be changed,* [52]*In a moment, in the twinkling of an eye, at the last trump: for the trumpet shall sound, and the dead shall be raised incorruptible, and we shall be changed.* [53]*For this corruptible must put on incorruption, and this mortal must put on immortality.*"
    d. Daniel 12:3 – "*And they that be wise shall shine as the brightness of the firmament; and they that turn many to righteousness as the stars for ever and ever.*"
    e. Hebrews 9:28 – "*So Christ was once offered to bear the sins of many; and unto them that look for him shall he appear the second time without sin unto salvation.*"
    f. I Peter 1:5 – "*Who are kept by the power of God through faith unto salvation ready to be revealed in the last time.*"
    g. Romans 13:11 – "*And that, knowing the time, that now it is high time to awake out of sleep: for now is our salvation nearer than when we believed.*"
    h. Ephesians 1:14 – "*Which is the earnest of our inheritance until the redemption of the purchased possession, unto the praise of his glory.*"

So you see, our spirits <u>have been redeemed</u>, our souls <u>are being redeemed</u>, and our bodies <u>will be redeemed</u>. This is our great and uttermost salvation!

Dr. Samuel Greene, Ph.D.
www.nwmin.org

Dr. Samuel Greene is president and founder of Narrow Way Ministries International (nwmin.org), an outreach missionary arm of the body of Christ, seeking to disciple and teach believers everywhere foundational truths and sound doctrine, helping the body of Christ grow up into Jesus in all things. Brother Sam was saved at the young age of 15, and he has walked with the Lord now for over 45 years. He was ordained into the ministry in 1976 and has pastored all over the United States, as well as started churches and bible schools all over the world. Dr. Greene has also written over 50 books to help solidify and found the body of Christ in basic sound doctrine, revelational truths about the coming Kingdom of God and the doctrine of the remnant. God spoke to him at the age of 15, telling him he was going to teach the doctrine to the remnant in the last days. Not knowing what this meant, he simply began to search the Scriptures as God brought into his life many men and women of God who taught him faithfully. Dr. Greene's guiding passion is for God to bring forth His people into the bride of Christ that He has called her to be with His image, carrying His glory all over the earth.

For information on obtaining **TABERNACLE OF MOSES AUDIO** to accompany this study manual, please contact us at **www.nwmin.org**

www.ingramcontent.com/pod-product-compliance
Lightning Source LLC
LaVergne TN
LVHW080333110826
845155LV00027B/233

* 9 7 8 1 9 3 7 1 9 9 5 6 2 *